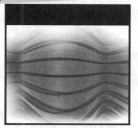

Ready-to-Run Java 3D™

Kirk Brown
Daniel Petersen

With a Foreword by James Gosling

Wiley Computer Publishing

John Wiley & Sons, Inc.

NEW YORK · CHICHESTER · WEINHEIM · BRISBANE · SINGAPORE · TORONTO

To Kendyl, Kevin, and Kate, for giving up some of their time with Dad for the sake of the project.

My thanks and love to Ellen to whom much is deserved.

Library of Congress Cataloging-in-Publication Data:

Brown, Kirk, 1958–
    Ready-to-run Java 3D / Kirk Brown, Daniel Petersen.
      p.   cm.
    "Wiley computer publishing."
    Includes index.
    ISBN 0-471-31702-0 (paper/CD-ROM)
    1. Java (Computer program language) I. Petersen, Daniel, 1965– .
II. Title.
QA76.73.J38B78   1999
005.7'2—dc21   98-31971
                                          CIP

Printed in the United States of America.

10 9 8 7 6 5 4 3 2 1

Contents

Acknowledgments

Many people deserve recognition and sincere thanks for all the hard work they put into making this book become a reality when at times it seemed it might have ended up in virtual reality. Many of the book's sections were expanded and improved because of their encouragement and participation.

Daniel Petersen, co-author and member of the Java 3D team at Sun, wrote several of the Java classes found throughout the book and managed to find some time in his busy Java 3D production schedule to author Chapter 7, "Behaviors, Interpolators, and Event Detection." Dan provided valuable advice and foresight that made the book clearer and more useful.

My sincere gratitude to James Gosling, inventor and architect of Java, for giving us all a peek into those early moments when Java was revealed and the final result which has been utterly fantastic. Completion of the Foreword is a story in itself and nothing less than a miracle. Amid flying around the world as Java's ambassador, delivering keynote addresses, personal projects, Java 2 reviews, designing meetings, and encountering harsh weather resulting in power failures that blew away a nearly composed Foreword, James never gave up and put up with my late phone call to a Tokyo hotel, weekly emails, several visits, and pending deadlines.

Senior Sun Systems Engineers Rolf Behrsing and Mike Williams provided technical manuscript review, helped spot my errors and shortcomings, and offered good advice on making the book understandable.

Thanks also to Tom Nevin for his advice and design in helping to create an advanced Java programming feature for the book's applets, known as, "dynamic class instantiation."

The Wiley team was just great. My personal thanks to Bob Elliott for taking on this project while putting up with the delays and glitches of new 3D technology and at the same time encouraging and leading the project forward to completion. Pam Sobotka provided a firm but encouraging hand in getting the manuscript pulled together by keeping me on track and setting production goals and schedules, and Emilie Herman helped tie up all the loose ends. Marnie Wielage was the Assistant Managing Editor who turned the raw bundle of manuscript pages and figures into the final product.

Finally I would like to thank Dan Berg for his advice, Matt Delcambre for supporting this project, and Matt Robinson, Douglas Pew, and Markus Roskothen for providing some of their own Java 3D work and tools for the book.

Foreword

The first public demonstration of the Java technology happened at the Technology, Education and Design (TED) conference in Monterey, California, at the beginning of 1995. Back then it was cool to have a Web page of even the simplest sort, because Web pages were very much like paper pages: text with simple images. The conference was buzzing with people who were excited just to be able to click on a link and see a document from the other side of the planet. When John Gage and I got on stage, we began our song and dance with static Web pages; but pretty soon we showed a Web page that contained what looked like a picture of a molecular model. I reached over with my mouse, grabbed the molecule, and spun it. The audience collectively inhaled and held their breath; then there was an excited buzz as they realized what they thought of as the laws of physics of Web pages had just been violated.

In 10 seconds, with some simple 3D graphics, the audience had come to understand what was so revolutionary about the technology. By appealing to the innate visual 3D orientation that we all share, we were able to get a compelling message across. After that, we had them hooked. We had their attention when we launched into the technical meat of the talk. And though the 3D applications I had written were done without the benefit of a real 3D library, and so were quite primitive, they were effective.

In the almost four years since then, the use of Java has exploded like nothing before. It has established itself as the premier language for building Web applications, and is used extensively in all other application areas. The Java programming language has proven to be a very effective way to write programs of all kinds, and to significantly enhance the productivity of developers.

Java itself has grown, too: While we have kept the language stable, the underlying runtime system has achieved a level of robustness and performance that makes it solid enough for the most demanding applications. The real growth has been in the application programming Interfaces (APIs)—there are interfaces to databases, file systems, the network, user interfaces, signatures, sophisticated 2D graphics, and many others.

And now there is the Java 3D library, a set of tools that allow applications to easily construct three-dimensional models and display images of them. In its full generality, 3D modeling is a very complex and sophisticated topic. Our human abilities may make three-dimensional imagery seem like a simple and natural thing, but what is actually going on in terms of light, texture, shadow, and form is innately complex. One of the design goals of Java 3D was to handle as much of this complexity as possible, to ease the task of developers.

Nonetheless, Java 3D can still be pretty intimidating, so this book is a gentle introduction to it. With it, you should be able to design applets that construct, manipulate, and display 3D models. I wish you many happy hours of hacking.

James Gosling

James Gosling is a Vice President and Fellow at Sun Microsystems whose early research work led to the Java programming language.

Getting Started

"Java is designed to solve a number of problems in modern programming practice."

—JAMES GOSLING

The computer industry has begun a process of reinventing itself, marked by innovations across the board. Computer processing power is on an exponential upward curve. A few months ago, 300 MHz computers were the talk of the techies over late-night, junk-food meals. The central processing unit (CPU) that is common to all computers continues to climb to more powerful clock speeds. All that processing power means more powerful and effective applications and solutions. Not only are the CPUs getting faster, but so are the memory and networking components. The internal "roadways" that connect the memory to the CPU to the graphics board and other system components have multiplied their capacity to carry more data (see Figure 1.1). That's like adding 32 more lanes to an existing 32-lane superhighway! Gordon Moore, one of the founders of Intel, years ago made the following prediction: The number of transistors that could be designed into a CPU would double every 18 months. The result, of course, would be faster and faster CPUs. This became known as Moore's Law, and it still applies today. Recently, gigahertz (GHz) clock speeds have been announced for availability before the year 2000. We're talking major "muscle desktops" that will blast us into the next century.

On the other hand, while hardware has continued to become faster,

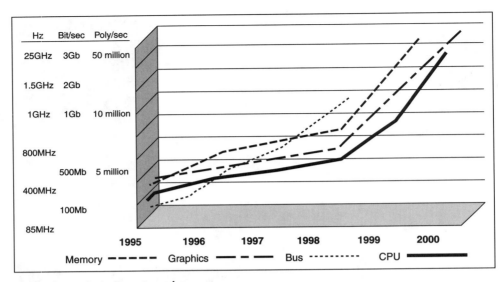

Figure 1.1 Component road maps.

smaller, and cheaper, software continues to be complex, bloated, and unreliable. Java, however, is one innovation that is changing software development. Java software is small and simple. That's its secret. And you can snap a bunch of these small and simple Java modules together to solve complex problems. And now Java has been extended to include 3D graphics.

This is great news for those of us in the graphics camp. Over the next few years, 3D graphics will explode onto desktops and over the Web. Andy Grove, former Intel CEO, stated that the Pentium II microprocessor was responsible for solving the graphics bottlenecks on the desktop. In fact, he is only partially correct. Sufficient CPU speeds are necessary to perform intense mathematical operations used by standard 3D software libraries today. Typically, the faster the CPU, the more polygons per second can be computed. The result (along with other 3D operations) enable users to create fantastic graphics. Maybe 2000 will be the year of 3D graphics. All of this is geared toward a growing consumer demand for innovations in software applications that incorporate computer graphics. Java is becoming an integrated component on the desktop, and 3D graphics will not be overlooked, thanks to the new Java 3D API (application programming interface).

Indeed, the software world is reengineering itself with Java, perhaps pointing to a Java-unified environment. Java in the browser, Java in the operating system, Java applications, dedicated Java hardware chips, and extension into the embedded consumer electronics market. Java is popping up everywhere, sometimes in unexpected places, such as the United States

Postal Service, one of the first organizations to deliver commercial Java postal statement forms over the Web to some 50,000 end users using JDK 1.0! Wouldn't you agree this is radical? Today, companies are even using Java 3D to implement new distributed MCAD packages and to improve oil/gas exploration.

Transmogrify is a great word to describe these changes. It is not as catchy as paradigm shift, revolution, or critical mass, but Java solicits the same reaction. Transmogrify means to "make over" to a radically different form, composition, state, or disposition. Software designs are evolving to accommodate innovative technology, faster computers, and worldwide digital connectivity. We are talking more than a face-lift here, which only refreshes an old product and whose results never fool anyone. This is a major technology shift, sometimes called a *dislocation.*

We have all found ourselves jumping on the latest software development bandwagon. Remember the ASCII application interface available with MSDOS? Aligning all of those asterisks or plus signs to represent the crude beginnings of a container on a computer screen called a "text screen." Well it was the only thing available at the time. And remember how Curses tried to take this to the next level? Or how about GKS or some of those other fleeting cross-platform graphics APIs over the years? But all would agree the success of Java is something we have never experienced before. And the Java 3D API is following the same track.

According to Herb Schildt, author of dozens of technical books on C programming, "Computer graphics ranks high on the list of exciting things that you can do with a computer. However, what all graphics applications have in common is the ability to draw points, lines and boxes." You can't help being struck by this simple explanation and definition of why we are fascinated by this technology. Although the statement was written 10 years ago, it still holds true, except that the geometry has expanded a little to include splines, triangles, and NURBS. It is the recent developments of modern computer graphics that go way beyond the ability to render just points, lines, and boxes. The scientific, educational, and entertainment value of computer graphics today is glorious and fantastic. We feel the same way about the future of the Java 3D application programming interface.

Overview of the Book and Technology

This book was written to assist Web content developers who want to use Java 3D right away to spice up their Web sites. These new and interesting 3D

Web applets are ready to use and designed to hold the viewer's interest and attention. The book also helps the Java professional who is looking to push himself or herself into the next level of experience. This is accomplished by revealing some new tricks and knowledge regarding 3D graphics, based on the Java 3D API. Most important, this book provides Java 3D applications that were designed for Web pages to attract and hold visitors.

We think the little GIF animation files are clever, but limited. A better effect can be produced with the Java 3D API with more interaction, entertainment, and visual navigation for a Web site. Some of the best Web sites are marked by their originality and creativity. We believe the Web developer and the Java programmer will take a keen interest in what the Java 3D API has to offer. For the Web developer, these applets come ready to use, with a documented HTML interface to make customizing a snap. For the programmer, there are tutorials on the major components of the Java 3D API and source code to explain various graphics effects. For everybody, there are useful utilities, tools, and Java classes, which have been collected in one place to make creating Java 3D programs, geometry, and special effects as easy as possible.

Media in the Browser

Until now, interactive media content within commercial Web sites has been limited to pictures with image maps and GIF animation. The goal of these media types is to increase the attractiveness of the interface that is presented to the visitor. You will notice that successful Web sites have very rich graphics and provide gamelike interfaces that are both visual and easy to access in the maze of data and links that await the surfer. As computers integrate cheaper and faster hardware, the result will be the explosive production of multimedia content onto the desktop. Also, this fast and cheap hardware will support 3D graphics. To date, there hasn't been a formal framework that manages combined media and logic; it had been accomplished by gluing and hacking CGI or PERL server scripts with static, repetitious GIF pictures to simulate a graphical user interface (GUI). Java 3D is a great solution and offers a very robust interface for the Web. The cartoon Java mascot Duke made Java famous and enhanced the HTML interface with animated graphics where before there were none. Documents on the Web evolved from text into a new combined media of text, audio, video, and logic.

Java 3D programs can be built to trigger additional activity based on what the user might do or on how they might react. Sounds can be launched, the viewpoint of the animation or scene can change; a visitor can fly around a

3D Duke, or touch him and get a reaction, or follow him to additional cool media that presents 3D menus or a virtual corporate campus. For about the same file size, relative to the height and width of the GIF animation, Java 3D is superior technology with additional features.

Other media innovations were released prior to Java 3D. For example, VRML is a 3D-scene medium, which can be viewed from a browser. But since the browser itself doesn't support VRML directly, users need a *plug-in*. The browser is configured to recognize a VRML data file (*.wrl) and will launch a separate helper application, or plug-in, to view this data file format on behalf of the browser. There are many types of plug-ins for many media data file types, such as multimedia files and audio and movie clips. Many of these features run outside of the browser and are independent of the browser application.

Java 3D in the Browser

Java 3D is a standard extension to Java. Several Internet browsers support Java, including Netscape Navigator and Microsoft Internet Explorer (IE). There is also a group of 30 or so independent software developers who are creating a universal browser in Java, which is expected to be available later this year or in early 2000. The browsers ship with a Java virtual machine (JVM) and logic that will run Java applets within the browser window. Here's how it works (see Figure 1.2): When you are surfing a particular Web site and you click on an HTML link that contains an HTML Java <APPLET> reference, the applet code is downloaded to your PC or workstation. The browser manages the window space and makes room to display the applet before invoking the applet program. The Java applet is able to run only because there is a JVM within the browser that handles starting and stopping the applet and executes whatever the program is supposed to perform.

The problem today is that browser developers and vendors are slow to track the new innovations of Java, including Java 3D; for example, the browser application is compiled and hard coded with old versions of Java and doesn't provide a method for replacing the old Java runtime environments with newer versions. There are also multiple Java versions between browser products. For example, the Java support in versions of Internet Explorer may be different from the Java version used in Netscape's browser. This makes distributing Java applets within browsers difficult—especially the programs based on the latest Java release, like Java 2, and with emerging Java APIs (like Java 3D), there may be other compatibility problems in the near future.

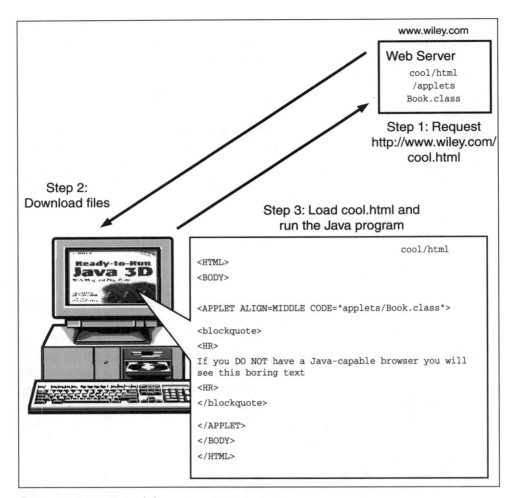

Figure 1.2 How a Web browser runs Java programs.

To solve this problem, Sun has created a plug-in for Java applets. But instead of launching from the browser as a separate window, the Java plug-in remains embedded within the browser window. The Java Plug-in is free and is distributed with the Java 2 runtime environment.

When the HTML file is created with a reference to one of the Java 3D applets in this book, end users will have to download and install one initial copy of Java 2, which includes the plug-in, on their system before they can run the Java 3D program. The entire process is a few point-and-click tasks and most surfers have already been through this process several times for other file types, like PDF, PostScript, or ShockWave. The Java Plug-in replaces the old Java runtime environment of the browser with the needed

Java 2 runtime environment to display 3D applets. Also, the Java 3D applet doesn't run in a separate browser window, but it is embedded into the main browser window just like any browser-compatible Java applet today. In order to accommodate Java 3D applets, some planning needs to be done before creating the HTML page containing the program, but the examples within this book have the HTML files already created and ready to use. The actual HTML syntax will be discussed in a few pages. Additional HTML templates have been added to better assist your end users in downloading necessary files (see Appendix B).

Java Plug-In for Internet Browsers

Since the early development of the first Internet browsers, browsers have been able to recognize various non-ASCII file format types. The *Multipurpose Internet Mail Extension* (*MIME*) allows the browser to view a variety of data file types, like audio, video, picture, binary, and VRML. MIME refers to the official Internet standard that specifies how Internet messages must be formatted so they can be exchanged between email programs. MIME is so flexible that any type of file or document can be sent as a message. The MIME format also happens to be similar to that exchanged between a Web browser connected to a Web server. The MIME format is also part of the HyperText Transfer Protocol (HTTP), the communication protocol used throughout the World Wide Web that enables Web sites to exchange information. MIME types can be associated with a helper application; for example, if you are surfing the Net and click on a *scene.wrl* link, the browser will try to invoke the file within a VRML helper application because the browser was set up to view all files ending in *.wrl with a specific helper application.

What does this all have to do with you and Java 3D? Some Web pages contain non-ASCII data types, like an audio file named *sample.wav*. Most of these special data types are not directly supported by the browser and so require the help of a plug-in application. Plug-ins are simply software applications that extend the browser's capabilities to view or hear the special data file. There are dozens of plug-ins for 3D and animation, business utilities, presentations, audio/video, image viewers, and more.

Now there is a new plug-in for Java. Similar to the audio file example, when the browser detects a Java applet, it will load the required Java environment to run the Java applet properly. This provides the ability to run special Java applets that use Java extensions not currently supported by Internet browsers, like the Java 3D API standard extension to Java. Again, why is this Java Plug-in needed? Well, the current and popular Internet browsers from Netscape and Microsoft were developed and shipped with older versions of Java. Java 3D programs are dependent on the latest Java 2 version (or later) from Sun. Eventually, browser development will catch up to the current Java version, but until then, a Java Plug-in is required to run the Java 3D applets. So, the Java Plug-in is software that allows the latest and greatest Java virtual machine (JVM) to run inside Netscape or Microsoft browsers in order to support the latest Java features. It doesn't destroy the browser's Java environment; rather, it coexists with the browser's JVM. Besides, the Java Plug-in is free from java.sun.com/products and most Web users have had to download one of the current 200 plug-ins used around the Web. The Netscape Navigator browser treats the Java Plug-in just like any other helper application. There is an initial download and self-installation session. Subsequent reliance on the plug-in goes unnoticed by the end user after the plug-in and Java 3D software are installed.

When users click on a Web page containing a Java 3D applet (see Figure 1.3) they are zapped to a server from which the plug-in can be downloaded. It's all point-and-click. The next time the same page is clicked on, the applet will be handled by the plug-in and launched. The Java 3D applet will appear in the browser like magic and use the Java environment pointed to by the Java Plug-in. A minor edit to the HTML file will disable the plug-in feature when browser development catches up to the latest Java wave. Also keep in mind Java 3D applets are restricted by the same security model that applies to standard Java applets (see Appendix B).

How to Put Java 3D onto Your Web Site

Use the following information when inserting Java 3D applets on your Web site:

On Internet Explorer. The first time a user's Web browser comes across a Web page that is enabled for the Java Plug-in product, it automatically downloads and installs the Java Plug-in software (and hence the latest implementation of the JRE-Java Runtime Environment) on the user's system. From that point forward, the browser will automatically invoke the Java Plug-in software every time it comes across Web pages that support the technology, which is completely transparent to the end user.

On Netscape Navigator. The first time a user's Web browser comes across a Web page that is enabled for the Java Plug-in product, it redirects the user to a Web page to download and install the Java Plug-in software on the user's system. From that point forward, the browser

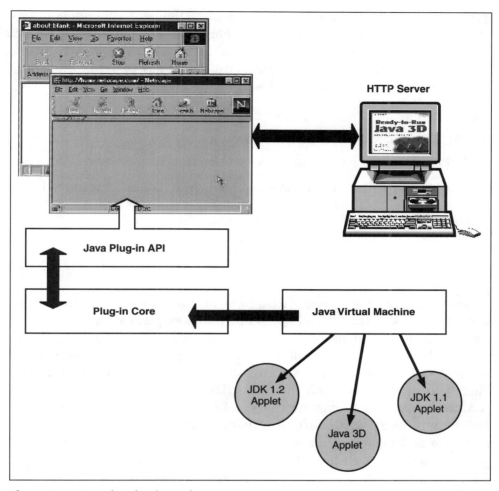

Figure 1.3   How the plug-in works.

will automatically invoke the Java Plug-in software every time it comes across Web pages that support the technology, which is completely transparent to the end user.

The Java Plug-in defines a "tag" that needs to be specified in the HTML page that will host the Java 3D applet. Instructions for Netscape-only or Microsoft-only environments in the Java Plug-in documentation can be referenced from its Web site (java.sun.com/products/plugin). The following will cover both environments to avoid confusion and to simplify the discussion; it was excerpted from the setup and installation notes.

In an Internet/intranet environment, an HTML page is likely to be browsed from many different platforms, for example, Microsoft Explorer or Netscape Navigator. You should activate Java Plug-in only on the correct browser and platform combination. Otherwise, you should use the browser's default JVM. (It is possible that some Web pages will have a mix of old Java and new Java 3D applets; you can achieve this using the Java Plug-in tags:

<OBJECT> for Microsoft Explorer browser.

<EMBED> for Netscape Navigator browser.

<APPLET> for the latest Sun Microsystems HotJava browser.

The original (before Java 3D was invented) Java APPLET tag looked like:

```
<APPLET code="XYZApp.class" codebase="html/" align="baseline"
width="200" height="200">
<PARAM NAME="model" VALUE="models/HyaluronicAcid.xyz">
</APPLET>
```

This will invoke the applet "XYZApp" inside the browser window with an area of 200×200 pixels and will pass one parameter called "model," which points to a local file named "HyaluronicAcid.xyz".

The following is an example using Java Plug-in tags. We'll be using a script to determine the browser environment so we can invoke the Java Plug-in correctly for multiple platforms. This example includes comments and can be used as a template that can be cut and pasted when creating Java Plug-in Web pages. Don't be intimidated by all these characters; their sequence and meaning can be mastered in a short period of time. And keep in mind that each Java 3D applet in the book is accompanied with an HTML template that is ready to go. Just cut and paste it into your favorite HTML page.

```
<!-- The following code is specified at the beginning of the <BODY> tag.
-->
<SCRIPT LANGUAGE="JavaScript"><!--
    var _info = navigator.userAgent; var _ns = false;
    var _ie = (_info.indexOf("MSIE") > 0 && _info.indexOf("Win") > 0
                        && _info.indexOf("Windows 3.1") < 0); //-->
</SCRIPT>
<COMMENT><SCRIPT LANGUAGE="JavaScript1.1"><!--
    var _ns = (navigator.appName.indexOf("Netscape") >= 0
        && ((_info.indexOf("Win") > 0 && _info.indexOf("Win16") < 0
        && java.lang.System.getProperty("os.version").indexOf("3.5") <
        0) || _info.indexOf("Sun") > 0)); //-->
</SCRIPT></COMMENT>
```

```
<!-- The following code is repeated for each APPLET tag -->
<SCRIPT LANGUAGE="JavaScript"><!--
    if (_ie == true) document.writeln('<OBJECT
    classid="clsid:8AD9C840-044E-11D1-B3E9-00805F499D93"
    width="200" height="200" align="baseline"
 codebase="http://java.sun.com/products/plugin/1.2/jinstall-12-win32.cab
#Version=1,1,0,0">
    <NOEMBED><XMP>');
    else if (_ns == true) document.writeln('<EMBED
    type="application/x-java-applet;version=1.2" width="200"
height="200"
    align="baseline" code="XYZApp.class" codebase="html/"
    model="models/HyaluronicAcid.xyz"
    pluginspage="http://java.sun.com/products/plugin/1.2/plugin-
install.html">
    <NOEMBED><XMP>');
 //--></SCRIPT>
    <APPLET code="XYZApp.class" codebase="html/" align="baseline"
        width="200" height="200"></XMP>
    <PARAM NAME="java_code" VALUE="XYZApp.class">
    <PARAM NAME="java_codebase" VALUE="html/">
    <PARAM NAME="java_type" VALUE="application/x-java-
applet;version=1.2">
    <PARAM NAME="model" VALUE="models/HyaluronicAcid.xyz">
    No Java 2 support for this APPLET!!
 </APPLET></NOEMBED></EMBED></OBJECT>

 <!--
<APPLET code="XYZApp.class" codebase="html/" align="baseline"
        width="200" height="200">
<PARAM NAME="model" VALUE="models/HyaluronicAcid.xyz">
    No Java 2 support for this APPLET!!
</APPLET>
    -->
```

Although this tag seems complicated compared to the old APPLET tag, actually, it is not. Most of the Java Plug-in tag is the same regardless of the applet used. Thus, for the majority of cases, a webmaster can just copy and paste the Java Plug-in tag.

The first block of the script extracts the browser and platform. It is recommended that you determine the browser and platform on which the applet is running. You do this by using JavaScript to extract first the browser name, then the platform. This is done once per HTML document. The second block of the script replaces the APPLET tag. You must replace each APPLET tag with a similar block of code. The script replaces the APPLET tag with either an EMBED or OBJECT tag, depending on the browser. It would be nice if everybody could agree on the same tag names, but since they can't, a little more work is needed. You use the OBJECT tag for Internet Explorer (IE) and the EMBED tag for Netscape Navigator. Finally, the original APPLET tag is included as a comment at the end. It is always a good idea to keep the original APPLET tag in case you want to remove the Java Plug-in invocation when browsers eventually support Java 2 or higher.

Let's review what we just said. The first JavaScript establishes the browser and the platform on which the browser is running. You must do this because the Java Plug-in currently supports only Windows 95/98, Windows NT 4.0, and Solaris. Note that Windows NT 3.51 is the only Win32 platform that Java Plug-in does not support. Java Plug-in should be invoked only on the supported browser and platform. The script sets the variable _ie to true if the browser is Internet Explorer. It sets the variable _ns to true if the browser is Navigator. (Note that all variable names in the JavaScript start with a single underscore. This is done to avoid conflict with other Java-Script variables in the same page.)

To detect the correct browser, the JavaScript evaluates three strings that are within the JavaScript's Navigator object: userAgent, appVersion, and appName. These strings contain information about the browser and the platform. By looking at some examples of the userAgent string, you can easily see how to evaluate userAgent and use it to determine the browser.

Remember that this block of JavaScript should be put at the top of the <BODY> of the HTML file, so that other JavaScripts can reference the variables _ie and _ns. This JavaScript is the same in all HTML files, and so it is needed only once for each HTML body.

The second block of HTML tags are actually the corresponding OBJECT and EMBED tags that are mapped from the data in the APPLET tag. Note that JavaScript outputs the OBJECT tag when the browser is IE running on Windows 95/98 or Windows NT 4.0. If the browser is Navigator 3/4 on Windows 95/98, Windows NT 4.0, or Solaris, then JavaScript also outputs the EMBED tag, though with a slightly different syntax. Recall that the mechanism for detecting the browser and the platform was described in the previous section. Finally, the symbols <!-- and --> are used to enclose comments in HTML.

How This Book Is Organized

This is really two books in one, centered on example applets for each chapter. Each chapter contains a User section and a Technical section. The User section describes how to configure the provided Java 3D programs and how to customize the programs by editing the HTML file with your favorite editor. The Technical section describes how the program was designed using Java 3D objects and classes. Many methods of creating special effects using Java 3D will be covered in depth. We also include cool tools that Sun Microsystems is shipping with the product to simplify much of the tedious, irksome work you occasionally face in creating computer 3D graphics programs. If you have ever counted pixels on the screen display, then you know what we are talking about.

Each chapter also presents the ready-to-run Java 3D applets with simple directions and step-by-step instructions on how to customize the applet to your needs. This is followed by a detailed technical tutorial that focuses on the Java 3D concepts and constructs used to create the Web applets. Webmasters will appreciate the front sections of each chapter and will be introduced to Java 3D programming in the back sections of each chapter. Beginner and intermediate programmers will gain understanding by studying the back sections of each chapter to learn how various special effects were created using the Java 3D API. This can be helpful when creating your own Java 3D programs.

In Chapter 2 we'll start off with a primer on 3D computer graphics concepts and an introduction to the Java 3D API. Both of these sections will provide a reference point supporting the content that is presented in the rest of the book. Geometry and trigonometry might not have been your thing in school, but don't worry; 3D graphics simply uses mathematics to push and organize colorful pixels around the display to make interesting pictures. The primer will take some of the mystery out of the 3D graphics engineering realm, which was previously reserved for nerdy programmers with oversized brain stems. Chapter 3 will take the perplexity out of the Java 3D design architecture and clear up some new terms. But be aware, this will take a few encounters before the "lightbulb stays lit." Just go with the flow for awhile and you'll soon catch on. Chapter 4 starts us out with a look at the foundation of 3D graphics, which can only be geometry. There are many useful utilities available with the book for creating your own custom shapes without having to know what CAD stands for. Chapter 5 discusses rotating, positioning, and animating the geometry that you created in Chapter 4.

Then things get a little more creative and the action never stops! Chapter 6 covers how to create and use lighting and transparency. Chapter 7 discusses behaviors, interpolators, and event handling. Chapter 8 details how to create a neat special effect: fog. With Chapter 9, you will be able to add realism using texture mapping and 3D sounds, which is covered in Chapter 10. Adding 2D and 3D text, such as logos and labels, is discussed in Chapter 11. Finally, tools and utilities to make creating Java 3D content easier are covered in Chapter 12.

The book's appendices include detailed installation and setup instructions, as well as a primer on the Java language. Memorize the concepts so you can impress your engineering friends at the next brown-bag lunch. No one can cover Java in a few dozen pages, so the attempt here is to introduce the Java language, which provides the foundation for our discussion on the Java 3D API. For those with an interest, there are hundreds of books on Java for you to study for more detail.

Who Should Read This Book?

The answer is, simply: computer professionals who are tasked with creating World Wide Web content, webmasters, computer graphics students, and software engineers who are considering Java 3D technology for their solutions. It might have been unnecessary to say that, but this book assumes you might be one of those working in a coffee shop, buying some time while planning your future. Day after day, you've been noticing very cool people with laptops, working with this computer thing called Java. One day, you bribe a cool patron with free latte refills only to learn that this person also has a cool job that produces a cool salary. Or you might be a database programmer who has been looking at all of those joins, tables, and strings for years and you can't take it anymore; you want to step out on the wild side and explore 3D graphics. In either case, this book was written with you in mind.

Tools You Will Need

Since vendor graphics accelerators are proprietary versus "open," special libraries have been created to twiddle the logic gates of these 3D hardware acceleration boards. There has been a movement to standardize the programming interfaces that run across popular graphics hardware. The most popular are OpenGL and Direct3D. The Java 3D API sits on top of these graphics libraries (see Figure 1.4).

As the Java 3D program executes on a Sun one day and on Windows another day, the idea is the same. Java code will execute in the same way

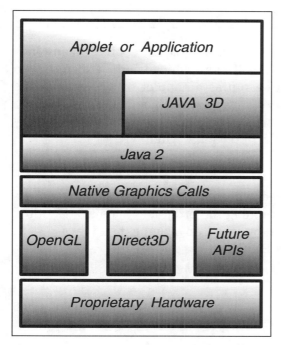

Figure 1.4 Java 3D software to hardware relationship.

across multiple 3D platforms. Somebody summarized this capability by changing the Java motto, "write once, run everywhere" to "write once, render everywhere." So besides OpenGL or Direct3D, the Java 3D API requires the Java 2 environment and JVM, in which case, the three components necessary to develop or run Java 3D programs are:

- Java 3D classes
- Java 2 or later
- OpenGL 1.1 or greater or Direct3D 5.0 or greater
- OpenGL or Direct3D supported graphics accelerator for best viewing

If you don't have any of this software, or if you are not sure what to do next, proceed to Appendix B, "What's on the CD-ROM?." Also, templates are provided to assist the installation process. You can access these templates by loading the following file into your browser:

file:///D:/index.html.

What's on the CD-ROM?

The CD-ROM that accompanies *Ready-to-Run Java 3D* contains many Java 3D programs and their companion HTML files, which can be added to Web sites. Each Java 3D program can be run as an applet or as a standalone application. The main reason the programs were designed to run standalone was so that you could quickly see what the Java 3D programs look like by simply typing the following in a DOS or terminal window:

```
% java -mx64m Morphing -demo
```

The same program can be invoked within a browser by clicking on the HTML file (Morphing.html) or by running the program inside a Java utility called appletviewer. Assuming the new Java 2 environment and Java 3D API have been installed (see Appendix B).

```
% appletviewer Morphing.html
```

The CD-ROM is divided into several directories. The chapter directories contain applets. The CD looks something like:

/programs	These are the Java 3D Web applets.
	/ch4 Applets start with Chapter 4.
	/ch5
	. . . Each chapter has related applets.
/util	This directory contains useful tools to build 3D Web pages.
/src	This directory contains source code listings for all Java 3D programs
/resources	This directory contains useful images, links, textures to help you create your 3D content.
	/ch4
	/ch5
	. . . Each chapter has related source listings.

Using the CD-ROM Programs

Once you decide which Java 3D program is to be used, the provided Java 3D applet *.html file and *.class file(s) must be located to the same directory on the Web server. The provided HTML files should be combined or edited to reflect the new Web environment. Please refer to Appendix B for installation information.

Summary

The Java 3D API has been designed to be detached from certain platform dependencies, just like "mother" Java. (Application distribution will be covered later in the book and will provide some strategies for rolling out your Java 3D programs.) In the next chapter, we'll take a short break and go over some basic 3D graphics concepts. Then we'll take on the Java 3D API and examine why Java 3D was created and how has it accomplished some of its design goals. The purpose of this book is to introduce you to Java 3D as a Web content format of choice. We think Java 3D has a lot to offer in the way of methods for spicing up your Web sites. Sure, it is a full-blown language capable of building commercial graphics applications and games, but it can also create small robust applets that are perfect for the Web.

CHAPTER
2

A 3D Graphics Primer

"No problemo."

—MODEL TERMINATOR T-101
IN *TERMINATOR 2*

Using three-dimensional graphics is just a lot of fun. At the lowest level is the realization of complex mathematical models that provide the ability to visualize geometric relationships. To a child, a 3D graphic becomes Buzz Light Year or Johnny Quest. It is also a wonderful and far-reaching discipline that can both entertain and expose important medical information or even be used to discover oil. Behind 3D graphics are mathematical engines performing, basically, two distinct functions: modeling and rendering.

Modeling is a term used to describe an object by a numerical representation of its shape, size, and dimensions. *Rendering* is the process of drawing the geometric model to the hardware display so the viewer can see the object's numerical representation.

Actually, 3D objects are nothing more than a bunch of points in space. These sets of data are held together by a coordinate system. This process goes back to some fundamental models invented by the French mathematician René Descartes in the seventeenth century. Wonder if René would believe that his work had made the *Terminator* movies possible? Anyway, Descartes invented the coordinate system called the *Cartesian plane*. It is a method of describing the placement of a point along a plane in space. In 3D graphics, several types of coordinate systems are used to store the picture data at various stages of modeling and rendering. All of these steps together are called the *graphics pipeline*.

Planes intersecting at right angles form the Cartesian plane (see Figure 2.1); the horizontal plane is called the x-axis, and the vertical plane is called the y-axis; the point of intersection is called the origin that is the center of four parts called quadrants. In 3D coordinate systems, another plane is added for the z-axis. It is at right angles to the x- and y-axes and would go in and out of this page if included in our diagram. Also plotted in Figure 2.1 is a 3D rectangle shape defined as 24 points (6 sides and 4 points to a side).

The real trick in 3D graphics is projecting a 3D model back to the hardware display, which is represented by a 2D coordinate system where the origin (0,0) is usually in the upper left-hand corner of the display. "No problemo," because mathematics are provided, like from our old friend René, to help solve all of our problems. It's all part of the graphics pipeline. Pay attention, and you'll be amazed at how a bunch of points and some math can produce graphics like those found in *Toy Story*.

Okay, you probably know that computer displays are made up of millions of little dots that get charged in such a way that each dot can produce a specified color value on command at some position on the screen. Each dot is called a picture element or *pixel*. How do they do this? Who cares. They just do. The amount of pixel information that an output device can display is called the *display resolution*. A monitor with a sharp resolution may have

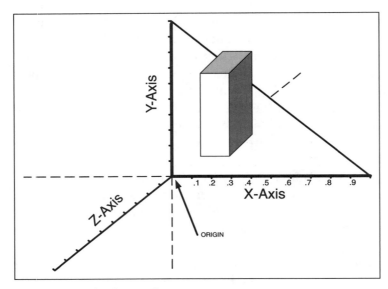

Figure 2.1   A basic coordinate system.

1,280 columns of pixels and 1,024 rows, or 1280×1024. The screen size, refresh scan rate, and resolution all affect the image quality.

What you need to know is that every computer has a *framebuffer*, a bunch of computer parts and memory, which stores picture information and instructs the computer monitor as to which pixels to activate to create a picture. The display has its own device coordinates; so does a printer, a projector, and every other kind of output device. Now, it would be very ugly to write a 3D application and try to accommodate every device coordinate system known to humankind. Some might be based on floating point while others are integer-based; some coordinate systems have the x-axis point up, while others have the y-axis up; some follow the left-hand rule and others the right-hand rule. The reality is, most of us view 3D virtual worlds through a 2D *portal* or device.

Many 3D systems use a *world coordinate system* to model objects. The object is unbounded and can be represented as the size of Texas, as tall as the highest mountain, or as small as an atomic particle. How the coordinate system is defined and how sets of points are modeled within its space determine the dimensions and scale. There is also a big difference if the coordinates are integer-based or floating point. The scale is infinite and only limited by the computing power running the software program. For example, let's say you wanted to plot the distance from the Earth (point A) to the moon (point B), and starting from Earth, you attempt to reach the moon by dividing the distance in half moving toward the moon, divide again, and so on. How long would it take to reach the moon? The task would be infinite, and the answer would be forever; you would never reach the moon. You might be dividing distance at the subatomic level, but you'd never reach the moon. Java 3D has a coordinate system that could represent this problem (but would eventually fail somewhere around the subatomic representation). That's a lot of simulated, virtual 3D room. The point is, if anybody asks, Java 3D has a fine precision coordinate system. Not that they will, but they might. Engineers attending a business cocktail party get a little wild once in awhile. Ask them to solve the problem we've posed after they have had a few drinks.

Creating Simple Objects

Now that you have an idea what a coordinate system is, it's time to create 3D shapes. This is called *modeling*. By plotting a collection of points (*vertices*) onto our 3D numerical coordinate system, it is easy to create 3D *wireframe* models. The sets of vertices are connected by *edges* to define the shape of the object. The data for the points can be stored as an array of values in the program, loaded from a file, or mathematically generated. Consider the basic shape of a cube that consists of a vertex list, which defines the points needed to model the shape (see Figure 2.2).

There you have it, a square cube. As you can see, creating complex models by hand results in very simple objects. There is *computer-aided design (CAD)* modeling software on the market to help, along with object scanners, real-time capturing systems, and several companies that sell models of every kind.

A Point, a Line, a Polygon

We've seen how to plot a point using 3D coordinates. We only need two sets of points and a function to draw a line between both points. The following Java 3D code accomplishes this basic *primitive.*

```
Point3f p1 = new Point3f(0.0f, 1.0f, 0.0f);
Point3f p2 = new Point3f(1.0f, 0.0f, 0.0f);
```

Two points have been established.

```
float[] coordinates = new float[6];
coordinate[0] = p1.x; coordinate[1] = p1.y; coordinate[2] = p1.z;
coordinate[3] = p2.x; coordinate[4] = p2.y; coordinate[5] = p2.z;
LineArray line = new LineArray(2, LineArray.COORDINATES);
line.setCoordinates(0, coordinates);
```

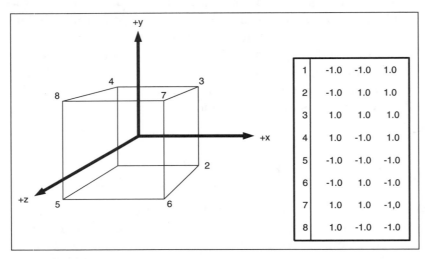

Figure 2.2   Six-sided cube vertex list.

Now we are getting into rendering primitives. There are many additional parameters to consider, such as line width, color, and line style (i.e., dash, solid) and *antialiasing*. These parameters are referred to as *primitive attributes.*

Antialiasing is a technique of smoothing the jagged edges on diagonal lines or curved shapes by calculating a halftone or faded color near the pixel that is part of the line or object. The human eye is fooled, and the edge appears more pleasing and smooth.

Solid Surfaces

You have seen how a 3D object is constructed from lines and points to form a wireframe model. Such objects look rather hollow and uninteresting because you can see right through the model, and it's difficult to tell which edges are closest from those further away. The whole object lacks a general sense of depth. If, however, we were to create solid surfaces, then the object would really begin to take on an attractive shape and to simulate volume.

This is accomplished by changing the object model from wireframe to a *polygonal mesh.* Mesh is a term used when an object is broken up into many polygons. A mesh approximates the surface shape of an object by providing the vertices of polygonal *faces.* The vertices for an object's facets are described in a face list.

The list for each face is determined by the object vertices, counterclockwise as seen from the outside of the object (see Figure 2.3). There are *face-culling* operations that can distinguish the inside from the outside surface. You wouldn't always want to draw outside and inside faces; it is unnecessary and consumes precious CPU cycles. Optimally, you only render the viewable faces and cull the rest. Another term for this is called *hidden surface removal.* There are two parts to HSR: First is to remove invisible faces

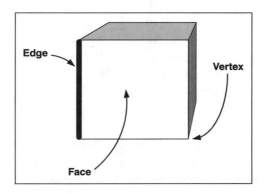

Figure 2.3   Simple box with identified faces.

called *backfaces*, surfaces that cannot be seen from the viewpoint of the viewer; Second is to render the *front faces* in a proper sequence in order for the picture to look correct.

The *Z-buffer* algorithm is a common method used for HSR. System memory is set aside to create a cache, and it acts like a framebuffer. An amount of data for each pixel is stored in the Z-buffer. A test is performed to determine if a pixel is covered by a face using a point-by-point calculation that involves the Z values of the polygons and the pixel color value. Only the pixel color information is passed onto the framebuffer if the pixel is to be rendered. Most advanced graphics hardware has dedicated Z-buffering hardware built in, so you don't have to worry about it.

In Figure 2.3, you see a type of *polyhedron* that is a connected mesh of simple polygons such that every edge is shared by exactly two faces. This law of symmetry is so harsh that only five such objects can exist: a 3D solid triangle, or *tetrahedron;* a six-sided solid cube, or *hexahedron;* and three other polyhedrons too difficult to describe with words called *octahedron, iscosahedron,* and *dodecahedron.*

The best 3D software modeling packages try to create a model from some physical object in a number of ways, using radar, X-ray, infrared, and a laser to scan the physical object and create its shape. These advanced software programs replicate the physical model in a polygonal mesh. The faces are defined and usually divided into the simplest polygon—triangles. Why? Usually, 3D graphics hardware is designed to render triangles very quickly using dedicated firmware algorithmic equations.

In summary, a geometry model is composed of several parts (see Figure 2.3). The vertex list, mentioned in the previous section, contains geometric information. The face list contains connectivity or topological information. The vertex list tells us where each corner lies in 3D space, and the face list tells us which vertices are connected in a face.

Since most hardware and graphics accelerators, optimally, can render the simplest polygon, a triangle, it is common for the graphics API to refine the polygonal mesh into a *triangle mesh* or a *quadrilateral.*

To reduce a polygonal shape into triangles (see Figure 2.4), we pick a vertex and its two adjacent vertices as in our polygon example. We have computed the first triangle. This is represented by the broken lines in Figure 2.4. We remove the triangle from the polygon and store the triangle data. This is the first step in creating a triangle mesh. This operation is repeated until the polygon has been converted into a mesh of triangles.

Sometimes, when dealing with a complex scene, the triangle list is enormous, and so is difficult for the hardware to process in a timely manner. Thus, there are additional operations to reduce the number of triangles,

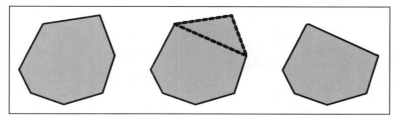

Figure 2.4 Creating a triangle mesh.

resulting in less work for the computer and fewer cycles to render the object. Though some realism or resolution is lost, the user doesn't have to wait an hour for the image to finish displaying on the screen.

Similarly, a 3D object may be composed of a large mesh made up of very small triangles. To speed up the performance during rendering, the number of triangles will be increased, with each side becoming 1 pixel in length. It is easier to draw a cluster of points for each triangle than a group of polylines. It takes fewer logical operations and CPU cycles on some hardware architectures.

Now it's time for the fun part: making our 3D objects move and dance across the screen. Lights (we'll be getting to that soon—you can't see anything in 3D without lighting), camera (we'll be working our way through the section on viewing later), action! That's what we want: movement, animation, and action!

Moving a 3D Object Around

As we mentioned, many coordinate systems are implemented in a complex scene. Each object or part may have its own coordinate system, called a *local coordinate* system. By manipulating the values of the local coordinates, we can perform *object transformation* and generate movement, like rotating the object.

There are other simulated movements, too. We can perform a *view transform* to change the viewpoint or vantage point in relationship to an object. At this point, we are virtually flying around an object to get a different view. There are three basic actions we can perform on a 3D object: translation, scaling, and rotation (see Figure 2.5). *Translating* a 3D object means taking a point (x, y, z) and changing it to (dx, dy, dz) by using matrix mathematics. When working with matrices, it is common to denote the matrix by a rectangular array of numbers or *scalars*.

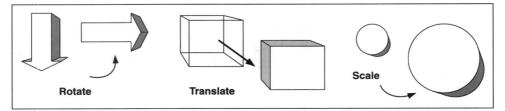

Figure 2.5   3D action operations.

$$
\begin{vmatrix} M00 & M01 & M02 & M03 \\ M10 & M11 & M12 & M13 \\ M20 & M21 & M22 & M23 \\ M30 & M31 & M32 & M33 \end{vmatrix}
\begin{vmatrix} x \\ y \\ z \\ w \end{vmatrix}
=
\begin{vmatrix} x' \\ y' \\ z' \\ w' \end{vmatrix}
= A
$$

Of course, the matrix array members (Mnn) are replaced with values. Some array elements will always be a 1 or 0 for common matrix operations. Other matrix elements may be defined by a variable (i.e., dx, dy, or dz) that may be updated by the program logic. For example, consider a 3D game in which the user moves the mouse around to manipulate a 3D object. The matrix applied to the specified object may be getting updated in near real time, as are specific matrix elements. When the matrix is multiplied by another matrix, the calculation result will be used as data to change the location, orientation, or position of our 3D object. This will involve additional logical operations in other parts of our 3D program illustration.

$$
\begin{vmatrix} 1 & 0 & 0 & 0 \\ 0 & 1 & 0 & 0 \\ 0 & 0 & 1 & 0 \\ dx & dy & dz & 1 \end{vmatrix}
\begin{vmatrix} x \\ y \\ z \\ 1 \end{vmatrix}
=
\begin{vmatrix} x' \\ y' \\ z' \\ w' \end{vmatrix}
= A
$$

$x' = M00 * x + M01 * y + M02 * z + M03 * w$

$y' = M10 * x + M11 * y + M12 * z + M13 * w$

$z' = M20 * x + M21 * y + M22 * z + M23 * w$

$w' = M30 * x + M31 * y + M32 * z + M33 * w$

To perform a translation using matrix multiplication:

dx = .10

dy = .10

dz = .10

$$
\begin{vmatrix} 1 & 0 & 0 & 0 \\ 0 & 1 & 0 & 0 \\ 0 & 0 & 1 & 0 \\ dx & dy & dz & 1 \end{vmatrix} \quad \begin{vmatrix} x \\ y \\ z \\ 1 \end{vmatrix} = \begin{vmatrix} x' \\ y' \\ z' \\ w' \end{vmatrix} = A
$$

where the instances of .10 are the translation scalars for dx, dy, and dz, respectively, and x', y', and z' are the product and new points after the operation. Using this notation, a displacement would be applied to every vertex that defines the object. This of course, would require additional logic to achieve. Another interesting use for a transformation is to create a distorted effect on the shape of an object, such as simulating the fish-eye camera lens.

Scaling changes the size of the scene or object and involves three scaling factors *Sx*, *Sy*, and *Sz*, where each point *P* is moved *Sx*, *Sy*, *Sz* times further from the origin in the X, Y, and Z directions. This is called *scaling about the origin*.

Here's the 4×4 matrix to do all of the work necessary to implement *uniform scaling*.

$$
\begin{vmatrix} Sx & 0 & 0 & 0 \\ 0 & Sy & 0 & 0 \\ 0 & 0 & Sx & 0 \\ 0 & 0 & 0 & 1 \end{vmatrix} \quad \begin{vmatrix} x \\ y \\ z \\ 1 \end{vmatrix} = \begin{vmatrix} x' \\ y' \\ z' \\ w' \end{vmatrix} = A
$$

Each vertex of the object is scaled by the same factor to produce a uniform enlargement of the 3D object.

If *S* were negative, then the object vertex would be *reflective*, which can produce a mirror image of the object. If |*S*| < 1, then the points will be moved closer to the origin to cause the desired *demagnification* effect.

Changing the factors for each X, Y, and Z will produce a *nonuniform* scaling operation. Nonuniform scale should be defined as a scale on which all the scale factors are *not* the same.

The following operation rotates a point parallel to the X-axis about the origin (0.0, 0.0, 0.0) (see Figure 2.6).

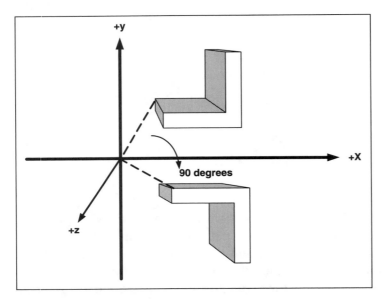

Figure 2.6 Rotating a shape.

$$
\begin{vmatrix} 1 & 0 & 0 & 0 \\ 0 & \cos r & \sin r & 0 \\ 0 & -\sin r & \cos r & 0 \\ 0 & 0 & 0 & 1 \end{vmatrix} \quad \begin{vmatrix} x \\ y \\ z \\ 1 \end{vmatrix} = \begin{vmatrix} x' \\ y' \\ z' \\ w' \end{vmatrix} = A
$$

The ones on a diagonal are the identity matrix. Without a specified identity matrix, the operation would fail. The value r represents the angle, in radians. Radians are a measure of angles or rotation. A complete rotation is broken down into (2*PI) radians. When dealing with computers or higher-level math, you will have to deal with angles in terms of radians instead of degrees. Figure 2.7 shows a full rotation broken down into eighths of a rotation. Note that the number of radians in a full circle is the same as the circumference of a circle divided by its radius. The formula for converting from degrees to radians is:

Radians = (degrees/360) * (2*PI)

Degrees are units of rotation; a degree is defined as being one 360th of a full rotation; therefore, there are 360 degrees in a full rotation. In computing and many of the sciences, it is more common to use radians as a method of defining angles and rotation. Figure 2.7 shows a full rotation broken down into eighths of a rotation. Note that 360 degrees is equal to 0 degrees, and

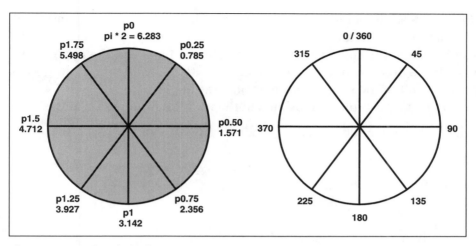

Figure 2.7   Units of rotation.

315 degrees is equal to –45 degrees. The formula for converting from radians to degrees is:

Degrees = (radians/(2*PI)) * 360

The mathematical function *cosine* is the ratio of the base and the hypotenuse of a right-angled triangle for any given angle between the base and the hypotenuse. Since all the possible angles are contained within a single rotation, we can plot the result of the cosine function against the angle (see Figure 2.8).

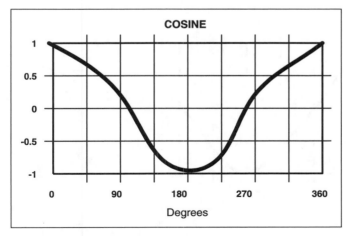

Figure 2.8   A cosine illustrated.

Figure 2.9 shows a full cosine curve through 360 degrees. The mathematical function *sine* is the ratio of the height and the hypotenuse of a right-angled triangle for any given angle between the base and the hypotenuse. Since all the possible angles are contained within a single rotation, we can plot the result of the sine function against the angle.

A small change in our operation and the rotation is about the Y-axis.

$$\begin{vmatrix} \cos r & 0 & -\sin r & 0 \\ 0 & 1 & 0 & 0 \\ \sin r & 0 & \cos r & 0 \\ 0 & 0 & 0 & 1 \end{vmatrix} \quad \begin{vmatrix} x \\ y \\ z \\ 1 \end{vmatrix} = \begin{vmatrix} x' \\ y' \\ z' \\ w' \end{vmatrix} = A$$

And, finally, a rotation about the Z-axis.

$$\begin{vmatrix} \cos r & \sin r & 0 & 0 \\ -\sin r & \cos r & 0 & 0 \\ 0 & 0 & 1 & 0 \\ 0 & 0 & 0 & 1 \end{vmatrix} \quad \begin{vmatrix} x \\ y \\ z \\ 1 \end{vmatrix} = \begin{vmatrix} x' \\ y' \\ z' \\ w' \end{vmatrix} = A$$

Mapping Worlds onto 2D Displays

Many of the 3D images seen on a screen are really a trick of the eye. The modeling is performed in 3D, but the rendering has to be converted to 2D

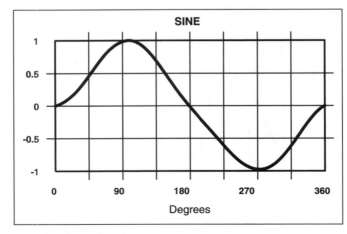

Figure 2.9   Full cosine curve.

because displays, screens, and video projection are 2D devices. The rendering of 3D pictures to a 2D device is accomplished through *projection;* that is, the image is projected onto a 2D plane. Head-mounted displays provide a view for each eye called *stereovision.* Each eye provides a different viewpoint, the brain registers depth, and the result is a more realistic 3D experience. There are two common types of projections: *parallel* and *perspective.*

In a parallel projection, the Z component is ignored, and the object's X and Y points and edges are projected to the device coordinates (see Figure 2.10). A perspective projection takes into account the relative distance of the eye and the viewplane and calculates the points and lines to be drawn on the display (see Figure 2.11).

Where Y and Z determine the viewplane, the eye, or E, is aligned with the X-axis and represents the *eye distance.* To calculate the projection, draw a line from the eye (E) with a straight line to the (x, y, z) point, or P. Where this line intersects the viewplane, that's where the point is rendered (see Figure 2.12).

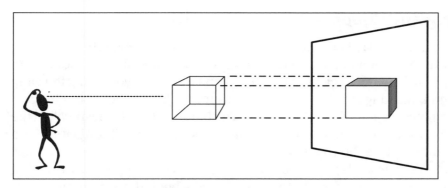

Figure 2.10   Parallel projection.

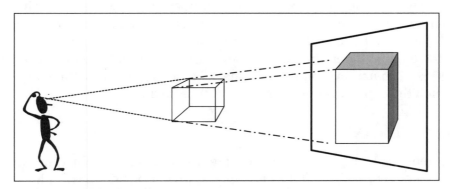

Figure 2.11   Perspective projection.

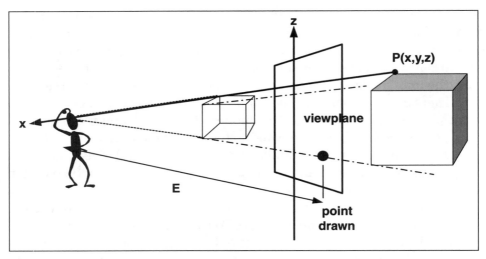

Figure 2.12   Perspective calculation.

Viewing and Clipping

The computer display is like a portal; you have the same experience looking through the lens of a camera, which results in a limited field of view. More imagery is in front of the camera lens than can be seen, so you swing the camera around, panning for the next subject to frame. The same is true in computer graphics displayed on a 2D screen. The limited field of view is called the *viewing volume*. Assume we could see a full picture of the Terminator, for a few seconds, before the frame zooms in on his robotic eye. The greater portion of the Terminator is squeezed off the display. What happens to the rest of him? Simply stated, the Terminator was clipped—but it didn't hurt much.

Objects or object parts within the viewing volume are visible. Portions outside the volume are *clipped*. A graphics operation defines a viewing plane and a clipping plane. As the user dynamically navigates a 3D scene, parts of the overall scene do not need to be drawn. In a heavy broken accent, the clipping operation looks to find a new victim, "You have been selected for termination. You are no longer in view. Hasta la vista, baby." From which the clipped geometry replies, "I'll be back."

Shading

Three-dimensional graphics primitives are used to create objects. But objects are not very realistic if they are only colored. Consider the rendered scene in Figure 2.13. Many of the shapes cast a shadow by blocking light reflected off the surface of the surrounding objects in the scene. A light

Figure 2.13 Example of shading.

source that is bounced off objects and distributed over a 3D scene is called *radiosity*. The light source appears to be coming from everywhere, rather than from an obvious source. A shadow (absence of light) is created in those areas that the light cannot penetrate. This type of reflected light is called *indirect lighting*, and this type of computer graphics effect adds *photorealism* to the picture scene.

Line drawing in the wireframe model can be separated into front-face edges or backface edges. Those toward the back can be contrasted to simulate depth and dimension, as seen in Figure 2.14. The edges of the front- and backfaces are drawn, but extra information, such as line color and line width, is used to render a 3D-like shape. *Filled wireframes* take a polygonal face and fill it with a solid color or a shade of color to give objects a solid appearance and distinguish the object's faces. This is also known as *flat shading* and provides some basic indication of a light source.

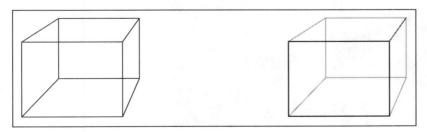

Figure 2.14 Shaded polygons.

Smooth shading varies the color at different points on the face (see Figure 2.15). Where the colors intersect, they are blended to create a smooth appearance. *Ray tracing* is an extension of smooth shading (refer back to Figure 2.13); each pixel of the display relates to the focal point or direction of view. A "ray," or line of sight, is cast from the camera position or eye position through a pixel point in a 3D object, and a shadow is cast onto the first surface the ray encounters. The effect is a colored, shaded drop shadow or a reflection.

Lighting

As mentioned, realistic 3D objects cannot be created unless lighting is used to provide depth and dimension. A couple of lighting types have specific functions, but share common characteristics. Light has a brightness or intensity value, a color, and reacts with the object surface by reflecting from the surface or by being absorbed by the surface.

Ambient lighting produces a constant source of illumination on all surfaces to create a uniform glow over the scene. Too little ambient light will create a scene dominated by shadows, and too much will wash out the scene entirely. A summer sun is a good analogy of ambient light; it spreads uniformly in all directions to illuminate the objects the light touches.

Each object of the 3D model is assigned a value called the *ambient reflection coefficient*. The light source is given an intensity value. If *P* is a point in 3D space, the amount of light on *P* is calculated by computing the product of the source intensity and the ambient reflection coefficient that returns the amount of light that reaches the eye (point of view) from point *P*.

Directional lighting provides light from a specific direction (see Figure

Figure 2.15   Smooth shading.

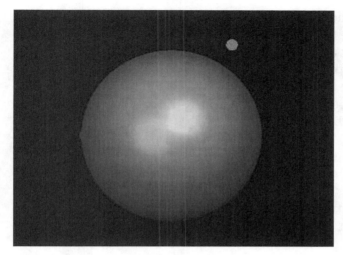

Figure 2.16   Directional lighting example.

2.16). The light from the source is parallel, and the direction of the light is the same for all objects, regardless of their positions. *Point lighting* (see Figure 2.15) also has a sense of direction, usually located close to the model, but light from the source is not parallel and the object's position will affect how the light ray strikes the object.

Texture Mapping

To simulate the patterns and textures of the real world, texture mapping is used (see Figure 2.17). The outcome is incredible realism. A digital picture

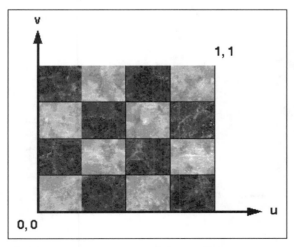

Figure 2.17   Texture mapping coordinates.

or *bitmap* is used to wrap the 3D object, like a Christmas package. Actually, the bitmap is attached to the surface of the polygonal model of the 3D object, the excess is cut away, and the seam is smoothed so it is not visible. Here's how texture mapping works: A coordinate system, U and V, references the bitmap where the values are between 0.0 and 1.0. The image is fitted to the model; it could be stretched in the *V* direction or multiplied (replicated) in the *U* direction to provide enough material to wrap the object's circumference. This is called *repetition*, or *tiling*, when the texture's coordinates are outside the coordinate range. For example, 0,0 to 1,2 would be a repetition of two tiles in the *U* direction that would be applied to the provided 3D object.

It is also possible to transform, scale, or rotate the texture to make the application look correct. Most of the time, the surfaces given a texture usually are not flat. So we need another coordinate system (see Figure 2.18), called the *texture surface space*, where coordinate *S* is the horizontal plane and coordinate *T* the vertical plane. *S* and *T* are mapped to *U*, *V* coordinates. Since the surface is irregular, *U* and *V* coordinates of the image are mapped to *S* and *T* coordinates that reference the vertices of the model (see Figure 2.19).

In summary, a texture is a digital image or bitmap with color information, which is mapped onto a polygon using texture mapping. Since a texture is flat or 2D (*V*, *U*), the relationship to 3D space is described with a special coordinate system (*T*, *S*) called *surface space*, *texture space*, *polygon space*, or *polygon coordinate space*. In turn, this 3D geometric system has to be

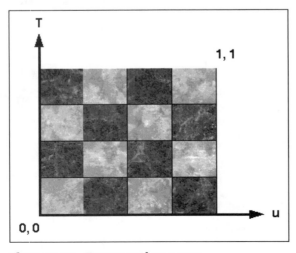

Figure 2.18 Texture surface space.

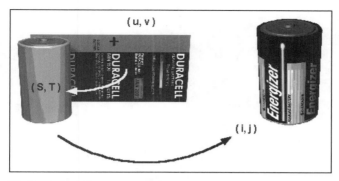

Figure 2.19   Texture mapping process.

mapped to the 2D space (i, j) of the display device. But you must have additional knowledge when using texture mapping, having to do with the creation of the texture images themselves. A good source of information can be found in the book written by Bill Fleming called *3D Photorealism Toolkit* (John Wiley & Sons, Inc., 1998; check out www.wiley.com/compbooks/fleming). Fleming will make you a master at planning and creating photorealistic 3D scenes, such as the realistic images found in this chapter. Although his book has nothing to do with Java 3D, the artistic concepts are educational and will improve your texture image quality.

The method by which the texture map source is created will have an immediate effect when it is applied to the 3D model. The most common undesired effect is stretching. In Java 3D, one trick when texturing a sphere or cylinder is to create a strip image map. The width should be 325 percent ($3.25 \times$ height) of its height. And don't forget that Java 3D requires texture dimensions to be a power of 2, such as 64×128. If there isn't enough material to cover the object, Java 3D will stretch the texture to fit the object, and you won't want the result. The image will lose quality and will not look correct. If the Java 3D object is a cube or freeform, then the image map may need to be sized, cropped, and designed properly. At some point, it may cost some trial-and-error time.

Hopefully, this primer has defined many of the terms and concepts that will be used in the following chapters. That wasn't a problem was it? Repeat after us, in a deep Arnold voice: "3D No Problemo," and move onto the next chapter imbued with new confidence.

CHAPTER

3

Meet the Java 3D API

"Any smoothly functioning technology will have the appearance of magic."

—ARTHUR C. CLARKE

Some talented engineers have created a very powerful graphics toolkit for use, and the best thing about it is that it's free! It must have cost somebody a few million bucks to build and many long days and weekends of relentless work. What else can we say except thanks!

The Java 3D API is extremely productive in use, and the benefits of the Java language structure and its portability have been passed on to the world of 3D graphics. This chapter will provide a quick overview of the Java 3D API classes and functionality.

The Java API provides a standard 3D graphics interface to a variety of hardware and serves as a framework from which to build software and Web applications. The Java API (Application Programming Interface) is divided into the Java Base API, which includes the core language, utility, I/O, network, GUI, and services support, and the Java Standard Extension API, which provides extensions to the base Java functionality. The Standard Extension includes additional interfaces for eCommerce, Security, Database Access, Telephony, Java Server, and the Java Media Framework.

The Java Media Framework API supports a broad range of multimedia and graphics technologies, such as, audio, video, 2D, animation, and 3D. One component of the Java Standard Extension is the Java 3D API.

Java 3D is an API used to create standalone 3D applications and 3D applets. Applications can describe very large virtual worlds in which 3D objects can be programmed with given behaviors to interact with other objects or user mouse/keyboard input and some virtual reality (VR) devices, like tracking devices. Java 3D also includes classes for 3D sound, similar to that found in THX theaters to provide remarkable sensory experiences. In the future, Java 3D may support other technology such as tactile input devices to further push the reality of the 3D experience. But the core Java 3D functionality provides 3D graphics application support.

History of Java 3D

Java 2D is part of the Java Media Framework, which was extended to include a 3D API that would be truly cross-platform. But building a graphics library that runs well on various hardware is not easy. To date, there has been wide acceptance of the Virtual Reality Markup Language (VRML), which needs a special Web browser extension. VRML is being used primarily to represent virtual companies and storefronts, but the language has never caught on in the computer mainstream as has Java. It has been said that the Java 3D API and VRML are close cousins, and there are some familiar components, but also many new ones. This chapter will try to provide a working knowledge of the "moving parts" to a Java 3D scene. The emphasis is on *scene* versus *API*. When you are looking at a Java 3D program running on the display, do you know what makes it all happen? That's the question we plan to answer in this chapter. How it all happened is another story.

Intel, Silicon Graphics, Apple, and Sun Microsystems worked in collaboration to define the Java 3D specification. Much input also was provided by licensed Java vendors and numerous early access sites. Together, they defined the Java 3D API version; and Sun posted its implementation of the specification on its Web site for downloading. There have also been a couple of other implementations of the Java 3D specification out there from other vendors, and more are expected in the future.

Java 3D is actually a common API layer on top of the graphics device libraries based on OpenGL and Direct3D, depending on which platform the program is running. Sun, SGI, Microsoft, and other platforms support the low-level graphics interface. But today, the Sun implementation of the Java 3D specification only runs on Solaris, Windows 95/98, and NT operating systems. OpenGL is supported on Sun, SGI, HP, and Microsoft and can be obtained from these vendors' sites (or www.opengl.org).

When to Use Java 3D

The API was designed for cross-platform portability, and the performance is fairly good because the API talks to the low-level graphic hardware interfaces. Java 3D is not intended to replace every API out there, but we firmly believe that Java 3D is an excellent choice to spice up your Web sites. This book is founded on that goal, and it includes many applets to follow that will give you a well-rounded impression of what the API can do. The API is nicely packaged and designed to simplify some common operations found in gaming and virtual reality program designs. Furthermore, it continues to follow Java's lead in providing a language that increases productivity and simplifies the implementation of 3D application development—in short, Java 3D delivers. The initial Java 3D implementation performs quite well if you help it along with a graphics accelerator and a fast CPU. Its speed will surprise some.

Extending the Java API

Many features and extensions have been identified but not yet defined, because the process is iterative and the goal was to get an API published as soon as possible. The Java community can hardly wait. In the interim, other 3D libraries have cropped up, serving as a stopgap to expedite functionality. A word of caution: These libraries are in general built using homemade classes and core JDK, so make sure you have the real thing when you start building Java 3D applications.

Java 3D Design Goals

The API borrowed common constructs from a group of popular APIs, such as VRML, OpenGL, and Direct3D. The architects have provided a good initial set of features for creating some interesting 3D applications, games, and effects. Other Java APIs may supplement whatever might be missing. Also, many of the vendor file formats are supported by runtime loaders, such as VRML and *.obj files.

The Java 3D API core framework is based on a scene graph programming model. Pictures rendered with Java 3D are called *scenes*. There is an underlying object class structure that defines the composition of the scene.

The scene, or "virtual universe," is broken into the following components that make up the scene's composition: behavior, model, object characteristics, sound, 3D coordinate, math, and everything else needed to create a complex world of 3D objects. At the center stage of our framework is the SceneGraph object. It contains a complete description of the scene, including model data, attributes, and viewing information.

Scene Graph Structure

Again, Java 3D is a scene graph-based API. That means a 3D picture is composed of a three-dimensional space with a set of prominent objects that have a connate relationship with a variety of special-purpose class objects. The scene comprises parts that retain their individuality, yet represent the measurable whole called the *virtual universe.* As the Java 3D program executes, a 3D scene is constructed. The first procedure a programmer implements is the creation of a Virtual Universe object; he or she then attaches one or more Locale objects. A *Locale* provides the coordinate system. The coordinate system is such that a 1.0f unit is equivalent to 1 meter in the physical world. A collection of one or more subgraphs is created and attached to the Locale object. There are two scene graph branches, or subgraphs, in Figure 3.1. Each contains additional created objects like behaviors, transforms, view objects, and 3D shape objects. They, in turn, are programmatically added to the scene. Next these objects are scheduled for rendering, after which the 3D scene comes to life on the display. Typically, each Java 3D program will have one BranchGroup node that contains 3D content (shapes, textures, lights, etc.) and another branch for scene-viewing related activity (zoom, panning, etc.).

At runtime, as soon as a scene graph containing a ViewPlatform object is attached to the Virtual Universe, the Java 3D's rendering engine cranks up and the scene begins to appear on the drawing canvas.

The terms used for the scene graph class hierarchy are constructs and terms borrowed from other object-oriented design patterns, such as VRML. As already noted, VRML is a close cousin of Java 3D in design concepts. A scene is composed of nodes in a treelike structure. Nodes have field values that describe their attributes; some nodes are predefined with appearance and shape properties. There are specialized nodes for behavior attributes of the scene, transform nodes to create object movement, and so on.

The BranchGroup serves as a parent to each subgraph, which consists of a collection of nodes and other types of classes. Only BranchGroup objects can descend from Local superclasses. This is a cast system—you know, my class is more powerful and important than your class.

Subgraphs contain objects to get the desired 3D job done. The objects could, for example, load VRML files, perform transforms, or define a shape and its appearance, in addition to many more effects that will be explored in

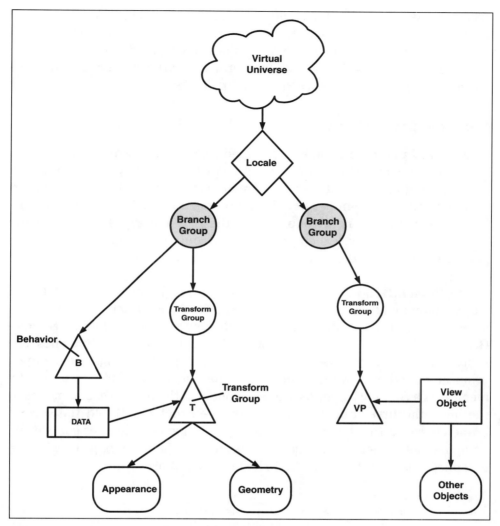

Figure 3.1   SceneGraph treelike structure.

examples in the following chapters. Mixed with data, geometry, and constructs, and you have a virtual 3D world that can be browsed, explored, and moved.

The Java 3D framework provides simplicity and efficiency, enabling the application developer to focus on scene composition and creativity, rather than on performance issues or triangle-strip compositions. The structure of the Java 3D scene graph is detailed in the next chapters; the intent here is to slowly transfer the information you need, to keep you from falling asleep.

Java 3D was designed for creating large, complex 3D scenes. The scope of this book, however, limits the application of Java 3D to small defined applet scenes that provide some interesting viewing and commercial value for today's Web sites. Before we look at a Java 3D scene case study, let's quickly cover some basic Java 3D building blocks.

Grouping Scene Components

Java 3D likes numerous objects grouped together to form multiple group scene components. This is a very useful way to organize your universe and map its design to the real world. There are several types of groupings, and each may have any number of children (components). So far, we have discussed only the BranchGroup. All of these group types belong to the general-purpose class, called, what else, Group. Children of a group are inserted or removed depending on what you are trying to accomplish in the scene.

The BranchGroup acts like a large supporting branch of a tree. It is a major component in the scene graph, which can be attached to the scene locale. A complex Java 3D scene is usually constructed of multiple Branch-Groups attached to the same Local object. Often these branches are switched or activated, based on what the user might be doing. For example, in an animated adventure game, the various levels could each be implemented as a BranchGroup. As the user conquers the first level and moves to the next, the first branch is simply removed (detached) and the second branch is added to the Local. For better performance, branches can also be compiled before being attached to the scene (via the Local object) using the compile() method. Java 3D will do its best to optimize your program.

```
Local   local  =  new Local (myuniverse);
Shape3D myshape  =  new  Shape3D(geometry, appearance);
BranchGroup branch1  =  new  BranchGroup( );
branch1.addChild(myshape);
branch1.compile( );
locale.addBranchGroup(branch1);
```

OrderedGroup(s) make sure their children are rendered in a first-to-last order. This is useful if you want the viewer to see a scene render in a specific sequence. For example, let's say we want to construct a virtual human, and each part, organ, and bone were a unique Java 3D object. How could we build it from the feet up? We would need to create each body part first then add them in order to the OrderedGroup object. That's it. Forget about managing the rendering process. Java 3D does that for you. Ordered groupings are also useful to render decal geometry (geometry that is placed on top of another, such as found in company logos), textures, or 3D text onto other shapes. *DecalGroup* extends OrderedGroup to do just that!

```
Shape3D  box  =  new Shape3D(boxgeometry, a);
Shape3D decal  =  new Shape3D(sunlogo, app);
DecalGroup logo =  new DecalGroup( );
logo.addChild(box);
logo.addChild(decal);
```

The *Switch* groupings are like a logical switch statement:

```
switch(instance) {
     case 0:
            // do not render
     case 1:
            // Render Child 1
     case 2:
            // Render Child 2
     default:
            // Render All
}
```

A Switch selects a child to render by referencing its index mask or its bit mask. This is a common trick to control the level of detail in a scene. The farther the viewer is from an object, the less detail. As the viewer moves closer to the object, an implemented behavior will calculate when to "switch" to render an object in greater detail. For example, let us say you wanted to approach the Earth from Venus. At first, Earth would be a speck, growing larger as you approached at light speed. When you reached 100 miles from the Earth's surface, the view would change, as would the resolution. At 25 miles, the view would change again along with the level of detail. You would use a Switch to accomplish this effect. We would also need to create a behavior (not shown) to index between levels of detail based upon predefined conditions.

```
Shape3D  tinyEarth  =  new  Shape3D(geometry, a1);
Shape3D 100Earth  =  new  Shape3D(geometry, a2);
Shape3D detailEarth  =  new  Shape3D(geometry, a3);
Switch  lodEarth  =  new Switch( );
lodEarth.addChild(tinyEarth);
lodEarth.addChild(100Earth);
lodEarth.addChild(detailEarth);

// Add a Java 3D behavior that indexes between these objects
// as a function of proximity to Earth.
```

We have discussed how it might be useful to group and manage objects. Use BranchGroups to organize your scene. Use OrderedGroups when you need the scene objects to be rendered in a specific order. Finally, use a Switch class when you want to represent multiple versions of the same scene. What if you wanted to move a group of objects together? The next section describes how Java 3D handles transformations of Java 3D objects.

Viewing Model

When a Java 3D scene is created, it gets viewed. The Java 3D API defines a new viewing model to incorporate the physical environment to influence control over the viewing parameters. The view model defines a separation between the virtual environment and the physical environment. In the virtual environment, the programmer will present to the view a bunch of 3D objects, as if you were sitting directly in front of them, like watching TV. You sit there and the objects on the screen float in front of you versus around you. You can't look around the television to see the backside of the actor, for example. This differs from the model that is influenced by a real person who can manipulate input devices to affect how the view model is placed and viewed. Likewise, the action of an object in view would affect the user's input device. Examples of this are pressure-feedback joysticks, haptic input devices, and head-mounted displays (HMD). This is a very different approach from camera-based view models, which attempt to emulate a camera in the virtual world. Programmers must tediously reposition the camera to simulate the human experience, which is different from a physical to virtual to physical correspondence within a common single space, called *the virtual world*.

What's the point of all of this rambling? To show that Java 3D provides a sophisticated viewing model that attempts (with the right extra input/output hardware) to support a framework for leading-edge virtual reality computing and simulation:

- The Screen3D object contains information that describes the display screen's physical properties.

- The PhysicalBody object contains calibration information for advanced input devices, which describe the user's proportions in order to accurately collect and display program interactions.

- The PhysicalEnvironment object contains calibration information to describe the physical environment associated with a hardware input device, such as a 6-degrees-of-freedom tracking device.

The Java 3D rendering engine uses all of these viewing components and information to construct the appropriate viewing matrices.

The ViewPlatform object (a viewpoint) is a leaf node within the Java 3D scene graph. This is the only object associated with the viewing model, which resides as a node within the scene graph structure. By changing the TransformGroup above a particular ViewPlatform object, this will move the view's location and orientation within the virtual world. The ViewPlatform defines a coordinate system within the virtual world. View objects use the ViewPlatform as a point of attachment in the virtual universe and as a reference for determining the view. Think of a ViewPlatform as a viewpoint for the virtual universe. The associated TransformGroup is used to move this viewpoint around and becomes a means for the end user to navigate the scene.

```
ViewPlatform  lookout  =  new  viewPlatform( );
Transform3D movehere  =  new  Transform3D( );
movehere.setTranslation(new Vector3D(0.0f, 2.0f, 0.0f));
TransformGroup navigator = new TransformGroup(movehere );
navigator.addChild(lookout);
```

The *View object* is the main Java 3D object for coordinating all aspects of the viewing model. All components that determine the viewing transform used to render to the 3D canvases are either contained within the View object or within objects referenced by a View object. It is possible in Java 3D to have multiple active View objects, each with control over its own set of canvases. The *Canvas3D* object is the 3D version of the Abstract Windowing Toolkit (AWT) Canvas class. It is an area on which Java 3D will render objects. Think of the View object as an entity, which describes a type of virtual camera, which is used to view the virtual universe from a specified view platform. It can define the horizontal field of view, like a wide-angle camera lens or a telephoto camera lens. It can control the perspective of objects and set a clipping policy that defines when objects are allowed to be in the scene. The View object, in addition to defining the properties of our virtual camera, can also specify the quality of the picture view.

```
View  virtualCamera  =  new  View( );
virtualCamera.setFieldOfView(0.333);
virtualCamera.setBackClipDistance(35.0);
virtualCamera.setFrontClipDistance(0.5);
virtualCamera.setSceneAntialiasingEnable(True);
virtualCamera.attachViewPlatform(lookout);
```

Rendering Model

The Java 3D API was designed as a Java initiative, so cross-platform operability drives the rendering model design. Performance, too, was a goal, but compromises must always be made when portability is the goal. The Java 3D rendering model also gives the programmer great freedom to either programmatically manipulate when and how a scene is created and drawn, or to let Java 3D do everything automatically. The API supports three different rendering modes:

Immediate Mode. Offers flexibility, in that the programmer can programmatically force geometry to be drawn immediately. This may lose some rendering optimizations as a trade-off. There are two immediate mode rendering styles. *Pure immediate mode rendering* prevents Java 3D from doing any automatic rendering. The Java 3D renderer is idle in this mode. The other style is *mixed-mode rendering*, which combines immediate mode and retained or compiled-retained modes. In this state, the Java 3D renderer is constantly running.

Retained Mode. In this mode, the underlying Java 3D logic is aware of how the program is structured. It tries to optimize by: constructing specialized data structures that hold geometry in a manner that enhances rendering speed; compiling objects so they run at maximum speed when invoked; flattening transform manipulations; and many other performance enhancements.

Compiled-Retained Mode. Builds on retained mode to offer advanced optimizations, such as geometry compression, geometry grouping, and scene graph flattening. This mode is accomplished by the programmer requesting Java 3D to compile an object or scene graph. The Java 3D Renderer, when invoked, performs the following jobs in a loop until the program exits:

- Process input.
- Check for collisions.
- Perform behaviors.
- Start playing sounds.
- Traverse the scene graph.
- Render "visible" objects.

Input Model

The Java 3D API uses the current AWT Java classes for keyboard and mouse interactions. Why reinvent the wheel? But AWT falls short of supporting real-time and 6-degrees-of-freedom devices. So the API invented its own real-time I/O class in an effort to support new input extensions to the mouse and keyboard devices.

Tracker Model

The Java 3D API supports 6-degrees-of-freedom tracking devices, such as head-mounted displays (HMD). Since the Java AWT Input Model doesn't support these types of devices, the Java 3D API provided them for the PC gaming and simulation market. In addition, a basic framework exists to support other important input devices, like joysticks and pressure-feedback devices.

Behavior and Event Handling

Java 3D provides a behavior object, which is used to perform actions, like animating objects and processing keyboard and mouse events. The application specifies one or multiple conditions that will "wake up" the behavior to start executing. Such conditions include an AWT event that occurred, time that elapsed, a specified number of frames that were drawn, a collision that was detected, or an object that passed through a specified region. Behavior objects are commonly associated with 3D objects and are used to manipulate their appearance attributes, orientation, position, and interaction with other geometric objects. The Java 3D API provides some easy-to-use classes to handle mouse events to perform mouse-picking of objects in a scene, zooming objects in and out, and changing the object's orientation.

```
import com.sun.j3d.utils.ui.*;

    //  Attach picking behavior utilities to the scene root.
    //  They will wake up when user manipulates a scene object
    //  with the mouse.

    PickDragBehavior behavior = new
        PickDragBehavior(3Dcanvas, objRoot, bounds);

    PickZoomBehavior behavior2 = new
        PickZoomBehavior(3Dcanvas, objRoot, bounds);

    PickTranslateBehavior behavior3 = new
        PickTranslateBehavior(3Dcanvas, objRoot, bounds);
```

Sound Model

Audio is managed within Java 3D programs spatially. The plush and sleek BMW 740il has a powerful audio system. But what's interesting, besides the banks of speakers surrounding the driver, are the controls available to manipulate the audio signal. You can, for example, load your favorite tune and command the CD player to simulate what the music would sound like in a jazz club or an amphitheater. Controls are available to design virtually any size or dimension of room in which you wish to hear the music played. Many home theater sound systems offer this capability. Many of us have had the wonderful experience of THX in a movie theater when *Jurassic Park* was released. The direction, amplitude, and modulation of the audio mix added a new dimension to our experience. Not only could we see the Dino running behind the jeep, looking for a midnight snack, but we could feel and sense action coming in all directions. Sometimes, this is referred to as 3D sound. The Java 3D API supports 3D sound and MIDI support, in addition to standard digital audio.

VRML

VRML is treated as a file format rather than a programming language. Java doesn't force a file format needed to describe a scene. *Loaders* are used to take an existing file, like *.wrl for VRML, and import it to the 3D scene by parsing the file and invoking associated Java 3D methods. There will be some important "plumbing" between Java 3D and VRML 3.0 in the future, but the details are still being worked out, though Java 3D by design interfaces nicely with VRML technology.

The Java 3D API Interfaces

Java elements, including the core language and emerging extensions, are grouped by functionality, which makes management of the class name space framework easier. A group of Java classes and interfaces aligned by common functionality are called *packages*. The Java 3D API requires two packages, *javax.vecmath* and *javax.media.j3d*.

Vector Math Library

The first interface (see Figure 3.2) is the Vector Math Library, a set of objects used to create and model other Java 3D objects. The library provides a useful set of methods for color and position components, volumes, vectors, and matrix mathematics. This package is set apart from the standard Java 3D package, but is required by Java 3D methods. Users can manipulate these mathematical constructs, which seem to be grouped outside Java 3D for use by other interfaces in the future. It has the components described in the following subsections.

Tuple Objects

Tuple objects specify two, three, and four element values used to represent points, coordinates, and vectors. Methods are provided to add, set, subtract, and get object attributes. Tuples are grouped by storage class.

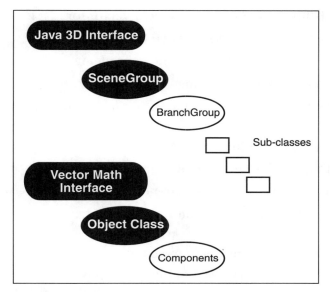

Figure 3.2 Java 3D structure.

Tuple2f. Used to manipulate two-element, single-precision, floating-point x, y coordinates with two variables for X and Y.

  + class java.vecmath.Point2f—a set of points for x, y

  + class java.vecmath.TexCoord2f—texture coordinates for x, y

  + class java.vecmath.Vector2f—a vector set for x, y

Tuple3b. Used to manipulate a three-element, coordinates in bytes for X, Y, and Z.

  + class java.vecmath.Color3b—defines 3-byte values for color. Java defines a byte as a signed integer from −128 to 127. This is *not* the common 0–255 for color values. Java 3D helps by treating the values in Color3b with a range 0–255.

Tuple3d. Used to manipulate three-element, double-precision floating-point x, y, z coordinates.

  + class java.vecmath.Point3d—defines a set of points for x, y, z

  + class java.vecmath.Vector3d—a vector set for x, y, and z

Tuple3f. Used to manipulate three-element, single-precision, floating-point x, y, z coordinates with three variables for X, Y, and Z.

  + class java.vecmath.Color3f—floats for RGB color values

  + class java.vecmath.Point3f—set of points as floats for x, y, z

+ class java.vecmath.TexCoord3f—three-element vector for x, y, z

+ class java.vecmath.Vector3f—vector created from x, y, z

Tuple4b.   Commonly used to compose color and alpha elements.

+ class java.vecmath.Color4b—four-element color in bytes

Tuple4d.   A four-element tuple for x, y, z, and w coordinates in double precision.

+ class java.vecmath.Point4d—creates a four-element point

+ class java.vecmath.Quat4d—a four-element quaternion for x, y, z, w

+ class java.vecmath.Vector4d—creates a four-element vector

Tuple4f.   A four-element tuple for x, y, z, and w coordinates in single precision.

+ class java.vecmath.Color4f—creates four-element color

+ class java.vecmath.Point4f—creates four-element point

+ class java.vecmath.Quat4f—a four-element quaternion for x, y, z, w

+ class java.vecmath.Vector4f—creates a four-element vector

AxisAngle4d.   A four-element axis angle in double-precision, floating-point values for x, y, z, and angle. A rotation in radians of an angle about the vector x, y, and z.

AxisAngle4f.   A four-element axis angle in single-precision, floating-point values for x, y, z, and angle. A rotation in radians of an angle about the vector x, y, and z.

Gvector.   Many entities in geometry and physics, such as force and velocity, involve both magnitude and direction, and cannot be fully characterized by a single real number. So a directed line segment is used, which has an initial point (P), a terminal point (Q), and a vector length. Vectors are denoted by lowercase bold letters such as **u, v,** and **w.**

Figure 3.3 describes two vectors (**u,v**) represented by directed line segments. Vector operations can be performed to calculate, for example, speed and direction. GVector would be used in programs that simulate real-world laws of physics, for example, to model an airplane descending at a speed of 100 miles per hour at an angle of 30 degrees below horizontal. (The *GVector* class provides a general double precision and dynamically resizable one-dimension vector representation.) As the plane reaches a certain point, let's assume it encounters a wind shear with a velocity of 30 miles per hour in the direction of N 45 degrees E. This might be part of a flight simulator game

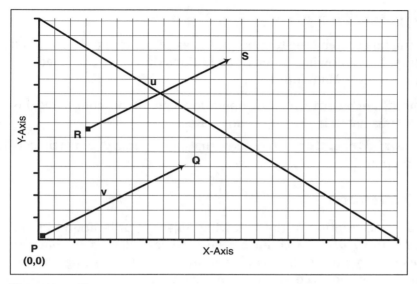

Figure 3.3 Vectors.

that provides conditions during a landing or take-off. The result would be a change to the plane's speed and direction that would cause a problem for the virtual pilot to solve. Many applications of vectors involve the use of triangles and trigonometry.

Matrix Objects

Matrix multiplication is used for many operations involving positional coordinates, such as 3D model rotation, translation, and scaling. Transforms are also used to map model data from 3D coordinate systems to 2D coordinate systems, and vice versa. As the 3D object progresses down the graphics pipeline, and ultimately gets drawn on the screen, matrices play a big role along the way. Java 3D has a tool chest of objects to simplify the work.

The Matrix objects come with many useful methods for performing desired operations:

Matrix3f. A single-precision, floating-point 3×3 matrix.

Matrix3d. A double-precision, floating-point 3×3 matrix.

Matrix4f. A single-precision, floating-point 4×4 matrix.

Matrix4d. A double-precision, floating-point 4×4 matrix.

Gmatrix. A double-precision and dynamically resizable two-dimensional $N \times M$ matrix class.

VectorMath Exception Classes

We all make mistakes from time to time, and most of us want to know when an error occurs. The following are error conditions that can be trapped and reported for the Vector Math interface.

MismatchedSizeException.   An operation cannot be completed because of a mismatch in the object attributes.

SingularMatrixException.   Indicates that the inverse of a matrix cannot be computed.

The Java 3D Interface

A more detailed description of the following objects can be found in *The Java 3D API Specification*, written by the core Java 3D team from Sun Microsystems (Henry Sowizral, Kevin Rushforth, Michael Deering, Warren Dale, and one of this book's coauthors, Dan Petersen).

Alpha.   Converts time values into alpha values [0.0 to 1.0]. For example, ObjectABC goes from (0,0,0) to (1,1,1) in the same amount of physical time, regardless of the frame rate between rendering the animated sequence. This keeps everything in sync within a scene.

Bounds.   An abstract class used to define a region of influence, an activation region, or a scheduling region for an object. Bounds are useful for collision detection and to trigger behavior or scene rendering. Bounds can be defined in the following ways:

    BoundingBox.   An axis-aligned box volume.

    BoundingPolytope.   A closed, convex polygonal volume.

    BoundingSphere.   A spherical bounding volume.

Canvas3D.   An extension of an AWT canvas for rendering. This is what the program draws on.

CompressedGeometry.   Used to store geometry in compressed format.

CompressedGeometryHeader.   Stores information specific to the compressed geometry that is used to decompress it.

Font3D.   Used to store extruded 3D glyphs to compose 3D text.

FontExtrusion.   Used to describe the extrusion path of the Font3D object.

GraphicsContext3D.   Created and used by a Canvas 3D object for rendering.

HiResCoord.   Specifies the location of scene components within the Virtual Universe.

Locale.   Acts as a container for a collection of subgraphs and specifies an originating point (or origin) in the Virtual Universe.

NodeReferenceTable.   Used as a parameter during the cloning operation of a tree subgraph. Cloning is a method enabling reuse of Java 3D code and parts of a Java 3D scene.

PhysicalBody.   Used to specify a user's body anomalies for tracking-device calibration. This class maps the physical realm with the virtual realm.

PhysicalEnvironment.   Describes the physical world for sensor object calibration.

PickShape.   Describes a pick shape for these subclasses:

> **PickPoint.**   A specified pickable point.
>
> **PickRay.**   A specified pickable ray.
>
> **PickSegment.**   Extends PickRay to define a pick line segment.

SceneGraphObject.   An abstract class that defines methods common to subclasses, such as node and component objects.

> **Node.**   Composed of two subclasses: Group and Leaf node objects. Objects in Java 3D are called "nodes."
>
> > **Group.**   Special classes that group one or more group child nodes as follows:
> >
> > > **BranchGroup.**   A parent of a subgraph in a scene graph.
> > >
> > > **OrderedGroup.**   Orders child rendering accordingly.
> > >
> > > > **DecalGroup.**   Used to define decal geometry, such as creating a decal for a shape.
> > >
> > > **SharedGroup.**   Allows sharing of subgraph parts.
> > >
> > > **Switch.**   Used to select among subgraphs for rendering.
> > >
> > > **TransformGroup.**   Used to transform a group of children or subgraphs to affect orientation and scale.
> >
> > **Leaf.**   An abstract class for nodes with no children, just components.
> >
> > > **Background.**   Specifies solid color or image to fill background.
> > >
> > > **Behavior.**   Framework for event handling and animation of objects with the following types:
> > >
> > > > **Billboard.**   Methods for billboard behavior.
> > > >
> > > > **Interpolator.**   Methods for interpolation behavior among multiple states.

ColorInterpolator.   Color interpolator behavior.

PathInterpolator.   Defines base class for all path interpolators:

> **PositionPathInterpolator.**   Position path behavior.
>
> **RotPosPathInterpolator.**   Position/orientation.
>
> **RotPosScalePathInterpolator.**   Rotate/position scale.
>
> **RotationPathInterpolator.**   Rotation path behaviors.

PositionInterpolator.   Position behavior.

RotationInterpolator.   Rotation behavior.

ScaleInterpolator.   Scaling behavior.

SwitchValueInterpolator.   Switch behavior.

TransparencyInterpolator.   Transparency behavior.

LOD.   Contains an ordered list of subgraphs and level-of-detail value.

> **DistanceLOD.**   Distance-based LOD class.

BoundingLeaf.   Bounding region references by other nodes.

Clip.   Defines the clipping region.

Fog.   Applies fog parameters to a specified region.

> **ExponentialFog.**   Defines how fog density is applied.
>
> **LinearFog.**   Defines fog density over distance.

Light.   Abstract class containing common constructs for all light subclasses.

> **AmbientLight.**   Defines an ambient light source object.
>
> **DirectionalLight.**   Defines a directional light source.
>
> **PointLight.**   Defines a fixed light source.
>
> **SpotLight.**   Defines a spotlight source object.

Link.   Used to link a specific SharedGroup node among multiple BranchGroups.

Morph.   Object changes form between geometry sets.

Shape3D.   Used to construct 3D objects from geometry.

Sound.   An abstract class that defines common properties to all sound objects.

BackgroundSound.   Plays background sound.

PointSound.   Sound spatially located at some point.

ConeSound.   Sound directed along a vector in space.

Soundscape.   Defines the listener's environment.

ViewPlatform.   Defines a viewing model that the viewer uses to navigate the Virtual Universe of the scene.

Component Attributes

The following classes are used to define object properties that will determine how 3D objects will look when rendered.

Appearance.   Defines rendering properties, such as color, and is used by other objects, like Shape3D.

AuralAttributes.   Defines properties for the Soundscape node.

ColoringAttributes.   Defines properties for color.

DepthComponent.   Defines a 2D array of Z values.

DepthComponentFloat.   A 2D Z array of floating points.

DepthComponentInt.   A 2D Z array of integers.

DepthComponentNative.   A 2D Z array in a device storage class.

LineAttributes.   Defines line attributes.

PointAttributes.   Defines the appearance of points.

PolygonAttributes.   Defines polygon characteristics.

RenderingAttributes.   Retrieves/sets rendering state information.

TextureAttributes.   Defines texture-mapping properties.

TransparencyAttributes.   Defines properties affecting transparency.

Appearance Components

The Appearance component class has additional properties that can be defined for a given object.

Bounds Object.   Defines a containing volume.

Material Object.   Defines properties used with lighting.

Texture Object.   Used to create a texture map object.

Texture2D Object.   Sets texture image in 2D.

Texture3D Object.   Sets texture in 3D.

TexCoordGeneration Object.   Coordinate system for texture mapping.

MediaContainer Object.   Component of Sound node that defines the sound data.

ImageComponent.   Classes used for textures and background images.

ImageComponent2D.   Defines a 2D array of pixels.

ImageComponent3D.   Defines a 3D array of pixels.

Geometry Components

A Shape Java 3D object consists of Appearance and Geometry components. The following are the provided properties that relate to geometry data formats.

Geometry.   Abstract class for geometry components used by the Shape3D node.

   CompressedGeometry.   Condenses geometric information to save space.

   GeometryArray.   Abstract class for common array components that contain vertex information.

   GeometryStripArray.   Abstract class for all strip constructs.

   LineStripArray.   Defines array of vertices as a set of connected line strips.

   TriangleFanArray.   Defines a triangle fan strip.

   TriangleStripArray.   Defines a triangle strip.

   IndexedGeometryArray.   Abstract class allows vertex data to be accessed via a level of indirection.

   IndexedGeometryStripArray.   Abstract class from which all indexed strip primitives are derived.

   IndexedLineStripArray

   IndexedTriangleFanArray

   IndexedTriangleStripArray

   IndexedLineArray.   A pair of indexed vertices that define a line.

   IndexedPointArray.   An array of indexed vertices as individual points.

IndexedQuadArray. Defines an array of index vertices as individual quadrilaterals.

IndexedTriangleArray. Indexed vertex array that defines individual triangles.

LineArray. A pair of vertices that define a line segment.

PointArray. An array of vertices that define a point.

QuadArray. An array of vertices that define a quadrilateral.

TriangleArray. An array of vertices that define a triangle.

Raster. Allows drawing of a raster image that is attached to a 3D point in space.

Text3D. 3D glyphs used to construct 3D text.

Screen3D. Provides a 3D version of the AWT screen object.

Sensor. Abstract concept of a hardware input device.

View. Coordinates rendering process and scene viewing.

ViewPlatform. Controls position, orientation, and scale of the view.

VirtualUniverse. Used to create a new Virtual Universe.

WakeupCondition. Abstract class for single notification condition.

WakeupAnd. Any number of conditions linked by the AND operator.

WakeupAndOfOrs. OR conditions linked by AND.

WakeupOr. Specifies wakeup conditions linked by the OR operator.

WakeupOrOfAnds. Specifies any number of AND conditions linked by OR.

WakeupCriterion. Abstract class for notification criteria. Any one or more of the following can be specified:

WakeupOnAWTEvent. AWT event occurred.

WakeupOnActivation. Activation region penetrated.

WakeupOnBehaviorPost. Specific event occurred.

WakeupOnCollisionEntry. Object collision event.

WakeupOnCollisionExit. Collision stops.

WakeupOnCollisionMovement. During collision.

WakeupOnDeactivation. Region no longer active.

WakeupOnElapsedFrames.   Wakeup after specified number of frames.

WakeupOnElapsedTime.   Wakeup after n milliseconds.

WakeupOnSensorEntry.   Wakeup on View boundary.

WakeupOnSensorExit.   Wakeup on boundary exit.

WakeupOnTransformChange.   Wakeup when transform group changes.

WakeupOnViewPlatformEntry.   Wakeup View platform intersection.

WakeupOnViewPlatformExit.   Wake on View platform exit.

For a detailed listing, consult the Java 3D API specification or HTML Javadoc contents for the API.

By now you should have a better understanding of what's included in the Java 3D API. The rest of this book contains useful applets that can be modified at a high level from the HTML interface. You don't even have to know how to program with Java and Java 3D to use these programs. The goal was to enable creativity for home pages, using 3D graphics, so that you can make your Web site more interesting and interactive. Visit any commercial Web site today, and you'll see GIF animations are heavily used. However, they are only cute static "movies," limited in functionality. For about the same size in space, Java 3D can replace this technology with increased functionality and interactivity that will hold visitors' attention to a particular Web page.

But first, let's replace the standard "Hello World" example with a robust scene graph application. The following example will give you a working knowledge of many of the 3D objects we just covered. If you are a programmer, dive right in. If not, you might want to just run the example from the CD and see what we are talking about before moving on to the next chapter.

Java 3D Case Study: Carnival

Most of the applets in this book use very small scene graphs. Their virtual worlds are on a visible scale from a single vantage point. Instead of a basic "Hello World" example, we decided to try an interesting case study of the larger variety. This scene has numerous active objects that are outside the user's view. Some navigation is provided, which not only allows the user to visit a virtual carnival but also presents an interesting study in scene navigation. We would have liked to replicate the opening scene in *Contact* by doing the visible universe fly-by (70 billion light years out from Earth), and throw in a few Klingon battle cruisers to shoot at, but then this book would have never been written on time. Nevertheless, we found a pretty good example to start the learning process.

Carnival (see Figure 3.4) was kindly contributed by Douglas Pew, a software engineer at Logicon Geodynamics, Inc. Doug received his Bachelors degree in Computer Science at George Mason University and wrote the Carnival applet while working toward his Masters degree in Computer Science there. He can be reached by email at http://access.digex.net/~dpew.

The Carnival program generates four virtual amusement rides: airplane, ferris wheel, pirate ship, and tea cup. All of these components are grouped into a single Virtual Universe. In Java 3D, a Virtual Universe represents a container and a coordinate system for associated objects. The program is organized in a very common sequence that provides constructs for running as an applet or as a standalone application.

Step 1: Specify Which Java Classes to Import

```
import java.applet.Applet;

import java.awt.BorderLayout;

import java.awt.event.*;

import java.util.ArrayList;
```

Figure 3.4 Carnival Java 3D application.

The classes that have the prefix "java" are part of the core Java API and thus are necessary for event handling, window layout, and applet creation. To avoid naming conflicts and to organize a group of related objects and their interface definitions, Java defines a class library and calls it a *package*. All of the Java 3D classes belong to the javax.media.j3d package because Java 3D is part of the Java Media API set. The *import* statement is similar to the *include* statement in C. The entire group of classes can be included by using the asterisk (*) wild card symbol following the class and interface name. The classes imported must have *public* access.

The core Java development environment provides several classes used to create Java programs. Various Java APIs, such as Java 3D, also provide reusable classes in addition to the JDK. In your 3D programs, both will be used. We recommend using the Java classes provided before building your own. Here is a short description of the JDK core packages. We also recommend reading a Java reference book to learn the details of each class and interface.

Java Platform Core API Packages

* package java.applet	// Java applet interface
* package java.awt	// Java Abstract Window Toolkit— GUI building
* package java.awt.datatransfer	// AWT Clipboard
* package java.awt.event	// Keyboard, mouse, window event handling
* package java.awt.image	// Image processing
* package java.beans	// JavaBeans—component building
* package java.io	// Input—output stream handling
* package java.lang	// Object class, class and thread support
* package java.lang.reflect	// Class member interface; that is, a public modifier
* package java.math	// Math routines
* package java.net	// Network, sockets, URL, content, MIME
* package java.rmi	// Remote method interface to remote objects
* package java.rmi.dgc	// Extends RMI; server-side garbage collection

| * package java.rmi.registry | // Database of remote objects; RMI registration |

* package java.rmi.registry // Database of remote objects; RMI registration

* package java.rmi.server // Remote server support; class loader

* package java.security // Certificate, private, and public key

* package java.security.acl // Access control list; guarded resource access

* package java.security.interfaces // Digital signature algorithm (DSA) support

* package java.sql // SQL support

* package java.text // Bidirectional iteration support over text

* package java.util // Date, random, observer interface, hash, and others

* package java.util.zip // Open/close *.zip files and other support

```
import javax.media.j3d.*;
import javax.vecmath.*;
import com.sun.j3d.utils.applet.MainFrame;
```

The Java 3D API classes prefixed by "javax" indicate packages belonging to the Standard Java Extension APIs. Java 3D also provides some convenience classes under the *com.sun.j3d* package. In this import statement we are going to use a class that will construct our Java 3D main window. This special Java class is called the *MainFrame* class.

```
import carnival.utils.view.*;
import carnival.utils.behaviors.mouse.*;
import carnival.rides.ViewPoint.ViewPoint;
import carnival.rides.DevilsWrath.DevilsWrath;
import carnival.rides.Plane.Plane;
import carnival.rides.Bueller.Bueller;
import carnival.utils.geometry.*;
import carnival.scenic.*;
```

In addition to the typical classes used within a Java 3D program, we have created our own package of classes, which are prefixed by "carnival."

The required classes and files are organized in the following manner: A directory is created to hold the program with a bunch of subdirectories:

```
Carnival
    \carnival
    \utils
        \behaviors
        \geometry
    \rides
        \ViewPoint
        \DevilsWrath
        \Plane
        \Bueller
    \scenic
```

In addition to the various custom classes for the program, the main class file can be located at the top level as well. Java 3D supports the Java archive format, so all of these loose files and components can be neatly tucked into one file and (optionally) compressed into a ZIP archive. Both the expanded model and the archive model will work. The JAR archive file would look like:

```
\Carnival
    Carnival.jar
```

The JAR archive format was designed mainly to facilitate the packaging of Java applets or applications into a single archive. When the components of an applet or application (class files, images, and sounds) are combined into a single archive, they can be downloaded by a Java agent (like a browser) in a single HTTP transaction, rather than requiring a new connection for each piece. This dramatically improves download time. The jar tool also compresses files and so further improves download time; in addition, it allows individual entries in a file to be assigned by the applet author so that their origin can be authenticated. Thus, Carnival.jar would contain a directory listing, plus all of the files:

```
steamboat% jar tvf Carnival.jar
    5889 Wed Apr 29 15:05:28 PDT 1998 META-INF/MANIFEST.MF
    5994 Wed Apr 29 09:58:36 PDT 1998 Carnival.class
     762 Wed Apr 29 09:42:14 PDT 1998 ControlPanel$1.class
     765 Wed Apr 29 09:42:14 PDT 1998 ControlPanel$2.class
    3481 Wed Apr 29 09:42:14 PDT 1998 ControlPanel.class
     521 Wed Apr 29 09:42:26 PDT 1998 ControlPanelBehavior.class
    1514 Wed Apr 29 09:42:16 PDT 1998 Ground.class
    3295 Wed Apr 29 09:58:38 PDT 1998 carnival/rides/DevilsWrath/
DevilsWrath.class
    2176 Wed Apr 29 09:58:40 PDT 1998 carnival/rides/DevilsWrath/
Platter.class
     946 Wed Apr 29 09:58:48 PDT 1998 carnival/rides/DevilsWrath/
InnerPlatter.class
```

```
   2898 Wed Apr 29 09:58:54 PDT 1998 carnival/rides/DevilsWrath/
RidePlatter.class
   3829 Wed Apr 29 09:58:56 PDT 1998 carnival/rides/DevilsWrath/
Teacup.class
206540 Wed Apr 29 01:43:38 PDT 1998 carnival/rides/DevilsWrath/
Teacup.3db
   4137 Wed Apr 29 09:58:40 PDT 1998 carnival/rides/Bueller/Bueller.class
   2594 Wed Apr 29 09:58:50 PDT 1998 carnival/rides/Bueller/Spoke.class
   1616 Wed Apr 29 09:58:56 PDT 1998 carnival/rides/Bueller/Gondola.class
   2044 Wed Apr 29 09:58:38 PDT 1998 carnival/rides/Plane/Plane.class
   2940 Wed Apr 29 09:58:50 PDT 1998 carnival/rides/Plane/PlaneArm.class
   3086 Wed Apr 29 09:58:54 PDT 1998 carnival/rides/Plane/Wildcat.class
182364 Wed Apr 29 01:43:58 PDT 1998 carnival/rides/Plane/p51.3db
   2020 Wed Apr 29 09:58:36 PDT 1998 carnival/rides/ViewPoint/
ViewPoint.class
   4130 Wed Apr 29 09:58:46 PDT 1998 carnival/scenic/Galleon.class
289236 Wed Apr 29 01:44:28 PDT 1998 carnival/scenic/galleon.3db
   1669 Wed Apr 29 09:58:52 PDT 1998 carnival/utils/io/ReadRawShape.class
   1570 Wed Apr 29 09:58:52 PDT 1998 carnival/utils/io/RawShape.class
    247 Wed Apr 29 09:58:40 PDT 1998 carnival/utils/view/Viewable.class
   1832 Wed Apr 29 09:58:42 PDT 1998 carnival/utils/view/
BillboardMgr.class
    447 Wed Apr 29 09:58:42 PDT 1998 carnival/utils/view/
ViewControl.class
   2503 Wed Apr 29 09:58:42 PDT 1998 carnival/utils/view/ViewSite.class
   1968 Wed Apr 29 09:58:46 PDT 1998 carnival/utils/view/
LookViewControl.class
    469 Wed Apr 29 09:58:50 PDT 1998 carnival/utils/view/
BillboardMgrNode.class
   1776 Wed Apr 29 09:58:54 PDT 1998 carnival/utils/view/
PlaneViewControl.class
   2022 Wed Apr 29 09:58:50 PDT 1998 carnival/utils/geometry/
ShapeBuffer.class
   2759 Wed Apr 29 09:58:50 PDT 1998 carnival/utils/geometry/Box.class
   1805 Wed Apr 29 09:58:42 PDT 1998 carnival/utils/behaviors/
mouse/MouseActivator.class
   2786 Wed Apr 29 09:58:52 PDT 1998 carnival/utils/behaviors/
mouse/MouseZoom.class
   2848 Wed Apr 29 09:58:52 PDT 1998 carnival/utils/behaviors/
mouse/MouseBehavior.class
   3238 Wed Apr 29 09:58:52 PDT 1998 carnival/utils/behaviors/
mouse/MouseLook.class
   3110 Wed Apr 29 09:58:56 PDT 1998 carnival/utils/behaviors/
mouse/MouseRotator.class
```

Now take a look at those "carnival.<path>.<class>" statements again. Do you see the correlation? In order for the execution environment to locate our program, we need to set up a path for the Java interpreter to look for when the applet is invoked. We need it to find our JAR archive.

On a PC:

```
SET CLASSPATH=%CLASSPATH%;Carnival.jar
```

This appends the JAR file to the current CLASSPATH variable. This means the user must be in the current Carnival directory for the interpreter to successfully start the program.

On a UNIX (Solaris):

```
CLASSPATH=$CLASSPATH:Carnival.jar
export CLASSPATH
```

The same task is accomplished in setting the CLASSPATH environment variable. The next job of the program is to tell us how it plans to run. This is a pretty simple Java programming concept.

Step 2: Declare the Program as an Applet to Run in a Browser

Within the file Carnival.java:

```
public class Carnival extends Applet {
    ** data **
    ** constructors **
    ** methods **
}
```

Java is both a *compiled* and *interpreted* language. After the programmer creates the program file, ending in *.java*, the compiler is invoked and the source code is compiled into a *bytecode*. This is an intermediate format that is interpreted by the JVM at runtime on the client machine. The compilers must adhere to a strict Java specification to ensure portability across multiple computer platforms. When the Java program is compiled into bytecode, a class file is generated with a (*.class*) suffix. The runtime interpreter reads the class files and executes its instructions.

Java applets are generally small, specific programs that run in a Web browser. Certain restrictions apply to applet programs, such as a tight security model to prevent unwanted system tampering. Java applications are designed to run outside the Web browser by invocation from the command line. Unlike applets, they have a *main( )* method. To run the program, the Java interpreter must be invoked:

```
% java -mx64m Carnival
```

The Java interpreter, by default, allocates 16 megabytes for the heap size, which is used when dynamically allocated objects and arrays are created. In our Carnival example, the default heap size is too small. The Java interpreter provides a command-line interface to increase the heap size, called *maxmem* or *-mx*. Appending a letter after the unit amount specifies the size. In our case, we have allocated 64 megabytes.

Step 3: Invoke the Standalone Option

```
public static void main(String[] args) {
        new MainFrame(new Carnival(args), 600, 450);
}
```

Java 3D provides its own main window frame that is invoked if the program is run from the command line. This is a nice feature because it can run as an application or as an applet. MainFrame is invoked when main( ) is called. The main method in turn will call other methods to perform some computation. The arguments are passed from main ( ) to the program all the way from the command line. An array of strings or command-line arguments are expected, then tested, after which some action is taken. In this case, Carnival is invoked with the array of command-line arguments and two values for window width and window height. The main( ) method is ignored when the program is run as an applet.

Step 4: Create a Scene and Attach It to a Virtual Universe

The first item of business is to specify a constructor for the Carnival class, which will create the BranchGraph to include 3D Shape objects and their behaviors. Then it adds this newly created BranchGraph to the Locale object, which was generated from the SimpleUniverse utility. This is also a good place to process command-line arguments, which might require certain state flags to be set that will be used later in the program.

```
187    public Carnival(String[] args) {
188        SimpleUniverse universe;
189        Locale          locale;
190        BranchGroup      scene;
191        View             view;
192
193        int i;
194        for (i = 0; i < args.length; i++) {
```

```
195          if (args[i].startsWith("-")) {
196              if (args[i].equals("-notea"))
197                  do_teacup = false;
198              if (args[i].equals("-help"))
199              {
200                  usage();
201                  System.exit(0);
202              }
203          }
204      }
205
206      sites = new ArrayList(5,5);
207      root = new BranchGroup();
208
209
210      createSceneGraph();
211      createControlCenter();
212      universe = new SimpleUniverse();
213      locale   = new Locale(universe);
214      locale.addBranchGraph(root);
215      panel.initialize();
216  }
```

This section of the program defines a constructor that is called when the applet is run from a browser or called from main( ) when it is run as a standalone program. The first section simply parses any command-line argument present that starts with an en (–) dash. This applies to the program only when it is run as a standalone, which uses the *argv* interface. Applets use a different interface. In lines 193–204, the user could specify two command-line options. The program argument "-help" will invoke the usage( ) method, then the program will exit. This is a common programming practice of documenting all of the possible arguments available to the user. In this case, there is only one:

```
Carnival -notea
```

If this is passed on the command-line argument, the program will not create the teacup ride for the scene. The Teacup component is fairly large and has many transforms, so it might hinder the program from running at all on lower performing computers.

The rest of the constructor will invoke high-level methods that will generate all of the components needed in our program to create a virtual carnival. Line 206 will create a multidimensional array that allocates five arrays, each holding 5 bytes. Next the BranchGroup is created, to serve as a parent to each subgraph, which consists of a collection of nodes and other types of classes that will be used to build our carnival.

The meat of the program is contained in the createSceneGraph( ) method. Carnival rides will be created with a ground for everything to sit on, and actions will be defined to operate the rides. That's right. The whole carnival operation will be automated. That means no expensive labor and benefits to pay; no overhead costs and no employees to manage. In order to do this, we need a control center (line 211). This will provide a means of navigating our carnival with predefined camera locations. That way, by a click of a button, we can check out what's happening on the ferris wheel or see if any kids are getting sick on the teacup ride.

Finally, we have nearly completed the creation of our carnival and will soon be open for business. The scene is formed of parts that retain their individuality, yet represent the measurable whole called the Virtual Universe. As the Java 3D program executes, a 3D scene is constructed. The first procedure a programmer implements is the Virtual Universe object (line 212); he or she next attaches one or more Locale objects (line 213). A Locale provides the coordinate system. The coordinate system is right-handed, where a 1.0f unit is equivalent to 1 meter in the physical world. A collection of one or more subgraphs is created and attached to the Locale object (line 214).

Step 5: Define Objects and Their Attributes

Inside the createSceneGraph( ) method, the virtual scene is organized; objects for the scene are defined and created; and controls over the scene objects are defined. Every Java 3D scene is composed of objects. Specifically, Scene Graph objects. These scene objects reference node component objects. For example, lights are node objects, and an Appearance object is a node component of the Light node.

Scene graph objects contain a bunch of Java 3D node and node component objects that are connected in a treelike branch structure called a subgraph. Once a subgraph has been created it can then be attached to a virtual universe, via the Locale object, making the objects "live." Optionally, the entire subgraph can be compiled for better performance, prior to being attached to the Virtual Universe.

So, inside the createSceneGraph( ) method, we said Node objects are defined and created. There are two kinds of Node objects: Group and Leaf. Group node objects "glue" scene graph elements together and are "proud parents" to several Group node "children." A good example of a Group node object is a TransformGroup object, which defines a single spatial transform used to position, orient, and scale all of its children. The TransformGroup Leaf Node objects define components of the scene, such as lights, sound, shapes (geometry), and how objects act (called behaviors). Defining a scene node object is simple:

```
141   BoundingSphere bounds;
142   bounds = new BoundingSphere(
new Point3d(0.0, 0.0, 0.0), 400.0);
143   AmbientLight aLgt = new AmbientLight(alColor);
144   aLgt.setInfluencingBounds(bounds);
145   root.addChild(aLgt);
```

Step 6: Define Behaviors and Event Handling

We are still trying to complete the creation of the scene graph. We need to handle mouse events, animations, and object behaviors in order to make our scene interesting and interactive.

Step 7: Define the Viewing Model

Java 3D provides a couple of objects to handle viewing the scene in our example. The View object is used to determine how transforms will be used when rendering to the Canvas3D (an extension of the AWT Canvas object). A Java 3D program can navigate within the Virtual Universe by modifying a ViewPlatform's parent (a TransformGroup object). A TransformGroup is used to move the viewpoint around the scene. We said that Java 3D scenes consist of subgraphs; they form a collection of objects, shapes, behaviors, and transforms.

Step 8: Add Everything to the Scene and Enjoy the Show

```
210   createSceneGraph();
211   createControlCenter();
212   universe = new SimpleUniverse();
213   locale   = new Locale(universe);
214   locale.addBranchGraph(root);
```

The SceneGraph has been created with defined objects and behaviors for our carnival (line 210). The user interface is built so that all the user has to do to move around is point and click and jump to predefined viewpoints of the Carnival universe (line 211). The next method uses a universe builder utility to establish a Virtual Universe with a single high-resolution Locale object (line 213). Think of a Locale as the provider of the coordinate system used by objects within the Carnival universe. As soon as the SceneGraph is attached to the Carnival's Virtual Universe (line 214), the Java 3D's rendering engine is invoked, and the scene will appear on the display.

There are a few hundred lines of code behind the scenes doing much more than we can cover here. But hopefully you'll start getting the hang of it. We'll go over much more of the Java 3D API in detail in the following chapters. So if your brain is aching a little bit now, hang in there. The book gets a lot more fun, and so do the sample applets.

Beautiful Geometry

"You're never too old to do goofy stuff."

—WARD CLEAVER

This is where it all starts. Geometry. The scaffolding of computer graphics. Smooth, computer-generated curves and surfaces were made popular by the famous teapot of Martin Newell (see Figure 4.1) based on cubic Bezier patches. The teapot has become the symbol of innovation in the field of computer graphics. Java 3D expands on this innovation by abstracting the interface to high-order objects. You can deal with objects instead of vertices. With Java 3D, you create content instead of worrying about the rendering process.

Morphing Description and Usage

The applet can take three geometry shapes and "mutate" from one shape to the other (see Figure 4.2). This is called *morphing*. The result is an interesting sequence that will keep people staring at the Web page. Some special geometry could be contracted from a number of companies or created internally to present more interesting effects, like a waving hand, a company logo, or even the famous dancing baby. There is also some CAD/MCAD software that you could purchase to build your own model sequence. Just make sure it supports *.obj and *.wrl output formats. Vertex and polygon

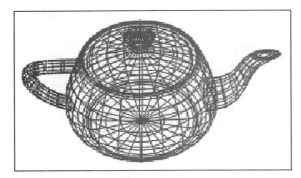

Figure 4.1 Newell's famous teapot.

reduction may be necessary because the Java 3D Morph object likes all three models to have the same vertex count.

This Web applet was designed to be an eye-catcher (see Figure 4.3). You can also define the 3D object shape for each sequence. This program can also be associated with a single URL link, or you can choose to have just an inactive URL link. This will be your decision when modifying the HTML interface. When the user clicks the morph object, by pressing the left mouse button over the picture, the Web browser will load the associated URL page and exit the program.

Morphing Parameters Explained

Since this will be the first sample program, let's go over some general information first. Each Java 3D applet will use the following HTML tags to change the Java 3D logic. That way you don't have to be a Java 3D programmer and spend weeks dealing with engineering the code.

Figure 4.2 Morphing multiple 3D objects.

Figure 4.3   Morphing applet.

```
<PARAM NAME="ObjectName1" VALUE="hand">
```

This parameter has the keyword "ObjectName" and can specify the name of the objects you intend to flip through during the 3D presentation. The ObjectName identifies the name of the morphing sequence. It refers to the names of the local files that will be used to create the Morph 3D object. For example, the demo uses the following local files: hand1.obj, hand2.obj, and hand3.obj. This applet only supports morphing three files, and they need to be in the WaveFront format (*.obj) or converted VRML2.0 (*.wrl) to Java classes (also refer to the CD directory for additional references). The internal program logic just looks for a group name (i.e., "hand1") in the PARAM field and increments the ending file extension ("hand" + ".obj") when Java 3D loads the geometry data from these files. Also note that all three files need to have the same number of vertices and polygon count to morph properly.

```
<PARAM NAME="ObjectPosition" VALUE="middle">
```

This option allows you to position the morphing sequence within the main window. You can place the action at the "top", "middle", or "bottom" of the window. This is so that you can move the morphing objects to place a Text Label below or above the action.

```
<PARAM NAME="TextLabel" VALUE="Enter #1 Network">
```

The TextLabel parameter creates a 2D string label for the scene. This program only supports a single text string per applet. You just type in your favorite string and be ready to specify color, font, style, and text size, with additional parameters. The following predefined colors are available: red, blue, green, yellow, purple, gold, orange, black, white, medblue (medium blue), and medgreen (medium green). The following fonts are used: Helvetica, Times, Courier, Monospaced, Serif, and Dialog. The styles that can be specified are bold, italic, and plain. The text can also be positioned at the top, middle, or bottom. Alternately, the actual floating-point number can be specified to position the text object for X, Y, and Z. You may use the "canned" TextPosition method, or if you understand the Java 3D coordinate system (a right-hand system, 0,0,0 in the middle, Y-axis pointing up), then you may want to use Text[X,Y,Z] parameters. The values take floating-point numbers.

```
<PARAM NAME="TextSize" VALUE="60">
<PARAM NAME="TextColor" VALUE="red">
<PARAM NAME="TextFont" VALUE="Times">
<PARAM NAME="TextStyle" VALUE="bold">
<PARAM NAME="TextPosition" VALUE="middle">
<PARAM NAME="TextX" VALUE="1.0">
<PARAM NAME="TextY" VALUE="0.0">
<PARAM NAME="TextZ" VALUE="-1.0">
<PARAM NAME="TextSpin" VALUE="true">
```

If a text label has been specified, the label can orbit around the window. You can control the orbit radius and speed with the following parameters. The lower the orbit speed, the faster the text loops around the scene. The higher the radius floating-point value, the further away the text orbits from the specified position.

```
<PARAM NAME="TextOrbitSpeed" VALUE="5000">
<PARAM NAME="TextRadius" VALUE="1.2">
```

Sometimes, it is hard to make the 3D objects fit the FIXED 300×300 window or to appear correctly when text is added. To give you greater control, a scaling factor interface has been added (see Figure 4.4). This will let you decrease or increase the size of the morphing objects. You can use the predefined values from less to more (1–5) to zoom out.

```
<PARAM NAME="Scale" VALUE="zoomout3">
```

When an applet is put on a Web page, most of the time you want to match the Web background color to the applet background color. This is what this parameter is used for: to set the Java 3D applet background color. The possible values are the following color names: red, blue, green, yellow, purple, gold, orange, black, white, medblue (medium blue), and medgreen (medium green).

Figure 4.4 Scaling.

```
<PARAM NAME="BackgroundColor" VALUE="black">
```

Once the morph is declared with the proper HTML parameter tag, you can associate a URL with the object by using the "URL" keyword. When the user clicks the mouse button over the morph, the browser will jump to the specified address and leave the Java 3D program.

```
<PARAM NAME="URL" VALUE="http://www.sun.com/">
```

Finally, there are color parameters for the two light sources and the morph object. You can use the predefined colors: red, blue, green, yellow, purple, gold, orange, black, white, medblue (medium blue), and medgreen (medium green). Changing the light colors will modify the special effect on the scene.

```
<PARAM NAME="DirectLightColor" VALUE="white">
<PARAM NAME="AmbientColor" VALUE="white">
<PARAM NAME="ObjectColor" VALUE="green">
```

Morphing HTML File Explained

The HTML file for the applet will look something like Source 4.1. Although it looks a bit scary and messy, it really is pretty straightforward when you take a closer look. Read through this and then we'll discuss the HTML tags line by line. This will be the file you will need to edit to create a custom effect for your Web site.

```
<HTML>
<TITLE>Morphing 3 Applet</TITLE>
<BODY>

<OBJECT classid="clsid:8AD9C840-044E-11D1-B3E9-00805F499D93"
     width="300" height="300" align="baseline"
     codebase="http://java.sun.com/products/plugin/1.2/jinstall-12-
win32.cab#Version=1,2,0,0">
   <PARAM NAME="code" VALUE="Morphing.class">

   <PARAM NAME="type" VALUE="application/x-java-applet;version=1.2">
   <PARAM NAME = "ObjectName1" VALUE  = "logo1">
   <PARAM NAME = "ObjectName2" VALUE  = "logo2">
   <PARAM NAME = "ObjectName3" VALUE  = "logo3">
   <PARAM NAME = "URL" VALUE = "http://www.wiley.com">
   <PARAM NAME = "ObjectPosition" VALUE  ="middle">
   <PARAM NAME = "TextLabel" VALUE  ="Click Here">
   <PARAM NAME = "TextSize" VALUE  ="72">
   <PARAM NAME = "TextColor" VALUE  ="purple">
   <PARAM NAME = "TextFont" VALUE  ="Monospaced">
   <PARAM NAME = "TextStyle" VALUE  ="bold">
   <PARAM NAME = "TextPosition" VALUE  ="middle">
   <PARAM NAME = "TextSpin" VALUE  ="true">
   <PARAM NAME = "TextOrbitSpeed" VALUE  ="5000">
   <PARAM NAME = "TextRadius" VALUE  ="0.5">
   <PARAM NAME = "Scale" VALUE  ="zoomout5">
   <PARAM NAME = "BackgroundColor" VALUE  ="black">
   <PARAM NAME = "DirectLightColor" VALUE  ="white">
   <PARAM NAME = "AmbientColor" VALUE  ="white">
   <PARAM NAME = "ObjectColor" VALUE  ="blue">

<COMMENT>
     <EMBED type="application/x-java-applet;version=1.2" width="300"
        height="300" align="baseline" code="Morphing.class"
        ObjectName1="logo1"
        ObjectName2="logo2"
        ObjectName3="logo3"
        URL="http://www.wiley.com"
        ObjectPosition="middle"
        TextLabel="Click Here"
        TextSize="72"
        TextColor="purple"
        TextFont="Monospaced"
        TextStyle="bold"
        TextPosition="middle"
        TextSpin="true"
```

Source 4.1   Morphing HTML File

```
            TextOrbitSpeed="5000"
            TextRadius="0.5"
            Scale="zoomout5"
            BackgroundColor="black"
            DirectLightColor="white"
            AmbientColor="white"
            ObjectColor="blue"

            pluginspage="http://java.sun.com/products/plugin/1.2/plugin-
install.html">
        <NOEMBED>
        </COMMENT>
             No JDK 1.2 (Java 2) support for APPLET!!
        </NOEMBED></EMBED>
  </OBJECT>

<!-- Save old syntax but comment out
   <APPLET  CODE = "Morphing.class" WIDTH = "300" HEIGHT = "200"
   ALIGN = "baseline" >
   <PARAM NAME = "ObjectName1" VALUE  = "logo1">
   <PARAM NAME = "ObjectName2" VALUE  = "logo2">
   <PARAM NAME = "ObjectName3" VALUE  = "logo3">
   <PARAM NAME = "URL" VALUE = "http://www.wiley.com">
   <PARAM NAME = "ObjectPosition" VALUE ="middle">
   <PARAM NAME = "TextLabel" VALUE ="Click Here">
   <PARAM NAME = "TextSize" VALUE  ="72">
   <PARAM NAME = "TextColor" VALUE  ="purple">
   <PARAM NAME = "TextFont" VALUE  ="Monospaced">
   <PARAM NAME = "TextStyle" VALUE  ="bold">
   <PARAM NAME = "TextPosition" VALUE  ="middle">
   <PARAM NAME = "TextSpin" VALUE  ="true">
   <PARAM NAME = "TextOrbitSpeed" VALUE  ="5000">
   <PARAM NAME = "TextRadius" VALUE  ="0.5">
   <PARAM NAME = "Scale" VALUE  ="zoomout5">
   <PARAM NAME = "BackgroundColor" VALUE  ="black">
   <PARAM NAME = "DirectLightColor" VALUE  ="white">
   <PARAM NAME = "AmbientColor" VALUE  ="white">
   <PARAM NAME = "ObjectColor" VALUE  ="blue">

   No Java 2 support for this APPLET!!

   </APPLET>
-->

</BODY>
</HTML>
```

Source 4.1 *Continued*

How to Interpret the HTML Tags

The original HTML Java interface used the APPLET tag that looked like:

```
<APPLET code="XYZApp.class" codebase="html/" align="baseline"
                    width="200" height="200">
<PARAM NAME="model" VALUE="models/HyaluronicAcid.xyz">
                    No Java 2 support for this APPLET!!
</APPLET>
```

When a Java-capable browser loads this portion of the HTML file, it would also load and invoke the referenced Java program ("XYZApp"). This Java program would then use the specified parameters (indicated by the tag name PARAM NAME and associated values) to modify the program upon initialization. That way users can pass the Java program needed data. For example, in the applet XYZApp, a model of hyaluric acid is being passed to the program for rendering.

There is some additional administration we have to plan for when dealing with Java 3D applets. Current Web browsers can handle plain Java applets, but they are not ready to run Java 3D applets, so they will need a little help from a plug-in called the Java Plug-in. This will provide the software environment needed to run Java 3D applets (assuming the end user also has OpenGL or Direct3D preinstalled on his or her system).

In the Web environment, you cannot dictate what the user will use for a browser. There are several types out there, including Netscape Navigator or Microsoft Internet Explorer (IE), so the HTML interface has to be set up to accommodate these various browsers. One common requirement is that the browser has to be Java-capable, meaning the browser software has been designed to run Java applets.

You should either activate the Java Plug-in only on the correct browser and platform combination, or use the browser's default JVM. (Note: It is possible that some Web pages will have a mix of old Java version applets and new Java 3D applets.) You can achieve this using these Java Plug-in tags:

<OBJECT> Use for Microsoft Explorer browser.

<EMBED> Use for Netscape Navigator browser.

<APPLET> Use for the latest Sun Microsystems HotJava browser.

We'll be using JavaScript to determine the browser environment so we can invoke the Java Plug-in correctly for multiple platforms. This example includes comments, so you might want to use it as a template that can be cut and pasted when creating Java Plug-in Web pages. And don't be freaked out by all of these characters. You will master the sequence and meaning in a short period of time. And keep in mind that each Java 3D applet in the book is accompanied with an HTML page that is all ready to go. You'll just have to modify the file's parameters.

The first block of the script extracts the browser and platform. You must determine the browser and platform on which the applet is running. You do this by using JavaScript to extract first the browser name, then the platform once per HTML document. The second block of the script replaces the APPLET tag. You must replace each APPLET tag with a similar block of code. The script replaces the APPLET tag with either an EMBED tag or OBJECT tag, depending on the browser. You use the OBJECT tag for Internet Explorer and the EMBED tag for Netscape Navigator. Finally, the original APPLET tag is included as a comment at the end. It is always a good idea to keep the original APPLET tag in case you want to remove the Java Plug-in invocation at a later date.

The first part of the JavaScript establishes the browser and the platform on which the browser is running. You must do this because, currently, Java Plug-in supports only Windows 95, Windows NT 4.0, and Solaris. Note that Windows NT 3.51 is the only Win32 platform that Java Plug-in does not support. Java Plug-in should be invoked only on supported browsers and platforms. The script sets the variable _ie to true if the browser is Internet Explorer. It sets the variable _ns to true if the browser is Navigator. (Note that all variable names in the JavaScript start with an underscore (_) to avoid conflict with other JavaScript variables in the same page.)

To detect the right browser, the JavaScript evaluates three strings within the JavaScript's Navigator object: userAgent, appVersion, and appName. These strings contain information about the browser and the platform. By looking at some examples of the userAgent string, you can easily see how to evaluate userAgent and use it to determine the browser.

Remember that this block of JavaScript should be put at the top of the <BODY> of the HTML file, so that other JavaScripts can reference the variables _ie and _ns. This JavaScript is the same in all HTML files, and it is only needed once for each HTML body.

The second block of HTML tags is actually the corresponding OBJECT and EMBED tags that are mapped from the data in the APPLET tag. Note that JavaScript outputs the OBJECT tag when the browser is IE running on Windows 95 or Windows NT 4.0. If the browser is Navigator 3.x/4.x on Windows 95, Windows NT 4.0, or Solaris, then JavaScript also outputs the EMBED tag, though with a slightly different syntax. Recall that the mechanism for detecting the browser and the platform has been described in the preceding subsection. (Tags <!-- and --> are used for comments in HTML.)

When the user surfs to the Web page that contains the Morphing applet, the program is invoked. One of the first things the applet program does is parse the list of attributes identified by the "param" keyword in the HTML file. Each parameter has an associated value. These values will set specific attributes in the Morphing demo that will be seen at runtime.

Geometry Concepts

The term *wireframe* comes from sculptured art. In order for a model to maintain its shape while the heavy clay is being applied by the artist, stiff wire is used to create a skeleton model. It supports the artwork in progress, which includes surface modeling, texture, and form. In 3D graphics, geometry is used in the same manner.

In this section, the creation of geometry is discussed in the context of using a special Java 3D API construct called the Shape3D node and associated Appearance objects. Appearance classes define such object properties as, color, line styles, points, and polygons. Combined with shape objects, these are the components Java 3D uses to create a 3D scene. The Shape3D Leaf node is made from two elements: the geometry and an appearance. So let's take a look at how to create some geometry. First, we need to order the geometrical data into a Java 3D construct, which will be used to render the vertices into some shape. Next, certain appearance attributes can be set up for the shape before it is rendered. These might include color, line type, shading model, or a solid filled surface (see Figure 4.5). The appearance attributes are constructed as a separate object, so it can be reused over and over again by multiple 3D shapes that share the same Appearance object.

For example, let's say a scene is created that displays a bag of 100 marbles

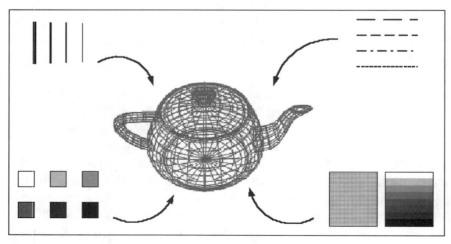

Figure 4.5 Shape properties.

spilled onto the floor. Each marble would be cloned from the same geometry object and reused 100 times. Think about it: Even in a real bag of marbles, there are generally fewer than a dozen varieties of marble types—cats' eyes, solids, swirls, and so forth. In Java 3D, these variety attributes could be represented by a couple of Appearance objects and randomly applied to the 100 replicated Shape3D marble objects.

Shape3D Class

In Chapter 2, we established that 3D objects are constructed from points and polygons in 3D space, and a coordinate system was used to establish position and depth. A list of points and their edges or vertices is the basic data used to create 3D shapes. The information can be computed mathematically or as a specified list of vertices and color information. The most common method is to use another software application modeler toolkit, which provides a "digital sketch pad," for the user to draw the 3D wireframe model (see Figure 4.6). It is saved into a file and passed to the 3D application for processing, then loaded into the Java 3D scene.

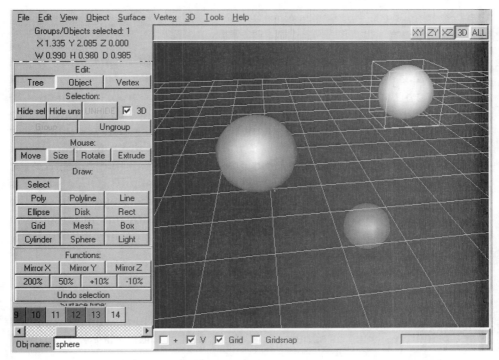

Figure 4.6 Modeling software (AC3D shown).

The Java 3D API also provides some basic geometric class objects, such as a sphere, cube, and a cone, but a modeler toolkit is really necessary to construct interesting virtual scenes with a higher level of detail. It is not as easy as it looks to create a virtual world that looks better than something your kid constructed out of building blocks. True, stacking these simple objects will result in a 3D scene, but it may prove uninteresting to the viewer. There are also many companies that will generate any shape you wish. The shape is saved to a file that can be imported into a Java 3D scene. The point is, it would be best to either purchase the geometry or use other available tools to create more complex geometric scenes.

Let's take a look at how 3D shape classes are created in Java 3D, given the following chunk of pseudo-code.

```
Shape3D = Geometry + Appearance
```

This formula is used to create the 3D shape but needs two important building blocks to do its job: The Geometry object, which contains additional components used to describe the geometrical properties of the shape; and the Appearance object, used to specify such properties as color and line style and how to draw the geometry.

```
Appearance looks = new Appearance();
Shape3D shape = new Shape3D(new MakeCube(), looks);
```

This is one example of how a shape might be created. *MakeCube()* is just a method that draws the vertices with their positional coordinates (vertex positions in 3D space), normals (used in lighting equations), texture coordinates (called *texel locations*) and color information (RGB values per vertex) used to render the boxlike shape. Point, line, or surface geometry is specified in an array, called a *Geometry Array*. There are four basic vertex formats: points, lines, triangles, and quads. The *looks* child object of the Appearance object will initialize everything using defaults. Once *shape* is added to the scene graph and the application is run, the viewer will see the cube dead-on. To see around the object's sides, transformation or rotation behaviors will have to be applied. That's basically all there is to making shapes of varied colors and attributes.

Geometry Convenience Classes

The Java 3D API provides some easier methods to generate some supplied shape primitives, such as sphere, box, cone, and cylinder classes.

```
Appearance a = new Appearance();
Primitive box1 = new Box(1.0f, 0.6f, 1.0f, a);
```

where X, Y, and Z are the dimensions of the box, cube, or rectangle created with a given length, width, and height. The shape is centered at the origin, and the values for the shape dimensions are in the Java 3D vertex format.

```
Primitive ball = new Sphere (1.0f, 45, a);
```

where the sphere is created with a specified radius and resolutions (divisions). It is centered at the origin (0.0f, 0.0f, 0.0f). The resolution defaults to 45 divisions along the sphere's axis. The greater the resolution (higher number of divisions), the finer the object detail. For example, Figure 4.6 shows what the sphere looks like with 7 divisions versus 20 divisions, shown in Figure 4.7.

```
Primitive cone = new Cone (1.0f, 2.0f, 40, 40, a);
```

where the cone is created with a specified radius, height, resolutions, and appearance. The default resolution is 50 divisions along the X and Y axes.

```
Primitive cyl = new Cylinder (1.0f, 2.0f, 60, 60, a);
```

where a radius, height, resolution, and appearance define the cylinder. It is capped at both ends. Resolution defaults to 50 divisions.

In addition to the provided shape classes in Java 3D, we have created a couple of tools that can be used to generate your own custom geometry. The description of and information regarding these tools can be found in the last chapter of this book. The first, the Surfacer, generates a 3D shape by using a profile sweep generator (see Figure 4.8). The user draws any given 2D profile of the desired object's shape, then the Surfacer program constructs the 3D object and saves it as a Java source. This generated file can then be compiled and reused over and over again as a Java 3D Shape object.

The second utility tool can convert 3D objects from VRML 1.0 and 2.0 formats to create Java 3D classes for each shape. Of course, Java 3D provides a VRML loader and export class to load entire scenes but it might be useful

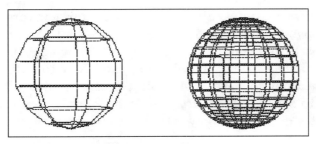

Figure 4.7   Resolution examples.

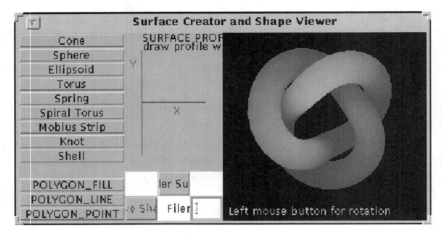

Figure 4.8 Surfacer shape tool.

to create dynamic classes of shapes to avoid certain Java security administration duties, like signed applets. Java 3D also provides a loader for other
graphics file formats, like WaveFront (*.obj) files. But our utility is a great
way to rip favorite objects out of an existing VRML scene file and reuse
them with the Java 3D Web applets.

Let's now take a look at some Java 3D source code that implements many
of the classes we have been discussing, or as it relates to geometry creation
and manipulation. (Refer to Chapter 12, "J3D Web Tools and Utilities," for
additional information.)

Appearance Component

The Appearance object defines all settable properties and rendering permissions of the object created as a Shape3D node. The Appearance object is
a component of the Shape3D object. The Appearance component is a subclass and a member of the Node Component objects. This object belongs to
a logical grouping of classes that provide geometry and appearance attributes. The Appearance component can define when a particular rendering
operation is allowed to modify a particular Shape3D object. Permissions are
given through the use of capability flags. At first, everything is set to NULL
until the flags are set to a particular state. For example, the following code
fragment creates an Appearance object that will be applied later to a 3D
Shape object. Let's say we want to have a 3D object constructed from
points. To do so, we have to set the *capability flag*, Poly_Point, which is
part of the PolygonAttributes class, and apply it to the Appearance object
we'll be using.

```
Appearance app = new Appearance( );
PolygonAttributes pa = new PolygonAttributes( );
pa.setPolygonMode(pa.Polygon_Point);
app.setPolygonAttributes(pa);
```

The following operations have two states: READ or WRITE. Only when the WRITE flag is set are you allowed to change the value after initialization (for example, on the fly when you want that text to turn red when clicked).

COLORING

LINE

MATERIAL

POINT

POLYGON

RENDERING

TEXGEN

TEXTURE

TRANSPARENCY

If the state variable is WRITE for a specific appearance property, then the application can change the information and effect a visible change on the 3D shape. READ means just what it says: The values are read-only because you don't want any part of the program to ever change them. It makes a lot of sense that there are times, during a 3D game for example, when conditions would warrant a change to the 3D scene and its rendering properties.

These capability flags can be enabled using the *setCapability( )* method. If an Appearance object is used with the provided Java 3D convenience classes (like *Sphere( )*), then some of the following default values are used. Sphere( ) just generates a ball with a given radius and Appearance object to use.

Color:	white (1,1,1)
Shade Model:	SHADE_SMOOTH
Polygon Mode:	POLYGON_FILL
Transparency Enable:	false
Point Size:	1.0
Line Width:	1.0
Line Pattern:	PATTERN_SOLID
Point Antialiasing:	false
Line Antialiasing:	false

There are *set* and *get* methods for each group of Appearance attributes. For example, *setPolygonAttributes( )* and *getPolygonAttributes( )* are used to modify and retrieve properties that affect the polygons of the Shape3D object. The following are some of the logical groupings that relate to the Appearance object.

ColoringAttributes.   Applies to color mapping and setting the shade model, like flat shading (SHADE_FLAT) or Gouraud (SHADE_ GOURAUD). Figure 4.9 illustrates their differences. The flat-shaded cylinder on the left looks pretty rough. Adding more geometry information could make it look better. Gouraud (pronounced "goo-row") shading costs more in CPU time, which affects application performance, so using flat shading on very distant objects in your scene would make a lot of sense, especially when the objects appear so small and distant that the shading model doesn't matter.

```
ColoringAttributes  ca  =  new ColoringAttributes(new Color3f(0.0f,
            1.0f, 0.0f), ColoringAttributes.SHADE_GOURAUD);
app.setColoringAttributes(ca);
```

LineAttributes.   Used to specify line-rendering options, such as PAT-TERN_SOLID, PATTERN_DASH, PATTERN_DOT, PATTERN_DASH_ DOT.

```
LineAttributes  la  =  new  LineAttributes( );
la.setLineWidth(1.5f);
la.setLinePattern(PATTERN_DOT);
la.setLineAntialiasingEnable(true);
app.setLineAttributes(la);
```

PointAttributes.   There's not much you can do to points except set their size in pixels and turn antialiasing on or off. The default point size is 1.0, and antialiasing is disabled.

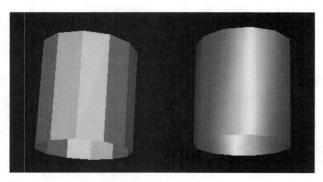

Figure 4.9   Gouraud shaded object.

```
PointAttributes pta  =  new PointAttributes(2.0f, true);
pta.setPointAntialiasingEnable(false);
app.setPointAttributes(pta);
```

PolygonAttributes. Attributes can be set for culling operations on polygons (CULL_NONE, CULL_FRONT, CULL_BACK). By default, CULL_BACK is set. That means if you create a rotating object, you won't see the back side. First, CULL_NONE needs to be set. Also, the lines drawn for the point list of a 3D object can be rendered as a line, as points, or as a filled polygon by setting POLYGON_POINT, POLY-GON_LINE, and POLYGON_FILL.

```
PolygonAttributes pa = new PolygonAttributes( );
pa.setPolygonMode(pa.Polygon_Point);
pa.setCullFace(pa.CULL_NONE);
app.setPolygonAttributes(pa);
```

Other attributes are used for Material, Texture, and Transparency properties, and they will be covered in a later chapter.

Geometry Component

In addition to its prebuilt utilities for rendering a cone, a cube, and so on, Java 3D provides a method to define some geometry the application creator might want to use. These methods are grouped by geometric type classes under the Geometry parent class. All are used to create *geometry objects*. Let's look at how to specify some geometry data as an array of vertices to construct a geometry object that is used to build a Shape3D node. We'll use the *QuadArray* class in our first example, which is a child of the Geometry-Array object. Along with the QuadArray are additional geometry components used to contain information for the Geometry object. There are three geometric types you can use:

GeometryArray

Text3D

Compressed Geometry

Each of these types defines one or more geometric objects. The Geome-tryArray object has several subclasses (see Figure 4.10) and is used to define a shape with vertex components, such as coordinates, normals, and color information, and texture coordinates.

We are going to look at the *Geometry Array* class in more detail. It contains a half dozen data array types, or children, that are commonly used. Remember, we said to build a 3D shape you need geometry and appearance components, which together form the Shape3D object.

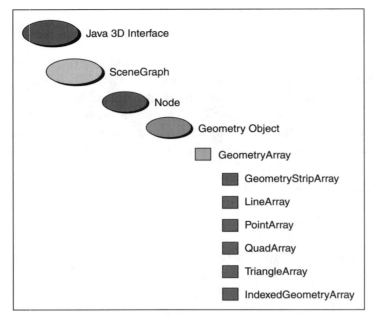

Figure 4.10 GeometryArray classes.

The GeometryArray class contains a data array for the following vertex components: coordinates, colors, normals, and texture coordinates. A bitmask tag is used to indicate which of these vertex components are present. Here are examples of some: COORDINATES, NORMALS, COLOR_3, and TEXTURE_COORDINATE_2.

The GeometryArray data itself can be represented in several primitive format types (as in Figure 4.11), including point array, line strip, quadrilat-

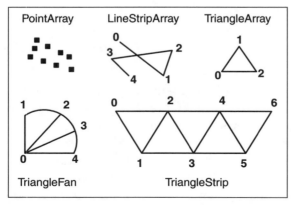

Figure 4.11 Geometry components and formats.

eral (quad), triangle strip, triangle fan, or triangle array. The GeometryArray object provides a class for a variety of data types, including indexed geometry data. There are several ways to create geometry. One is to create separate arrays to hold vertex information, such as coordinates and colors. The arrays can also hold normals and texture-mapping coordinate information.

Quadrilateral Array

The following code example uses a *quadrilateral array* (see Figure 4.12) to present the data to the renderer. Objects of this class draw the array of vertices as individual quadrilaterals. Each group of four vertices in the array defines a quadrilateral to be drawn.

```
public QuadArray(int vertexCount, int vertexFormat)
```

vertexCount = the number of vertex elements in the array.

vertexFormat = the mask indicating the type of per-vertex information that is included: in other words, coordinates, color, and texture coordinates. The flags are ORed together if more than one is present.

The following constructs an empty QuadArray for 24 vertices and the vertex format for coordinates. Then a method is called to initialize the object with the vertices information.

```
QuadArray box = new QuadArray(24, COORDINATES);
box.setCoordinates(0, boxverts);

private static final float[] boxverts = {
        // front face
         1.0f, -1.0f,  1.0f,
         1.0f,  1.0f,  1.0f,
        -1.0f,  1.0f,  1.0f,
        -1.0f, -1.0f,  1.0f,
        // backface
        -1.0f, -1.0f, -1.0f,
        -1.0f,  1.0f, -1.0f,
```

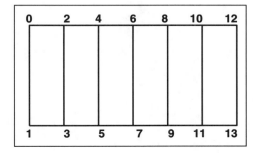

Figure 4.12 Quad format.

```
     1.0f,   1.0f, -1.0f,
     1.0f, -1.0f, -1.0f,
// right face
     1.0f, -1.0f, -1.0f,
     1.0f,   1.0f, -1.0f,
     1.0f,   1.0f,   1.0f,
     1.0f, -1.0f,   1.0f,
// left face
    -1.0f, -1.0f,   1.0f,
    -1.0f,   1.0f,   1.0f,
    -1.0f,   1.0f, -1.0f,
    -1.0f, -1.0f, -1.0f,
// top face
     1.0f,   1.0f,   1.0f,
     1.0f,   1.0f, -1.0f,
    -1.0f,   1.0f, -1.0f,
    -1.0f,   1.0f,   1.0f,
// bottom face
    -1.0f, -1.0f,   1.0f,
    -1.0f, -1.0f, -1.0f,
     1.0f, -1.0f, -1.0f,
     1.0f, -1.0f,   1.0f,
};
```

To add color or texture-mapping coordinates, additional arrays need to be created. For example, adding color information would look like:

```
private static final float[] boxcolors = {
        // front face (red)
        1.0f, 0.0f, 0.0f,
        1.0f, 0.0f, 0.0f,
        1.0f, 0.0f, 0.0f,
        1.0f, 0.0f, 0.0f,
        // backface (green)
        0.0f, 1.0f, 0.0f,
        0.0f, 1.0f, 0.0f,
        0.0f, 1.0f, 0.0f,
        0.0f, 1.0f, 0.0f,
        // right face (blue)
        0.0f, 0.0f, 1.0f,
        0.0f, 0.0f, 1.0f,
        0.0f, 0.0f, 1.0f,
        0.0f, 0.0f, 1.0f,
        // left face (yellow)
        1.0f, 1.0f, 0.0f,
        1.0f, 1.0f, 0.0f,
        1.0f, 1.0f, 0.0f,
        1.0f, 1.0f, 0.0f,
        // top face (magenta)
        1.0f, 0.0f, 1.0f,
```

```
        1.0f,  0.0f,  1.0f,
        1.0f,  0.0f,  1.0f,
        1.0f,  0.0f,  1.0f,
        // bottom face (cyan)
        0.0f,  1.0f,  1.0f,
        0.0f,  1.0f,  1.0f,
        0.0f,  1.0f,  1.0f,
        0.0f,  1.0f,  1.0f,
    };

QuadArray box = new QuadArray(24, COORDINATES|COLOR_3);
box.setCoordinates(0, boxverts);
box.setColor(0,boxcolors);
```

COORDINATES are ORed with COLOR_3, which comprises bit masks used by the method to indicate the presence of coordinate and color information.

Getting the hang of it? The most difficult part is getting the 3D object you want into the Java 3D vector format so it can be rendered. Hopefully, third-party vendors will write more robust tools in the near future. As already noted, Java 3D does offer file loaders for VRML and *.obj file formats, and we have provided a couple of useful tools to generate your own 3D shapes. Again, these topics are covered in the last chapter.

The other cool thing you can do with Java 3D geometry is morph and compress it. Morphing between geometry models makes interesting effects. Compression is just a useful utility when dealing with moving data over a network. Let's take a look at these more closely.

Morphing

Morphing, as we mentioned earlier, was made famous in movies like *Terminator 2*, in which a shape or face would be transformed into another. Sometimes, morphing is done by merging two photo images, pixel by pixel, over a period of time. In Java 3D, there is a class called the *morph node* that allows an application to morph among multiple geometric arrays. We just covered GeometricArrays, but as a reminder, these are objects whose descriptions are formatted into separate arrays for coordinates, colors, normals, and texture coordinates. Together, these arrays form the vertex components for the Shape 3D object.

You'll need a few components in order to implement morphing in your program. First, you're going to need an array of multiple GeometryArray objects. We'll use one of the GeometryArray "kids," the QuadArray, to create our data sets of three 3D forms that Java 3D will morph from Form1 to Form2 to Form3 (refer to Figure 4.2).

```
QuadArray  geometry[ ]  =  new  QuadArray[3];
geometry[0]  =  new Form1( );
geometry[1]  =  new Form2( );
geometry[2]  =  new  Form3( );
```

Three QuadArray objects were just created and then initialized with some specific geometry information (Form1–3 classes). The Form classes would be declared in a file called *Form[n].java* with the following example structure:

```
class Form1 extends QuadArray {
    private static final float[] verts = {
    }
    private static final float[] colors = {
    }
    Form1( ) {
        super(nVertices, QuadArray.COORDINATES |
                         QuadArray.COLOR_3);
        setCoordinates(0, verts);
    setColors(0, colors);
    }
     }
```

Each Form class file would contain:

■ An array of floating-point vertices.

■ An array of floating-point color values for each vertex.

■ A constructor that creates the array and sets coordinates and color information.

Besides the input geometry arrays, our morphing program will need to create a morph node. This specialized class will require an Appearance node, our array of GeometryArray objects, and an array of corresponding weights. The weights are used by the Morph node to apply a morph weight vector component; this will help create the morphing effect we desire. Changing the weight values also changes the effect.

```
Appearance app  =  new  Appearance( );
Morph  terminator  =  new  Morph((GeometryArray[]) geometry, app);
terminator.setCapability(Morph.ALLOW_WEIGHTS_READ);
terminator.setCapability(Morph.ALLOW_WEIGHTS_WRITE)
objTrans.addChild(terminator);
```

The Morph node has now been created and added to a transform object, because we might want to position, orient, or scale the Morph node within the scene. Notice that we have added two flags that will allow us to access and modify the weight values. This is so we can fiddle with the weights to create a desired effect. It is very common to set up a behavior object that will do this for us and an Alpha object to control the speed of the morphing operation. First the Alpha object:

```
Alpha morphAlpha = new Alpha(-1, Alpha.INCREASING_ENABLE |
                             Alpha.DECREASING_ENABLE,
                             0, 0,  4000, 1000, 500, 4000, 1000, 500);
```

To specify and create the morphing behavior:

```
MorphingBehavior mBehavior = new MorphingBehavior(morphAlpha, morph);
mBehavior.setSchedulingBounds(bounds);
objRoot.addChild(mBehavior);
```

Don't forget to specify the scheduling bounds on the Behavior object, otherwise it will never take place. Bounds is a bounding volume, and indicates a given region where action should take place—in this case, where the created Behavior class will perform its operation. Behavior and Alphas are discussed later in the book because they are much too complex to cover here. But basically, Behaviors and Alphas make a Java 3D world come alive. They provide the dynamics used to gather user input and provide motion to objects in a Java 3D scene. Behaviors allow us to specify that an action should occur based on a particular set of events—what Java 3D calls a WakeupCondition. A WakeupCondition is a combination of another Java 3D object called a WakeupCriterion. These WakeupCriterion cover a wide range of activities from waiting for a certain number of frames to trapping AWT events to our Java 3D Canvas3D object.

Alphas (or Interpolators) are specialized versions of a Behavior. They use a time-generated value that is in the range of [0.0–1.0] to modify some characteristic of a Java 3D object. The Alpha object takes time (measured in milliseconds) and maps it onto a floating-point value in the range [0.0–1.0] inclusive. It's like your own personal waveform: It waits, ramps up, waits, ramps down, and waits. We're going to use an Alpha to perform timing for our morphing operation. This is much better than sticking in a bunch of sleeps, while loops, or conditions.

Morphing Code Example

The following Morphing applet (shown in Source 4.2) takes three Wave-Front *.obj files, and the file interpolates the geometry between the files to produce animation and action. The code is well commented, and it would be useful to spend some time reading how it was constructed.

```
import java.applet.*;
import java.awt.BorderLayout;
import java.awt.Font;
import java.awt.event.*;
import java.net.URL;
import java.net.MalformedURLException;
import javax.media.j3d.*;
import javax.vecmath.*;
import java.io.*;
import com.sun.j3d.utils.geometry.Text2D;
import com.sun.j3d.utils.applet.MainFrame;
import com.sun.j3d.utils.universe.*;
import com.sun.j3d.loaders.objectfile.ObjectFile;
```

Source 4.2   Complete Morph Applet

```
import com.sun.j3d.loaders.*;

public class Morphing extends Applet {

 /** -------------------------------------------------------------
    *  Credits: This applet was based on work from a Sun Microsystems
    *           Java 3D example.
    *
    * %W% %E%
    * @Author: Modifications in version 2.0 made by Kirk Brown
    *
    *      Morphing allows you to specify 3 geometry objects (created
    *      with CAD/MCAD modelling software, like Pixel3D) that mutate
    *      from one to the other. Each model MUST contain the same
    *      number of vertices and polygons. The HTML interface allows
    *      the user to change the 3 objects for the program to
    *      use (One can contract 3D content providers to create,
    *      for example, a company logo sequence, position a text
    *      label that can rotate, and scale the morphing objects to
    *      fit the window.) When run in a browser, clicking the mouse
    *      will load an associated URL document passed from the HTML
    *      PARAM interface.
    *
    *      The program, in "-demo" mode will use hard coded models
    *      to demonstrate the Java 3D effect.
    *
    *      The program, when run as an Applet, requires additional
    *      pre-planning. To avoid having to perform file I/O (which
    *      would require the end user and applet distributor to perform
    *      security certification and authentication) this Applet has
    *      been designed to provide a trusted Applet without the security
    *      hoops to jump through. The Applet requires the following:
    *              1. 3 provided VRML (*.wrl) models that must have
    *                 the same polygon and vertex count in order for
    *                  the Morph class to operate properly.
    *              2. Use the conversion tool, from Markus Roskothen,
    *                 to convert the *.wrl files to Java 3D Shape
    *                 objects. (get from www.vruniverse.com)
    *              3. Pass the new Java 3D object names to the Applet
    *                 using the HTML PARAM tag "ObjectName[n]".
    *
    *      The conversion tool is called VrmlFacesToJ3d and is invoked:
    *          % java VrmlFacesToJ3d someVRMLfile(leave off the *.wrl)
    *      This will generate a "someVRMLfile.java" file that needs to
    *      be compiled (Java 2 JDK and Java 3D 1.1 development) with:
    *          % javac someVRMLfile.java
```

continues

Source 4.2 *Continued*

```
*
*        The result will be 3 models (someVRMLfile1,..2,..3) that
*        have an equivalent *.class file. (See Appendix B for info)
*
*        Finally modify the HTML file, locate the new classes in the
*        same directory as this program and load the HTML file with
*        A Java-enabled browser running Java Plug-in.
*/

// Class variables.
//
// The following is the defined HTML interface to this program:
//
//    <PARAM NAME="ObjectName1" VALUE="hand1">
//        Value Options: ObjectName[1-3] VALUE="[name][n]"
//    <PARAM NAME="ObjectPosition" VALUE="middle">
//        Value Options: ObjectPosition VALUE="[top, middle, bottom]"
//    <PARAM NAME="TextLabel" VALUE="Enter #1 Network">
//        Value Options: TextLabel VALUE="[some text]"
//    <PARAM NAME="TextSize" VALUE="60">
//        Value Option: TextSize VALUE="[font size number]"
//    <PARAM NAME="TextColor" VALUE="red">
//        Value Option: red,blue,green,yellow,purple,gold,
//                       orange,black,white,medblue,medgreen
//    <PARAM NAME="TextFont" VALUE="Times">
//            Value Options: TextFont VALUE="[times, helvetica, serif,
//                           monospaced, courier, dialog]"
//    <PARAM NAME="TextStyle" VALUE="bold">
//            Value Options: TextStyle VALUE="[bold, italic, plain]"
//    <PARAM NAME="TextPosition" VALUE="top">
//        Value Options: TextPosition VALUE="[top, middle, bottom]"
//     OR
//    <PARAM NAME="TextX" VALUE="1.0">
//    <PARAM NAME="TextY" VALUE="0.0">
//    <PARAM NAME="TextZ" VALUE="-1.0">
//        Value Options: Text[axis] VALUE="[floating-point number]"
//
//    <PARAM NAME="TextSpin" VALUE="true">
//        Value Option: TextSpin VALUE="[true, false]"
//    <PARAM NAME="TextOrbitSpeed" VALUE="5000">
//        Value Options: TextOrbitSpeed  VALUE="[low number = fast]"
//    <PARAM NAME="TextRadius" VALUE="1.2">
//        Value Options: TextRadius VALUE="[orbit radius as float]"
//    <PARAM NAME="Scale" VALUE="zoomout3">
//            Value Options: Scale Value=zoomout[1-5]
//    <PARAM NAME ="BackgroundColor" VALUE="black">
//        Value Options: red,blue,green,yellow,purple,gold,
```

Source 4.2 Complete Morph Applet (*Continued*)

```
//                orange,black,white,medblue,medgreen
   //          <PARAM NAME="URL" VALUE="http://www.wiley.com/" >
   //             Value Options: URL VALUE="[url reference]"
   //          <PARAM NAME="DirectLightColor" VALUE="red">
   //             Value Options: red,blue,green,yellow,purple,
//                gold,orange,black,white,medblue,medgreen
   //          <PARAM NAME="AmbientColor" VALUE="blue">
   //             Value Options: (same as DirectLightColor)
   //          <PARAM NAME="ObjectColor" VALUE="green">
   //             Value Options: (same as DirectLightColor)


// Pre-defined colors
Color3f white = new Color3f(1.0f, 1.0f, 1.0f);
Color3f black = new Color3f(0.0f, 0.0f, 0.0f);
    Color3f gray = new Color3f(0.6f, 0.6f, 0.6f);
    Color3f red   = new Color3f(1.0f, 0.0f, 0.0f);
Color3f ambientred = new Color3f(0.4f, 0.1f, 0.0f);
    Color3f medred = new Color3f(0.80f, 0.4f, 0.3f);
    Color3f green   = new Color3f(0.0f, 0.80f, 0.2f);
Color3f ambientgreen = new Color3f(0.0f, 0.3f, 0.1f);
    Color3f medgreen = new Color3f(0.0f, 0.5f, 0.1f);
Color3f orange   = new Color3f(0.7f, 0.4f, 0.0f);
Color3f ambientorange = new Color3f(0.5f, 0.02f, 0.0f);
    Color3f medorange = new Color3f(0.5f, 0.2f, 0.1f);
    Color3f blue   = new Color3f(0.1f, 0.3f, 0.9f);
Color3f ambientblue = new Color3f(0.0f, 0.1f, 0.4f);
    Color3f medblue = new Color3f(0.0f, 0.1f, 0.4f);
    Color3f gold = new Color3f(1.0f, 0.8f, 0.0f);
    Color3f yellow = new Color3f(1.0f, 1.0f, 0.6f);
    Color3f purple = new Color3f(0.5f, 0.2f, 0.8f);
    Color3f medpurple = new Color3f(0.5f, 0.2f, 0.5f);
Color3f ambient = new Color3f(0.2f, 0.2f, 0.2f);
Color3f diffuse = new Color3f(0.7f, 0.7f, 0.7f);
Color3f specular = new Color3f(0.7f, 0.7f, 0.7f);


    // Objects name which will be followed by a number 1-3,
// for example,"hand1","hand2", "hand3". This applet only supports
// morphing 3 files which HAVE TO BE WaveFront format or *.obj.
// This program will use these files only in "-demo" mode.
    String objName1 = new String("hand1.obj");
String objName2 = new String("hand2.obj");
String objName3 = new String("hand3.obj");


// Used only if running as an Applet
String[] newclass = new String[3];
```

continues

Source 4.2   *Continued*

```
boolean applet = false;
boolean pick = false;

// Morph object position
int objPos = 1;

// Scale the group of objects by specified factor
float scale = (float) 0.7;

// Url information
URL[] link;

// Background color
Color3f bgcolor = new Color3f(0.0f, 0.0f, 0.0f);

// Text properties: label, color, size, position, spin?
String label = new String("Java 3D");
String tfont = new String("Helvetica");
int tstyle = Font.BOLD;
Color3f tcolor = red;
int tsize = 72;
Float x = new Float("0.0");
Float y = new Float("0.6");
Float z = new Float("0.0");
float xPos = x.floatValue();
float yPos = y.floatValue();
float zPos = z.floatValue();
boolean spin = true;
int ospeed = 5000;
Float r = new Float("0.5");
float oradius = r.floatValue();

    // Direct Light color
    Color3f dcolor = white;

    // Ambient Light  color
    Color3f acolor = white;

    // Objects color
    Color3f objcolor = blue;


// Examines all parameters that can be passed in to this
// applet and updates the global state to reflect any
// non-default settings.
private void lookForParameters() {
```

Source 4.2 Complete Morph Applet (*Continued*)

```
                    // Used to read in the parameters for the applet.
                    String paramValue;

        // Running as an applet.
        applet = true;

        // Look for the object group name
        paramValue = getParameter("ObjectName1");
        if (paramValue != null) {
            newclass[0] = new String(paramValue);
        }
        paramValue = getParameter("ObjectName2");
        if (paramValue != null) {
            newclass[1] = new String(paramValue);
        }
        paramValue = getParameter("ObjectName3");
        if (paramValue != null) {
            newclass[2] = new String(paramValue);
        }


    // Look for morph object position
    paramValue = getParameter("ObjectPosition");
                if (paramValue != null) {
            if (paramValue.equalsIgnoreCase("top") == true)
                                objPos = 0;
                    else if (paramValue.equalsIgnoreCase("middle") ==
true)
                                    objPos = 1;
            else if (paramValue.equalsIgnoreCase("bottom") == true)
                    objPos = 2;
            else
                    objPos = 1;
    } else {
            System.out.println("Using default objPos=1");
            objPos = 1;
    }


                // Look for the scaling factor to fit the objects to the
    // window. Factor zoomout1 is large to zoomout10 is scaled
    // way down.
                //
                paramValue = getParameter("Scale");
                if (paramValue != null) {
        if (paramValue.equalsIgnoreCase("zoomout1") == true)
                                scale = (float) 1.0;
        else if (paramValue.equalsIgnoreCase("zoomout2") == true)
```

continues

Source 4.2 *Continued*

```
                                             scale = (float) 0.9;
                else if (paramValue.equalsIgnoreCase("zoomout3") == true)
                                             scale = (float) 0.8;
                else if (paramValue.equalsIgnoreCase("zoomout4") == true)
                                             scale = (float) 0.7;
                else if (paramValue.equalsIgnoreCase("zoomout5") == true)
                                             scale = (float) 0.6;
                else if (paramValue.equalsIgnoreCase("zoomout6") == true)
                                             scale = (float) 0.5;
                else if (paramValue.equalsIgnoreCase("zoomout7") == true)
                                             scale = (float) 0.4;
                else if (paramValue.equalsIgnoreCase("zoomout8") == true)
                                             scale = (float) 0.3;
                else if (paramValue.equalsIgnoreCase("zoomout9") == true)
                                             scale = (float) 0.2;
                else if (paramValue.equalsIgnoreCase("zoomout10") == true)
                                             scale = (float) 0.1;
                else
                                             scale = (float) 0.5;
                    } else {
              System.out.println("Using default scale=0.5");
                            scale = (float) 0.5;
        }


                    // Look for URLs to associate with the applet
                    //
                    paramValue = getParameter("URL");
        if (paramValue != null) {
          try {
                link = new URL[1];
                link[0] = new URL(paramValue);
            }
                    catch (Exception e) {
                // Bad URL.
                              System.out.println("ERROR: reading value for
URL");
                        }
            }
        else {
            // We don't need a pick mouse behavior if there's
            // not a URL to pick.
            pick = true;
        }

    // Look for Background Color
    paramValue = getParameter("BackgroundColor");
    if (paramValue != null)
```

Source 4.2 Complete Morph Applet (*Continued*)

```
                       if (paramValue.equalsIgnoreCase("red") == true)
                                bgcolor = red;
                   else if (paramValue.equalsIgnoreCase("green") == true)
                                bgcolor = green;
                   else if (paramValue.equalsIgnoreCase("blue") == true)
                                bgcolor = blue;
                   else if (paramValue.equalsIgnoreCase("medred") == true)
                                bgcolor = medred;
                   else if (paramValue.equalsIgnoreCase("medgreen") == true)
                                bgcolor = medgreen;
                   else if (paramValue.equalsIgnoreCase("medblue") == true)
                                bgcolor = medblue;
                   else if (paramValue.equalsIgnoreCase("black") == true)
                                bgcolor = black;
                   else if (paramValue.equalsIgnoreCase("gray") == true)
                                bgcolor = gray;
                   else if (paramValue.equalsIgnoreCase("white") == true)
                                bgcolor = white;
                   else if (paramValue.equalsIgnoreCase("yellow") == true)
                                bgcolor = yellow;
                   else if (paramValue.equalsIgnoreCase("gold") == true)
                                bgcolor = gold;
                   else if (paramValue.equalsIgnoreCase("purple") == true)
                                bgcolor = purple;
                   else if (paramValue.equalsIgnoreCase("medpurple") == true)
                                bgcolor = medpurple;
                   else if (paramValue.equalsIgnoreCase("orange") == true)
                                bgcolor = orange;
                   else if (paramValue.equalsIgnoreCase("medorange") == true)
                                bgcolor = medorange;
                   else
                             bgcolor = black;
        else
              bgcolor = black;

      // Look for the text label
      paramValue = getParameter("TextLabel");
      if (paramValue != null)
              label = new String(paramValue);
      else
                        label = new String("Morphing Demo");

      // Look for morph text position
      paramValue = getParameter("TextPosition");
              if (paramValue != null) {
          if (paramValue.equalsIgnoreCase("top") == true) {
```

continues

Source 4.2   *Continued*

```
                                        xPos = (float) -0.7;
                yPos = (float) 1.1;
        }
                 else if (paramValue.equalsIgnoreCase("middle") ==
true) {
                                        xPos = (float) -0.7;
                yPos = (float) -0.1;
        }
        else if (paramValue.equalsIgnoreCase("bottom") == true) {
                                xPos = (float) -0.7;
                yPos = (float) -1.0;
        }
        else {
                tsize = Integer.parseInt(paramValue);
                xPos = (float) -0.7;
                yPos = (float) 1.4;
        }
    } else {
            System.out.println("Using default X = -0.7");
            System.out.println("Using default Y = -0.1");
            xPos = (float) -0.7;
            yPos = (float) -0.1;
    }

    // Look for morph text position in finer detail
    paramValue = getParameter("TextX");
    if (paramValue != null) {
            Float x = new Float(paramValue);
            xPos = x.floatValue();
    } else {
            xPos = (float) -0.7;
    }

    paramValue = getParameter("TextY");
    if (paramValue != null) {
            Float y = new Float(paramValue);
            yPos = y.floatValue();
    } else {
            yPos = (float) -0.1;
    }

    paramValue = getParameter("TextZ");
    if (paramValue != null) {
            Float z = new Float(paramValue);
            zPos = z.floatValue();
    } else {
            zPos = (float) 0.0;
```

Source 4.2 Complete Morph Applet (*Continued*)

```
        }

        // Do we need to spin the text?
        paramValue = getParameter("TextSpin");
        if (paramValue != null)
            if (paramValue.equalsIgnoreCase("true") == true)
                spin = true;
            else
                spin = false;
        else
            spin = true;

        // What is the orbiting Text radius?
        paramValue = getParameter("TextRadius");
        if (paramValue != null) {
            Float r = new Float(paramValue);
            oradius = r.floatValue();
        }

        // What is the orbiting Text speed?
        paramValue = getParameter("TextOrbitSpeed");
        if (paramValue != null)
            ospeed = Integer.parseInt(paramValue);
        else
            ospeed = 5000;


        // Look for the text Font
        paramValue = getParameter("TextFont");
        if (paramValue != null)
            if (paramValue.equalsIgnoreCase("TimesRoman") == true)
                tfont = new String(paramValue);
                else if (paramValue.equalsIgnoreCase("Helvetica") ==
true)
                tfont = new String(paramValue);
            else if (paramValue.equalsIgnoreCase("Serif") == true)
                tfont = new String(paramValue);
            else if (paramValue.equalsIgnoreCase("Monospaced") == true)
                tfont = new String(paramValue);
            else if (paramValue.equalsIgnoreCase("Courier") == true)
                tfont = new String(paramValue);
            else if (paramValue.equalsIgnoreCase("Dialog") == true)
                tfont = new String(paramValue);
            else
                tfont = new String("Helvetica");
        else
```

continues

Source 4.2 *Continued*

```
                tfont = new String("Helvetica");

        // Look for the text Style
        paramValue = getParameter("TextStyle");
        if (paramValue != null)
            if (paramValue.equalsIgnoreCase("bold") == true)
                tstyle = Font.BOLD;
            else if (paramValue.equalsIgnoreCase("italic") == true)
                tstyle = Font.ITALIC;
            else if (paramValue.equalsIgnoreCase("plain") == true)
                tstyle = Font.PLAIN;
            else
                tstyle = Font.PLAIN;
        else
            tstyle = Font.BOLD;

         // Look for the text Size
        paramValue = getParameter("TextSize");
        if (paramValue != null)
            tsize = Integer.parseInt(paramValue);
        else
                        tsize = 60;

            // Look for Text color
           paramValue = getParameter("TextColor");
        if (paramValue != null)
            if (paramValue.equalsIgnoreCase("red") == true)
                tcolor = red;
            else if (paramValue.equalsIgnoreCase("green") == true)
                tcolor = green;
            else if (paramValue.equalsIgnoreCase("blue") == true)
                tcolor = blue;
            else if (paramValue.equalsIgnoreCase("medred") == true)
                tcolor = medred;
            else if (paramValue.equalsIgnoreCase("medgreen") == true)
                tcolor = medgreen;
            else if (paramValue.equalsIgnoreCase("medblue") == true)
                tcolor = medblue;
            else if (paramValue.equalsIgnoreCase("black") == true)
                tcolor = black;
            else if (paramValue.equalsIgnoreCase("gray") == true)
                tcolor = gray;
            else if (paramValue.equalsIgnoreCase("white") == true)
                tcolor = white;
            else if (paramValue.equalsIgnoreCase("yellow") == true)
                tcolor = yellow;
            else if (paramValue.equalsIgnoreCase("gold") == true)
```

Source 4.2   Complete Morph Applet (*Continued*)

```
                        tcolor = gold;
              else if (paramValue.equalsIgnoreCase("purple") == true)
                        tcolor = purple;
              else if (paramValue.equalsIgnoreCase("medpurple") == true)
                        tcolor = medpurple;
              else if (paramValue.equalsIgnoreCase("orange") == true)
                        tcolor = orange;
              else if (paramValue.equalsIgnoreCase("medorange") == true)
                        tcolor = medorange;
              else
                        tcolor = red;
        else
              tcolor = red;

// Look for a new Direct Lighting color
paramValue = getParameter("DirectLightColor");
if (paramValue != null)
    if (paramValue.equalsIgnoreCase("red") == true)
                dcolor = red;
    else if (paramValue.equalsIgnoreCase("green") == true)
                dcolor = green;
    else if (paramValue.equalsIgnoreCase("blue") == true)
                dcolor = blue;
    else if (paramValue.equalsIgnoreCase("medred") == true)
                dcolor = medred;
    else if (paramValue.equalsIgnoreCase("medgreen") == true)
                dcolor = medgreen;
    else if (paramValue.equalsIgnoreCase("medblue") == true)
                dcolor = medblue;
    else if (paramValue.equalsIgnoreCase("black") == true)
                dcolor = black;
    else if (paramValue.equalsIgnoreCase("gray") == true)
                dcolor = gray;
    else if (paramValue.equalsIgnoreCase("white") == true)
                dcolor = white;
    else if (paramValue.equalsIgnoreCase("yellow") == true)
                dcolor = yellow;
    else if (paramValue.equalsIgnoreCase("gold") == true)
                dcolor = gold;
    else if (paramValue.equalsIgnoreCase("purple") == true)
                dcolor = purple;
    else if (paramValue.equalsIgnoreCase("medpurple") == true)
                dcolor = medpurple;
    else if (paramValue.equalsIgnoreCase("orange") == true)
                dcolor = orange;
    else if (paramValue.equalsIgnoreCase("medorange") == true)
```

continues

Source 4.2 *Continued*

```
                          dcolor = medorange;
                  else
            dcolor = white;
       else
           dcolor = white;

 // Look for Ambient Light color
 paramValue = getParameter("AmbientLightColor");
       if (paramValue != null)
           if (paramValue.equalsIgnoreCase("red") == true)
               acolor = red;
           else if (paramValue.equalsIgnoreCase("green") == true)
               acolor = green;
           else if (paramValue.equalsIgnoreCase("blue") == true)
               acolor = blue;
           else if (paramValue.equalsIgnoreCase("medred") == true)
               acolor = medred;
           else if (paramValue.equalsIgnoreCase("medgreen") == true)
               acolor = medgreen;
           else if (paramValue.equalsIgnoreCase("medblue") == true)
               acolor = medblue;
           else if (paramValue.equalsIgnoreCase("black") == true)
               acolor = black;
           else if (paramValue.equalsIgnoreCase("gray") == true)
               acolor = gray;
           else if (paramValue.equalsIgnoreCase("white") == true)
               acolor = white;
           else if (paramValue.equalsIgnoreCase("yellow") == true)
               acolor = yellow;
           else if (paramValue.equalsIgnoreCase("gold") == true)
               acolor = gold;
           else if (paramValue.equalsIgnoreCase("purple") == true)
               acolor = purple;
          else if (paramValue.equalsIgnoreCase("medpurple") == true)
               acolor = medpurple;
           else if (paramValue.equalsIgnoreCase("orange") == true)
               acolor = orange;
          else if (paramValue.equalsIgnoreCase("medorange") == true)
               acolor = medorange;
            else
               acolor = white;
       else
           acolor = white;

           // Look for the morphing Object's color
           paramValue = getParameter("ObjectColor");
       if (paramValue != null)
```

Source 4.2   Complete Morph Applet (*Continued*)

```
            if (paramValue.equalsIgnoreCase("red") == true)
                objcolor = red;
            else if (paramValue.equalsIgnoreCase("green") == true)
                objcolor = green;
            else if (paramValue.equalsIgnoreCase("blue") == true)
                objcolor = blue;
            else if (paramValue.equalsIgnoreCase("medred") == true)
                objcolor = medred;
            else if (paramValue.equalsIgnoreCase("medgreen") == true)
                objcolor = medgreen;
            else if (paramValue.equalsIgnoreCase("medblue") == true)
                objcolor = medblue;
            else if (paramValue.equalsIgnoreCase("black") == true)
                objcolor = black;
            else if (paramValue.equalsIgnoreCase("gray") == true)
                objcolor = gray;
            else if (paramValue.equalsIgnoreCase("white") == true)
                objcolor = white;
            else if (paramValue.equalsIgnoreCase("yellow") == true)
                objcolor = yellow;
            else if (paramValue.equalsIgnoreCase("gold") == true)
                objcolor = gold;
            else if (paramValue.equalsIgnoreCase("purple") == true)
                objcolor = purple;
            else if (paramValue.equalsIgnoreCase("medpurple") == true)
                objcolor = medpurple;
            else if (paramValue.equalsIgnoreCase("orange") == true)
                objcolor = orange;
            else if (paramValue.equalsIgnoreCase("medorange") == true)
                objcolor = medorange;
            else
                objcolor = blue;
        else
            objcolor = blue;

    } // END LookForParameters

    private BranchGroup createSceneGraph(Canvas3D c,
                                        AppletContext context) {

        // Create the root of the branch graph
        BranchGroup objRoot = new BranchGroup();

        // Create a Transformgroup to scale all objects so they
        // appear in the scene.
        TransformGroup objScale = new TransformGroup();
```
continues

Source 4.2 *Continued*

```
        objScale.setCapability(TransformGroup.ENABLE_PICK_REPORTING);
           Transform3D t3d = new Transform3D();
           t3d.setScale(scale);
           objScale.setTransform(t3d);
           objRoot.addChild(objScale);

           // Create a bounds for the background and lights
           BoundingSphere bounds =
                   new BoundingSphere(new Point3d(0.0,0.0,0.0), 100.0);

           // Set up the background
           Background bg = new Background(bgcolor);
           bg.setApplicationBounds(bounds);
           objScale.addChild(bg);

           // Set up the vector for directional light
           Vector3f lDir1  = new Vector3f(-1.0f, -1.0f, -1.0f);

    // Create 2 light sources
           AmbientLight al = new AmbientLight(acolor);
           al.setInfluencingBounds(bounds);
           DirectionalLight dl = new DirectionalLight(dcolor, lDir1);
           dl.setInfluencingBounds(bounds);
           objScale.addChild(al);
           objScale.addChild(dl);

           //
           // Create the transform group nodes to position Text labels
           // and the morphed object.  Add them to the root of the
           // branch graph.
           //
           TransformGroup objTrans[] = new TransformGroup[3];

           for(int i=0; i<3; i++) {
           objTrans[i] = new TransformGroup();
           objScale.addChild(objTrans[i]);
           }

           Transform3D tr = new Transform3D();
           Transform3D rotX90 = new Transform3D();
           rotX90.rotX(90.0 * Math.PI / 180.0);

    // Top location
    //
           objTrans[0].getTransform(tr);
           tr.setTranslation(new Vector3d(0.0, 0.7, 0.0));
           tr.mul(rotX90);
```

Source 4.2   Complete Morph Applet (*Continued*)

```
        objTrans[0].setTransform(tr);

// Middle location
//
    objTrans[1].getTransform(tr);
    tr.setTranslation(new Vector3d(0.0, 0.0, 0.0));
    tr.mul(rotX90);
    objTrans[1].setTransform(tr);

// Bottom location
//
    objTrans[2].getTransform(tr);
    tr.setTranslation(new Vector3d(0.0, -0.7, 0.0));
    tr.mul(rotX90);
    objTrans[2].setTransform(tr);

// Now load the object files
    Scene s[] = new Scene[3];
    GeometryArray g[] = new GeometryArray[3];
    Shape3D shape[] = new Shape3D[3];
    ObjectFile loader = new ObjectFile(ObjectFile.RESIZE);

 // Initialize object arrays
    for(int i=0; i<3; i++) {
        s[i] = null;
        g[i] = null;
        shape[i] = null;
    }

// Use the loader for *.obj imported models. For
// Applets, Shape 3D class files have to be pre
// generated and compile and the class name passed
// from the HTML interface.
//
if (applet != true) {
  try {
    s[0] = loader.load(objName1);
    s[1] = loader.load(objName2);
    s[2] = loader.load(objName3);
  }
  catch (FileNotFoundException e) {
        System.err.println(e);
        System.exit(1);
  }
  catch (ParsingErrorException e) {
        System.err.println(e);
```

continues

Source 4.2   *Continued*

```
                        System.exit(1);
            }
        catch (IncorrectFormatException e) {
                System.err.println(e);
                System.exit(1);
        }
    }

    for(int i=0; i<3;i++) {

        if (applet != true) {
            BranchGroup b = s[i].getSceneGroup();
            shape[i] = (Shape3D) b.getChild(0);
        }
        else {
            // This is how a class can be dynamically instatiated.
            // forName and newInstance is like "new Class()"
            // And getShape() will return the reference
            // to the provided Shape3D object that was passed as
            // a String from the HTML interface. Avoids signing
            // JAR files to prevent security violations and is
            // fully Java security compliant.
            //  ** Note the Shape3D class was generated with
            //      the VRMLFacesToJ3d tool and compiled, then
            //      co-located to the same directory (or unsigned
            //      JAR file) as this Applet.
            //
            try {
                DynamicShape dynamo = (DynamicShape)
                Class.forName(newclass[i]).newInstance();
                shape[i] = (Shape3D) dynamo.getShape();
            }
            catch (ClassNotFoundException e) {
                        System.err.println(e);
                        System.exit(1);
            }
            catch (IllegalAccessException e) {
                        System.err.println(e);
                        System.exit(1);
            }
            catch (InstantiationException e) {
                        System.err.println(e);
                        System.exit(1);
            }
        }

        g[i] = (GeometryArray) shape[i].getGeometry();
```

Source 4.2   Complete Morph Applet (*Continued*)

```
        shape[i].setGeometry(g[i]);

    }  // END of FOR loop


// Create a Morph node, and set the appearance and input
// geometry arrays.  Set the Morph node's capability bits
// to allow the weights to be modified at runtime.
// "weights" are what control the morph effect. But they
// are hard coded in the MorphBehavior class.
//
    Appearance app = new Appearance();
    app.setMaterial(new Material(objcolor,
            black, objcolor, white, 80.0f));
    Morph morph = new Morph( (GeometryArray[]) g, app);
    morph.setCapability(Morph.ALLOW_WEIGHTS_READ);
    morph.setCapability(Morph.ALLOW_WEIGHTS_WRITE);

    objTrans[objPos].addChild(morph);

    // Now create the Alpha object that controls the speed of the
    // morphing operation.
    Alpha morphAlpha = new Alpha(-1, Alpha.INCREASING_ENABLE |
                    Alpha.DECREASING_ENABLE,
                    0, 0,
                    2000, 1000, 200,
                    2000, 1000, 200);

    // Finally, create the morphing behavior
    MorphingBehavior mBeh =
        new MorphingBehavior(morphAlpha, morph);
    mBeh.setSchedulingBounds(bounds);
    objScale.addChild(mBeh);

// Create text label, if specified.
//
if (label != null) {

        Shape3D textObj = new Text2D(label,
                            tcolor,
                            tfont,
                            tsize,
                            tstyle);

    Appearance tapp = textObj.getAppearance();
    PolygonAttributes pa = tapp.getPolygonAttributes();
```

continues

Source 4.2 *Continued*

```
                    if (pa == null)
                        pa = new PolygonAttributes();
          pa.setCullFace(PolygonAttributes.CULL_NONE);
                    if (tapp.getPolygonAttributes() == null)
                        tapp.setPolygonAttributes(pa);



          // Don't Spin the Text, just put it at the given position
          //
          if (spin != true ) {

              // step 1. Create a transform object for the label.
              // step 2. Set up its properties.
              // step 3. Define a transform matrix to manipulate.
              // step 4. Modify the matrix parts for translation.
              //         This is done with convenience methods to
              //         position, rotate, pitch/yaw/roll and
              //         scale. We'll be using the setTranslation
              //         method.
              // step 5. Add the transform group to the root branch
              //         group.
              // step 6. Add the Text object below the transform
              //         object.
              //
              TransformGroup textObjTrans = new TransformGroup();
              textObjTrans.setCapability(
                        TransformGroup.ALLOW_TRANSFORM_WRITE);
              Transform3D text3d = new Transform3D();
              text3d.setTranslation(new Vector3f(xPos,yPos,zPos));
              objRoot.addChild(textObjTrans);
              textObjTrans.addChild(textObj);
          }
          else {
              // Orbit the Text around the Morph
              //
              TransformGroup orbit = new XZorbit(ospeed,
                          oradius, new Point3d(xPos,yPos,zPos));
              objScale.addChild(orbit);
              orbit.addChild(textObj);
          }
      }

   if (pick = true) {
      // Setup mouse picking behavior.
      //
      PickURL pickURL = new PickURL(c, objRoot,
                  bounds, link, context);
```

Source 4.2 Complete Morph Applet (*Continued*)

```
                    pickURL.setSchedulingBounds(bounds);
                    objRoot.addChild(pickURL);
          }


                return objRoot;
       }


       // Morphing() will be invoked by the browser because the <APPLET>
       // HTML tag contains a pointer to this object
       // "code=Morphing.class". The applet arguments are passed in the
       // form of <PARAM> tags to a convenience method lookForParameters
       // when the applet is started.
       //
       public void init() {

           AppletContext context = null;

          // If we are running as an applet we need to
          // initialize values according to the user settings in
          // the HTML file accomplished by lookForParameters().
          // Otherwise we'll just use the values used to initialize
          // the local variable declarations at the top of the block.
          //
          if (getParameter("ObjectName1") != null) {
                    context = getAppletContext();
                    lookForParameters();
          }

          // Create a Canvas3D object and add it to the applet
               setLayout(new BorderLayout());
               Canvas3D c = new Canvas3D(null);
               add("Center", c);

               // Create a simple scene.
          BranchGroup scene = createSceneGraph(c, context);

          // attach the scene to the virtual universe
               SimpleUniverse u = new SimpleUniverse(c);

               // This will move the ViewPlatform back a bit so the
               // objects in the scene can be viewed.
               u.getViewingPlatform().setNominalViewingTransform();

          // Add the branch graph to the Locale object to
          // make the branch "live".
               u.addBranchGraph(scene);
```
                                                            continues

Source 4.2   *Continued*

```
        }

    public static void main(String[] args) {
        if (args.length > 0) {
            // Parse Input Arguments
            for (int i = 0; i < args.length; i++) {

                if (args[i].equals("-demo")) {
                    new MainFrame(new Morphing(), 300, 300);
                } else {
                            System.out.println("Usage: java Morphing -
demo");
                    System.exit(0);
                    }
                }
        } else {
            System.out.println("Usage: java Morphing -demo");
            System.exit(0);
        }
    } // END Main

} // END Applet
```

Source 4.2   Complete Morph Applet (*Continued*)

Moving On

This chapter has given an overview of how geometrical data is imported into a Java 3D program. Although Java 3D provides some primitive shapes, like a sphere, box, and so on, it does not help with creating the geometry. To display more complicated geometry it is recommended that you obtain a 3D modelling software program that saves objects as WaveFront *.obj files. Use these applications to create your own custom geometry or pay one of the several vendors to create some geometry for you. Next, we will take a closer look at how to move our geometry objects around in a scene.

Translation, Rotation, and Scaling

"The primary purpose of the DATA statement is to give names to constants. Instead of referring to π (pi) as 3.141592653589793 at every appearance, the variable PI can be used instead. This also simplifies the program, should the value of π (pi) change."

—EXCERPT FROM A FORTRAN MANUAL

Planets Applet Description and Usage

The Planets applet (see Figure 5.1) is designed to provide a mechanism or model that allows visitors to navigate an internal or external Web site. The theme is our solar system, in which each planet can have an associated label and URL. When visitors click on planets or moons, they are whisked away to the specified Web page. The scene consists of multiple planetary objects orbiting the Sun, and each planet has its own rotation. The Earth object not only orbits while rotating, but it has a moon that orbits and rotates the Earth at the same time. The scene has many interesting objects, with detailed planet surface maps that create a rich and realistic solar system 3D menu. Three-dimensional text is used to identify the item associated with a planet in our virtual solar system. You might want to present an organizational chart or major "jump-off" point in your Web site.

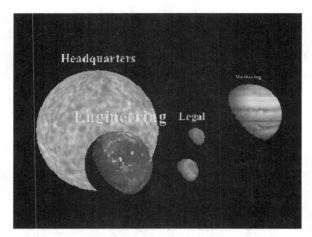

Figure 5.1   Java 3D planets example.

Planets Applet Parameters Explained

The following is the defined HTML interface to this program. How to read the syntax of the provided HTML file (Planets.html) is covered in Chapter 4, "Beautiful Geometry," in great detail so we will not repeat the material here.

First, the program must know how many planets to create. When thinking about the usage of the applet, consider having some of the planets or moons inactive just for effect. Of course, other objects in the scene will be used like a virtual 3D menu that references URL links.

```
<PARAM NAME="Planets" VALUE=2>
```

To match the applet to the created HTML page, you can specify the background color that uses predefined colors named: red, blue, green, yellow, purple, gold, orange, black, white, medblue (medium blue), and medgreen (medium green).

```
<PARAM NAME="BackgroundColor" VALUE="black">
```

Besides naming a color background, each planet can have a specific color. But you don't need to create a planet color if you will be using a picture over the planet, called a *texture*. The color choices are: red, blue, green, yellow, purple, gold, orange, black, white, medblue (medium blue), and medgreen (medium green).

```
<PARAM NAME="PlanetColor1" VALUE="blue">
```

Each planet will rotate the first created planet (Planet1). By design, this was intended to be the Sun. But you could make the center of the solar system anything you want—say, the Earth or some other representation. Each planet will have an orbit speed, except Planet1 which will stay fixed. Use the following predefined speeds: slow, medium, fast, and xfast.

```
<PARAM NAME="PlanetSpeed1" VALUE="slow">
```

In addition, to orbit velocity, you will need to specify the distance of the planet's orbit from the center of the solar system. This number will increment by the value you provide in order to calculate all planets' orbit radii. For example, using the value of 2, as shown in the following example, the first planet will orbit at a distance of N from the center of the solar system (see Figure 5.2). Our scale could be equal to the real universe (1.0 = 1 meter), but then it would be pretty hard to fit the solar system into the Web browser window. You will want to see all of the planets within the program window, so we suggest you do a little trial and error. Start off small, like 0.3, and see what that looks like first before returning to adjust this parameter.

```
<PARAM NAME="PlanetOrbit" VALUE="2.0">
```

Each of the planets can also have a defined size using the following predefined values: small, medium, large, xlarge.

```
<PARAM NAME="PlanetSize1" VALUE="large">
```

For this program, surface pictures are supplied, which you can use to texture your planets; or you might want to create your own textures to use. The image is applied to the 3D object by the process called texture mapping. By using the keyword "PlanetImage" and the planet identifier "1," you pass the file name of the image you would like to use.

```
<PARAM NAME="PlanetImage1"
VALUE="http://www.wiley.com/images/earth.jpg">
```

Figure 5.2 Planet orbit value calculation.

If you will need to associate a URL link that is loaded when the user clicks on the planet, then use the keyword "PlanetImage" with the planet number, and provide a URL address.

To create a text label over the planet object, use "PlanetText" and pass a string as its value. There are a number of other attributes you can set on the text, such as color, font type (Times, Courier, Helvetica, Monospaced, Serif, and Dialog), size (8, 10, 12, 14, 18, 24, 36, 72) and font style (plain, bold, and italic).

```
<PARAM NAME="PlanetText1" VALUE="Engineering">
<PARAM NAME="PlanetTextColor1" VALUE="red">
<PARAM NAME="PlanetTextFont1" VALUE="Times">
<PARAM NAME="PlanetTextSize1" VALUE="32">
<PARAM NAME="PlanetTextStyle1" VALUE="bold">
```

You also have the option of creating moons, which orbit a planet. Here's how: First specify the planet objects you want created; these parameters are specified in the HTML file. For example, let us assume you have created three planets and you want a moon to orbit Planet2. Use the keyword "Moon" and associate it with Planet2 using the same identification number. The HTML file would contain the following definition. Setting the value to "true" just means you want the moon to be created. What happened to Moon1 and Moon3? You could have specified them in the HTML file and set the value to "false", but this extra work is unnecessary.

```
<PARAM NAME="Moon2" VALUE="true">
```

Similar properties apply to moons, and in the same manner, so review the planet value options for this information; we won't restate it here.

```
<PARAM NAME="MoonImage1" VALUE="http://www.sun.com/images/ito.jpg">
<PARAM NAME="MoonURL1" VALUE="http://www.sun.com/">
<PARAM NAME="MoonColor1" VALUE="green">
<PARAM NAME="MoonSpeed1" VALUE="slow">
<PARAM NAME="MoonSize1" VALUE="large">
<PARAM NAME="MoonText1" VALUE="Engineering">
<PARAM NAME="MoonTextColor1" VALUE="red">
<PARAM NAME="MoonTextFont1" VALUE="Times">
<PARAM NAME="PlanetTextSize1" VALUE="24">
<PARAM NAME="PlanetTextStyle1" VALUE="bold">
```

Planets HTML File Explained

The HTML file for the applet will look like the following. Don't be intimidated; it really is pretty straightforward upon closer inspection. And remember, a line-by-line discussion of the HTML tags was given in Chapter 4 if you get confused. Source 5.1 is the HTML file you will need to edit to create a custom applet for your Web site.

```
<HTML>
<TITLE>Planet 1 Applet</TITLE>
<BODY>


<!--"CONVERTED_APPLET"-->
<!-- CONVERTER VERSION 1.0 -->
<OBJECT classid="clsid:8AD9C840-044E-11D1-B3E9-00805F499D93"
WIDTH = "600" HEIGHT = "400" ALIGN = "baseline"
codebase="http://java.sun.com/products/plugin/1.2/jinstall-12-
                    win32.cab#Version=1,2,0,0">
<PARAM NAME = CODE VALUE = "Planets.class" >

<PARAM NAME="type" VALUE="application/x-java-applet;version=1.2">
<PARAM NAME = "Planets" VALUE      = "3">
<PARAM NAME = "PlanetOrbit" VALUE      = "1.75">
<PARAM NAME = "BackgroundColor" VALUE      = "black">
<PARAM NAME = "PlanetColor1" VALUE      = "blue">
<PARAM NAME = "PlanetImage1" VALUE = "http://www.wiley.com/sun.jpg">
<PARAM NAME = "PlanetURL1" VALUE   = "http://www.sun.com">
<PARAM NAME = "PlanetSpeed1" VALUE      = "slow">
<PARAM NAME = "PlanetSize1" VALUE      = "large">
<PARAM NAME = "PlanetText1" VALUE      = "CORPORATE">
<PARAM NAME = "PlanetTextColor1" VALUE      = "yellow">
<PARAM NAME = "PlanetTextFont1" VALUE      = "Helvetica">
<PARAM NAME = "PlanetTextSize1" VALUE      = "60">
<PARAM NAME = "PlanetTextStyle1" VALUE      = "bold">
<PARAM NAME = "PlanetColor2" VALUE      = "purple">
<PARAM NAME = "PlanetSpeed2" VALUE      = "15000">
<PARAM NAME = "PlanetSize2" VALUE      = "small">
<PARAM NAME = "PlanetText2" VALUE      = "PRODUCTS">
<PARAM NAME = "PlanetTextColor2" VALUE      = "yellow">
<PARAM NAME = "PlanetTextFont2" VALUE      = "Helvetica">
<PARAM NAME = "PlanetTextSize2" VALUE      = "60">
<PARAM NAME = "PlanetTextStyle2" VALUE      = "bold">
<PARAM NAME = "PlanetColor3" VALUE      = "red">
<PARAM NAME = "PlanetSpeed3" VALUE      = "28000">
<PARAM NAME = "PlanetSize3" VALUE      = "medium">
<PARAM NAME = "PlanetText3" VALUE      = "SUPPORT">
<PARAM NAME = "PlanetTextColor3" VALUE      = "yellow">
<PARAM NAME = "PlanetTextFont3" VALUE      = "Helvetica">
<PARAM NAME = "PlanetTextSize3" VALUE      = "60">
<PARAM NAME = "PlanetTextStyle3" VALUE      = "bold">
<PARAM NAME = "Moon3" VALUE      = "true">
<PARAM NAME = "MoonColor3" VALUE      = "blue">
<PARAM NAME = "MoonSpeed3" VALUE      = "10000">
<PARAM NAME = "MoonSize3" VALUE      = "small">
<PARAM NAME = "MoonText3" VALUE      = "Eng">
```

continues

Source 5.1   Planet HTML Listing

```
<PARAM NAME = "MoonTextColor3" VALUE    = "yellow">
<PARAM NAME = "MoonTextFont3" VALUE     = "Helvetica">
<PARAM NAME = "MoonTextSize3" VALUE     = "48">
<PARAM NAME = "MoonTextStyle3" VALUE    = "bold">
<COMMENT>
<EMBED type="application/x-java-applet;version=1.2"
java_CODE = "Planets.class" WIDTH = "600" HEIGHT = "400"
ALIGN = "baseline"
Planets =   "3"
PlanetOrbit =   "1.75"
BackgroundColor =   "black"
PlanetColor1 =   "blue"
PlanetImage1 =   "http://www.wiley.com/sun.jpg"
PlanetURL1 =   "http://www.sun.com"
PlanetSpeed1 =   "slow"
PlanetSize1 =   "large"
PlanetText1 =   "CORPORATE"
PlanetTextColor1 =   "yellow"
PlanetTextFont1 =   "Helvetica"
PlanetTextSize1 =   "60"
PlanetTextStyle1 =   "bold"
PlanetColor2 =   "purple"
PlanetSpeed2 =   "15000"
PlanetSize2 =   "small"
PlanetText2 =   "PRODUCTS"
PlanetTextColor2 =   "yellow"
PlanetTextFont2 =   "Helvetica"
PlanetTextSize2 =   "60"
PlanetTextStyle2 =   "bold"
PlanetColor3 =   "red"
PlanetSpeed3 =   "28000"
PlanetSize3 =   "medium"
PlanetText3 =   "SUPPORT"
PlanetTextColor3 =   "yellow"
PlanetTextFont3 =   "Helvetica"
PlanetTextSize3 =   "60"
PlanetTextStyle3 =   "bold"
Moon3 =   "true"
MoonColor3 =   "blue"
MoonSpeed3 =   "10000"
MoonSize3 =   "small"
MoonText3 =   "Eng"
MoonTextColor3 =   "yellow"
MoonTextFont3 =   "Helvetica"
MoonTextSize3 = "48"
MoonTextStyle3 = "bold"
```

Source 5.1 Planet HTML Listing (*Continued*)

```
No Java 2 support for this APPLET!!
</NOEMBED></EMBED>
</OBJECT>


<!--
<APPLET  CODE = "Planets.class" WIDTH = "600" HEIGHT = "400"
ALIGN = "baseline" >

<PARAM NAME = "Planets" VALUE    = "3">
<PARAM NAME = "PlanetOrbit" VALUE    = "1.75">
<PARAM NAME = "BackgroundColor" VALUE    = "black">
<PARAM NAME = "PlanetColor1" VALUE    = "blue">
<PARAM NAME = "PlanetImage1" VALUE = "http://www.wiley.com/sun.jpg">
<PARAM NAME = "PlanetURL1" VALUE   = "http://www.sun.com">
<PARAM NAME = "PlanetSpeed1" VALUE    = "slow">
<PARAM NAME = "PlanetSize1" VALUE    = "large">
<PARAM NAME = "PlanetText1" VALUE    = "CORPORATE">
<PARAM NAME = "PlanetTextColor1" VALUE    = "yellow">
<PARAM NAME = "PlanetTextFont1" VALUE    = "Helvetica">
<PARAM NAME = "PlanetTextSize1" VALUE    = "60">
<PARAM NAME = "PlanetTextStyle1" VALUE    = "bold">
<PARAM NAME = "PlanetColor2" VALUE    = "purple">
<PARAM NAME = "PlanetSpeed2" VALUE    = "15000">
<PARAM NAME = "PlanetSize2" VALUE    = "small">
<PARAM NAME = "PlanetText2" VALUE    = "PRODUCTS">
<PARAM NAME = "PlanetTextColor2" VALUE    = "yellow">
<PARAM NAME = "PlanetTextFont2" VALUE    = "Helvetica">
<PARAM NAME = "PlanetTextSize2" VALUE    = "60">
<PARAM NAME = "PlanetTextStyle2" VALUE    = "bold">
<PARAM NAME = "PlanetColor3" VALUE    = "red">
<PARAM NAME = "PlanetSpeed3" VALUE    = "28000">
<PARAM NAME = "PlanetSize3" VALUE    = "medium">
<PARAM NAME = "PlanetText3" VALUE    = "SUPPORT">
<PARAM NAME = "PlanetTextColor3" VALUE    = "yellow">
<PARAM NAME = "PlanetTextFont3" VALUE    = "Helvetica">
<PARAM NAME = "PlanetTextSize3" VALUE    = "60">
<PARAM NAME = "PlanetTextStyle3" VALUE    = "bold">
<PARAM NAME = "Moon3" VALUE    = "true">
<PARAM NAME = "MoonColor3" VALUE    = "blue">
<PARAM NAME = "MoonSpeed3" VALUE    = "10000">
<PARAM NAME = "MoonSize3" VALUE    = "small">
<PARAM NAME = "MoonText3" VALUE    = "Eng">
<PARAM NAME = "MoonTextColor3" VALUE    = "yellow">
<PARAM NAME = "MoonTextFont3" VALUE    = "Helvetica">
<PARAM NAME = "MoonTextSize3" VALUE    = "48">
<PARAM NAME = "MoonTextStyle3" VALUE    = "bold">
```

continues

Source 5.1   *Continued*

```
No Java 2 support for this APPLET!!

</APPLET>
-->

<!--"END_CONVERTED_APPLET"-->

</BODY>
</HTML>
```

Source 5.1   Planet HTML Listing (*Continued*)

How to Interpret the HTML Tags

Go back to Chapter 4 and review the detailed discussion regarding the syntax of this HTML file. The parameter definitions are discussed at the beginning of this chapter.

Java 3D Translation Concepts

In this section, we continue our discussion of the SceneGraph model with some information on transforming hierarchical objects utilizing the 3D methods provided by the Java 3D API. As we have been seeing, a scene is constructed from a group of objects. Some are shape objects; others specify appearance properties; and some have unique functionality, like transformations. Let's stop for a moment and examine how objects are moved around the scene.

The symbol PI is used regularly in our formulas to calculate orbits and rotations. And we assure you it hasn't changed its value in the Java 3D API implementation, the humorous excerpt that opens the chapter notwithstanding! Remember, *PI* represents the ratio of the circumference to the diameter of a circle. We'll be using the value of PI in many of the methods used to create the orbit and rotation transforms in the Planet applet.

Usually, the position and orientation of rotating objects are described in degrees, as in, "the object has rotated 180 degrees." Although Java 3D and most graphics commonly use another metric to describe orientation, called radians, degrees are easier to deal with conceptually than radians. At the Olympics in Nagano, Japan, during the ice skating event, the announcer didn't praise the champion performance with, "Wow, what a fantastic negative triple 6.28 radians toe loop! Unbelievable performance! Just look at the double precision we have going here tonight! What do you think about that performance

Peggy?" "I don't know Dick. I'm just amazed at the number of radians these skaters can achieve today. I could only do 3.00056 radians at the peak of my career, and it's just amazing how far the sport has come today."

It is helpful to convert everything into degrees, assign it to a variable, and then plug it back into your method. PI is defined in the java.lang.Math class; 360 degrees equals 6.28 radians, or Math.PI*2 radians, where:

radians = degrees/(180/Math.PI)

Also, positive angles will result in a counterclockwise rotation. Use a negative value for the degree variable if you want a clockwise rotation.

The transformation of 3D objects involves translation, rotation, and scaling of the graphical object (see Figure 5.3). *Translation* is the change in position of an object without changing its shape, size, or orientation. *Rotation* is a geometric transformation that causes points to be reoriented about the X, Y, or Z axis in 3D space. And *scaling* changes the size of an object without affecting its location or orientation. The view zooms toward or away from the object, and the object increases or decreases in size.

In addition, the applet in this book includes some simplified classes for performing desired scaling, rotation, and translation to make the developer's job easier; they can be reused in other applications. Reminder: A full description of these utilities is included in the last chapter.

Basic Steps to Perform Translation

There is a basic pattern, or recipe, to follow to enable 3D objects to spin, orbit, and move along a predefined path. Here are the basic steps:

1. Create a Transform Group. Set needed properties.

```
TransformGroup sphereScale = new TransformGroup();
sphereScale.setCapability(TransformGroup.ALLOW_TRANSFORM_WRITE);
objRoot.addchild(sphereScale);
```

2. Create some geometry.

```
Sphere planet = new Sphere();
```

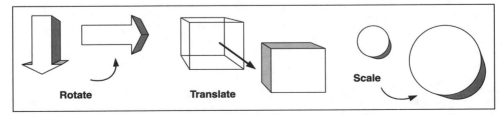

Figure 5.3   Rotation, Translation, and Scaling.

3. Add a behavior to the transform group to rotate the 3D object (discussed later in the book).

or

Modify the transform matrix that will perform a rotation, scale, or translation.

```
Transform3D t3d = new Transform3D();
t3d.setScale(0.16);
scaleSphere.setTransform(t3d);
objRoot.addChild(scaleSphere);
```

4. Add the created Sphere object under the transform. The result will be a scaled, enlarged spherical planet. If a behavior was created, like Orbit, then just add the planet under the behavior and it will orbit. Amazing.

```
ScaleSphere.addChild(planet);
```

The Behavior node will modify values in the TransformGroup node (see Figure 5.4), which is over the Shape3D object, thus creating new transforms that in return move the object around the scene. Since this is done on the fly, the transform needs the capability to WRITE values in the new matrix that will point to the next position to which we'll be sending the object. That's

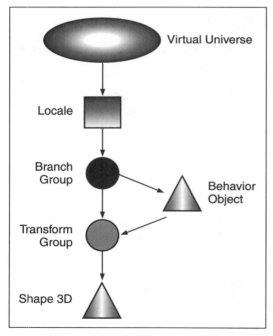

Figure 5.4 BranchGroup with a transform and behavior.

why we had to set "sphereScale.setCapability(TransformGroup.ALLOW_ TRANSFORM_WRITE)" as shown in step 1. In the following case, Rotator contains the behavior to create planet rotation.

```
Transform3D yAxis = new Transform3D();

Alpha rotationAlpha = new Alpha(-1, Alpha.INCREASING_ENABLE,
        0,0,4000,0,0,0,0,0);

RotationInterpolator rotator = new RotationInterpolator(
        rotationAlpha, objTrans, yAxis,
        0.0f, (float) Math.PI*2.0f);
BoundingSphere bounds = new BoundingSphere(
        new Point3D(0.0,0.0,0.0),100.0);

rotator.setSchedulingBounds(bounds);

objTrans.addChild(rotator);
```

These chunks of code would create a rotating sphere at a constant rate of PI/2 radians per second. We could fiddle with the speed (4,000 milliseconds) in the Alpha constructor to moderate the rate of spin along the Y-axis. We'll go through the various methods later in the chapter, but now let's take a look at the applet class for this chapter and its supporting utilities.

Applet Example Explained

When creating an applet with motion in Java 3D, you can follow a basic template, delineated here:

1. Use an AWT layout manager to position components within a container object. Specify which layout manager to use. In this case BorderLayout versus GridBagLayout or Container.

2. Create a 3D Canvas component to draw on.

3. Add the Canvas 3D component to the AWT container, and center it.

4. Create a scene graph, which is constructed of a collection of objects and organized in a tree structure.

5. Establish a Virtual Universe with a hi-res Locale coordinate system. Essentially, *SimpleUniverse( )* performs the following shortcut:

```
VirtualUniverse u = new VirtualUniverse();
Local local = new Locale(u);
```

6. Eventually, the objects in the BranchGroup are attached to the Virtual Universe, making the object live; the user sees the rendered scene.

That is basically the 10,000-foot view of creating the framework for a Java 3D program. Now let's look a little closer at step 4, which encompasses establishing and performing translation.

First we need to create a BranchGroup that establishes the root of a subgraph in a scene. Children or objects will be added to the subgraph as we go along. The SceneGraph can be altered at runtime, which is why subgraphs are created in this manner. A subgraph might be cloned, reparented, or removed.

Next we need to create a bounding or containing volume of the spherical type with its origin at 0 along the X, Y, and Z axes. The specified dimension is a radius of 100 meters. This should be sufficient to contain any movement we might perform. None of the effects or behaviors will work unless included within its boundaries. So we simply set it very large since we are not using the boundary region to initiate notification of specific conditions in order to cause an effect. If we wrote a complex game, however, and as the player's position changed, certain bounding regions could trigger various actions. Certainly a complex game would have numerous BranchGroups and bounding volumes; intersections would cause starships to blow up or monsters to attack, for instance. Now let's create a backdrop in a specified color; it will be the first object we'll add to the scene.

Pay attention, because we are going to explain and use our first utility, which provides a shortcut in creating a TransformGroup with a specific behavior. *Rotator* is a class that spins 3D shapes along the Y-axis. Basically, this class will follow the pattern described earlier in the chapter:

1. Create a transform group.

2. Create a behavior.

3. Create geometry (we'll create some geometry outside of this class and apply the class constructs to it).

4. Add the transform above the behavior to the root BranchGroup node (which is later added as a group to the scene graph).

5. Add the behavior to the transform group above the Shape object. Now everything that happens (transforms and behaviors) will apply to our 3D shape.

Source 5.2 lists the source code and comments for the *Rotator class*. It is called with the following syntax:

```
TransformGroup yRotate = new Rotator(new Transform3D(),Rotator.SLOW);
```

The first parameter establishes an identity matrix necessary for translation operations. The second parameter specifies the speed of the rotation, SLOW, MEDIUM, or FAST.

```
 1    // Import the Java 3D classes and the vector mathematics classes.
 2    import javax.media.j3d.*;
 3    import javax.vecmath.*;
 4
 5    /**
 6     * The Rotator class is used to set up a bevavior that continuously
 7     * rotates about a given axis. The Rotator class acts just like
 8     * a TransformGroup - add a Rotator to the scene graph and then any
 9     * children added to the Rotator will be rotated.
10     *
11     * @version 1.0
12     */
13    public class Rotator extends TransformGroup {
14
15        /**
16         * Predefined rotation speed value. Must be preceded by the
17         * class name to use: Rotator.SLOW.
18         */
19        public static final int SLOW = 8000;
20
21        /**
22         * Predefined rotation speed value. Must be preceded by the
23         * class name to use: Rotator.MEDIUM.
24         */
25        public static final int MEDIUM = 4000;
26
27        /**
28         * Predefined rotation speed value. Must be preceded by the
29         * class name to use: Rotator.FAST.
30         */
31        public static final int FAST = 1000;
32
33        /**
34         * Creates and initializes the objects used to create
35         * the rotation behavior. This includes creating the Alpha,
36         * the RotationInterpolator and the Bounds object.
37         *
38         * @param axis The axis to rotate about. The default
39         *    RotationInterpolator rotates about the Y-axis.
40         * @param speed The time for one complete roatation to
41         *    occur (in milliseconds).
42         */
43        protected void initRotator(Transform3D axis, int speed) {
44
45            // Must set this to allow the TransformGroup's Transform
```

continues

Source 5.2 Rotator Class Code

```
46              // to be updated when the scene graph is made live.
47              // If this value is not set, a CapabilityNotSetException
48              // will be thrown once the node is made live.
49              setCapability(TransformGroup.ALLOW_TRANSFORM_WRITE);
50
51              // Create an alpha to use with the RotationInterpolator.
52              // The following values are used for each parameter:
53              //    loopCount
54              //          Specifies the number of times to cycle the alpha.
55              //          A -1 means to cycle it infinitely.
56              //    mode
57              //          Specifies what part of the waveform (going from
58              //          0.0 to 1.0 or 1.0 to 0.0 or both) to use. The Rotator
59              //          alpha will go from 0.0 to 1.0 and then start over at
60              //          0.0.
60              //    triggerTime
61              //          Defines when (in milliseconds) to begin the
62              //          alpha waveform. For the Rotator class no delay is
63              //          necessary.
64              //    phaseDelayDuration
65              //          Defines a time period when the alpha value does not
66              //          change. For this time alpha will be either 0.0 or
67              //          1.0
67              //          depending on the waveform of the alpha created.
68              //    increasingAlphaDuration
69              //          The time (in milliseconds) to vary alpha from 0.0
70              //          to its 1.0 value. This value is changed in the
71              //          Rotator
71              //          class to change how fast an object is rotating.
72              //    increasingAlphaRampDuration
73              //          Used to change the rate at which alpha increases over
74              //          time. For the Rotator class, a constant rate is
74              //          desired
75              //          so this value is set to 0.
76              //    alphaAtOneDuration
77              //          The time (in milliseconds) to keep alpha at its 1.0
77              //          value.
78              //          The Rotator class wants a continuous rotation so
78              //          this value
79              //          is set to 0 so no delay occurs.
80              //    decreasingAlphaDuration
81              //          The time (in milliseconds) to vary alpha from 1.0 to
81              //          0.0.
82              //          The Rotator class does not use decreasing alpha so this
83              //          value is ignored.
84              //    decreasingAlphaRampDuration
```

Source 5.2   Rotator Class Code (*Continued*)

```
85       //          Used to change the rate at which alpha decreases over
86       //          time. The Rotator class does not use decreasing
         //          alpha so
87       //          this value is ignored.
88       //     alphaAtZeroDuration
89       //          The time (in milliseconds) to keep alpha at its 0.0
         //          value.
90       //          The Rotator class wants a continuous rotation so
         //          this value
91       //          is set to 0 so no delay occurs.
92       Alpha rotationAlpha = new Alpha(-1, Alpha.INCREASING_ENABLE,
93          0, 0, speed, 0, 0, 0, 0, 0);
94
95       // Create the RotationInterpolator. The following values
96       // are used for each parameter:
97       //     alpha
98       //          The alpha value to use for this interpolator.
99       //     target
100      //          The TransformGroup to modify by this interpolator.
101      //          Because Rotator is a subclass of TransformGroup,
102      //          the Rotator class will be modifying its own
103      //          TransformGroup.
104      //     axisOfRotation
105      //          The RotationInterpolator always does its rotation
106      //          about the Y-axis. This transform is used to
107      //          orient this local coordinate system in the desired
108      //          manner before performing the rotation.
109      //     minimumAngle
110      //          The starting angle of the interpolator. The Rotator
111      //          class will be generating a complete 360-degree
         //          rotation
112      //          so the start value is 0.0 (in radians).
113      //     maximumAngle
114      //          The final angle of the interpolator. Since the
         //          Rotator
115      //          class wants one rotation to happen for every alpha
         //          cycle,
116      //          the final angle is 2*PI.
117      RotationInterpolator rotator = new RotationInterpolator(
118         rotationAlpha, this, axis, 0.0f, (float)Math.PI*2.0f);
119
120      // Allocate the bounding sphere to be used with this Rotator.
121      // The assumption is that all Rotators should be active all
122      // the time. The bounds center is set to the origin and
123      // then a radius of 100 is assumed to be "sufficiently large" so
124      // that this interpolator will always be active. For large
```

continues

Source 5.2 *Continued*

```
125          // scene graphs this bounds should be adjusted so that the
126          // Interpolator is only active when the viewer is close enough
127          // to see the object being rotated.
128          BoundingSphere bounds =
129             new BoundingSphere(new Point3d(0.0, 0.0, 0.0), 100.0);
130          rotator.setSchedulingBounds(bounds);
131
132          // Add the Rotator Interpolator to this TransformGroup. Now
133          // all objects added to the TransformGroup will be rotated.
134          addChild(rotator);
135      }
136
137      /**
138       * Creates a Rotator object rotating about the given axis, rotating
139       * at the specified speed.
140       *
141       * @param axis The transform used to orient the
             * RotationInterpolator's
142       *  Y-axis (the axis the rotation is performed on).
143       * @param speed The time (in milliseconds) for one complete
             * rotation
144       *  to occur. Three predefined values are provided:SLOW, MEDIUM and
145       *  FAST.
146       */
147      public Rotator(Transform3D axis, int speed) {
148          // Call the initRotator routine with the given parameters.
149          initRotator(axis, speed);
150      }
151
152      /**
153       * Creates an uninitialized Rotator object. Only routines that
154       * subclass the Rotator need this method.
155       */
156      Rotator() {
157          // initRotator must be called manually
158      }
159 }
```

Source 5.2 Rotator Class Code (*Continued*)

Now back to the main section of our demo applet. What we have so far is behavior that will rotate our planet object about the Y-axis to simulate a part of our virtual solar system. Next we want to create an orbiting moon, which also rotates about its Y-axis. For this we'll use a new class to accomplish the job. The *YZorbit* constructor is called with the following parameters:

```
TransformGroup moonOrb = new YZorbit(OrbitBehavior.SLOW, 1.7f,
          new Point3d(0.0,0.0,0.0));
```

The first parameter specifies the speed of the orbit; the second defines the radius of orbit from a given point, which is specified in the last parameter. Source 5.3 lists code for our XZorbit class.

The XZorbit class is a method from the *OrbitBehavior* class, shown in Source 5.4.

We continue to work our way through the demo applet. If you have been able to follow along, congratulations! Your brain stem is all powerful. At this juncture, we are in the middle of creating our SceneGraph components. So far we have:

- A BranchGroup root object
- A bounding sphere containing volume
- A color Background object
- A Y rotate transform and behavior
- A YZ orbit transform and behavior

Finally, we'll create Planet and Moon objects and add the components to the scene. A 3D shape in the Java 3D API is composed of rendering properties and geometry. We'll need an Appearance object for the planets and moon shapes. The Appearance object is used to define rendering attributes, such as color, texture, and line properties.

In this case, we are creating two objects with the following default values:

color: white

shade mode: smooth shading

polygon mode: polygon fill

transparency disabled

cull backfaces

point size: 1.0

line width: 1.0

line pattern: solid

antialiasing disabled

Next, the user specifies GIF/JPEG images to use as textures that will create the planet and moon surfaces. Details of how texture mapping works and some helpful hints on how to create your texture maps properly are in

```
1
2    // package ThreDimensionalJava;
3
4    // Import the Java 3D a vector mathematics classes.
5    import javax.media.j3d.*;
6    import javax.vecmath.*;
7
8    /**
9     * The YZorbit class is used to set up a behavior that causes
10    * objects to have a circular "orbit" about a given point.
11    * The orbit is within the YZ plane.
12    * Any children added to an YZorbit object will have this
13    * behavior.
14    *
15    * @(#)YZorbit.java 1.2 98/03/11 11:17:59
16    * @version 1.0
17    */
18   public class YZorbit extends TransformGroup {
19
20       // The OrbitBehavior that will modify this TransformGroup.
21       OrbitBehavior ob;
22
23       /**
24        * Constructs a YZorbit object with OrbitBehavior.MEDIUM speed,
25        * a radius of 1.0 and centered about the origin.
26        */
27       YZorbit() {
28           // Just call alternate constructor with the default speed.
29           this(OrbitBehavior.MEDIUM, 1.0f, new Point3d(0.0, 0.0, 0.0));
30       }
31
32       /**
33        * Constructs a YZorbit object with OrbitBehavior.MEDIUM speed,
34        * the specified radius and centered about the origin.
35        *
36        * @param radius The radius the YZorbit object should have.
37        */
38       YZorbit(float radius) {
39           // Just call alternate constructor with the default speed.
40           this(OrbitBehavior.MEDIUM, radius, new Point3d(0.0, 0.0, 0.0));
41       }
42
43       /**
44        * Constructs a YZorbit object using the specified speed, radius
45        * and center point.
46        *
```

Source 5.3 XZorbit Class

```
47        * @param speed The time (in milliseconds) for one complete orbit
48        *   to occur. Three predefined values are
          *   provided:OrbitBehavior.SLOW,
49        *   OrbitBehavior.MEDIUM and OrbitBehavior.FAST.
50        * @param radius The radius of the orbit.
51        * @param center The point about which to center the orbit.
52        */
53       YZorbit(int speed, float radius, Point3d center) {
54
55           // Allow the transform to be updated when the scene is made
             // live.
56           setCapability(TransformGroup.ALLOW_TRANSFORM_WRITE);
57
58           // Create the OrbitBehavior object that will modify the
59           // Transform3D of this TransformGroup object.
60           ob = new OrbitBehavior(this, speed, radius, center,
61                                  OrbitBehavior.YZ_PLANE);
62
63           // Add the OrbitBehvior to this TransformGroup.
64           addChild(ob);
65       }
66   }
```

Source 5.3 *Continued*

Chapter 2, "A 3D Graphics Primer." How the geometry is created for the Sun, planets, and Moon is covered in Chapter 4, "Beautiful Geometry."

Our SceneGraph is almost complete. All that remains to be done is to add everything to the root branch node in a tree structure sequence. The objects will be invoked in the order they are added. Now the viewer should see a sun with rotating planets and a moon rotating the Earth.

Related Translation Constructs

The Java 3D API includes a special node called the *TransformGroup*, which provides affine matrices (defined shortly) that position, orient, and can scale children associated with a particular transform group. The Transform-Group is one of seven components used to construct a scene graph. Remember, transforms are the foundation for making objects move, rotate, and scale. This is accomplished using mathematical matrix calculations. This was explained in Chapter 2, but we'll give you a short math lesson here on matrix multiplication.

```
 1
 2   import javax.media.j3d.*;
 3   import javax.vecmath.*;
 4   import java.util.Enumeration;
 5
 6
 7   /**
 8    * The OrbitBehavior class is used to create circular "orbit"
 9    * animations.
10    * When linked up with a TransformGroup node, objects can be made to
11    * circle around a given point in space along the three standard
12    * planes
13    * (XY, XY, YZ). This class is a demonstration of how to use the
14    * generic Behavior class.
15    *
16    * @version 1.0
17    * @(#)OrbitBehavior.java 1.5 98/03/11 09:25:04
18    */
19   class OrbitBehavior extends Behavior {
20
21       /**
22        * Predefined orbit speed value. Must be preceded by the
23        * class name to use: Rotator.SLOW.
24        */
25       public static final int SLOW = 8000;
26
27       /**
28        * Predefined orbit speed value. Must be preceded by the
29        * class name to use: Rotator.MEDIUM.
30        */
31       public static final int MEDIUM = 4000;
32
33       /**
34        * Predefined orbit speed value. Must be preceded by the
35        * class name to use: Rotator.FAST.
36        */
37       public static final int FAST = 1000;
38
39       /**
40        * The circular orbit should be in the XY plane.
41        */
42       public static final int XY_PLANE = 1;
43
44       /**
45        * The circular orbit should be in the XZ plane.
46        */
```

Source 5.4 OrbitBehavior Class

```
45        public static final int XZ_PLANE = 2;
46
47        /**
48         * The circular orbit should be in the XY plane.
49         */
50        public static final int YZ_PLANE = 3;
51
52        // The alpha to use for the motion.
53        private Alpha OrbitAlpha;
54
55        // Holds the matrix that will be modified to create the orbit
56        // movement.
57        private Transform3D orbitTransform;
58
59        // Holds the current translation value to load into the axis
60        // transform.
60        private Vector3d vec;
61
62        // The wakeup criteria - will wake up on every frame.
63        private WakeupOnElapsedFrames wakeUp;
64
65        // Local copy of TransformGroup node this behavior will modify.
66        private TransformGroup orbitNode;
67
68        // The radius of the orbit.
69        private float radius;
70
71        // The center point of the orbit.
72        private float xCenter, yCenter, zCenter;
73
74        // The orbit plane, one of XY_PLANE, XZ_PLANE, YZ_PLANE.
75        private int orbitPlane;
76
77        // The time (in milliseconds) of one complete orbit.
78        private int speed;
79
80        // One complete revolution in radians.
81        static private final float twoPi = (float)Math.PI * 2.0f;
82
83        /**
84         * Creates a new OrbitBehavior object. All children of the
         * TransformGroup
85         * associated with this node will move in a circular "orbit".
86         *
87         * @param node The TransformGroup node this behavior will
         * modify.
```

continues

Source 5.4   *Continued*

```
 88           * @param speed The time, in milliseconds for one complete orbit
              *  to
 89           *  occur.
 90           * @param radius The radius of the orbit.
 91           * @param center The position the orbit will be centered about.
 92           * @param orbitPlane The plane in which the orbit will take
              *  place.
 93           *  Must be one of: XY_PLANE, XZ_PLANE, or YZ_PLANE.
 94           */
 95          public OrbitBehavior(TransformGroup node, int speed, float
              *  radius,
 96            Point3d center, int orbitPlane) {
 97
 98              // Save all parameters into local storage.
 99              orbitNode = node;
100              this.speed = speed;
101              this.radius = radius;
102              this.orbitPlane = orbitPlane;
103              xCenter = (float) center.x;
104              yCenter = (float) center.y;
105              zCenter = (float) center.z;
106
107              // Allocate the bounding sphere to be used with this
                 // OrbitBehavior.
108              // The assumption is that all orbits should be active all
109              // the time. The bounds center is set to the origin and
110              // then a radius of 100 is assumed to be "sufficiently
                 // large" so
111              // that this behavior will always be active. For large
112              // scene graphs this bounds should be adjusted so that the
113              // behavior is only active when the viewer is close enough
114              // to see the object in orbit.
115              setSchedulingBounds(new BoundingSphere(new Point3d(0.0, 0.0,
                 // 0.0),
116                100.0));
117          }
118
119      public void initialize() {
120              // Create an Alpha to use with the OrbitBehavior node.
121              // The following values are used for each parameter:
122              //   loopCount
123              //         Specifies the number of times to cycle the alpha.
124              //         A -1 means to cycle it infinitely.
125              //   mode
126              //         Specifies what part of the waveform (going from
127              //         0.0 to 1.0 or 1.0 to 0.0 or both) to use. The
                 // Orbit
```

Source 5.4   OrbitBehavior Class (*Continued*)

```
128        //        alpha will go from 0.0 to 1.0 and then restart at
           //        0.0,
129        //        so only an increasing alpha value is used.
130        //   triggerTime
131        //        Defines when (in milliseconds) to begin the
132        //        alpha waveform. For the OrbitBehavior no delay is
133        //        necessary.
134        //   phaseDelayDuration
135        //        Defines a time period when the alpha value does
           //        not
136        //        change. For this time alpha will be either 0.0 or
           //        1.0
137        //        depending on the waveform of the alpha created.
           //        This is
138        //        not used for the OrbitBehavior - it is set to 0.
139        //   increasingAlphaDuration
140        //        The time (in milliseconds) to vary alpha from 0.0
141        //        to its 1.0 value. This value determines the speed
           //        of
142        //        the orbit.
143        //   increasingAlphaRampDuration
144        //        Used to change the rate at which alpha increases
           //        over
145        //        time. For OrbitBehavior class, a constant rate is
           //        desired
146        //        so this value is set to 0.
147        //   alphaAtOneDuration
148        //        The time (in milliseconds) to keep alpha at its
           //        1.0 value.
149        //        OrbitBehavior class defines a continuous orbit so
           //        the value
150        //        is set to 0 so no delay occurs.
151        //   decreasingAlphaDuration
152        //        The time (in milliseconds) to vary alpha from 1.0
           //        to 0.0.
153        //        OrbitBehavior class does not use decreasing alpha
           //        so this
154        //        value is ignored.
155        //   decreasingAlphaRampDuration
156        //        Used to change the rate at which alpha decreases
           //        over
157        //        time. OrbitBehavior class does not use decreasing
           //        alpha so
158        //        this value is ignored.
159        //   alphaAtZeroDuration
160        //        The time (in milliseconds) to keep alpha at its
           //        0.0 value.
```

continues

Source 5.4   *Continued*

```
161          //            OrbitBehavior class defines a continuous orbit so
             //            this value
162          //            is set to 0 so no delay occurs.
163          OrbitAlpha = new Alpha(-1, Alpha.INCREASING_ENABLE,
164            0, 0, speed, 0, 0, 0, 0);
165          vec = new Vector3d();
166          orbitTransform = new Transform3D();
167
168          // Create and register the WakeUp behavior. This object will
             // use
169          // the ElapsedFrames criterion to wake up. A value of 0 means
             // wake
170          // this object up every frame. A frame is defined as one
171          // complete rendering of the scene graph.
172          wakeUp = new WakeupOnElapsedFrames(0);
173          wakeupOn(wakeUp);
174
175      }
176
177      public void processStimulus(Enumeration criteria) {
178          // Retrieve the current alpha value - this is used to
             // determine
179          // the position along the orbit the object will be at for
             // this frame.
180          float alphaVal = OrbitAlpha.value();
181
182          // Calculate sine and cosine values - these are used to
183          // generate the circular positions.
184          double sVal = Math.sin(twoPi * alphaVal);
185          double cVal = Math.cos(twoPi * alphaVal);
186
187          // Select the proper plane and create the translation "vector".
188          switch(orbitPlane) {
189              case XY_PLANE:
190                  vec.set(cVal*radius+xCenter, sVal*radius+yCenter,
zCenter);
191                  break;
192
193              case XZ_PLANE:
194                  vec.set(cVal*radius+xCenter, yCenter,
sVal*radius+zCenter);
195                  break;
196
197              case YZ_PLANE:
198                  vec.set(xCenter, cVal*radius+yCenter,
sVal*radius+zCenter);
199                  break;
```

Source 5.4 OrbitBehavior Class (*Continued*)

```
 200            }
 201
 202            // Update the Transform's translational components by the
 203            // circular offsets.
 204            orbitTransform.set(vec);
 205            orbitNode.setTransform(orbitTransform);
 206
 207            // Re-register the wakeup criterion so this object will be
waked
 208            // up on the next frame.
 209            wakeupOn(wakeUp);
 210        }
}
```

Source 5.4 *Continued*

A matrix is a rectangular array of elements; the elements are numbers. A matrix with m rows and n columns is described as an $m \times n$ matrix. A matrix is square if it has the same number of rows as columns. Consider the following 3×3 matrix equation:

$$
\begin{matrix}
x' \\
y' \\
z'
\end{matrix}
\;=\;
\begin{matrix}
A\,B\,C \\
D\,E\,F \\
G\,H\,I
\end{matrix}
\;*\;
\begin{matrix}
x \\
y \\
z
\end{matrix}
$$

In 3D graphics, applications commonly use 3×3 and 4×4 congruent (scales by 2) matrices. Two common square matrices are the *zero matrix* and the *identity matrix*. All of the elements in a zero matrix have the value of 0. An identity matrix consists of ones on its main diagonal and zeros elsewhere. A matrix of numbers may be scaled by a number or scaling factor. Matrices can be added and multiplied and generally manipulated to perform translation calculations. Review Chapter 2, "A 3D Graphics Primer" for specific matrix computations used in 3D graphics.

```
public class Transform3D( )
```

This class provides a general transform object and provides the following 4×4 matrices:

AFFINE.   Used to provide mathematical transformation of coordinates equivalent to a translation, rotation, expansion, or reflection, with respect to a fixed origin and coordinate system, by an amount that is uniform in all directions.

CONGRUENT. An angle and length-preserving matrix, meaning that it can translate, rotate, and reflect about an axis, and scale by an amount that is uniform in all directions.

IDENTITY. A matrix that consists of one's on its main diagonal and zeros elsewhere.

NEGATIVE_DETERMINANT. This matrix has a negative determinant; an orthogonal matrix with a positive determinant is a rotation matrix; an orthogonal matrix with a negative determinant is a reflection and rotation matrix.

ORTHOGONAL. The four row vectors that make up an orthogonal matrix form a basis, meaning that they are mutually orthogonal; an orthogonal matrix with a positive determinant is a pure rotation matrix; a negative determinant indicates a rotation and a reflection.

RIGID. This matrix is a rotation and a translation with unity scale; the upper 3×3 of the matrix is orthogonal, and there is a translation component.

SCALE. A uniform scale matrix with no translation or other off-diagonal components.

TRANSLATION. A translation-only matrix with ones on the diagonal.

ZERO. A matrix in which all of the elements are zero.

The type of constructed transform will be classified automatically depending on the parameter values specified at creation. Java 3D keeps track internally of the type of matrix being used. The scope of this book precludes coverage of the many adaptations of this constructor. For more information, reference the HTML documentation that ships with Java 3D. Transform3Ds are used to perform translations, rotations, and scaling and shear effects.

```
ALLOW_TRANSFORM_WRITE
```

This constant must be enabled using the *setCapability( )* method in order to allow the application to update the position, orientation, or scale of the shape object associated with the transform group.

```
public TransformGroup( )
void setTransform(Transform3D  trans)
```

This construct is used to initialize a new transformGroup node to an identity matrix. Transform groups are used to build new coordinates systems for 3D components that are relative to the parent. The idea is that if you translate this newly created coordinate system organized with 3D shapes underneath it, then the shapes associated with the transform group will move, too. Again, we need these components to perform the calculations that result in our 3D object moving around in our Virtual Universe.

```
Transform3D( )
Transform3D(Matrix4d  matrix)
Transform3D(Matrix3d  rotate, Vector3d translate, double scale)
```

Java 3D uses matrix objects to perform rotations and 3D transforms. Generally, Java 3D uses 3×3 matrices to store rotations and 4×4 matrices to perform 3D transforms. Both forms support both single-precision and double-precision floating-point representations. Usually, the method invocation without any parameters will create a TransformGroup node and initialize it with an identity matrix. The ALLOW_TRANSFORM_WRITE constant is enabled so that the behavior object can modify the transform group during runtime.

```
Shape3d  shape  =  new  Shape3D(geometry, a);
Transform3D positionRight  =  new  Transform3D( );
positionRight.set(New Vector3D(1.0, 0.0, 0.0));
TransformGroup  g  =  new  TransformGroup( );
g.setTransform(positionRight);
g.addChild(shape);
```

The TransformGroup object is added to the root of the subgraph. Any objects added below it will be affected or modified when the transform group is modified. And that is pretty cool! By providing this sort of API, Java 3D has made it easy to specify a position, orientation, and scale of the geometric objects within the application's Virtual Universe. In our case, a 3D shape is being translated to vector 1,0,0 by adding the shape to the transform group. Whenever the position of the transform is updated (by calling *set* methods), our example shape will also be visibly changed.

There are many ways to create transforms to position, orient, or scale objects in a scene. Java 3D provides helper methods that simplify setting the transform to an identity; setting the translation; setting the rotation for X, Y, and Z; and setting uniform and nonuniform scaling:

setIdentity( )	Sets transform to an identity.
set(Vector3d trans)	Sets transform to a translation.
rotX(double angle)	Sets rotation about X.
rotY(double angle)	Sets rotation about Y.

rotZ(double angle)   Sets rotation about Z.

setScale(Vector3d scale)   Sets scale factor.

In summary, a Transform3D object describes the transform being used by a transform group (TransformGroup). Any objects added to a transform group will be affected by changes performed on the Transform3D object. Such effects include scaling, positioning, translating, and shearing of the 3D shape.

Applet Example (Planets.java)

The following applet, shown in Source 5.5, supplies an interesting method to provide site navigation and links to other Web pages.

```java
import java.applet.*;
import java.awt.BorderLayout;
import java.awt.Font;
import java.lang.String;
import java.net.MalformedURLException;
import java.net.URL;
import com.sun.j3d.utils.applet.MainFrame;
import com.sun.j3d.utils.geometry.*;
import com.sun.j3d.utils.universe.*;
import com.sun.j3d.utils.image.TextureLoader;
import javax.media.j3d.*;
import javax.vecmath.*;
import java.util.Enumeration;


/**------------------------------------------------------------------

    Credits:
    Planets program by Kirk Brown.
    Orbit/Rotate Behaviors provided by Dan Petersen.

    Planets is a solar system theme to be used as a navigational
    map or menu for the top level of a Web site. It could also
    represent an organization of multiple business units. There
    is at the core, a Sun which is orbited by planets and moons.
    Each object can have a label and URL associated with it.

    ------------------------------------------------------------------*/

public class Planets extends Applet {
```

Source 5.5   Complete Planets.java Applet Example

```
// Class variables.  The default values can be overridden
// by using the PARAMS tag when invoking the applet.
//
// The following is the defined HTML interface to this program:
//
//      <PARAM NAME="Planets" VALUE=2>
//              Value Options: 0 to n
//      <PARAM NAME ="BackgroundColor" VALUE="black">
//            Value Options: red,blue,green,yellow,purple,
//                    gold,orange,black
//                    white,medblue,medgreen
//      <PARAM NAME ="PlanetColor1" VALUE="blue">
//            Value Options: red,blue,green,yellow,
//                    purple,gold,orange,black
//                    white,medblue,medgreen
//      <PARAM NAME ="PlanetSpeed1" VALUE="slow">
//            Value Options: PlanetSpeed[n]
//            VALUE="[slow, medium, fast, xfast]"
//      <PARAM NAME ="PlanetOrbit" VALUE="2.0">
//            Value Options: ( a floating point number to
//                    increase the orbit's radius incrementally.)
//      <PARAM NAME="PlanetSize1" VALUE="large">
//            Value Options: PlanetSize
//            VALUE="[small, medium, large, xlarge]"
//      <PARAM NAME="PlanetImage1" VALUE="earth.jpg">
//            Value Options: Image[n] VALUE="[image file]"
//      <PARAM NAME="PlanetURL1" VALUE="http://www.sun.com/">
//            Value Options: PlanetURL[n] VALUE="[url reference]"
//      <PARAM NAME="PlanetText1" VALUE="Engineering">
//            Value Options: PlanetText[n] VALUE="[text string]"
//      <PARAM NAME="PlanetTextColor1" VALUE="red">
//            Value Options: PlanetTextColor[n]
//            Value=[red,blue,green,yellow,
//               purple,gold,orange,black,
//               white,medblue,medgreen]
//      <PARAM NAME="PlanetTextFont1" VALUE="Times">
//            Value Options: PlanetTextFont[n]
//            VALUE="[system font name]"
//      <PARAM NAME="PlanetTextSize1" VALUE="60">
//            Value Options: PlanetTextSize[n] VALUE="[font size]"
//      <PARAM NAME="PlanetTextStyle1" VALUE="bold">
//            Value Options: PlanetTextStyle[n]
//            VALUE="[bold, italic, plain]"
//      <PARAM NAME="Moon3" VALUE="true">
//            Value Options: Moon[n]
//            VALUE="[true creates a moon around Planets[n]"
```

continues

Source 5.5   *Continued*

```
//      <PARAM NAME="MoonImage1" VALUE="ito.jpg">
//          Value Options: MoonImage[n] VALUE="[image file]"
//      <PARAM NAME="MoonURL1" VALUE="http://www.sun.com/">
//          Value Options: MoonURL[n] VALUE="[url reference]"
//      <PARAM NAME="MoonColor1" VALUE="green">
//          Value Options: MoonColor[n]
//           Value=[red,blue,green,yellow,purple,gold,orange,black,
//                    white,medblue,medgreen]
//      <PARAM NAME ="MoonSpeed1" VALUE="slow">
//          Value Options: MoonSpeed[n]
//          VALUE="[slow, medium, fast, xfast]"
//      <PARAM NAME="MoonSize1" VALUE="large">
//          Value Options: MoonSize
//          VALUE="[small, medium, large, xlarge]"
//      <PARAM NAME="MoonText1" VALUE="Engineering">
//          Value Options: MoonText[n] VALUE="[text string]"
//      <PARAM NAME="MoonTextColor1" VALUE="red">
//          Value Options: MoonTextColor[n]
//          Value=[red,blue,green,yellow,
//                    purple,gold,orange,black,
//                    white,medblue,medgreen]
//      <PARAM NAME="MoonTextFont1" VALUE="Times">
//          Value Options: MoonTextFont[n]
//          VALUE="[system font name]"
//      <PARAM NAME="PlanetTextSize1" VALUE="60">
//          Value Options: MoonTextSize[n] VALUE="[font size]"
//      <PARAM NAME="PlanetTextStyle1" VALUE="bold">
//          Value Options: MoonTextStyle[n]
//          VALUE="[bold, italic, plain]"

 // Pre-defined colors
Color3f white = new Color3f(1.0f, 1.0f, 1.0f);
Color3f black = new Color3f(0.0f, 0.0f, 0.0f);
Color3f gray = new Color3f(0.6f, 0.6f, 0.6f);
Color3f red   = new Color3f(1.0f, 0.0f, 0.0f);
Color3f ambientred = new Color3f(0.4f, 0.1f, 0.0f);
Color3f medred = new Color3f(0.80f, 0.4f, 0.3f);
Color3f green   = new Color3f(0.0f, 0.80f, 0.2f);
Color3f ambientgreen = new Color3f(0.0f, 0.3f, 0.1f);
Color3f medgreen = new Color3f(0.0f, 0.5f, 0.1f);
Color3f orange   = new Color3f(0.7f, 0.4f, 0.0f);
Color3f ambientorange = new Color3f(0.5f, 0.02f, 0.0f);
Color3f medorange = new Color3f(0.5f, 0.2f, 0.1f);
Color3f blue   = new Color3f(0.1f, 0.3f, 0.9f);
Color3f ambientblue = new Color3f(0.0f, 0.1f, 0.4f);
Color3f medblue = new Color3f(0.0f, 0.1f, 0.4f);
```

Source 5.5   Complete Planets.java Applet Example (*Continued*)

```
Color3f gold = new Color3f(1.0f, 0.8f, 0.0f);
Color3f yellow = new Color3f(1.0f, 1.0f, 0.6f);
Color3f purple = new Color3f(0.5f, 0.2f, 0.8f);
Color3f medpurple = new Color3f(0.5f, 0.2f, 0.5f);
Color3f ambient = new Color3f(0.2f, 0.2f, 0.2f);
Color3f diffuse = new Color3f(0.7f, 0.7f, 0.7f);
Color3f specular = new Color3f(0.7f, 0.7f, 0.7f);

// Background color
private Color3f bgcolor = black;

// Planet "-demo" mode default attributes
private float position = 0.0f;
private int numPlanets = 3;        // number of planets
private float porbit = 1.75f;      // orbit radius
private float scale = 0.22f;        // scene scale factor
private int[] pspeed =              // orbit speed
     {OrbitBehavior.SLOW,15000,28000};
private float[] psize =            // planet size
     {1.5f, 0.3f, 0.45f};
private Color3f[] pcolor =         // planet color (if no image)
     {white, medpurple, white};
private String[] pimage =          // planet texturemap
     {"sun.jpg", null, "earth.jpg"};
private URL[] purl =               // planet URL link
      {null, null, null};
private String[] ptext =           // planet text label
     {"CORPORATE", "PRODUCTS", "SUPPORT"};
Point3d ppoint1 = new Point3d(0.1, 0.7, 0.0);
Point3d ppoint2 = new Point3d(0.65, -0.75, 0.0);
Point3d ppoint3 = new Point3d(0.4, -0.51, 0.0);
private Point3d[] ptextpos =       // planet text position
     {ppoint1, ppoint2, ppoint3};
private Color3f[] ptcolor =        // planet text color
     {yellow, yellow, yellow};
private String[] ptfont =          // planet text font type
     {"Helvetica", "Helvetica", "Helvetica"};
private int[] ptstyle =            // planet text font style
     {Font.BOLD, Font.BOLD, Font.BOLD};
private int[] ptsize =             // planet text label size
      {60, 60, 60};

// Default "-demo" mode Moon attributes
private int numMoons = 3;          // number of moons
private boolean[] moons =          // associate moon with planet
      {false, false, true};
```

continues

Source 5.5 *Continued*

```
    private int[] mspeed =            // orbit speed
          {0, 0, 10000};
    private float[] msize =           // moon size
          {0.0f, 0.0f, 0.2f};
    private float morbit = 1.0f;      // orbit radius around planet
    private String[] mimage =         // moon texturemap
          {null, null, null};
    private URL[] murl =              // moon URL link
          {null, null, null};
    private Color3f[] mcolor =        // moon color (if no image)
          {null, null, blue};
    private String[] mtext =          // moon text label
          {null, null, "Eng"};
    Point3d mpoint1 = new Point3d();
    Point3d mpoint2 = new Point3d();
    Point3d mpoint3 = new Point3d(0.2,-0.5,0.0);
    private Point3d[] mtextpos =      // moon text position
          {mpoint1, mpoint2, mpoint3};
    private Color3f[] mtcolor =       // moon text color
          {null, null, yellow};
    private String[] mtfont =         // moon text font type
          {null, null, "Helvetica"};
    private int[] mtstyle =           // moon text style
          {Font.BOLD, Font.BOLD, Font.BOLD};
    private int[] mtsize =            // moon text label size
          {0, 0, 48};

    // Pre-defined Text Positions
    private Point3d smallTPOS = new Point3d(0.2, -0.6, 0.0);
    private Point3d mediumTPOS = new Point3d(0.2, -0.5, 0.0);
    private Point3d largeTPOS = new Point3d(0.2, -0.1, 0.0);
    private Point3d xlargeTPOS = new Point3d(0.2, 0.6, 0.0);

    URL[] pimageURL;
    URL[] mimageURL;
    boolean applet = false;

    // Examines all parameters that can be passed in to this
    // applet and updates the global state to reflect any
    // non-default settings.
    private void lookForParameters() {

      // Used to read in the parameters for the applet.
      String paramValue;

      // Reset
```

Source 5.5   Complete Planets.java Applet Example (*Continued*)

```
      numMoons = 0;
      float morbit = 1.0f;

      // Running as an applet.
      applet = true;

      // Find out the total number of planets.
      //
      paramValue = getParameter("Planets");
      if (paramValue != null)
          numPlanets = Integer.parseInt(paramValue);
      else
          numPlanets = 2;

      // Allocate the needed array space based on
      // the number of planets.
      //
      pspeed = new int[numPlanets];
      psize = new float[numPlanets];
      pimageURL = new URL[numPlanets];
      purl = new URL[numPlanets];
      ptext = new String[numPlanets];
      ptextpos = new Point3d[numPlanets];
      pcolor = new Color3f[numPlanets];
      ptcolor = new Color3f[numPlanets];
      ptfont = new String[numPlanets];
      ptstyle = new int[numPlanets];
      ptsize = new int[numPlanets];
      moons = new boolean[numPlanets];
      msize = new float[numPlanets];
      mspeed = new int[numPlanets];
      mimage = new String[numPlanets];
      murl = new URL[numPlanets];
      mtext = new String[numPlanets];
      mtextpos = new Point3d[numPlanets];
      mtcolor = new Color3f[numPlanets];
      mtfont = new String[numPlanets];
      mtstyle = new int[numPlanets];
      mimageURL = new URL[numPlanets];
      mcolor = new Color3f[numPlanets];

          // Look for Background Color
          paramValue = getParameter("BackgroundColor");
          if (paramValue.equalsIgnoreCase("red") == true)
                bgcolor = red;
          else if (paramValue.equalsIgnoreCase("green") == true)
                bgcolor = green;
```

continues

Source 5.5 *Continued*

```
        else if (paramValue.equalsIgnoreCase("blue") == true)
            bgcolor = blue;
        else if (paramValue.equalsIgnoreCase("medred") == true)
            bgcolor = medred;
        else if (paramValue.equalsIgnoreCase("medgreen") == true)
            bgcolor = medgreen;
        else if (paramValue.equalsIgnoreCase("medblue") == true)
            bgcolor = medblue;
        else if (paramValue.equalsIgnoreCase("black") == true)
            bgcolor = black;
        else if (paramValue.equalsIgnoreCase("gray") == true)
            bgcolor = gray;
        else if (paramValue.equalsIgnoreCase("white") == true)
            bgcolor = white;
        else if (paramValue.equalsIgnoreCase("yellow") == true)
            bgcolor = yellow;
        else if (paramValue.equalsIgnoreCase("gold") == true)
            bgcolor = gold;
        else if (paramValue.equalsIgnoreCase("purple") == true)
            bgcolor = purple;
        else if (paramValue.equalsIgnoreCase("medpurple") == true)
            bgcolor = medpurple;
        else if (paramValue.equalsIgnoreCase("orange") == true)
            bgcolor = orange;
        else if (paramValue.equalsIgnoreCase("medorange") == true)
            bgcolor = medorange;
        else
            bgcolor = black;

// Planet Orbit radius factor
//
paramValue = getParameter("PlanetOrbit");
if (paramValue != null) {
        Float f = new Float(paramValue);
        porbit = f.floatValue();
}
else
        porbit = 1.75f;

   // Look for the scaling factor to fit the objects to the
   // window. Factor zoomout1 is large to zoomout10 is scaled
   // way down.
   //
   paramValue = getParameter("Scale");
   if (paramValue != null) {
       if (paramValue.equalsIgnoreCase("zoomout1") == true)
                scale = (float) 1.0;
```

Source 5.5   Complete Planets.java Applet Example (*Continued*)

```
             else if (paramValue.equalsIgnoreCase("zoomout2") == true)
                     scale = (float) 0.9;
             else if (paramValue.equalsIgnoreCase("zoomout3") == true)
                     scale = (float) 0.8;
             else if (paramValue.equalsIgnoreCase("zoomout4") == true)
                     scale = (float) 0.7;
             else if (paramValue.equalsIgnoreCase("zoomout5") == true)
                     scale = (float) 0.6;
             else if (paramValue.equalsIgnoreCase("zoomout6") == true)
                     scale = (float) 0.5;
             else if (paramValue.equalsIgnoreCase("zoomout7") == true)
                     scale = (float) 0.4;
             else if (paramValue.equalsIgnoreCase("zoomout8") == true)
                     scale = (float) 0.3;
             else if (paramValue.equalsIgnoreCase("zoomout9") == true)
                     scale = (float) 0.2;
             else if (paramValue.equalsIgnoreCase("zoomout10") == true)
                     scale = (float) 0.1;
             else
                     scale = (float) 0.5;
    } else {
         scale = (float) 0.2;
    }

for (int i=0; i < numPlanets; i++) {

    // Look for the Planet Speed
    paramValue = getParameter("PlanetSpeed" + (i + 1));
    if (paramValue.equalsIgnoreCase("slow") == true)
         pspeed[i] = 32000;
    else if (paramValue.equalsIgnoreCase("medium") == true)
         pspeed[i] = 20000;
    else if (paramValue.equalsIgnoreCase("fast") == true)
         pspeed[i] = 10000;
    else if (paramValue.equalsIgnoreCase("xfast") == true)
         pspeed[i] = 1000;
    else
         pspeed[i] = Integer.parseInt(paramValue, 10);

    // Look for Planet's Size
    paramValue = getParameter("PlanetSize" + (i + 1));
    if (paramValue.equalsIgnoreCase("small") == true) {
         psize[i] = 0.2f;
         ptextpos[i] = smallTPOS;
    }
    else if (paramValue.equalsIgnoreCase("medium") == true) {
         psize[i] = 0.45f;
```

continues

Source 5.5   *Continued*

```
                ptextpos[i] = mediumTPOS;
          }
      else if (paramValue.equalsIgnoreCase("large") == true) {
            psize[i] = 0.80f;
            ptextpos[i] = largeTPOS;
      }
      else if (paramValue.equalsIgnoreCase("xlarge") == true) {
            psize[i] = 1.25f;
            ptextpos[i] = xlargeTPOS;
      }
      else {
        psize[i] = 0.80f;
        ptextpos[i] = largeTPOS;
      }

      // Look for Planet images files to create. They need
      // to be fully qualified URLs to avoid generating a
      // security violation from the browser.
      //
      paramValue = getParameter("PlanetImage" + (i + 1));
      if (paramValue != null) {

          try {
             pimageURL[i] = new URL(paramValue);
          }
          catch (MalformedURLException e) {
            System.out.println("ERROR: reading image URL: " +
                                   paramValue);
          }
      }

      // Look for URLs to associate with each object. We
      // will stuff this value into a UserData class that
      // will associate the URL with our 3D object. The
      // getURL method is called in our mouse behavior (PickURL)
      // and the document is loaded. If the HTML file does
      // not contain a URL for a planet, we need to hack
      // some temp value as place holder and we'll test
      // for a valid URL in the behavior later.
      //
      paramValue = getParameter("PlanetURL" + (i + 1));
      if (paramValue != null) {
         try {
            purl[i] = new URL(paramValue);
         }
         catch(MalformedURLException e) {
```

Source 5.5   Complete Planets.java Applet Example (*Continued*)

```
                    System.out.println("ERROR: reading value for URL: " +
                                        paramValue);
        }
      }
      else {
        try {
          purl[i] = new URL("http://stub");
        }
        catch(MalformedURLException e) {
          System.out.println("ERROR: reading value for URL: " +
                              paramValue);
        }
      }

      // Look for a new Planet color
      paramValue = getParameter("PlanetColor" + (i + 1));
      if (paramValue != null)
          if (paramValue.equalsIgnoreCase("red") == true)
              pcolor[i] = red;
          else if (paramValue.equalsIgnoreCase("green") == true)
              pcolor[i] = green;
          else if (paramValue.equalsIgnoreCase("blue") == true)
              pcolor[i] = blue;
          else if (paramValue.equalsIgnoreCase("medred") == true)
              pcolor[i] = medred;
          else if (paramValue.equalsIgnoreCase("medgreen") == true)
              pcolor[i] = medgreen;
          else if (paramValue.equalsIgnoreCase("medblue") == true)
              pcolor[i] = medblue;
          else if (paramValue.equalsIgnoreCase("black") == true)
              pcolor[i] = black;
          else if (paramValue.equalsIgnoreCase("gray") == true)
              pcolor[i] = gray;
          else if (paramValue.equalsIgnoreCase("white") == true)
              pcolor[i] = white;
          else if (paramValue.equalsIgnoreCase("yellow") == true)
              pcolor[i] = yellow;
          else if (paramValue.equalsIgnoreCase("gold") == true)
              pcolor[i] = gold;
          else if (paramValue.equalsIgnoreCase("purple") == true)
              pcolor[i] = purple;
          else if (paramValue.equalsIgnoreCase("medpurple") == true)
              pcolor[i] = medpurple;
          else if (paramValue.equalsIgnoreCase("orange") == true)
              pcolor[i] = orange;
          else if (paramValue.equalsIgnoreCase("medorange") == true)
```

continues

Source 5.5   *Continued*

```
                pcolor[i] = medorange;
        else
                pcolor[i] = blue;
    else
        pcolor[i] = blue;

    // Look for the Planet's text label
    paramValue = getParameter("PlanetText" + (i + 1));
    if (paramValue != null)
            ptext[i] = new String(paramValue);
    else
        ptext[i] = null;

    // Look for the Planet's text Font
    paramValue = getParameter("PlanetTextFont" + (i + 1));
    if (paramValue != null)
        if (paramValue.equalsIgnoreCase("TimesRoman") == true)
            ptfont[i] = new String(paramValue);
        else if (paramValue.equalsIgnoreCase("Helvetica") == true)
            ptfont[i] = new String(paramValue);
        else if (paramValue.equalsIgnoreCase("Serif") == true)
            ptfont[i] = new String(paramValue);
        else if (paramValue.equalsIgnoreCase("Monospaced") == true)
            ptfont[i] = new String(paramValue);
        else if (paramValue.equalsIgnoreCase("Courier") == true)
            ptfont[i] = new String(paramValue);
        else if (paramValue.equalsIgnoreCase("Dialog") == true)
            ptfont[i] = new String(paramValue);
        else
            // Let's see if we can get other system loaded fonts
            ptfont[i] = new String(paramValue);
            if (ptfont[i] == null)
                ptfont[i] = new String("Serif");
    else
        ptfont[i] = new String("Helvetica");

    // Look for the Planet's text Style
    paramValue = getParameter("PlanetTextStyle" + (i + 1));
    if (paramValue != null)
        if (paramValue.equalsIgnoreCase("bold") == true)
            ptstyle[i] = Font.BOLD;
        else if (paramValue.equalsIgnoreCase("italic") == true)
            ptstyle[i] = Font.ITALIC;
        else if (paramValue.equalsIgnoreCase("plain") == true)
            ptstyle[i] = Font.PLAIN;
        else
```

Source 5.5   Complete Planets.java Applet Example (*Continued*)

```
                    ptstyle[i] = Font.PLAIN;
        else
            ptstyle[i] = Font.BOLD;

        // Look for the Planet's text Size
        paramValue = getParameter("PlanetTextSize" + (i + 1));
        if (paramValue != null)
            ptsize[i] = Integer.parseInt(paramValue);
        else
            ptsize[i] = 60;

    // Look for Text color
    paramValue = getParameter("PlanetTextColor" + (i + 1));
    if (paramValue != null)
        if (paramValue.equalsIgnoreCase("red") == true)
            ptcolor[i] = red;
        else if (paramValue.equalsIgnoreCase("green") == true)
            ptcolor[i] = green;
        else if (paramValue.equalsIgnoreCase("blue") == true)
            ptcolor[i] = blue;
        else if (paramValue.equalsIgnoreCase("medred") == true)
            ptcolor[i] = medred;
        else if (paramValue.equalsIgnoreCase("medgreen") == true)
            ptcolor[i] = medgreen;
        else if (paramValue.equalsIgnoreCase("medblue") == true)
            ptcolor[i] = medblue;
        else if (paramValue.equalsIgnoreCase("black") == true)
            ptcolor[i] = black;
        else if (paramValue.equalsIgnoreCase("gray") == true)
            ptcolor[i] = gray;
        else if (paramValue.equalsIgnoreCase("white") == true)
            ptcolor[i] = white;
        else if (paramValue.equalsIgnoreCase("yellow") == true)
            ptcolor[i] = yellow;
        else if (paramValue.equalsIgnoreCase("gold") == true)
            ptcolor[i] = gold;
        else if (paramValue.equalsIgnoreCase("purple") == true)
            ptcolor[i] = purple;
        else if (paramValue.equalsIgnoreCase("medpurple") == true)
            ptcolor[i] = medpurple;
        else if (paramValue.equalsIgnoreCase("orange") == true)
            ptcolor[i] = orange;
        else if (paramValue.equalsIgnoreCase("medorange") == true)
            ptcolor[i] = medorange;
        else
            ptcolor[i] = red;
```

continues

Source 5.5   *Continued*

```
        else
            ptcolor[i] = red;

    } // END of Planet Loop

    for (int x=0; x < numPlanets; x++) {
        // Look for Moons associated with planets and flag the index.
        // For example, if the user specifies Moon3==true, then we'll
        // need to create a moon that orbits the 3rd planet. Does not
        // support multiple moons per planet.
        //
        paramValue = getParameter("Moon" + (x + 1));
        if (paramValue != null) {
            moons[x] = true;
            // Keep track of the number of moons
            numMoons = numMoons + 1;
        }
        else {
            moons[x] = false;
        }

        // Look for Moon URL image files to create
        //
        paramValue = getParameter("MoonImage" + (x + 1));
        if (paramValue != null) {
            try {
                mimageURL[x] = new URL(paramValue);
            }
            catch (MalformedURLException e) {
                System.out.println("ERROR: reading image URL: " +
                                        paramValue);
            }
        }

        // Look for URLs to associate with each Moon.
        // (See PlanetURL for what does this mean?)
        //
        paramValue = getParameter("MoonURL" + (x + 1));
        if (paramValue != null) {
            try {
                murl[x] = new URL(paramValue);
            }
            catch(MalformedURLException e) {
                System.out.println("ERROR: reading value for URL: " +
                                        paramValue);
            }
```

Source 5.5 Complete Planets.java Applet Example (*Continued*)

```
            }
            else {
              try {
                murl[x] = new URL("http://stub");
              }
              catch(MalformedURLException e) {
                System.out.println("ERROR: reading value for URL: " +
                                        paramValue);
              }
            }

            // Look for the Moon Speed
            paramValue = getParameter("MoonSpeed" + (x + 1));
            if (paramValue != null)
              if (paramValue.equalsIgnoreCase("slow") == true)
                  mspeed[x] = 32000;
              else if (paramValue.equalsIgnoreCase("medium") == true)
                  mspeed[x] = 20000;
              else if (paramValue.equalsIgnoreCase("fast") == true)
                  mspeed[x] = 10000;
              else if (paramValue.equalsIgnoreCase("xfast") == true)
                  mspeed[x] = 1000;
              else
                  mspeed[x] = Integer.parseInt(paramValue, 10);
            else
                  mspeed[x] = 15000;

            // Look for Moon's Size
            paramValue = getParameter("MoonSize" + (x + 1));
            if (paramValue != null) {
              if (paramValue.equalsIgnoreCase("small") == true) {
                  msize[x] = 0.2f;
                  mtextpos[x] = smallTPOS;
              }
              else if (paramValue.equalsIgnoreCase("medium") == true) {
                  msize[x] = 0.45f;
                  mtextpos[x] = mediumTPOS;
              }
              else if (paramValue.equalsIgnoreCase("large") == true) {
                  msize[x] = 0.80f;
                  mtextpos[x] = largeTPOS;
              }
              else if (paramValue.equalsIgnoreCase("xlarge") == true) {
                  msize[x] = 1.25f;
                  mtextpos[x] = xlargeTPOS;
              }
```

continues

Source 5.5   *Continued*

```
    else {
        msize[x] = 0.2f;
        mtextpos[x] = smallTPOS;
    }
}
else {
  msize[x] = 0.2f;
  mtextpos[x] = smallTPOS;
}

// Look for a new Moon color
paramValue = getParameter("MoonColor" + (x + 1));
if (paramValue != null)
    if (paramValue.equalsIgnoreCase("red") == true)
        mcolor[x] = red;
    else if (paramValue.equalsIgnoreCase("green") == true)
        mcolor[x] = green;
    else if (paramValue.equalsIgnoreCase("blue") == true)
        mcolor[x] = blue;
    else if (paramValue.equalsIgnoreCase("medred") == true)
        mcolor[x] = medred;
    else if (paramValue.equalsIgnoreCase("medgreen") == true)
        mcolor[x] = medgreen;
    else if (paramValue.equalsIgnoreCase("medblue") == true)
        mcolor[x] = medblue;
    else if (paramValue.equalsIgnoreCase("black") == true)
        mcolor[x] = black;
    else if (paramValue.equalsIgnoreCase("gray") == true)
        mcolor[x] = gray;
    else if (paramValue.equalsIgnoreCase("white") == true)
        mcolor[x] = white;
    else if (paramValue.equalsIgnoreCase("yellow") == true)
        mcolor[x] = yellow;
    else if (paramValue.equalsIgnoreCase("gold") == true)
        mcolor[x] = gold;
    else if (paramValue.equalsIgnoreCase("purple") == true)
        mcolor[x] = purple;
    else if (paramValue.equalsIgnoreCase("medpurple") == true)
        mcolor[x] = medpurple;
    else if (paramValue.equalsIgnoreCase("orange") == true)
        mcolor[x] = orange;
    else if (paramValue.equalsIgnoreCase("medorange") == true)
        mcolor[x] = medorange;
    else
        mcolor[x] = gray;
else
        mcolor[x] = gray;
```

Source 5.5 Complete Planets.java Applet Example (*Continued*)

```
                        // Look for the Moon's text label
            paramValue = getParameter("MoonText" + (x + 1));
            if (paramValue != null)
                    mtext[x] = new String(paramValue);
            else
                    mtext[x] = null;


            // Look for the Moon's text Font
            paramValue = getParameter("MoonTextFont" + (x + 1));
            if (paramValue != null)
                if (paramValue.equalsIgnoreCase("TimesRoman") == true)
                    mtfont[x] = new String(paramValue);
                else if (paramValue.equalsIgnoreCase("Helvetica") == true)
                    mtfont[x] = new String(paramValue);
                else if (paramValue.equalsIgnoreCase("Serif") == true)
                    ptfont[x] = new String(paramValue);
                else if (paramValue.equalsIgnoreCase("Monospaced") == true)
                    mtfont[x] = new String(paramValue);
                else if (paramValue.equalsIgnoreCase("Courier") == true)
                    mtfont[x] = new String(paramValue);
                else if (paramValue.equalsIgnoreCase("Dialog") == true)
                    mtfont[x] = new String(paramValue);
                else
                    // Let's see if we can get other system loaded fonts
                    mtfont[x] = new String(paramValue);
            else
                mtfont[x] = new String("Helvetica");


            // Look for the Moon's text Style
            paramValue = getParameter("PlanetTextStyle" + (x + 1));
            if (paramValue != null)
                if (paramValue.equalsIgnoreCase("bold") == true)
                    mtstyle[x] = Font.BOLD;
                else if (paramValue.equalsIgnoreCase("italic") == true)
                    mtstyle[x] = Font.ITALIC;
                else if (paramValue.equalsIgnoreCase("plain") == true)
                    mtstyle[x] = Font.PLAIN;
                else
                    mtstyle[x] = Font.PLAIN;
            else
                mtstyle[x] = Font.PLAIN;


             // Look for the Moon's text Size
            paramValue = getParameter("MoonTextSize" + (x + 1));
            if (paramValue != null)
                mtsize[x] = Integer.parseInt(paramValue);
            else
```

continues

Source 5.5 *Continued*

```
                mtsize[x] = 36;

        // Look for Moon Text color
        paramValue = getParameter("MoonTextColor" + (x + 1));
        if (paramValue != null)
            if (paramValue.equalsIgnoreCase("red") == true)
                mtcolor[x] = red;
            else if (paramValue.equalsIgnoreCase("green") == true)
                mtcolor[x] = green;
            else if (paramValue.equalsIgnoreCase("blue") == true)
                mtcolor[x] = blue;
            else if (paramValue.equalsIgnoreCase("medred") == true)
                mtcolor[x] = medred;
            else if (paramValue.equalsIgnoreCase("medgreen") == true)
                mtcolor[x] = medgreen;
            else if (paramValue.equalsIgnoreCase("medblue") == true)
                mtcolor[x] = medblue;
            else if (paramValue.equalsIgnoreCase("black") == true)
                mtcolor[x] = black;
            else if (paramValue.equalsIgnoreCase("gray") == true)
                mtcolor[x] = gray;
            else if (paramValue.equalsIgnoreCase("white") == true)
                mtcolor[x] = white;
            else if (paramValue.equalsIgnoreCase("yellow") == true)
                mtcolor[x] = yellow;
            else if (paramValue.equalsIgnoreCase("gold") == true)
                mtcolor[x] = gold;
            else if (paramValue.equalsIgnoreCase("purple") == true)
                mtcolor[x] = purple;
            else if (paramValue.equalsIgnoreCase("medpurple") == true)
                mtcolor[x] = medpurple;
            else if (paramValue.equalsIgnoreCase("orange") == true)
                mtcolor[x] = orange;
            else if (paramValue.equalsIgnoreCase("medorange") == true)
                mtcolor[x] = medorange;
            else
                mtcolor[x] = yellow;
        else
            mtcolor[x] = white;

    } // END for Moon loop
} // END LookForParameters


public BranchGroup createSceneGraph(Canvas3D c,
                                    AppletContext context) {
```

Source 5.5 Complete Planets.java Applet Example (*Continued*)

```
Color3f sunlight = new Color3f(1.0f, 1.0f, 1.0f);
Vector3f Vsun  = new Vector3f(0.0f, 0.0f, -1.0f);

// Transform array for Planet rotations
TransformGroup[] planetRot;

// Transform array for Planet orbits
TransformGroup[] planetOrb;

// Planet appearance objects
Appearance[] papp;

// Planet objects
Sphere[] planet;

// Transform array for Planet text labels
TransformGroup[] ptextOrb;

// Text label array for Planet
Shape3D[] plabel;

// Transform array for Moon rotations
TransformGroup[] moonRot;

//Transforms for Moon orbits
TransformGroup[] moonOrb;

// Moon appearance objects
Appearance[] mapp;

// Moon objects
Sphere[] moon;

// Transform array for Moon text labels
TransformGroup[] mtextOrb;

// 2D Text label array for Moon
Shape3D[] mlabel;

// Initialize Object arrays
planetRot = new Rotator[numPlanets];
planetOrb = new XZorbit[numPlanets];
papp = new Appearance[numPlanets];
planet = new Sphere[numPlanets];
ptextOrb = new XZorbit[numPlanets];
plabel = new Shape3D[numPlanets];
```

continues

Source 5.5 *Continued*

```
            moonRot = new Rotator[numPlanets];
            moonOrb = new XZorbit[numPlanets];
            mapp = new Appearance[numPlanets];
            moon = new Sphere[numPlanets];
            mtextOrb = new XZorbit[numPlanets];
            mlabel = new Shape3D[numPlanets];

        // Create the root of the branch graph
        BranchGroup objRoot = new BranchGroup();

        // Create a bounds for the background, behavior and lights
        BoundingSphere bounds =
            new BoundingSphere(new Point3d(0.0,0.0,0.0), 100.0);

        // This Transform Group scales the objects so
        // they fit the scene
        TransformGroup objScale = new TransformGroup();
        Transform3D t3d = new Transform3D();
        t3d.setScale(scale);
        objScale.setTransform(t3d);
        objRoot.addChild(objScale);

        // Set up the background color
        Background bg = new Background(bgcolor);
        bg.setApplicationBounds(bounds);
        objRoot.addChild(bg);

        // Needed by the texture loader utility.
        String rgb = new String("RGB");

        //  Create the Solar System with Planets, Moons and Text
        //
        for (int i=0; i < numPlanets; i++) {

           // These transforms will ROTATE objects around the Y-axis.
           planetRot[i] = new Rotator(new Transform3D(),
                                      Rotator.MEDIUM);

           // These transforms will ORBIT planet objects around
           // the Z-axis. All Planets orbit around the same origin
           // point, 1, -1, 0 position is really the radius from
           // the origin point. Speed is how fast the object swings
           // around and around.
           //
           planetOrb[i] =  new XZorbit(pspeed[i],
                                       position,
```

Source 5.5 Complete Planets.java Applet Example (*Continued*)

```
                            new Point3d(1.0,-1.0,0.0));

// Specify the transforms that will position the text label
// for each Planet and orbit at the same velocity. Make sure
// we have a text label before we create a transform since
// planet labels are optional.
//
if (ptext[i] != null)
    ptextOrb[i] = new XZorbit(pspeed[i],
                    position,
                    ptextpos[i]);
else
    ptextOrb[i] = null;


// The first "planet" will have a "zero" radius orbit so
// one can create a Sun for the first position. As more
// planets are added, the radius increases by the offset
// value.
// *** Note, the user can change the offset value to bunch
//     the orbits tightly together or spread them apart.
// In any case, the radius of the orbit increases with
// every planet. Position was initialized to zero when
// first created, so the first loop the position will be
// zero.
//
position = position + porbit;


// initialize the Appearance node
papp[i] = new Appearance();

if (pcolor[i] != null) {
    // Maybe a shiny planet color is specified instead.
    //
    Color3f objColor = pcolor[i];
    papp[i].setMaterial(new Material(objColor,
                black, objColor, white, 80.0f));
}
else {
    // Set the planet color to purple by default
    //
    Color3f objColor = medpurple;
    papp[i].setMaterial(new Material(objColor,
                black, objColor, white, 80.0f));
}

// Texturemap an image onto the Planet if specified.
```

continues

Source 5.5 *Continued*

```
            //
            if (applet == true) {
                if (pimageURL[i] != null) {
                    //   Param pimage[i] is the URL of a texture image
                    //   Param rgb is the format which channels to use
                    //   Param this is the associated image observer
                    //
                    TextureLoader t = new TextureLoader(pimageURL[i],
                                                    rgb, this);
                     if (t != null)
                        papp[i].setTexture(t.getTexture());

                    // Set up material properties so we can light the
                    // textured planet
                    papp[i].setMaterial(new Material(gray, black,
                                        gray, white, 1.0f));
                }
            }
            else if (pimage[i] != null) {

                // Load a local image file
                //
                TextureLoader t = new TextureLoader(pimage[i],
                                                rgb, this);
                 if (t != null)
                    papp[i].setTexture(t.getTexture());

                // Set up material properties so we can light the
                // textured planet
                papp[i].setMaterial(new Material(gray, black,
                                    gray, white, 1.0f));
            }

            // Create the Planet
            //
            planet[i] = new Sphere(psize[i],
                            Sphere.GENERATE_NORMALS |
                            Sphere.GENERATE_TEXTURE_COORDS,
                            60,  papp[i]);

            // Store URL in LocalData object and assign to this
            // primitive. Don't execute this if running -demo.
            //
            if (applet == true) {
                LocalData ld = new LocalData(purl[i]);
                planet[i].setUserData(ld);
            }
```

Source 5.5 Complete Planets.java Applet Example (*Continued*)

```
            // Create Planet text label, if specified.
            //
            if (ptext[i] != null)
                plabel[i] = new Text2D(ptext[i],
                                    ptcolor[i],
                                    ptfont[i],
                                    ptsize[i],
                                    ptstyle[i]);

         // If there is a Moon that orbits this planet, create the
         // moon's attributes.
         if (moons[i] != false) {

             // Create orbit transforms about the planet's
             // center point. The moon's orbit radius around
             // a planet can be specified from the HTML
             // interface. mspeed is how fast it orbits.
             //
             moonOrb[i] =  new XZorbit(mspeed[i],
                                morbit,
                                new Point3d(0.0,0.0,0.0));

             // Rotation transform for the moon at medium speed.
             //
             moonRot[i] = new Rotator(new Transform3D(),
                                        Rotator.MEDIUM);

             // Specify the transforms that will position the
             // text labels for each Planet and orbit at the
             // same velocity. Make sure we have a text label
             // before we create a transform since planet labels
             // are optional.
             //
             if (mtext[i] != null)
                 mtextOrb[i] = new XZorbit(mspeed[i],
                                morbit,
                                mtextpos[i]);
             else
                 mtextOrb[i] = null;

             // Create an Appearance object.  This will be used to
             // place the texture map onto the object.
             mapp[i] = new Appearance();

             if (mcolor[i] != null) {
                 // Maybe a shiny moon color is specified instead.
                 //
```

continues

Source 5.5   *Continued*

```
            Color3f objColor = mcolor[i];
            mapp[i].setMaterial(new Material(objColor,
                            black, objColor, white, 80.0f));
       }
       else {
            // Set the moon color to purple by default
            //
            Color3f objColor = medpurple;
            mapp[i].setMaterial(new Material(objColor,
                        black, objColor, white, 80.0f));
       }


       // Texture map or color the Moon if specified or use
       // default settings.
       //
       if (applet == true) {
           if (mimageURL[i] != null) {
               // Param pimage[i] is the string of a texture
               // image Param rgb is the format which channels
               // to use Param this is the associated image
               // observer
               //
           TextureLoader t = new TextureLoader(mimageURL[i],
                                        rgb, this);
               if (t != null)
                   mapp[i].setTexture(t.getTexture());

               // Set up material properties so we can light
               // the textured planet
               mapp[i].setMaterial(new Material(gray, black,
                                    gray, white, 1.0f));
           }
       }
       else if (mimage[i] != null) {
           TextureLoader t = new TextureLoader(mimage[i],
                                        rgb, this);
               if (t != null)
                   mapp[i].setTexture(t.getTexture());

               // Set up material properties so we can light
               // the textured planet
               mapp[i].setMaterial(new Material(gray, black,
                                    gray, white, 1.0f));
       }

       // Create the Moon
```

Source 5.5 Complete Planets.java Applet Example (*Continued*)

```
                    //
                    moon[i] = new Sphere(msize[i],
                                    Sphere.GENERATE_NORMALS |
                                    Sphere.GENERATE_TEXTURE_COORDS,
                                    60,  mapp[i]);


                    // Store URL in LocalData object and assign to this
                    // primitive. Don't execute this if running -demo.
                    //
                    if (applet == true) {
                        LocalData ld = new LocalData(murl[i]);
                        moon[i].setUserData(ld);
                    }

                    // Create Moon text label, if specified.
                    //
                    if (mtext[i] != null)
                                mlabel[i] = new Text2D(mtext[i],
                                                mtcolor[i],
                                                mtfont[i],
                                                mtsize[i],
                                                mtstyle[i]);

            } // END if moons statement

        }   // END for loop

// Simulate the source of light from a direction
//
DirectionalLight lgt1 = new DirectionalLight(sunlight, Vsun);
lgt1.setInfluencingBounds(bounds);
objScale.addChild(lgt1);

// Add everything to the Scene that was passed from the HTML
// file or if we are running in demo mode
//
for (int i=0; i < numPlanets; i++) {
    objScale.addChild(planetOrb[i]);
    planetOrb[i].addChild(planetRot[i]);
    planetRot[i].addChild(planet[i]);

    // If it has a text label then add it
    if (plabel[i] != null) {
        objScale.addChild(ptextOrb[i]);
        ptextOrb[i].addChild(plabel[i]);
```

continues

Source 5.5 *Continued*

```
                }

                // If a moon was created then add it
                if (moon[i] != null) {
                    planetOrb[i].addChild(moonOrb[i]);
                    moonOrb[i].addChild(moonRot[i]);
                    moonRot[i].addChild(moon[i]);
                }

                // If the moon had a text label then add it
                if (mlabel[i] != null) {
                    planetOrb[i].addChild(mtextOrb[i]);
                    mtextOrb[i].addChild(mlabel[i]);
                }
            }

        // Setup picking URLs.
        if (applet == true) {
            PickURL pickURL = new PickURL(c, objRoot, bounds, context);
            pickURL.setSchedulingBounds(bounds);
            objRoot.addChild(pickURL);
        }

        return objRoot;
    }

    public void init() {

        AppletContext context = null;

        // If we are running as an applet we need to
        // initialize values according to the user settings in
        // the HTML file accomplished by lookForParameters().
        // Otherwise we'll just use the values used to initialize
        // the local variable declarations at the top of the block.
        //
        if (getParameter("Planets") != null) {
            context = getAppletContext();
            lookForParameters();
        }

        // Create a Canvas3D object and add it to the applet
        setLayout(new BorderLayout());
        Canvas3D c = new Canvas3D(null);
        add("Center", c);
```

Source 5.5   Complete Planets.java Applet Example (*Continued*)

```java
        // Create a simple scene.
        BranchGroup scene = createSceneGraph(c, context);

        // attach the scene to the virtual universe
        SimpleUniverse u = new SimpleUniverse(c);

        // Move the ViewPlatform back a bit so the
        // objects in the scene can be viewed.
        u.getViewingPlatform().setNominalViewingTransform();

        // Add the branch graph to the Locale object to
        // make the branch "live".
        u.addBranchGraph(scene);
    }


    //
    // The following allows Planets to be run as an application
    // as well as an applet
    //
    public static void main(String[] args) {

        if (args.length > 0) {
            // Parse Input Arguments
            for (int i = 0; i < args.length; i++) {

                if (args[i].equals("-demo")) {
                    new MainFrame(new Planets(), 500, 400);
                } else {
                    System.out.println("Usage: java Planets -demo");
                    System.exit(0);
                }
            }
        } else {
            System.out.println("Usage: java Planets -demo");
            System.exit(0);
        }

    }  // END main

} // END Class
```

Source 5.5 *Continued*

Moving On

So far we have covered how to put 3D objects into a scene and move them around. We can forget about PI calculations and worry about more artistic concepts, like where to place a light source to provide the best visual response. If you have never taken art appreciation classes you are just about to get a crash course as we begin the study and application of light and transparent attributes.

Light and Transparency

"Oh, cut the bleeding heart crud, will ya? We've all got our switches, lights, and knobs to deal with, Striker. I mean, down here there are literally hundreds and thousands of blinking, beeping, and flashing lights, blinking and beeping and flashing—they're flashing and they're beeping. I can't stand it anymore! They're blinking and beeping and flashing! Why doesn't somebody pull the plug!"

—BUCK MURDOCK, PILOT IN *AIRPLANE II*

The art instructor, during a course lecture on portrait painting, emphasized that the figure would appear real if the eyes were rendered properly. Upon close examination of the subject's eyes in the painting, two bright reflections could be identified, revealing a very old secret. The instructor's work looked flawless, and the canvas had a depth and a rich dimension. Her work was like that of the baroque masters Caravaggio and his famous student Gerard van Honthorst. Their trick was to invoke a study of light and dark, which produced new realism in art, such as Caravaggio's *Supper at Emmaus* (see Figure 6.1).

These artists' secret was fairly simple: They would place one or two hidden light sources in the painting. The attenuated light source would cause deep dark areas to form in the corners of the picture (again, see Figure 6.1). The light source in turn would reflect off any shiny metallic or glass surfaces and create specular highlights onto the nearby objects—especially on the subjects' eyes! The result is realism and depth.

Figure 6.1 Caravaggio's *Supper at Emmaus.*

This chapter will discuss the role and usage of lights in a scene to produce higher levels of realism. Although currently Java 3D does not provide ray tracing or drop shadows, but the scene lighting is created in such a way as to simulate shadows.

ShowTime Description and Usage

The ShowTime applet is an interesting special effect that provides an attention grabber in the form of a type of slide show (see Figure 6.2). The idea is to take a rotating directional light and orbit it around the sphere shape. The light color is directed back at the sphere and illuminates only one half of the ball as it orbits around the sphere. "Slides" are groups of parameters that consist of a light color, an image to paste on the ball, and an associated URL. This is the interesting part. With each orbit, the slide group increments to the next set. Your viewer will see an interesting slide show or sequence of animation. Once the user picks a slide to view, he or she clicks on the ball, and the current URL is loaded into the browser frame.

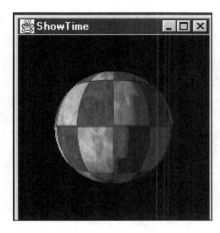

Figure 6.2   ShowTime applet.

This applet will be very useful, as it provides a creative way to present a new 3D menu of Web pages to visit in your site. ShowTime is designed with user navigation in mind. The applet could also be used on every page, to replace the typical bar menus or image maps that are implemented to get the user from the bottom to the top, or vice versa.

ShowTime Applet Parameters Explained

The interface is very simple; a basic template is provided on the CD-ROM (called ShowTime.html). When the user surfs to the Web page that contains the ShowTime applet, the program is invoked. One of the first things the applet program does is parse the list of attributes identified by the "param" keyword in the HTML file. Each parameter has an associated value. These values set specific attributes in the ShowTime demo that will be seen at run-time. If the user doesn't have the Java plug-in, an alternative site will be presented to the user so he or she can obtain the free plug-in in a relatively short time. The next time the user reloads the Web page containing the ShowTime applet, the program will appear in the browser.

Let's discuss how the parameter values affect the visual rendering of the demo.

> **ShowNumSlides.**   Used to specify the number of groupings, or slides, that will be described by following parameters. To do this, you provide an integer number from 1 to some reasonable number, say 12. The point is, you don't want the viewer to have to sit there for hours waiting for the applet to cycle back to slide one.

Example:

```
<PARAM NAME="ShowNumSlides" VALUE=2>
```

This example creates two slide groupings.

ShowColor[n].   Used to specify the color of the directional light; [n] is the slide grouping number this color belongs to. ShowColor takes the following predefined color names: red, green, blue, black [note, if you use black, you won't see anything, but this could be used as a spacer (discussed shortly) or delay between slides], white and gray.

Example:

```
<PARAM NAME="ShowColor1" VALUE="RED"
<PARAM NAME="ShowColor2" VALUE="BLUE">
```

The first parameter assigns a red light to the first slide grouping. The second example assigns a blue light to the second slide grouping, assuming we have specified two (as in the previous example).

ShowTexture[n].   Used to specify the desired image to texture the sphere; [n] is the slide grouping number the image is associated with. If no image is specified, the sphere will be lit with the specified light color. If no light color is indicated, the default green is used.

Example:

```
<PARAM NAME="ShowTexture1"
VALUE="http://www.wiley.com/images/logo1.jpg">
```

The parameter is assigned a value of a text string or the name of the picture file. Note that the image *must* have a height and a width that is a power of 2, such as 128×128, 64×64, and so on. You can use your favorite graphics editor to change the image size—Adobe Photoshop does a nice job. We would also suggest making the width 325 percent greater than the image height. This will generate text that looks appropriate when applied to the sphere, and will prevent "texture stretching."

ShowURL[n].   Used to associate a URL with a particular slide grouping. When the user clicks on the sphere with the correct active slide, the assigned URL will be loaded into the browser; [n] is the slide group number associated with the URL. If no URL is assigned, then nothing happens when the user clicks on the sphere.

Example:

```
<PARAM NAME="ShowURL1" VALUE="www.sun.com/about.html">
```

Creating Spaces between Slides

In certain situations, for effect, you may want to insert blank slides between active slides, to make the overall applet more interesting. Blank slides do not have a URL or image associated with them, only a solid light color on the sphere. During the first orbit, the user sees a color light moving across the surface of the sphere. In the next orbit, a picture appears that can be picked and linked to jump to another URL. The next slide could be another blank but with a different color. The next slide would be an active slide and so on. For example, consider the following HTML containing the ShowTime applet parameters:

```
<PARAM NAME="ShowNumSlides" VALUE=4>
<PARAM NAME="ShowColor1" VALUE="RED">
<PARAM NAME="ShowTexture1" VALUE="http://www.sun.com/logo1.jpg">
<PARAM NAME="ShowURL1" VALUE="www.sun.com/about.html">
<PARAM NAME="ShowColor2" VALUE="BLACK">
<PARAM NAME="ShowColor3" VALUE="BLUE">
<PARAM NAME="ShowTexture3" VALUE="logo2.jpg">
<PARAM NAME="ShowURL3" VALUE="www.sun.com/products.html">
<PARAM NAME="ShowColor4" VALUE="GRAY">
```

There are three slide groupings in the example. Slide number 2 will cause the scene to go completely black until the next slide is inserted after one orbit of the light object. Again, the light object is black so you will never see it. The next slide pastes a picture onto the sphere; when the user clicks the ball, the assigned URL will be loaded. The last slide will simply light the ball with a gray color before the entire program cycles back through the slides again.

Light Concepts

The human eye can see objects because light reflects off the object and back to our eyes, at the approximate speed of 186,000 miles per second. When light bounces off an object, it is *reflected*. The effect of this reflection is variable. For example, light reflecting off a smooth mirror will look much different from light reflecting off a rough granite boulder. Light normally travels in straight lines. But when light passes from one transparent medium to another, it becomes bent, or refracted. Light is also refracted as it passes through air.

Light must be present before the human eye can see anything, unless the person is wearing infrared vision goggles. The same is true for a scene in Java 3D. A synthetic light source must illuminate solid 3D models. Lighting in 3D graphics is implemented using complex mathematics, which compute factors in creating the specific effect, such as the angle and direction of the light source, the light source distance from the object, and specular and refractive characteristics.

There are numerous types of Java 3D light objects. *Ambient* light shines onto various surfaces of an object. It is the average light of the scene projected in all directions (see Figure 6.3). For example, the solar Sun provides

Figure 6.3   Ambient light.

ambient light by day, and the Moon provides ambient light by night. The light interacts with the object's surface in three possible ways: One, the light is absorbed by the surface and converted into heat; two, the light is reflected from the object's surface; and three, some of the light illuminates the interior of an object, such as sunlight illuminating an opalescent vase sitting on a windowsill.

There are two types of light reflection. *Diffused light* occurs when some of the light penetrates the surface, and the rest is scattered in all directions in a uniform pattern (see Figure 6.4). The color of the object is affected by this phenomenon. *Diffused color* is the true color of the object, revealed under pure white light. It is the perceived color of the object, rather than the color of the reflected light. Diffused color is the luminous color of an object. The surface material has a direct impact on how the surface color will be perceived.

Specular reflection is highly directional, as shown in Figure 6.5; the light does not penetrate the object's surface. This action generates highlights and makes a surface appear shiny. This is also called *specular highlights*, where the reflected light off of the object will be the same color as the light source itself.

Why should you care about ambient light? Because this is the first trick we use to greatly improve the realism of a picture. Ambient light illuminates the solid surfaces of an object with a shade. Highlights increase the realism of the picture and guide the viewer's perception as to what the surface construction might be and the types of material used. It is important for virtual scenes to look lifelike. And isn't it fun to trick the viewer? Hollywood is famous for its "how'd they do that?" movies that fooled the audience and blurred the line between reality and fantasy.

Figure 6.4   Diffused light.

Figure 6.5 Specular highlights.

Lighting is a big help in adding realism to your scene. There are other lighting effects we can use and many types of lighting calculations. *Local lighting*, or *spot lighting* (see Figure 6.6), is a concentration of a source of light, located at some point in space, and radiating to a specific location in the picture. For example, if you turn on a spotlight in a dark theater, only the objects that the spotlight illuminates can be seen. Usually, the light beam is fairly narrow and illuminates a specific area at the same intensity. Of course, adding multiple light sources can result in interesting "show biz" artistry. The typical movie set has dozens of light sources, positioned at various distance and angles to the action. There is back lighting, spotlighting, color lighting, lighting above and below. The purpose is to enhance the objects on the stage.

In the same way, Java 3D lighting is used to enhance our virtual stage of 3D objects. *Positional lighting*, or a *point light* (see Figure 6.7), defines a light source located at some position in 3D space, which radiates in all directions uniformly. *Directional light* defines the orientation of a light, located at some point in space and directed in a specific direction or vector.

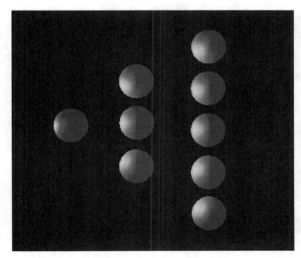

Figure 6.6 Spot light.

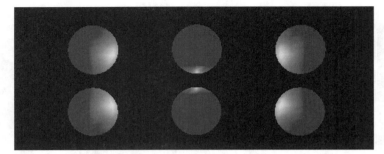

Figure 6.7 Point light.

The Light Node

The Java 3D API provides a class that defines the properties common to all light objects, including color, a state (on or off?), and a bounding volume. (Objects whose bounding regions intersect the light node's bounding region are lit by the defined light source, so don't forget to schedule the bounding region of the object if you ever hope to see it lit at runtime.) The Light node also provides a grouping node that indicates the hierarchical scope of the specified light. This allows you to constrain a light source to a specified scene object or branch group, and to specify certain properties for a particular grouping node; for example, to dim some of the lights in a group while cranking the Kelvin rating on others (see Figure 6.8). If no scoping is specified, then the light, by default, applies to the entire scene universe (Virtual

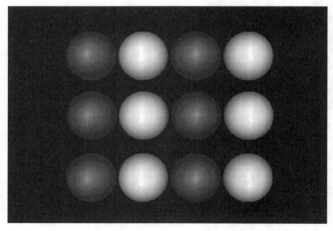

Figure 6.8 Light scoping.

Universe), and the objects within the light's region of influence, or bounds, will be lit.

All other Java 3D Light class types are derived from the Light node; for example:

```
public class PointLight extends Light
```

Here is the Light class hierarchy:

java.lang.Object

    javax.media.j3d.SceneGraphObject

      javax.media.j3d.Node

        javax.media.j3d.Leaf

          javax.media.j3d.Light

            javax.media.j3d.AmbientLight

            javax.media.j3d.DirectionalLight

            javax.media.j3d.PointLight

            javax.media.j3d.SpotLight

All lights in the Light class share these common attributes:

ON or OFF STATE

A DEFINED COLOR

A DEFINED BOUNDING VOLUME (only shapes in the volume are lit)

Related Constants

To change various parameters of a Light node, the following constants must be set using the *setCapability( )* method when the node is created. By default, everything is off until enabled.

ALLOW_INFLUENCING_BOUNDS_WRITE.   Allows the program to modify the bounding volume at runtime. A *READ* flag can also be enabled.

ALLOW_STATE_WRITE.   Allows the program to modify the light state to ON/OFF during runtime. A *READ* flag can also be enabled for the same attribute.

ALLOW_COLOR_WRITE.   When enabled, this allows the program to modify the Light node's color during runtime. It, too, supports a *READ* operation.

Related Constructors

```
public Light( )
public Light(Color3f color)
public Light(boolean state, Color3f color)
```

A Light node has three possible constructors: The first initializes the Light node with defaults; the second specifies a color; and the third defines the state of the light and a color. Usually, these constructors are not as commonly used as the specific light types themselves. Most programmers know what they want for a particular scene light object and construct it directly, such as an AmbientLight object or a PointLight object, and so on.

Related Methods

If the correct constant flags are enabled for the Light node, the following set/get methods can be used to modify the light properties. These methods turn the light on or off.

```
public final void setEnable(boolean state)
public final void getEnable()
```

These methods set the color of the light.

```
public final void setColor(Color3f color)
public final void getColor()
```

And these methods are used to modify the bounding volume of the light. This defines the region around the Light node. The light is applied to any object intersecting this region.

```
public final setInfluencingBounds(Bounds region)
public final Bounds getInfluencingBounds()
```

For some applications, there is a need to group Light nodes according to a hierarchical scope. The following are used to accomplish this task.

```
public final void setScope(Group scope, int index)
public final Group getScope(int index)
```

(See the API documentation for additional scoping methods.)

The Ambient Light Node

The AmbientLight class defines a light source that projects light uniformly in all directions. The light from the source is so scattered by active forces

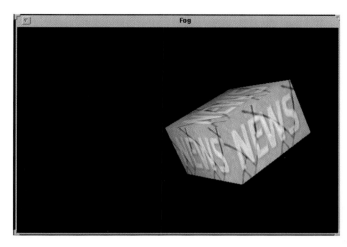

1. A 3D menu of Web news links is provided from a 3D object.

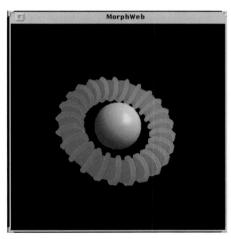

2. Multiple Java 3D geometry objects that mutate due to a Java 3D Morph object.

3. A 3D shape disappears into a thick fog bank and reappears with a new picture and shape that can load a URL when selected.

4. Interesting "slide-show" of images that are revealed by a rotating light that can load a URL when selected. A favorite image or logo can be textured onto the 3D sphere.

5. A Java 3D tool that creates geometry which is saved as a Java 3D class.

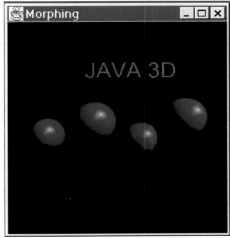

6. Morph between multiple object files with generated 3D text.

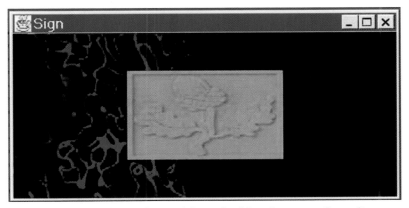

7. A rotating billboard provides a holder for your favorite product message or logo.

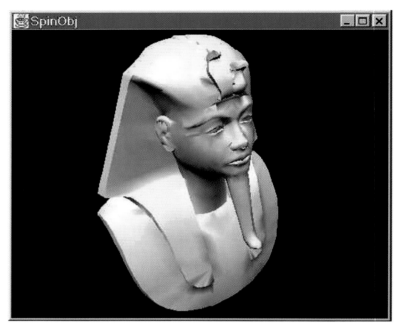

8. Load a WaveFront object file (*.obj) that is lit and rotates.

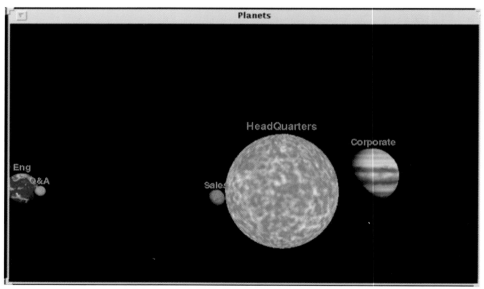

9. Create an unusual Web site navigation map (or menu) out of a solar system theme.

that it is impossible to determine the direction of the origin. It has the same constants and methods as its parent Light node class, which makes sense, since it is an extension to the Light node class.

```
public AmbientLight()
public AmbientLight(Color3f color)
public AmbientLight(boolean lighton, Color3f color)
```

For example:

```
Color3f red = new Color3f(1.0f, 0.0f, 0.0f);
AmbientLight amblight = new AmbientLight(red);
amblight.setInfluencingBounds(bounds);
amblight.setEnabled(true);
branchGroup.addChild(amblight);
```

This code will generate a red light source that will illuminate any object contained within the bounding volume "bounds" of the BranchGroup "branchGroup" for a particular scene. You use ambient lighting to provide some general lighting for a scene.

The Directional Light Node

This class defines a light with a given orientation and that has the same attributes as the Light node, in addition to a direction vector parameter. Parallel light rays travel in one direction along the specified vector (see Figure 6.9).

```
ALLOW_DIRECTION_WRITE
```

When enabled, this constant allows the vector information to be modified at runtime. An additional flag is set to *READ*-only capability.

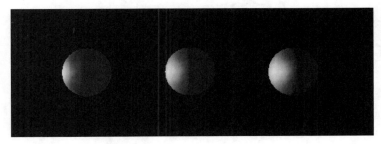

Figure 6.9 Directional light.

```
public DirectionalLight()
public DirectionalLight(Color3f color, Vector3f vector)
public DirectionalLight(boolean LightOn, Color3f color, Vector3f vector)
```

These constructors create a new directional Light node. In addition to the methods found in the Light node class, methods are used to set the direction of the light. These methods access or change the Light node's current direction. Let's quickly discuss vectors. We have covered the coordinate system and defining points, whereby 0.1f, 0.0f, 0.0f is a triplet of floating numbers representing X, Y, and Z. This can also be represented in the following way, where,

```
P = (Px, Py, Pz)
```

Two points and the difference between P1 to P2 naturally define the v vector, where:

```
P1 = (x1, y1, z1) and P2 = (x2, y2, z2)
v = (x2 - x1, y2 - y1, z2 - z1)
```

The vector is called "the vector from P1 to P2" and is bound to P1 (see Figure 6.10).

Vectors themselves do not have fixed locations, but you will often see them drawn as emanating from a specified point. Vectors are very important in computer graphics and for creating Java 3D objects. They are used to find the correct angle between the light and the object's surface, to produce the correct effect. Imagine standing directly in front of an object, and there is a bright light above your head. The object's surface you see should be bright and clear. Now imagine you walk around to the backside of the

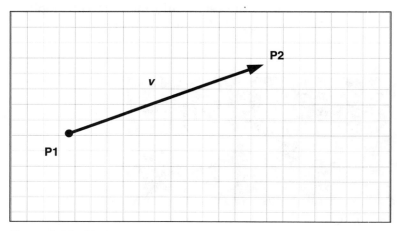

Figure 6.10   Vectors.

object to view the object's surface. You will see that the surface is very dark, nearly black. That's because light is blocked by the object mass, and light doesn't fall onto the back surface. How does a computer simulate this? How does it know which surface areas are facing toward or away from the light source? The process is complicated, but basically involves the use of vectors to find the correct angle between the light source and the given surface.

```
public final void setDirection(Vector3f direction)
public final void setDirection(float x, float y, float z)
public final void getDirection(Vector3f direction)
```

Let's look at an example:

```
Vector3f dir = new Vector3f(-1.0f, -1.0f, -1.0f);
DirectionalLight dl = new DirectionalLight(new Color3f(1.0f, 1.0f,
1.0f, dir);
dl.setInfluencingBounds(bounds);
branchGroup.addChild(dl);
```

This code specifies a vector that will direct light in a specific direction; the color of the light is white.

The Point Light Node

A point light source defines a light located at some point in space and that radiates in all directions. The light intensity is attenuated; as distance from the light source increases, the brightness of the light decreases. Attenuation is controlled by three variables: constant, linear, and quadratic coefficients.

$$\text{brightness} = \frac{\text{light intensity}}{\text{constant} + \text{linear} * \text{distance} + \text{quadratic} * \text{distance}^2}$$

It has the same attributes as the Light node class, in addition to location and attenuation parameters. We need to be able to set the following during runtime:

```
public static final int ALLOW_POSITION_WRITE (and READ)
public static final int ALLOW_ATTENUATION_WRITE (and READ)
```

We set the flags using the setCapability( ) method.

```
public PointLight()
```

This creates a new point light at the position 0.0, 0.0, 0.0.

```
public PointLight(Color3f color, Point3f pos, Point3f attenuation)
public PointLight(boolean lighton, Color3f color,
Point3f pos, Point3f att)
```

These methods create a position light at the specified position, color, and attenuation. We can modify the light's position with *setPosition(Point3f position)*, and set the light's attenuation with *setAttenuation(Point3f attenuation)*. Here is an example:

```
Color3f Color1 = new Color3f(1.0f, 0.0f, 0.0f);
Point3f Point1 = new Point3f(0.0f, 0.0f, 0.0f);
Point3f atten = new Point3f(1.0f, 0.0f, 0.0f);
PointLight pointlight = new PointLight(Color1, Point1, atten);
pointlight.setInfluencingBounds(bounds);
branchGroup.addChild(pointlight);
```

The Spotlight Node

Defining a point light source located at some point in space and radiating in a specific direction creates a spotlight. The light emits radially from a point within a cone. You can control the cone's angle to define a wide or narrow spotlight, and you can set the concentration factor to focus the light. The less focused the light, the softer the spotlight edges. Concentrations vary from sharp (128.0) to soft (0.0). This class has the same attributes as the Point Light node, but in addition to the direction of the radiation, you can set a spread-of-field angle to specify its limits, and a concentration factor. Again, some flags must be set when you want to modify the class.

```
ALLOW_SPREAD_ANGLE_WRITE ( and READ)
ALLOW_CONCENTRATION_WRITE (and READ)
ALLOW_DIRECTION_WRITE (and READ)
```

Remember, the spotlight's direction and spread angle are defined in the local coordinates of the node.

```
public SpotLight()
```

To create a spotlight with default properties:

```
        public SpotLight(Color3f color, Point3f position, Point3f
attenuation,
            Vector3f direction, float spreadAngle, float concentration)
```

And use the following to set various unique properties:

```
setSpreadAngle(float spreadAngle)
setConcentration(float concentration)
setDirection(float x, float y, float z)
setDirection(Vector3f direction)
```

Along with the associated capability flags, set:

```
ALLOW_SPREAD_ANGLE_WRITE
ALLOW_CONCENTRATION_WRITE
ALLOW_DIRECTION_WRITE
```

```
SpotLight bluespot = new SpotLight(new Color3f(0.0f,0.0f,1.0f),
         new Point3f(0.0f,0.0f,-5.0f),              // position
         new Point3f(0.1f,0.1f,0.1f),           // attenuation
         new Vector3f(0.0f, 0.0f, 0.0f),           // direction
         new Float(0.5f),                    // spread angle
         new Float(50.0f);                   // concentration
```

Setting Influencing Bounds

A region of influence controls the behavior of the Java 3D light model, which means that a bounding volume is associated with each light object that is created and added to a scene. The light object will illuminate any 3D shapes that intersect this specified volume. Another term for this is *influencing bounds*. This is very useful for managing and designing lighting for a large, complex scene. By default, lights do not establish their own bounding region, so if you forget to do this, nothing in your scene will be illuminated.

There are two types of bounding volumes you can use with lights: Bounds and BoundingLeaf. Bounds is commonly used to set a large volume over the entire scene when using simple lighting techniques, and is relative to the light's coordinate system. The volume is centered on the light; when the light moves, so does the volume.

```
Bounds bounds  =  new  Bounds(100.0f);
PointLight  pt  =  new PointLight( );
pt.setInfluencingBounds(bounds);
```

On the other hand, Bounding Leaf volumes are relative to their own coordinate system. When the light moves, the volume stays put. As the Leaf node moves, so does the volume.

```
TransformGroup  trans  =  new  TransformGroup( );
BoundingLeaf  leaf  =  new  BoundingLeaf(new Bounds(10.0f));
trans.addChild(leaf);
PointLight  pt  =  new  PointLight( );
pt.setInfluencingBoundingLeaf(leaf);
```

Scoping

Java 3D provides a method of masking the light's application to scene objects. This is useful when you want only specific shapes in the scene to be lit by a certain light, while other shapes are left alone (see Figure 6.8). This is accomplished by scoping the light object to one or more groups of shapes, and has to be specified using one of the scoping methods. Scoping is a good way to perform advanced scene lighting techniques. For example, let's say that in a complex home walk-through scene, three sets of light sources are created, one to simulate dawn's early light, one for dusk, and another for night. Each light set has a different scope grouping list and illuminates different parts of the scene with different properties. Each light in a set would be able to illuminate specified shape objects while avoiding other scene objects' lights.

```
        Group group1 = new Group( );
        Group group2 = new Group( );
  //  Create group 1's shapes with Sphere( ) or Box( ) or something
        ( geometry creation not shown)
  // Add geometry to group
        group1.addChild(sphere1);
        group1.addChild(sphere2);
  // Create group 2's geometry
        (geometry creation not shown)
  // Add geometry/shapes to group 2
        group2.addChild(box1);
        group2.addChild(box2);
  // Create 2 lights
        DirectionalLight light1 = new DirectionalLight( );
        DirectionalLight light2 = new DirectionalLight( );
        (adding properties and color not shown. Don't forget to set the
          scheduling bounds on the lights when you create them.)
  // Light Scoping
        light1.addScope(group1);
        light2.addScope(light2);
```

The attributes for lights 1 and 2 would of course be more interesting and have a color, but the basic programming template is demonstrated. Scoped lights can also be removed, inserted, and set.

```
setScope(Group group, int index)
addScope(Group group)
insertScope(Group group, int index)
removeScope(int index)
```

Transparency

The TransparencyAttributes object defines all properties affecting the transparency of the object. This is very useful in creating virtual glass objects, screen doors and windows, glass windows and silhouetted shades, and other objects for which you want the viewer to see the background through an object. This effect is very simple to create. It is part of the Appearance object applied to a particular 3D shape.

```
Appearance app = new Appearance( );
TransparencyAttributes ta = new TransparencyAttributes( );
ta.setTransparency(0.5f);
ta.setTransparencyMode(TransparencyAttributes.BLENDED);
app.setTransparencyAttributes(ta);
```

Now when a shape is created with the "app" Appearance object, it will be transparent. That's all there is to it, although there are a few modes to go over:

FASTEST.   Use for performance optimization.

NICEST.   Use when quality counts.

SCREEN_DOOR.   A stipple pattern used to provide a screen effect.

BLENDED.   Use alpha blend equation: alpha*src+(1-alpha)*dst.

NONE.   Implement no transparency.

Concepts Summary

Lighting is the most important aspect of 3D scene creation. Hollywood lighting professionals make a living knowing how to light performers and objects with different types of light sources to create the most fantastic and sometimes surreal scenes. This area is for the artist, not the programmer. We have introduced the types of lighting and transparency properties you can apply to a 3D scene. Later in the book, we discuss fog, which will enable you to invoke additional tricks to simulate depth and realism.

ShowTime Source Code (ShowTime.java)

Source 6.1 is the code for the applet with detailed comments that demonstrate how lighting is used.

```java
// Import needed JDK classes.
import java.applet.*;
import java.awt.*;
import java.awt.event.*;
import java.net.MalformedURLException;
import java.net.URL;

// Import the Java 3D API & vector mathematics API.
import javax.media.j3d.*;
import javax.vecmath.*;

// Import the needed Java 3D utility classes.
import com.sun.j3d.utils.applet.MainFrame;
import com.sun.j3d.utils.universe.*;
import com.sun.j3d.utils.geometry.*;
import com.sun.j3d.utils.image.TextureLoader;

public class ShowTime extends Applet {

    // Class variables.  The default values can be overridden
    // by using the PARAMS tag when invoked as the applet.
    //
    // The following is the defined HTML interface to this program:
    //
    //        <PARAM NAME="ShowNumSlides" VALUE=2>
    //        <PARAM NAME="ShowColor1" VALUE="RED" or "1.0 0.0 0.0">
    //        <PARAM NAME="ShowTexture1" VALUE="logo1.jpg">
    //        <PARAM NAME="ShowURL1" VALUE="www.sun.com/about.html">
    //            <PARAM NAME="ShowColor2" VALUE="BLUE" or "0.0 0.0 1.0">
    //            <PARAM NAME="ShowTexture2" VALUE="logo2.jpg">
    //        <PARAM NAME="ShowURL2" VALUE="www.sun.com/products.html">
    //                <PARAM NAME="ShowColor3" VALUE="RED" or "1.0 0.0 0.0">
    //                    note there is no URL or texture for 3. This is like
    //                    a spacer in between pictures by using a default slide

    // Switch group that will cycle through each
    // texture.
    Switch slides;

    // Array of lighting color
    private Color3f[] ltcolor =
     { new Color3f(0.0f, 0.0f, 1.0f),
           new Color3f(0.0f, 0.0f, 1.0f),
           new Color3f(0.0f, 0.2f, 0.6f),
           new Color3f(0.0f, 0.0f, 1.0f),
           new Color3f(0.6f, 0.6f, 0.6f)};
```

Source 6.1   Complete ShowTime.java Code

```
// Array of texture names used by each "slide".
// We'll use imageURL when running as applet.
private String[] texture =
  { "tdemo1.jpg",
        "circuit.jpg",
        "tdemo2.jpg",
        "circuit.jpg",
    "tdemo3.jpg" };

// Array of URLs associated with each "slide".
private URL[] link =
     {null, null, null, null, null};

// Total number of slides(default).
private int numSlides = 5;

// Every object that needs a Bounds will share
// the same bounds object.
BoundingSphere bounds;

private URL[] imageURL;
boolean applet = false;

// lookForParameters()
// Examines all parameters that can be passed in to this
// applet and updates the global state to reflect any
// non-default settings.
//
private void lookForParameters() {

    // Used to read in the parameters for the applet.
    String paramValue;

    // Running as an applet.
    applet = true;

    paramValue = getParameter("ShowNumSlides");
    if (paramValue != null)
            numSlides = Integer.parseInt(paramValue);
    else
            numSlides = 1;

    // Allocate the needed array space.
    ltcolor = new Color3f[numSlides];
    imageURL = new URL[numSlides];
    link = new URL[numSlides];
```

continues

Source 6.1   *Continued*

```java
    // Look for the parameter values for each slide or set defaults
for (int i = 0; i < numSlides; i++) {

    // Looks for lighting color
      paramValue = getParameter("ShowColor" + (i + 1));
      if (paramValue != null)
            if (paramValue.equalsIgnoreCase("red") == true)
          ltcolor[i] = new Color3f(1.0f, 0.0f, 0.0f);
      else if (paramValue.equalsIgnoreCase("green") == true)
          ltcolor[i] = new Color3f(0.0f, 1.0f, 0.0f);
      else if (paramValue.equalsIgnoreCase("blue") == true)
          ltcolor[i] = new Color3f(0.0f, 0.0f, 1.0f);
      else if (paramValue.equalsIgnoreCase("white") == true)
          ltcolor[i] = new Color3f(1.0f, 1.0f, 1.0f);
      else if (paramValue.equalsIgnoreCase("black") == true)
          ltcolor[i] = new Color3f(0.0f, 0.0f, 0.0f);
      else if (paramValue.equalsIgnoreCase("gray") == true)
          ltcolor[i] = new Color3f(0.4f, 0.4f, 0.4f);
    else
          ltcolor[i] = new Color3f(0.0f, 1.0f, 0.0f);

        // Looks for texture file
    paramValue = getParameter("ShowTexture" + (i + 1));
    if (paramValue != null) {
        URL linkURL;
        try {
                      linkURL = new URL(paramValue);
        }
        catch (MalformedURLException e) {
            // Bad URL.
            linkURL = null;
        }
        imageURL[i] = linkURL;
    }
    else {
                // set it to blank
                imageURL[i] = null;
    }

        // Look for URL link parameter value
    paramValue = getParameter("ShowURL" + (i + 1));
    if (paramValue != null) {
        URL linkURL;
        try {
                      linkURL = new URL(paramValue);
        }
```

Source 6.1 Complete ShowTime.java Code (*Continued*)

```
                    catch (MalformedURLException e) {
                        // Bad URL.
                        linkURL = null;
                    }
                    link[i] = linkURL;
                }
                else {
                    // Default Value
                    URL weblink;
                    try {
                        weblink = new URL("http://stub");
                        link[i] = weblink;
                    }
                                      catch(MalformedURLException e) {
                                          System.out.println("ERROR:" +
paramValue);
                                      }
                }

        }  // END of for loop

    } // END lookForParameters

    // Creates all the objects to be inserted in the scene graph.
    //
    public BranchGroup createSceneGraph(Canvas3D c,
                                        AppletContext context) {

        Color3f aColor  = new Color3f(0.1f, 0.1f, 0.1f);
            Color3f eColor  = new Color3f(0.0f, 0.0f, 0.0f);
            Color3f dColor  = new Color3f(0.2f, 1.0f, 0.6f);
            Color3f sColor  = new Color3f(1.0f, 1.0f, 1.0f);
        Color3f lColor1 = new Color3f(0.7f, 0.7f, 0.7f);
            Vector3f lDir1  = new Vector3f(-1.0f, -0.3f, -1.0f);
            Color3f alColor = new Color3f(1.0f, 1.0f, 0.0f);

        /// objects
        Sphere[] sphere = new Sphere[numSlides];

            // Create the root of the branch graph
            BranchGroup objRoot = new BranchGroup();

            // Create a bounding volume
            bounds = new BoundingSphere(new Point3d(0.0,0.0,0.0), 100.0);

            // This Transform Group scales the objects
```

continues

Source 6.1 *Continued*

```
    // so they fit the scene
    //
    TransformGroup objScale = new TransformGroup();
    Transform3D t3d = new Transform3D();
    t3d.setScale(0.5f);
    objScale.setTransform(t3d);
    objRoot.addChild(objScale);

      //
      // Create the transform group node for the lights and initialize
      // it to the identity.Enable the TRANSFORM_WRITE capability so
// that our behavior code can modify it at runtime.  Add it to
// the root of the subgraph via the Scaled group.
      //
      TransformGroup lightTrans = new TransformGroup();
      lightTrans.setCapability(TransformGroup.ALLOW_TRANSFORM_WRITE);
      objRoot.addChild(lightTrans);

// Create the slides switch node - it will initially
// display slide 0, the first slide.
slides = new Switch(0);

  // Set needed capabilities:
  //  ALLOW_SWITCH_WRITE will allow the currently selected switch
  //     node child to be changed.
  //  ALLOW_CHILDREN_READ will allow the switch node to call the
  //     numChildren() and getChild() methods.  Needed during
  //     picking to find the picked node and associated URL.
  //
  slides.setCapability(Switch.ALLOW_SWITCH_WRITE);
  slides.setCapability(Group.ALLOW_CHILDREN_READ);

  // Needed by the texture loader utility.
      String rgb = new String("RGB");

  for (int i = 0; i < numSlides; i++) {

      // Create an Appearance object.  This will be used to
      // place the texture map onto the object.
      Appearance a = new Appearance();
          Material m = new Material(aColor,
                  eColor, ltcolor[i], sColor, 0.0f);
          m.setLightingEnable(true);
          a.setMaterial(m);

      if (applet == true) {
```

Source 6.1 Complete ShowTime.java Code (*Continued*)

```
                    if (imageURL[i] != null) {
                        TextureLoader t = new TextureLoader(imageURL[i],
                                                    rgb, this);
                if (t != null)
                            a.setTexture(t.getTexture());

                // Set up material properties so we can light the
                // textured planet
                a.setMaterial(new Material(aColor,
                        eColor, ltcolor[i], sColor, 0.0f));
            }
        }
        else if (texture[i] != null) {
            TextureLoader t = new TextureLoader(texture[i],
                                                rgb, this);

            if (t != null)
                        a.setTexture(t.getTexture());

            // Set up material properties so we can light the
            // textured planet
            a.setMaterial(new Material(aColor,
                    eColor, ltcolor[i], sColor, 0.0f));
        }

        sphere[i] = new Sphere(1.0f,
                Sphere.GENERATE_NORMALS |
                Sphere.GENERATE_TEXTURE_COORDS,
                60, a);

        slides.addChild(sphere[i]);

        // Store URL in LocalData object and assign to this
        // primitive. Don't execute this if running -demo.
        if (applet == true) {
            LocalData ld = new LocalData(link[i]);
            sphere[i].setUserData(ld);
        }

    } // END For loop

    AmbientLight algt = new AmbientLight(alColor);
    algt.setInfluencingBounds(bounds);

    DirectionalLight dlgt = new DirectionalLight(lColor1, lDir1);
    dlgt.setInfluencingBounds(bounds);
```

continues

Source 6.1   *Continued*

```
      objRoot.addChild(algt);
      lightTrans.addChild(dlgt);

      // Create a new Behavior object that will perform the desired
      // operation on the specified transform object.
      //
      Transform3D yAxis = new Transform3D();
      Alpha rotoralpha = new Alpha(-1, Alpha.INCREASING_ENABLE,
                                    0, 0,
                                    5900, 0, 0,
                                    0, 0, 0);


      RotationInterpolator rotator =
              new RotationInterpolator(rotoralpha,
                                lightTrans,
                                yAxis,
                                0.0f, (float) Math.PI*2.0f);

  rotator.setSchedulingBounds(bounds);

    // Create a new Alpha object for the Switch
    //
    Alpha alpha = new Alpha(-1, Alpha.INCREASING_ENABLE,
                              0, 0,
                   23745, 7000, 0,
                   0, 0, 0);

    // This interpolator will continuously switch between all child
    // nodes of the Switch group node "slides".
    //
    SwitchValueInterpolator slideSwitch =
        new SwitchValueInterpolator(alpha,
                            slides, 0, numSlides);
    slideSwitch.setSchedulingBounds(bounds);


    // Add everything to the scene graph
    lightTrans.addChild(rotator);
    objScale.addChild(slides);
  objScale.addChild(slideSwitch);

  if (applet == true) {
    PickURL pickURL = new PickURL(c, objRoot, bounds, context);
    pickURL.setSchedulingBounds(bounds);
    objRoot.addChild(pickURL);
  }
```

Source 6.1 Complete ShowTime.java Code (*Continued*)

```
                return objRoot;
    }


public void init() {

    AppletContext context = null;

  // If we are running as an applet we need to
   // initialize values according to the user settings in
   // the HTML file accomplished by lookForParameters().
   // Otherwise we'll just use the values used to initialize
   // the local variable declarations at the top of the block.
   //
   if (getParameter("ShowNumSlides") != null) {
            context = getAppletContext();
            lookForParameters();
   }

   setLayout(new BorderLayout());
   Canvas3D c = new Canvas3D(null);
   add("Center", c);
   BranchGroup scene = createSceneGraph(c, context);
   SimpleUniverse u = new SimpleUniverse(c);

   // This will move the ViewPlatform back a bit so the
   // objects in the scene can be viewed.
   u.getViewingPlatform().setNominalViewingTransform();

   u.addBranchGraph(scene);
}


//
// The following allows ShowTime to be run as an application
// as well as an applet
//
public static void main(String[] args) {

    if (args.length > 0) {
       // Parse Input Arguments
       for (int i = 0; i < args.length; i++) {

            if (args[i].equals("-demo")) {
               new MainFrame(new ShowTime(), 300, 300);
            } else {
                    System.out.println("Usage: java ShowTime -demo");
               System.exit(0);
```

continues

Source 6.1   *Continued*

```
                    }
                }
            } else {
                System.out.println("Usage: java ShowTime -demo");
                System.exit(0);
            }

        }   // END Main
    } // END Class
```

Source 6.1 Complete ShowTime.java Code (*Continued*)

Moving On

The next chapter will provide continued action and fun. It's time to add interactivity and additional behaviors that will really impress your visitors and applet users.

CHAPTER

7

Behaviors, Interpolators, and Event Detection

"Generally, you don't see that kind of behavior in a major appliance."

—DR. PETER VENKMAN, IN *GHOSTBUSTERS*

So far, we have learned how to make static 3D worlds using the Java 3D API. We have documented how to create a basic scene graph that contains BranchGroup nodes, Locales, ViewPlatforms, TransformGroup nodes, and Shape3D nodes with Appearance node components. Really cool, but (yawn) that's not going to impress the friends and neighbors (and all those surfers). What catches people's eyes these days is action! People want to see objects moving around the screen, flying from side to side, and buzzing around their heads. They also want to be able to interact with the objects they see, to grab them and turn them so they can be viewed from every possible angle. They want collisions and changing colors. They want to feel that the 3D world they are viewing is alive, so they can be completely captivated by it. Finally, their experience culminates with the ultimate expressive compliment: Wow!!

But can Java 3D meet these expectations? Can we give the attention-deficit generation what they want, nay, even demand from every Web site they visit? Is Java 3D up to this challenge? Of course it is.

Shuffle Applet Description and Usage

This chapter's applet (see Figure 7.1) provides an interactive behavior with which the user can control the action. Like channel surfing with a remote, the user clicks over a stack of cards to reveal the next selection. The discarded slide card peels off to the side then flips toward the back of the stack, revealing the next selection. The user can hit any keyboard button to load the associated URL for a particular card. The program exits as the browser loads the selected link. Variations can be achieved by modifying the HTML file.

Shuffle Parameters Explained

When the user surfs to the Web page that contains the applet, the program is invoked. One of the first things the applet program does is parse the list of attributes identified by the "param" keyword in the HTML file. Each parameter has an associated value. These values set specific attributes in the applet that will be seen at runtime.

Let's discuss how the parameter values affect the visual rendering of the demo:

CardNum. You will need to specify how many card images you intend to flip through and provide the appropriate parameters for each. For example, if you specify three, you will also need to include CardTex-

Figure 7.1 The Shuffle applet.

ture1, 2, and 3; and CardURL1, 2, and 3. If you forget any of these supporting parameters, the program logic will fill in the gaps where it can and use default settings. These are probably *not* what you have in mind, and you will notice your oversight right away.

CardTexture[n]. Specifies an image to lay over the provided 3D shape. This is known as texture mapping. The image or picture must be in the GIF or JPEG format.

```
value="http://www.sun.com/images/logo.gif"
```

CardURL[n]. Associates a URL address or local HTML file with a specific 3D object in the 3D scene. When the user clicks the *left* mouse button over the card, the browser loads the page to the specified location. When the user clicks the *right* mouse button over the card, the program will flip to a new card.

```
value="http://www.sun.com"
```

Shuffle HTML File Explained

The HTML file for the applet is included on the book's CD. You use this to run the applet in a browser, but you'll need to edit the parameter portions in the HTML to specify your changes. Consult Chapter 4 for details on interpreting the syntax of this file.

Scene Behavior Concepts

The Java 3D API has two types of objects designed for the purpose of providing user interaction and action: behaviors and interpolators. Behaviors and interpolators are what make a Java 3D world come alive. They provide the dynamics used to gather user input and provide motion to objects in a Java 3D scene. *Behaviors* allow us to specify that an action should occur based on a particular set of events, in what Java 3D calls a WakeupCondition. A WakeupCondition is a combination of another Java 3D object called a WakeupCriterion. These WakeupCriterion cover a wide range of activities from waiting for a certain number of frames to trapping keyboard and mouse events over our Java 3D Canvas3D.

Interpolators are a specialized version of a behavior. They use a time-generated value in the range of 0.0–1.0 to modify some characteristic of a Java 3D object. That might not sound like much, but interpolators can add many interesting effects to a Java 3D world; in fact, they're so handy that we will be describing them in full detail.

All behavior types contain code to run when the behavior is triggered. Trigger events are called *wakeup conditions*. When the viewer's activation radius collides with the scheduling bounds of a behavior, the behavior is activated to do whatever it is programmed to do. Behaviors can do all sorts of things, like do computations, update a state machine, modify the scene graph, transform an object, or create new shapes. Let's take a closer look at some of these behaviors.

Interpolators

Because they are more specialized, we will start with interpolators. Again, an interpolator takes a value in the range of 0.0–1.0 and uses this value to modify an object in the Java 3D scene graph. Most interpolators modify a transform associated with a TransformGroup node, but some take a Shape3D node's Material node component object or a Switch node. You tell Java 3D the starting and ending values, and the object to effect it does the rest.

Interpolators can be made to transition continuously from their starting value to their ending value, or the number of times this transition is to occur can be specified. We can, for example, specify that the transition go from the start value to the ending value and then restart at the beginning value; or we can have it interpolate from the end value back to the starting value. We can also have the interpolation be at a constant rate or vary over time. In short, we have a lot of control as to how our objects will be interpolated by Java 3D. But have no fear, this power is easily handled by the Java 3D API.

Interpolator Coding Template

No matter what type of interpolator is being created, they all follow a basic pattern:

1. Create an Alpha object that describes how to map time to the range 0.0–1.0.
2. Create the interpolator object using this Alpha.
3. Specify the object to interpolate.
4. Specify how the Alpha float value will map to the range of the interpolator.
5. Assign the proper bounds to this object.
6. Add the interpolator to the scene graph.

Now watch and enjoy. That's all there is to it. Now let's dive into the details. We will start with our first interpolator called the Alpha class.

Alpha Objects

The Alpha class is a simple yet powerful object that will help our Java 3D worlds come alive. It should be stated that this class has nothing to do with the alpha value used in images to create transparency! Keep that in mind when working late nights just before the big deadline.

A simple description of the Alpha class is this: It takes time (measured in milliseconds) and maps it onto a floating-point value in the range 0.0–1.0 inclusive. When we create the Alpha object, we have a great deal of flexibility on how this mapping occurs. But this flexibility comes in the form of a rather daunting constructor and equivalent methods. But fear not! As we go through the various parameters of the constructor, you will see that the Alpha class isn't really that intimidating at all.

We like to think of an Alpha object as a mathematical function that generates different values over time, similar to plotting the values of the sine function over time to get the familiar oscillating waveform. Alpha objects let you generate your own personal waveform. To aid us in our quest to master the Alpha class, we have created a very simple Java 3D world, shown in Source 7.1. We can use this world to plug in different values for the Alpha constructor and see how they affect our world.

We will be modifying the constructor for the Alpha object and looking at what effect that has on the PositionInterpolator. We haven't discussed the PositionInterpolator class yet, so for now just think of it as translating an object from position 0.0 on the X-axis to 1.0. The PositionInterpolator created will use the Alpha value to map an Alpha value of 0.0 to the position 0.0 along the X-axis. An Alpha value of 1.0 will map to a position of 1.0. By using the PositionInterpolator in this way, we can cause objects to move back and forth along the X-axis over time.

Now on to the Alpha object. We will be looking at the various parameters in the Alpha constructor class. To start, let's construct a basic Alpha object and go over a few parameters:

```
Alpha simpleAlpha = new Alpha(1, Alpha.INCREASING_ENABLE,
    0, 0, 7000, 0, 0, 0, 0, 0);
```

Hold on; it's not that bad! Remember, we are going to ignore most of the parameters for now. In fact, we will skip almost all parameters with a zero value. To further aid us, let's also draw the "graph" of this Alpha object (see Figure 7.2).

```java
// Import needed JDK classes.
import java.applet.Applet;
import java.awt.BorderLayout;

// Import the Java 3D API.
import javax.media.j3d.*;
import com.sun.j3d.utils.applet.MainFrame;

// Import the vector mathematics API.
import javax.vecmath.*;

// Import the SimpleUniverse classes.
import com.sun.j3d.utils.universe.*;

// Import the Box geometry object - this will be
// the object we animate.
import com.sun.j3d.utils.geometry.Box;

/**
 * Simple applet used to demonstrate the use of the Alpha class.
 * A scene graph consisting of a TransformGroup, a
 * PositionInterpolator and a Box (geometry) are constructed.
 * When the parameters to the Alpha constructor are changed, the      *
 effects can be seen by the change
 * in the box's movement.
 */
 public class AlphaTest extends Applet {

     // Creates all the objects to be inserted in the scene graph.
     public BranchGroup createSceneGraph() {

         // Create the root of the branch graph.
         BranchGroup objRoot = new BranchGroup();

         // Allocate the bounding sphere to be used with the all nodes.
         // The assumption is that the all nodes should be active all
         // the time. The bounds center is set to the origin and
         // then a radius of 100 is assumed to be "sufficiently large" so
         // that all the nodes will always be within specified bounds.
         //
         BoundingSphere bounds = new BoundingSphere(
                 new Point3d(0.0,0.0,0.0),100.0);

         // This is the TransformGroup we will be modifying with
         // our interpolator.
         TransformGroup objTrans = new TransformGroup();
```

Source 7.1   A Very Simple Java 3D World

```
        // Must allow the Transform3D to be writeable after the
        // scene graph is made live.
        objTrans.setCapability(TransformGroup.ALLOW_TRANSFORM_WRITE);
        objRoot.addChild(objTrans);

        // This is our alpha to experiment with!
        Alpha alpha = new Alpha(1, Alpha.INCREASING_ENABLE,
                    0, 0, 7000, 0, 0, 0, 0, 0);

        // We will use the Alpha object with a position interpolator.
        // By default, this will move the object from (0.0, 0.0, 0.0),
        // when Alpha = 0.0, to (1.0, 0.0, 0.0) when ALpha = 1.0.
        PositionInterpolator p = new PositionInterpolator(alpha,
                                                  objTrans);

        // Don't forget to set the bounds or else nothing will happen!
        p.setSchedulingBounds(bounds);

        // Add the Interpolator to the scene graph.
        objTrans.addChild(p);

        // Create a small box. Use default Appearance attributes for now.
        // Later on we will see an Interpolator classes that affects
        // the created TransparencyAttributes object.
        //
        Appearance boxAppearance = new Appearance();
        TransparencyAttributes boxTransparency = new
                                TransparencyAttributes();
        boxAppearance.setTransparencyAttributes(boxTransparency);
        Box box = new Box(0.4f, 0.4f, 0.2f, boxAppearance);
        // Add the box to the scene graph.
        objTrans.addChild(box);

        return objRoot;
    }


    public AlphaTest()
    {
        // Initialize the Layout Manager and create the Canvas3D
        // object.
        setLayout(new BorderLayout());
        Canvas3D c = new Canvas3D(null);
        add("Center", c);

        // Create a simple scene and attach it to the virtual universe
        BranchGroup scene = createSceneGraph();
```

continues

Source 7.1 *Continued*

```
            SimpleUniverse u = new SimpleUniverse(c);

            // This will move the ViewPlatform back a bit so the
            // objects in the scene can be viewed.
            u.getViewingPlatform().setNominalViewingTransform();

            // Add the created scene graph to our universe.
            u.addBranchGraph(scene);
    }
      //
      // The following allows program to be run as an application
      // as well as an applet
      //
      public static void main(String[] args) {
              new MainFrame(new AlphaTest(), 212, 212);
      }
}
```

Source 7.1 A Very Simple Java 3D World (*Continued*)

As you can see, this Alpha object generates a single ramp from 0.0 to 1.0. This ramp takes 7,000 milliseconds (that's 7 seconds to you and me) to complete. After the 7,000 milliseconds are up, the Alpha object stays at its final value, 1.0. When we run the alphaTest applet, we see a 3D box inside the Canvas3D window moving slowly to the right. When half of the box is outside the window, the box stops moving (see Figure 7.3).

Visually, this makes sense. The quick description of the PositionInterpolator tells us that it will interpolate position based on the current Alpha value. Our simple test applet positions the box in the middle of the window—that is, (0.0, 0.0, 0.0). The PositionInterpolator is going to interpolate the X coordinate from 0.0 to 1.0. The position (1.0, 0.0, 0.0) will be on the right edge of our window. So the object should start in the center of the window and move to the right—which is exactly what we see.

From the graph of the Alpha "wave," we can see that is exactly what should happen. The Alpha starts at 0.0, smoothly goes to 1.0, and then remains at 1.0 for eternity (barring any year 2000 problems!).

From now on, we are going to insert a delay in our Alpha (see Figure 7.4). This will delay the Alpha from starting up right away. We will do this to ensure that Java 3D has enough time to bring up the window so we can see what is going on. (When you ran the sample applet, your initial view of the cube may not have had an X position of 0.0. The box may have already been

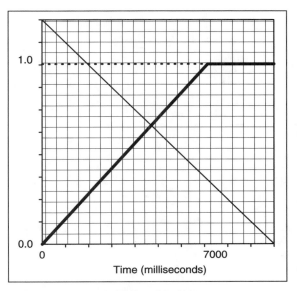

Figure 7.2   Simple Alpha object.

partially moved to the right side of the screen. This has to do with the mul-
tithreading nature of Java 3D. Java 3D can start to render objects before the
JDK has time to create the window in which to display our applet.) Luckily,
there is a parameter in the Alpha constructor to allow us to delay when an
Alpha starts to generate its wave. We will use this delay to give Java some
time to create the window and let us view the initial Java 3D scene. This
delay is specified in the triggerTime parameter. The triggerTime parameter

Figure 7.3   AlphaTest applet.

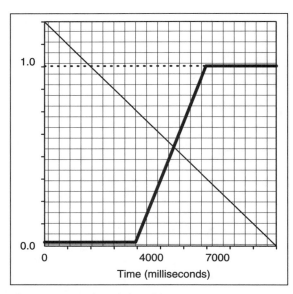

Figure 7.4 Delay Alpha object.

is the number of milliseconds to wait before starting to generate the alpha value. So now our Alpha value looks like:

```
Alpha delayAlpha = new Alpha(1, Alpha.INCREASING_ENABLE,
        4000,0,7000, 0, 0, 0, 0, 0);
```

The waveform generated by this Alpha object looks like Figure 7.4.

When we run our test program with this Alpha object, we see that the cube comes up in the center of the window as a stationary object, then starts to move to the right, exactly as our initial Alpha object.

Now let's look at some of the parameters. The first nonzero parameter we see is the 1 in the loopCount parameter. This parameter tells Java 3D how many times to perform this Alpha. A loop count of 1 tells Java 3D to generate our Alpha "wave" once and then stop. This is why after the alpha value reaches 1.0, it stays at 1.0. We have effectively done one cycle of our wave. If we change the loopCount value to 2, what will happen? Well, we should see our Alpha "wave" repeated twice (see Figure 7.5).

```
Alpha 2loopAlpha = new Alpha(2, Alpha.INCREASING_ENABLE,
        4000, 0,7000, 0, 0, 0, 0, 0);
```

Once the Alpha object finishes its 0.0 to 1.0 transition, it has completed one loop. To start the next loop, the Alpha value is reset to 0 and again will

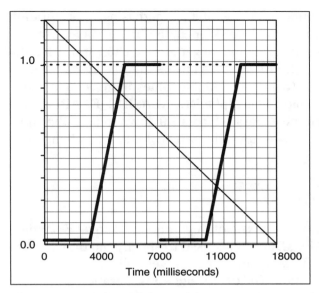

Figure 7.5   Two-loop Alpha.

smoothly increase to 1.0, completing the second loop and stopping. If we change the loopCount in our applet from 1 to 2, we will see the cube travel to the right side of the window, then immediately pop back to the center of the window where, once again, it will slowly start moving to the right side of the window. Once the cube is halfway out of the right side of the window, it will stop and remain in that position. This is exactly what we would expect, based on the graph of the previous Alpha. We can set the loopCount field to any positive number we want, and our Alpha will repeat for that amount.

If we want the Alpha to continuously generate its waveform forever, we can use the special value of −1 to tell Java 3D that this Alpha should continuously loop. What will that do to our bland, old cube? If you're not sure, try it and see.

See, that one wasn't so hard. Let's move on to the parameter with the value of 7,000 in our Alpha constructor. Why are we skipping one? Because to demonstrate the use of that parameter we need to change some other parameters as well. The increasingAlphaDuration field is used to specify how long the transition from 0.0 to 1.0 = 20 takes to occur. This time is also specified in milliseconds. Our initial Alpha says to take 7 seconds to evenly generate values from 0.0 to 1.0. To speed up the object, all we need to do is put in a smaller number for the increasingAlphaDuration. To slow it down, we enter a larger number.

Now that you have an understanding of the increasingAlphaDuration parameter, we can go back to the field we skipped, the "mode" field, which is used to describe which way values should be generated. Our Alpha uses the constant Alpha.INCREASING_ENABLE. This means that the alpha values = 20 will be generated from 0.0 to 1.0—the Alpha values increase over time. The other possible value for this field is Alpha.DECREASING_ENABLE. This will cause the Alpha values to be generated from 1.0 down to 0.0—the alpha value decreases over time. To see how that would look, let's change our AlphaTest values to:

```
Alpha alpha = new Alpha(2, Alpha.DECREASING_ENABLE,
        4000, 0, 7000,0, 0, 0, 0, 0);
```

What will this do to our favorite box? Nothing! It doesn't move! What happened? Well, as increasingAlphaDuration is used to specify the time it takes to go from 0.0 up to 1.0, there is a similar parameter called, appropriately enough, decreasingAlphaDuration. The decreasingAlphaDuration parameter is the time, in milliseconds, for the Alpha "wave" to transition from 1.0 down to 0.0. Because we currently have a decreasingAlphaDuration value of 0, our Alpha object will not generate any value. All we need to do is specify a value for this parameter and our trusty cube is off and moving (see Figure 7.6).

```
Alpha alpha = new Alpha(2, Alpha.DECREASING_ENABLE,
        4000, 0, 7000, 0, 0, 7000, 0, 0);
```

This causes the cube to move from the right side of the screen to the center of the screen. Because our loopCount is still 2, the square immediately jumps to the right side of our window, then moves back to the center, where it will stay indefinitely. As you can see, even though we specified a value for

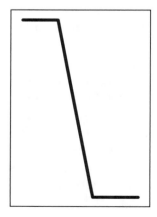

Figure 7.6   Alpha decreasing.

the increasingAlphaDuration parameter, it is ignored because our mode field specifies that our Alpha "wave" should generate only values going from 1.0 down to 0.0. The other important item to note, both in the Alpha wave graph and from observing the applet, is that while the Alpha is paused because of the triggerTime value we specified, it is now on the right side of the window. This is due to the fact that a DECREASING_ENABLE wave is defined as starting at 1.0 and then moving down to 0.0.

Having objects move to one side and then suddenly wrap back to their starting position isn't too realistic. By combining the mode flags we can move an object steadily from side to side. We do this by using the single-loop, bitwise OR operation.

```
Alpha Oralpha = new Alpha(1, Alpha.DECREASING_ENABLE |
    Alpha.INCREASING_ENABLE, 4000, 0, 7000, 0, 0, 7000, 0, 0);
```

The Alpha wave associated with this is shown in Figure 7.7. Can you guess what our trusty cube will do next?

We have covered a lot of ground; we have seen how the increasingRampDuration and decreasingRampDuration fields, mode, and loopCount parameters generate different Alpha waves. We have used the triggerTime parameter to delay our Alpha wave to ensure that the window we are rendering to is up before our interpolator starts executing. We have also

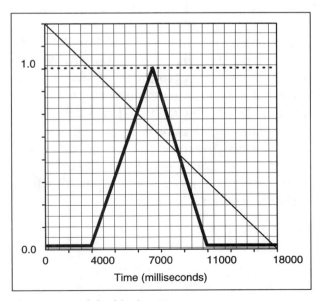

Figure 7.7 Alpha bitwise OR.

learned how to graph an Alpha wave and how to interpret that graph to see how it affects our PositionInterpolator. There are just a few more fields to describe to have complete control over how our Alpha generates values—and through our Alpha, how interpolators affect objects in our scene graph.

To this point, we have been using an Alpha with a constant velocity. Our cube moves to the left and right at a constant rate of speed. Sometimes, however, this might not yield the desired results. Often, we prefer an effect where an object starts out slow, then accelerates over a period of time before reaching its final, constant speed. Then the object slows down, eventually coming to a complete stop. This is typical of a car speeding up and then slowing down at a stop sign. The increasingAlphaRampDuration and decreasingAlphaRampDuration parameters are used to create this effect with our Alpha object. The increasingAlphaRampDuration parameter affects the INCREASING_ALPHA wave; likewise, the decreasingAlphaRamp-Duration parameter affects the DECREASING_ALPHA wave. Thanks to this symmetry, we can describe both parameters at once, knowing they have the same effect, albeit on different sides of the wave.

To understand how these two parameters affect our Alpha wave and, in turn, our faithful cube, let's briefly diverge into simple mechanical physics. Don't panic, even if you dropped out of physics; we won't be going into too much detail here. So far, our Alpha wave has gone from 0.0 to 1.0 (and sometimes back to 0.0) at a constant rate, or velocity. Velocity is measured by distance divided by time. When you hear numbers expressed as miles per hour, feet per minute, or meters per second, you are hearing a velocity measurement.

The speedometer in a car measures the current velocity of the vehicle. We have seen how to alter this velocity by changing the appropriate increasingAlphaDuration or decreasingAlphaDuration parameter. If we were to calculate the velocity of our cube, we would measure the distance it moved over a period of time and divide that distance by the time period. We would find that this number would be the same for our cube no matter where along the path we computed it (barring any system hiccups), because our cube is moving at a constant velocity, and the distance the object moves over any given period of time is always the same. From our initial Alpha, this illustration would be charted with the values found in Figure 7.8.

```
Alpha simpleAlpha = new Alpha(1, Alpha.INCREASING_ENABLE,
        4000, 0,7000, 0, 0, 0, 0, 0);
```

The maximum value of the velocity graph will be the increasing AlphaDuration/decreasing AlphaDuration parameter divided by the total distance the object moves.

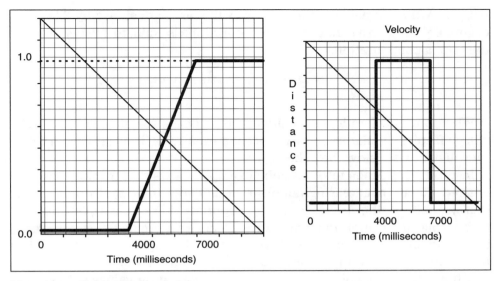

Figure 7.8 Alpha velocity model.

Now, as most of us have probably observed, the real world doesn't work like that. When was the last time you were in a car that was at a dead stop and then suddenly was cruising at the posted speed limit? More than likely (actually, certainly), you saw the speedometer (remember this is a measurement of velocity) quickly move (or in my car's case, slowly move) toward the desired speed. This change in velocity is called *acceleration.* Just as we can measure velocity as the change in distance divided by the change in time, we can calculate acceleration by measuring the change in velocity divided by the change in time. To avoid any migraine headaches, that's all the detail we will cover here.

In summary, by assigning a value to the increasingAlphaRampDuration and/or decreasingAlphaRampDuration parameter, we can vary the velocity over time—that is, we are assigning it acceleration. The AlphaRampDuration parameters are also assigned in milliseconds. By choosing a value that is less than half the equivalent increasingAlphaDuration or decreasingAlphaDuration time, we are allowing the Alpha velocity to change (accelerate and decelerate) over time. Our velocity will start at 0 and will then get faster and faster. After the specified increasingAlphaRampDuration or decreasingAlphaRampDuration period of time, our Alpha will be at full speed (specified by increasingAlphaDuration or decreasingAlphaDuration, remember?). Then, once there is increasingAlphaRampDuration (for Alpha.INCREAS-ING_ENABLE) or decreasingAlphaRampDuration (for Alpha.DECREAS-

ING_ENABLE) remaining, the velocity will start to decrease by 2,000 and eventually come to a gentle stop when our Alpha is equal to 1.0. Let's look at this Alpha configuration.

```
Alpha velocityAlpha = new Alpha(1, Alpha.INCREASING_ENABLE,
    4000, 0, 7000, 2000, 0, 0, 0, 0);
```

When our acceleration is positive, the velocity will increase (our cube will go faster). Similarly, where the acceleration graph is negative, the velocity will decrease (slow the cube down).

Inserting this Alpha into our cube example shows that we now have the desired affect. An increasingRampDuration/decreasingRampDuration value that is half of the value of the appropriate increasingAlphaDuration/ decreasingAlphaDuration parameter will cause the Alpha velocity to reach its maximum value exactly halfway through the Alpha wave. It will then immediately start to decelerate. Any RampDuration values that are over half the value (time) of their respective AlphaDuration values will be truncated to be half of the appropriate value.

```
Alpha moreAlpha = new Alpha(1, Alpha.INCREASING_ENABLE,
    4000, 0, 7000, 6000, 0, 0, 0, 0);
```

That's all the major parts of the Alpha constructor and, consequently, our Alpha wave. There are just a few more parameters to go, none of which should be too difficult. The phaseDelayDuration is the time period during which Alpha does not change; it is either 0.0 for INCREASING_ALPHA (or a combination INCREASING_ALPHA and DECREASING_ALPHA wave) or 1.0 for DECREASING_ALPHA waves.

```
Alpha simpleAlpha =3D new Alpha(1, Alpha.INCREASING_ENABLE,
    0, 4000, 7000, 0, 0, 0, 0, 0);
```

or

```
Alpha simpleAlpha =3D new Alpha(1, Alpha.INCREASING_ENABLE |
    Alpha.DECREASING_ENABLE, 0, 4000,7000, 0, 0, 0, 0, 0);
```

If you think this sounds an awful lot like the triggerTime parameter described long ago, you are right. So what's the difference? Well, there isn't any, really. Currently, the semantics of both parameters are the same, so feel free to use either one. The alphaAtOneDuration is the number of milliseconds for the Alpha value to remain at 1.0. It is a pause between the increasingAlpha and decreasingAlpha components. Similarly, the alphaAtZeroDuration parameter is the time for which the Alpha component remains at 0.0.

Figure 7.9 has a complete graph of our Alpha wave with all the parts labeled:

0 to a = triggerTime/phaseDelayDuration

a to b = increasingAlphaDuration

b to c = alphaAtOneDuration

c to d = decreasingAlphaDuration

d to e = alphaAtZeroDuration

The actual graph would be repeated by the number of times specified in the loopCount parameter. The increasingAlphaRampDuration and decreasingAlphaRampDuration are not graphed here because, well, it would be too hard to do. Those values would have an effect on how steep the lines were between points a and b and points c and d. This is also the place to point out that, for every parameter in the Alpha constructor, there are equivalent get and set methods. For instance, for loopCount, there is:

```
int getLoopCount( )
void setLoopCount(int loopCount)
```

These allow for retrieving and setting these values after the Alpha object has been constructed. A final method to look at in the Alpha class is the finished( ) method.

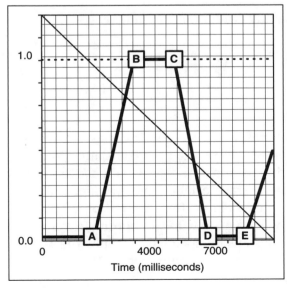

Figure 7.9 Alpha model.

```
boolean finished( )
```

This method can be used to determine if the Alpha has completed generating our Alpha wave. As long as we don't specify −1 for our loopCount parameter, the finished( ) method will eventually return True, indicating that our Alpha is complete. Whew! That should make us pretty much experts on the Alpha class. Now that we know how to construct Alpha objects with a variety of characteristics, let's look at how to use them.

Advanced Interpolators

We have seen only one use of an Alpha object: the PositionInterpolator. In fact, the Java 3D API provides a wide variety of interpolators that base their behavior on a given Alpha object. In this section, we will look at these objects in more detail.

PositionInterpolator

As demonstrated, a PositionInterpolator uses a given Alpha value to affect the translation component of an object. For all the preceding Alpha examples, we supplied only the minimum number of parameters needed, the Alpha object, and the TransformGroup the PositionInterpolator should modify. As we saw, this resulted in our object moving along the X-axis, starting at the center of our Java 3D window and moving to the right.

There is also a constructor that takes additional parameters:

```
PositionInterpolator(Alpha alpha,
TransformGroup target,
Transform3D axisOfTranslation,
          float startPosition,
          float endPosition) ;
```

The axisOfTranslation parameter allows us to specify any axis (think of it as a line oriented in 3D space) on which we want the translation to occur. For instance, to create a PositionInterpolator that would move objects along the Y-axis, we would create a Transform3D object (which will start out with the identity transform) and then perform a rotation of PI/2 (90 degrees) about the Z-axis. This will cause our local coordinate system to have a vertical X-axis (from the viewer's perspective, it is now the Y-axis). We comment out the PositionInterpolator in the previous Alpha example and replace it with the following lines:

```
Transform3D axis = new Transform3D();
axis.rotZ(Math.PI/2.0);
PositionInterpolator p = new
        PositionInterpolator(alpha,
            objTran s, axis, 1.0f, -1.0f);
```

Running this applet shows us that the cube does indeed move up and down in our window. The startPosition and endPosition parameters allow us to specify the beginning and ending positions over which the interpolation will occur. By default, these are set to 0.0 and 1.0, respectively. In our example here, they are set to 1.0 and −1.0 so that the box moves across the entire screen. Simply by reversing these two parameters can cause our box to move in the opposite direction. The toolkit provided with this book has interpolators for all three coordinate axes (Xoscillator, Yoscillator, and Zoscillator). The oscillators are a good place to start when experimenting with the use of PositionInterpolators.

RotationInterpolator

The RotationInterpolator will use the given Transform3D object (the target) to perform a rotation. Like the PositionInterpolator, there are two constructors. The first just takes our friendly Alpha object and a reference to the TransformGroup we want the interpolator to modify.

```
RotationInterpolator(Alpha alpha, TransformGroup target)
```

By default, this will perform a rotation about the Y-axis; and one Alpha wave (a complete $0.0 \to 1.0$ or $1.0 \to 0.0$ transition) will result in a rotation of 2 PI radians (360 degrees, or one complete circle).

The second constructor allows us to specify all the gory details.

```
RotationInterpolator(Alpha alpha,  TransformGroup target,
                Transform3D axisOfRotation,
                float minimumAngle,
                float maximumAngle)
```

The axisOfRotation is analogous to the axisOfTranslation of the previous PositionInterpolator. The minimumAngle and maximumAngle allow us to specify a range for the interpolation to occur. These values are specified in radians not degrees! To convert from degrees to radians, take your value and multiply by PI then divide by 180.

```
TransformGroup   group  =  new  TransformGroup( );
Alpha upRamp =  new Alpha;
```

```
upramp.setIncreasingAlphaDuration(10000);
upramp.setLoopCount(-1);   // -1 equals infinite loop

RotationInterpolator spinner = new
RotationInterpolator(upramp,group);
spinner.setAxisOfRotation(new Transform3D());
spinner.setMinimumAngle(0.0f);
spinner.setMaximumAngle((float) (Math.PI*2.0));
spinner.setSchedulingBounds(bounds);
group.addChild(spinner);
```

The last of the very specialized interpolators is the ScaleInterpolator. As you might imagine, the ScaleInterpolator affects the scale component of the specified Transform3D target object. The ScaleInterpolator has two constructors:

```
ScaleInterpolator(Alpha alpha, TransformGroup target)

ScaleInterpolator(Alpha alpha,
     TransformGroup target,
     Transform3D axisOfScale,
     float minimumScale,
     float maximumScale);
```

You can modify one of the toolkit's interpolator objects if you want to see the effects of this interpolator on geometry. The next set of interpolators affects the visual appearance of objects, rather than their position in our Java 3D window.

TransparencyInterpolator

The TransparencyInterpolator affects the transparency value of the specified TransparencyAttribute. The TransparencyAttributes are used to define how "see through" an object appears. Instead of the Alpha wave being used to affect the object's position, it is now used to affect the transparency value of a TransparencyAttribute object. As different Alpha values are generated, these are used to set the current transparency value. Again, these are the standard type of interpolator constructors:

```
TransparencyInterpolator(Alpha alpha,
                         TransparencyAttributes target)
```

Using this constructor will create a TransparencyInterpolator that maps an Alpha value of 1.0 to a transparency value of 1.0 (completely transparent); an Alpha of 0.0 maps to a transparency value of 0.0 (completely opaque).

```
TransparencyInterpolator(Alpha alpha,
                          TransparencyAttributes target,
                          float minimumTransparency,
                          float maximumTransparency)
```

This constructor gives us the added flexibility of specifying how to map the Alpha values to the transparency value. An Alpha of 1.0 will map to the maximum Transparency value, and a value of 0.0 will give us a transparency value of minimum transparency. Our standard Alpha test program is already set up to add a TransparencyInterpolator. Go to the line marked:

```
// Add TransparencyInterpolator code here
```

and add the following code:

```
 // Have the cube fade in and out of view by creating a
// TransparencyInterpolator.
TransparencyInterpolator ti = new TransparencyInterpolator(alpha,
                                  boxTransparency);
ti.setSchedulingBounds(bounds);
objTrans.addChild(ti);
```

PositionInterpolator

We are using the same Alpha object as the PositionInterpolator, so you should see the cube slowly fade to the background color (black, unless you've changed it) as it moves toward the right side of the screen (because the Alpha value is moving toward 1.0). The PositionInterpolator is very similar to the RotationInterpolator just explained above, including a code fragment example. Instead of setting a rotation angle, you set a starting and ending position. The interpolator will fill in all of the values in between to move an object from point A to point B. This is very cool for programming that next unmanned spacecraft with some predefined navigation through the Virtual Universe. Or, if you really need a lot of left and right turns, pitches and yaws, then you might want to use a PathInterpolator.

ColorInterpolator

The ColorInterpolator modifies the diffuse color of a Material object by interpolating between two colors. It works much like the TransparencyInterpolator we just looked at. The ColorInterpolator uses the Alpha wave to calculate the new diffuse color to set in the Material object. Like the TransparencyInterpolator, it has two constructors:

```
ColorInterpolator(Alpha alpha,
                     Material target)

ColorInterpolator(Alpha alpha, Material target,
       Color3f startColor, Color3f endColor)
```

These work as you would expect. The startColor will be the color for the object when the Alpha value is at 0.0, and the endColor will be the diffuse color of the object when the Alpha value reaches 1.0.

SwitchValueInterpolator

SwitchValueInterpolator interpolates over a specified set of child indices. This is good to use for simple animations, such as a walking Duke. Each geometry segment is created and organized as a range from 0 to n children, which is then switched. Another way to do animatronics is using the Morph node. Switch objects are another method for creating level of detail modes.

Understanding Behaviors

Like interpolators, behaviors bring our Java 3D worlds alive. Behaviors, however, are more generic than interpolators and therefore enable us to have much more control over when an event happens and what occurs once the specified event triggers our behavior. All behaviors share a basic structure. Each user-defined behavior must subclass the abstract Behavior class provided by the Java 3D API. Further, there are methods in this class that must be implemented by our subclassed Behavior object.

The method we must override is an initialization method:

```
public abstract void initialize()
```

This method is called for every behavior when it is made "live." That means the object is part of a live scene graph and is ready to be traversed and invoked by the Java 3D runtime process. In this routine, we can set some default state for our behavior and register our first WakeupCondition. A WakeupCriterion is a single event or logical combination of events that we tell Java 3D to alert our Behavior object about when they occur. These events can be an AWT event, a specified amount of time, or a certain number of frames. We inform Java 3D about the events our Behavior is interested in by calling:

```
public void wakeupOn(WakeupCondition condition)
```

This method will register the WakeupCriterion that we have constructed once an event that we specified interest in occurs (and we are in the behavior's schedulingBounds or schedulingBoundingleaf, of course).

The processStimulus method of our behavior is called:

```
public abstract void processStimulus(Enumeration criteria)
```

The Enumeration will list all WakeupCriterion that caused our behavior to be called. We can then perform specific actions based on which criteria occurred. Once we have done all our desired processing, it is necessary to tell Java 3D when our behavior should be called again. This is done by calling the wakeupOn method again. We can use the same or different WakeupCriteria, depending on the functionality we wish to achieve with our behavior. Once the new WakeupCriterion are registered, our behavior will again "go to sleep" and will awaken via a call to processStimulus, whenever an event we registered interest in occurs.

In order for any behavior to occur, we must specify the WakeupCriterion that our behavior is interested in. The Java 3D API provides a rich set of WakeupCriterion, or events that we can base our behaviors on. A behavior can wake up when some AWT event arrives to trigger the behavior action. Here are some of the criteria that can be specified:

WakeupOnAWTEvent	Mouse, keyboard, and AWT events
WakeupOnBehaviorPost & postId	A behavior or an AWT posts an event
WakeupOnActivation/Deactivation	Relative to condition
ElapsedFrames	After a number of rendering passes
ElapsedTime	After a period of time
SensorEntry/Exit	Penetrating a volume or boundary
CollisionEntry/Exit/Movement	Collisions with shapes/bounds
ViewPlatformEntry/Exit	Penetrating viewing volumes
TransformChange	A transform is modified

Some behaviors can be very complex, like in a battling game. In such cases, multiple wakeup criteria can be ANDed and ORed together to form wakeup conditions for the gaming behaviors. In addition to AWT events, behaviors can be activated when a shape's geometry collides with another shape. Collision detection can be estimated by using bounding volumes rather than geometry. One favorite trick is to shrink the bounding volume by 10 percent. That way, when the asteroid collides with the mother ship, on that close-up view, the wreck looks real and believable.

Creating Custom Behavior Classes

Often, you will want to create a specialized behavior that can be reused. The best thing to do is to put it into its own class and instantiate it when needed. The following is a discussion on how to lay out this Behavior class. We'll leave the fill-in-the-blanks to you. The first item of business is to create a file (i.e., CardBehavior.java) and to declare the class.

```
class CardBehavior extends Behavior {
}
```

You're going to need some basic imported Java classes and a neat little trick that we'll share with you. Consider the code example in Source 7.2. It provides a very good framework for doing just about any kind of behavior. It may become a staple when you start building your custom behavior classes.

Collision Detection

What's the value of Java 3D without a little destruction and mayhem? The following code fragment is your basic *Deep Impact* scenario. It's Armageddon time. The Earth has looped into the path of Jupiter and is about to be pulverized. You want to detect when the bounding volume of Jupiter intersects Earth's before activating the largest Fourth of July fireworks show this side of the Virtual Universe—just for the folks back home on Mars. Usually, the collision behavior is stuffed into its own file and class.

```
class Collide extends Behavior {

       // initialize colors, state, appearance components
       // needed to spark, fragment, crunch and explode
       // the scene.
       private boolean  impact = false;

       // Set up collision criteria
```

```
import javax.media.j3d.*;
import java.util.*;
import java.applet.*;
import java.net.URL;
import java.net.MalformedURLException;
import java.awt.*;
import java.awt.event.*;
import java.awt.AWTEvent;
import java.awt.event.MouseEvent;
import com.sun.j3d.utils.geometry.*;
import com.sun.j3d.utils.behaviors.picking.*;
import javax.vecmath.*;

/**
 *
 * The following behavior will process raw InputEvent subclass AWT
 * events, such as mouse and keyboard events. This behavior could
 * easily be modified to handle component and window events, but
 * only mouse and keyboard event handling are shown.
 *
 * Below are various event categories.
 *
 * KEYBOARD constants:
 *           Event.KEY_FIRST            Event.KEY_LAST
 *           Event.KEY_PRESSED          Event.KEY_RELEASED
 *           Event.KEY_TYPED
 * COMPONENT constants:
 *           ComponentEvent.COMPONENT_FIRST
 *           ComponentEvent.COMPONENT_HIDDEN
 *           ComponentEvent.COMPONENT_LAST
 *           ComponentEvent.COMPONENT_MOVED
 *           ComponentEvent.COMPONENT_RESIZED
 *           ComponentEvent.COMPONENT_SHOWN
 * MOUSE constants
 *           MouseEvent.MOUSE_PRESSED
 *           MouseEvent.MOUSE_RELEASED
 *           MouseEvent.MOUSE_CLICKED
 *           MouseEvent.MOUSE_DRAGGED
 *           MouseEvent.MOUSE_MOVED
 *           MouseEvent.MOUSE_ENTERED
 *           MouseEvent.MOUSE_EXITED
 * WINDOW constants
 *           WindowEvent.WINDOW_ACTIVATED
 *           WindowEvent.WINDOW_CLOSED
 *           WindowEvent.WINDOW_CLOSING
 *           WindowEvent.WINDOW_DEACTIVATED
```

continues

Source 7.2 Template for Building Custom Behavior Classes

```
*            WindowEvent.WINDOW_DEICONIFIED
*            WindowEvent.WINDOW_FIRST
*            WindowEvent.WINDOW_ICONIFIED
*            WindowEvent.WINDOW_LAST
*            WindowEvent.WINDOW_OPENED
*
*   (There are additional event types. Consult a Java resource.)
*
*------------------------------------------------------------
*    Credits:
*    CardBehavior program by Kirk Brown
*
*  ------------------------------------------------------------
*/

public class CardBehavior extends Behavior {

  // Declare any class variables and constants here
  //
  AppletContext acontext;
  BoundingSphere bounds;
  Switch newdeck;
  int count=0;
  int numcards=0;
  int x=0;
  int y=0;


  //
  // Portion of the scene graph to operate picking on. This
  // has been added so when the user presses RIGHT mouse down.
  //
  protected PickObject pickScene;

  // Define the triggers that will wake up the class methods to do
  // something. Add or subtract from this array. Add additional
  // tiggers and then fill out the appropriate code sections below
  // with additional methods. To disable, simply remove the trigger
  // from the WakeupCriterion array below.
  //
  // Notice the behavior will do something after 15 seconds
  // (15000 msecs) have elapsed. Yes I have included even a
  // useful timer to keep things active when the user is not.
  // Other triggers can be added as criterion below such as:
  //       Event.KEY_PRESS
  //       MouseEvent.MOUSE_DRAGGED
  //       ComponentEvent.COMPONENT_RESIZED
  //       ComponentEvent.COMPONENT_SHOWN
```

Source 7.2 Template for Building Custom Behavior Classes (*Continued*)

```
//          WindowEvent.WINDOW_ACTIVATED
//
WakeupCriterion criterion[] = {
  new WakeupOnAWTEvent(MouseEvent.MOUSE_PRESSED),
  new WakeupOnAWTEvent(WindowEvent.WINDOW_ACTIVATED),
  new WakeupOnElapsedTime( 15000 ) };

WakeupCondition conditions = new WakeupOr(criterion);

 /*-----------------------------------------------
  * Declared class constructors
  *---------------------------------------------*/

//
// It might be useful to pass this constructor scene
// graph transform group (the highest transform in the tree)
// and the Canvas3D object reference.
//
public CardBehavior(int numslides,
                    Switch deck,
                    AppletContext context,
                    Canvas3D canvas,
                    BranchGroup root) {

    // Pass needed info
    numcards = numslides;
    newdeck = deck;
    acontext = context;
    pickScene = new PickObject(canvas, root);
}


// Every Behavior class has to have an initialization method.
// This method is invoked by the Java 3D behavior scheduler.
// Classes that extend Behavior must provide their own init
// method.
//
public void initialize() {
        bounds = new BoundingSphere(
                new Point3d(0.0, 0.0, 0.0), 100);
        initialize(bounds);
}
public void initialize(BoundingSphere boundry) {
  count = 0;
  wakeupOn(conditions);
  setSchedulingBounds(boundry);
```

continues

Source 7.2 *Continued*

```
    }

/**
  *------------------------------------------------
  * Declared class methods
  *------------------------------------------------
  */

    // Create a method that animates the scene when
    // button is clicked or timer expires.
    //
    public void flipCard() {

        // Flip the card deck
        //
        if (count < numcards) {

            // Make sure the alpha is done and deal
            // a new card.
            //
            newdeck.setWhichChild(count);

            // Increment card count.
            count++;
        }
        else {
            count=0;
            newdeck.setWhichChild(0);
        }

        return;
    }

    // Create a method that will determine which Primitive object
    // was selected when the user clicked the LEFT mouse button and
    // then load the associated URL, if any.
    //
    public void loadURL() {

        Primitive shape;
        boolean result = false;

        // Find the currently selected "card" which is a Box
        // subclass of Primitive.
        shape = (Primitive)pickScene.pickNode(
            pickScene.pickClosest(x, y, PickObject.USE_BOUNDS),
            PickObject.PRIMITIVE);
```

Source 7.2   Template for Building Custom Behavior Classes (*Continued*)

```
            // Get the associated URL for this shape object which was set
            // earlier in the applet using the LocalData constructor.
            //
            if (shape != null) {
                URL shapeURL = ((LocalData)shape.getUserData()).getURL();

                try {
                  URL stub = new URL("http://stub");
                  result = shapeURL.sameFile(stub);
                }
                catch (MalformedURLException e) {
                        System.out.println("ERROR: PickURL URL");
                }

                // Valid URL to load.
                if (result == false) {

                    // Cause the browser to load the referenced URL
                    acontext.showDocument(shapeURL);
                }
            }

        return;
    }

// Declare and specify methods that will handle certain
// categories of events, like Mouse, Keyboard & Component.
//  Included are some code fragments to give you some ideas.
//
public void processMouseEvent(MouseEvent evt) {

    // Uses super class InputEvent to filter raw user input
    // event types of MouseEvent and KeyEvent. The method
    // getModifiers is used to determine which keys or mouse
    // buttons were down when the event occurs. But for our
    // applet behavior, we are only concerned with a single
    // mouse press to advance the next card. Be careful if
    // MOUSE_CLICKED is used. If the user drags the mouse at
    // the same time the click occurs, the event may go
    // undetected.

    // LEFT Mouse pressed. Ignore everything else.
    //
    if (evt.getID()==MouseEvent.MOUSE_PRESSED &&
            evt.getModifiers()==MouseEvent.BUTTON1_MASK) {
```

continues

Source 7.2   *Continued*

```
                    // Left mouse will cause the URL to be loaded
                    // but we first need the location of the pick
                    // which is used in our loadURL method.
                    //
                    switch (evt.getModifiers()) {
                        case MouseEvent.BUTTON1_MASK:
                            // Left Button generates X & Y
                            x = evt.getX();
                            y = evt.getY();
                            break;
                    }

                    // Load a URL reference document in the browser.
                    //
                    loadURL();
                    return;
            }

        // RIGHT Mouse Button pressed.
        //
        if (evt.getID()==MouseEvent.MOUSE_PRESSED &&
            evt.getModifiers()==MouseEvent.BUTTON3_MASK ) {

            // RIGHT mouse or the second button on most PC
            // mice will cause the card to shuffle.
            flipCard();
            return;
        }

/**
 *------------------------------------------------------------
 * Other logic that can be added shown here for reference
 *------------------------------------------------------------
 */
        // MIDDLE Mouse DRAG
        //
        //if (evt.getID()==MouseEvent.MOUSE_DRAGGED &&
        //    evt.getModifiers()==MouseEvent.BUTTON2_MASK ) return;

        // RIGHT Mouse Button pressed.
        //
        //if (evt.getID()==MouseEvent.MOUSE_PRESSED &&
        //    evt.getModifiers()==MouseEvent.BUTTON3_MASK ) return;

        // RIGHT Mouse DRAG
        //
        //if (evt.getID()==MouseEvent.MOUSE_DRAGGED &&
```

Source 7.2   Template for Building Custom Behavior Classes (*Continued*)

```
//       evt.getModifiers()==MouseEvent.BUTTON3_MASK ) return;

// Convenience methods for determining the state of the
// following keyboard modifiers. Shown here for instructional
// purpose.
//
//if (evt.isShiftDown()) return;
//if (evt.isAltDown()) return;
//if (evt.isControlDown()) return;
//if (evt.isMetaDown()) return;

// Sample switch to test button modifiers if that's all
// you need. Also notice you can get the location of an
// event. See Left button case.
//
//switch (evt.getModifiers()) {
//   case MouseEvent.BUTTON1_MASK:
//        // Left Button generates X & Y
//        x = evt.getX();
//        y = evt.getY();
//        break;
//
//   case MouseEvent.BUTTON2_MASK:
//        // Middle Button
//        break;
//   case MouseEvent.BUTTON3_MASK:
//        // Right Button
//        break;
//
// Example of looking for a double click
//
//if (evt.getClickCount() == 2) return;

return;

}  // END processMouseEvent

// Handles user events, such as a pressed or released key
// or a specific keyboard key or keyboard event. This will
// not be active unless the Event.KEY_PRESS wake up criterion
// has been specified. But we'll leave the code intact for
// instructional purposes.
//
// EVENT TYPE CONSTANTS:
//      KEY_FIRST     KEY_LAST         KEY_PRESSED
//      KEY_RELEASED  KEY_TYPED
```

continues

Source 7.2   *Continued*

```
// UNDEFINED KEY and CHARACTER CONSTANTS:
//      VK_UNDEFINED          CHAR_UNDEFINED
// ALPHANUMERIC CONSTANTS:
//      VK_A through VK_Z      VK_SPACE    VK_0 through VK_9
//      VK_NUMPAD0 through VK_NUMPAD9
// CONTROL KEY CONSTANTS:
//      VK_BACK_SPACE      VK_ENTER        VK_ESCAPE    VK_TAB
//      VK_ALT             VK_CAPS_LOCK    VK_CONTROL   VK_META
//      VK_SHIFT
// FUNCTION KEY CONSTANTS:
//      VK_F1 through VK_F12    VK_PRINTSCREEN    VK_SCROLL_LOCK
//      VK_PAUSE        VK_DELETE       VK_INSERT     VK_PAGE_DOWN
//      VK_PAGE_UP      VK_DOWN         VK_LEFT       VK_RIGHT
//      VK_UP           VK_END          VK_HOME       VK_ACCEPT
//      VK_NUM_LOCK     VK_CANCEL       VK_CLEAR      VK_CONVERT
//      VK_FINAL        VK_HELP         VK_KANA       VK_KANJI
//      VK_MODECHANGE   VK_NONCONVERT
// PUNCTUATION KEY CONSTANTS:
//      VK_ADD, VK_BACK_QUOTE, VK_BACK_SLASH, VK_CLOSE_BRACKET
//      VK_COMMA, VK_DECIMAL, VK_DIVIDE, VK_EQUALS, VK_MULTIPLY
//      VK_OPEN_BRACKET, VK_PERIOD, VK_QUOTE, VK_SEMICOLON,
//      VK_SEPARATOR, VK_SLASH, VK_SUBTRACT
//
private void processKeyEvent(KeyEvent evt) {

  int key;

  key = evt.getKeyCode();

  //if (key == KeyEvent.VK_UP) {
  //     System.out.println("DEBUG: VK_UP");
  //     return;
  //} else if ( key == KeyEvent.VK_DOWN) {
  //     System.out.println("DEBUG: VK_DOWN");
  //     return;
  //} else if ( key == KeyEvent.VK_LEFT) {
  //      System.out.println("DEBUG: VK_LEFT");
  //      return;
  //} else if ( key == KeyEvent.VK_RIGHT) {
  //      System.out.println("DEBUG: VK_RIGHT");
  //      return;
  //} else if ( key == KeyEvent.VK_PERIOD ) {
  //      System.out.println("DEBUG: VK_PERIOD");
  //      return;
  //} else if ( key == KeyEvent.VK_A ) {
  //      System.out.println("DEBUG: VK_A");
  //      return;
```

Source 7.2 Template for Building Custom Behavior Classes (*Continued*)

```
    //} else if (key==KeyEvent.VK_B ) {
    //      System.out.println("DEBUG: VK_B");
    //      return;
    //}

    return;

  }   // END processKeyEvent

// This method get called in a loop during runtime
// execution by the Behavior scheduler when the WakeUpCondition
// is detected. Classes that extend Behavior must provide
// their own processStimulus method. Notice have added a
// built-in timer. If the user just sits there, we will force
// an event to be posted after 15 seconds and the variable "timer"
// will be set to true.
//
public void processStimulus(Enumeration criteria) {

  // Define state variables
  WakeupCriterion wakeup;
  AWTEvent[] evt=null;
  boolean timer=false;

  while( criteria.hasMoreElements() ) {

    wakeup = (WakeupCriterion)criteria.nextElement();

    if (wakeup instanceof WakeupOnAWTEvent) {
       evt=((WakeupOnAWTEvent)wakeup).getAWTEvent();
       timer = false;
    }
    else if (wakeup instanceof WakeupOnElapsedTime) {
       timer = true;
    }

    // When an event has been detected, filter the event
    // type and call the appropriate method to handle the
    // event. Included is a stop watch in case something needs
    // to be accomplished by the user in a certain amount of
    // time.
    //
    if (evt!=null)
       for(int i=0; i<evt.length; i++) {
          if (evt[i] instanceof KeyEvent) {
             processKeyEvent((KeyEvent)evt[i]);
```

continues

Source 7.2   *Continued*

```
                                    timer = false;
                }
                if (evt[i] instanceof MouseEvent)  {
                    processMouseEvent((MouseEvent)evt[i]);
                    timer = false;
                }
                // Add IF statements here to add window and
                // component event filters.

            } // END for loop

        // If the timer has not expired don't animate. If the user
        // just sits there for 15 seconds, then we will animate.
        // If the user clicks the key/mouse button we disable the
        // timer.
        //
        if (timer) {
                flipCard();
        }

        // Inform the Java3D scheduler to wake up on specified
        // conditions. We're just kicking it to get some attention
        // on each loop.
        //
        wakeupOn(conditions);

    } // END WHILE loop

  }  // END ProcessStimulus

} // END Class
```

Source 7.2   Template for Building Custom Behavior Classes (*Continued*)

```
        WakeupOnCollisionEntry  enter;

        public Collide(Shape3D shape) {
                Appearance a = shape.getAppearance();

                // manipulate later
                impact = false;
        }

        public void initialize() {
                enter = new WakeUpOnCollisionEntry(shape);
                wakeupOn(enter);
```

```
        }

        public void processStimulus(Enumeration criteria) {

                if (impact) {

                        // fX action here. Planets blowing
                        // apart, etc.
                }
        }

}   // end of Collide behavior
```

Now the hard part is over: The basic behavior structure has been created. It would have been much more exciting to create some geometry morphing action that fragments and sends chunks of rock and fire in all directions while playing audio that goes kaboom! But we need to get back to reality so this chapter can end. Once the behavior has been created, it needs to be added to the scene.

```
public BranchGroup createSceneGraph() {
        // Create BranchGroup object
        // Create Earth and Jupiter shapes
        // Create transform groups for each and add behaviors to
        // animate the planets moving about in orbit

        // Create a collision behavior
        Collision bang = new Collision(earthShape);
        BoundingSphere bounds = new BoundingSphere(new
                Point3d(0.0,0.0,0.0), 2.0f);
        bang.setSchedulingBounds(bounds);

        // Add behavior to the scene
        objTrans.addChild(bang);
}
```

Finally, let's include the source code listing for the Shuffle program. The code is well documented and will provide some helpful insight. When you create animation for your scene, a behavior or multiple behaviors will most of the time control it. One behavior might signal other behaviors and so on. Source 7.3 will show how to create and invoke your custom behaviors. It uses multiple alphas and interpolators to get the animation job done.

```java
// Import needed JDK classes.
import java.applet.*;
import java.awt.BorderLayout;
import java.net.MalformedURLException;
import java.net.URL;

// Java 3D classes
import javax.media.j3d.*;
import com.sun.j3d.utils.applet.MainFrame;
import javax.vecmath.*;
import com.sun.j3d.utils.universe.*;
import com.sun.j3d.utils.geometry.*;
import com.sun.j3d.utils.image.TextureLoader;


/**-------------------------------------------------------------------
   Credits:
   Shuffle program by Kirk Brown

   A deck of cards with specified images can be shuffled in an
   animated fashion. The user can click on any card and jump to
   an associated URL which will load in the browser. This program
   is a type of 3D menu. Remember the images need to have widths
   and height in a power of 2 to work as textures in Java 3D. For
   example, 64x64, 128x128, etc. GIF and JPEG image formats are
   supported.

   -------------------------------------------------------------------*/
 public class Shuffle extends Applet {

   // Class variables.  The default values can be overridden
   // by using the PARAMS tag when invoking the applet.
   //
   // The following is the defined HTML interface to this program:
   //
   //        <PARAM NAME="numCards" VALUE="8">
   //                Value Options: "[number of defined cards]"
   //        <PARAM NAME="CardTexture1" VALUE="http://sun.com/card1.jpg">
   //                Value Options: "[path to *.jpg or *.gif]"
   //        <PARAM NAME="CardURL1" VALUE="http://www.sun.com">
   //                Value Options: "[HTML page associated
   //                                    with card]"

   // Array of texture names used by each "card".
   String[] texture =
       { "card1.gif", "card2.gif", "card3.gif" };

   URL[] imageURL = {null, null, null};
```

Source 7.3 Complete Shuffle Applet Code

```
    // Array of URLs associated with each "card".
    URL[] link = {null, null, null};

    // Total number of card.
    private int numCards = 3;

    // Every object that needs a Bounds will share
    // the same bounds object.
    BoundingSphere bounds;

    // Switch group that will cycle through each
    // Shape3D card object.
    Switch deck;

    // Array of card objects
    Box[] card = new Box[3];

    boolean applet = false;

    // Examines all parameters that can be passed in to this
    // applet and updates the global state to reflect any
    // non-default settings.
    private void lookForParameters() {

        // Used to read in the parameters for the applet.
        String paramValue;

        // Running as an applet.
        applet = true;

        // Find out the total number of "cards" or the number of
        // objects to switch in the scene.
        paramValue = getParameter("numCards");
        if (paramValue != null)
            numCards = Integer.parseInt(paramValue);
        else
            numCards = 3;

        // Allocate the needed array space.
        texture = new String[numCards];
        imageURL = new URL[numCards];
        link = new URL[numCards];

         //
         //Looks for parameter values for each "card".
         //
```

continues

Source 7.3   *Continued*

```
    for (int i = 0; i < numCards; i++) {

        // Look for the texture parameters.
        paramValue = getParameter("CardTexture" + (i + 1));
        if (paramValue != null) {
            URL linkURL;
            try {
                linkURL = new URL(paramValue);
            }
            catch (MalformedURLException e) {
                // Bad URL.
                linkURL = null;
            }
            imageURL[i] = linkURL;
        }
        else {
            // set it to blank
            imageURL[i] = null;
        }

        // Look for URL parameters.
        paramValue = getParameter("CardURL" + (i + 1));
        if (paramValue != null) {
            URL linkURL;
            try {
                linkURL = new URL(paramValue);
            }
            catch (MalformedURLException e) {
                // Bad URL.
                linkURL = null;
            }
            link[i] = linkURL;
        }
        else {
            // Default Value
            URL weblink;
            try {
                weblink = new URL("http://stub");
                link[i] = weblink;
            }
            catch(MalformedURLException e) {
                System.out.println("ERROR:" + paramValue);
            }
        }

    } // END FOR loop
} // END lookForParameters
```

Source 7.3 Complete Shuffle Applet Code (*Continued*)

```
        // Creates all the objects to be inserted in the scene graph.
        public BranchGroup createSceneGraph(Canvas3D c,
                                        AppletContext context) {

            Color3f aColor  = new Color3f(0.1f, 0.1f, 0.1f);
            Color3f eColor  = new Color3f(0.0f, 0.0f, 0.0f);
            Color3f dColor  = new Color3f(0.2f, 1.0f, 0.6f);
            Color3f sColor  = new Color3f(1.0f, 1.0f, 1.0f);
            Color3f lColor1 = new Color3f(0.7f, 0.7f, 0.7f);
            Vector3f lDir1  = new Vector3f(-1.0f, -0.3f, -1.0f);
            Color3f alColor = new Color3f(1.0f, 1.0f, 0.0f);
            Color3f ltcolor = new Color3f(1.0f, 1.0f, 1.0f);
            float rknots[] = {0.0f, 0.25f, 0.50f, 0.75f,
                            0.85f, 0.95f, 1.0f, 1.0f};
            Point3f exitRight[] = new Point3f[8];

            // Create the root of the branch graph.
            BranchGroup objRoot = new BranchGroup();

            // Scale all of the objects in the scene to
            // fit better.
            TransformGroup objScale = new TransformGroup();
            Transform3D t3d = new Transform3D();
            t3d.setScale(0.6);
            objScale.setTransform(t3d);
            objRoot.addChild(objScale);

            // Allocate the bounding sphere to be used with the all nodes.
            BoundingSphere bounds = new BoundingSphere(
                    new Point3d(0.0,0.0,0.0),100.0);

        // Create the card deck switch node - it will initially
        // display card 0, the first card in the deck until an event
        // advances the switch to the next card in the deck.
        //
        deck = new Switch(0);

        // Set needed capabilities:
        //  ALLOW_SWITCH_WRITE will allow the currently selected
        //     switch node child to be changed.
        //  ALLOW_CHILDREN_READ will allow the switch node to call
        //     the numChildren() and getChild() methods.  Needed
        //     during picking to find the picked node and
        //     associated URL.
        deck.setCapability(Switch.ALLOW_SWITCH_WRITE);
        deck.setCapability(Group.ALLOW_CHILDREN_READ);
```

continues

Source 7.3 *Continued*

```
          // This is the TransformGroup we will be modifying with
          // our spin interpolator to make the card spin as it is
          // shuffled. The interpolator is defined in the CardBehavior
          // class because we consider it "behavior-like", but it
          // could have been defined here. We must also allow the
          // Transform3D to be writeable after the scene graph is
          // made live so our behaviors can cause animation.
          //
          TransformGroup  spinTrans = new TransformGroup();
          spinTrans.setCapability(TransformGroup.ALLOW_TRANSFORM_WRITE);
          objScale.addChild(spinTrans);

          // While the previous transform spins the card, this
          // transform will move the spinning card along a path
          // using an alpha controlled position path interpolator
          // that is defined in the CardBehavior class file.
          //
          TransformGroup  flipTrans = new TransformGroup();

          // Must allow the Transform3D to be writeable after the
          // scene graph is made live so our behaviors can cause
          // animation. Add to the ordered tree structure which now
          // looks like objRoot->ObjScale->spinTrans->flipTrans. Any
          // object that is added to the flipTrans node will flip and
          // spin and will be scaled.
          flipTrans.setCapability(TransformGroup.ALLOW_TRANSFORM_WRITE);
          spinTrans.addChild(flipTrans);

          // Create the number of cards. Use a textured
          // appearance with a file the user interface
          // provided us with.
          //
          card = new Box[numCards];

          for (int i = 0; i < numCards; i++) {

              Appearance a = new Appearance();

              // Prepare possible solid lit color card
              Material m = new Material(aColor,
                          eColor, ltcolor, sColor, 0.0f);
              m.setLightingEnable(true);
              a.setMaterial(m);

              // If applet then expect URL references for the
              // images, else we are in "-demo" mode and we'll
              // be passing strings to the TextureLoader class.
```

Source 7.3   Complete Shuffle Applet Code (*Continued*)

```
            // If no image is specified, then we have prepared
            // a solid lit card surface (above).
            //
            if (applet == true) {
               if (imageURL[i] != null) {
                 TextureLoader t =
                           new TextureLoader(imageURL[i],
                                    new String("RGB"), this);
                   if (t != null)
                         a.setTexture(t.getTexture());
                }
            }
            else if (texture[i] != null) {
                   TextureLoader t =
                           new TextureLoader(texture[i],
                                    new String("RGB"), this);
                   if (t != null)
                         a.setTexture(t.getTexture());
            }

            card[i] = new Box(0.45f, 0.55f, 0.01f,
                           Box.GENERATE_NORMALS |
                           Box.GENERATE_TEXTURE_COORDS,
                           a);

            // Store URL in LocalData object and assign to this
            // primitive. Don't execute this if running -demo.
            if (applet == true) {
                LocalData ld = new LocalData(link[i]);
                card[i].setUserData(ld);
            }

            deck.addChild(card[i]);

    } // END for loop

    // Add Switch node to Transform Group
    flipTrans.addChild(deck);

    // The Switch node alpha. This is a simple alpha object that
    // will be used to cycle through each child node under the
    // switch node.  Each child node is considered one "card".
    //
    Alpha alpha = new Alpha();
    alpha.setPhaseDelayDuration(7000);
    alpha.setIncreasingAlphaDuration(8000);
```

continues

Source 7.3 *Continued*

```
            alpha.setLoopCount(-1);

            // Make the card spin by the modification of
            // the spinTrans object triggered by the alpha
            // timer. Add to the spin Transform Group.
            RotationInterpolator spin =
                        new RotationInterpolator(alpha, spinTrans);
            spin.setAxisOfRotation(new Transform3D());
            spin.setMinimumAngle(0.0f);
            spin.setMaximumAngle( (float)(Math.PI * 8.0) );
            spin.setSchedulingBounds(bounds);
            spinTrans.addChild(spin);

            // Setup a pre-determined flight path for the card after
            // the user clicks the top card on the deck and we send it
            // flying to the right and to the back of the pile.
            //
            exitRight[0] = new Point3f(0.0f, 0.0f, 0.0f);
            exitRight[1] = new Point3f(0.0f, 0.0f, 0.0f);
            exitRight[2] = new Point3f(1.0f, 0.0f, -0.3f);
            exitRight[3] = new Point3f(1.0f, 0.5f, -0.5f);
            exitRight[4] = new Point3f(1.0f, 1.0f, -0.75f);
            exitRight[5] = new Point3f(1.0f, 3.0f, -1.0f);
            exitRight[6] = new Point3f(1.0f, 8.0f, -1.0f);
            exitRight[7] = new Point3f(0.0f, 0.0f, 0.0f);

            // Flip the card according to our flight path.
            //
            PositionPathInterpolator shuffle =
                    new PositionPathInterpolator(alpha,
                                        flipTrans,
                                        new Transform3D(),
                                        rknots,
                                        exitRight);

            shuffle.setSchedulingBounds(bounds);
            flipTrans.addChild(shuffle);

            // We are going to have a deck of cards that peels off to the
            // right, spins a few times and ends up at the back of the deck
            // after each mouse click over the window or after 20 seconds
            // of user inactivity. To hyperlink to the associated URL with
            // each card, the user presses the key "w" on the keyboard, for
            // Web, and the linked URL web page is loaded.
            //
            CardBehavior flipper = new CardBehavior(numCards,
                                                    deck,
```

Source 7.3 Complete Shuffle Applet Code (*Continued*)

```
                                                 context,
                                                 c,
                                                 objRoot);
        objRoot.addChild(flipper);

        AmbientLight algt = new AmbientLight(alColor);
        algt.setInfluencingBounds(bounds);

        DirectionalLight dlgt = new DirectionalLight(lColor1, lDir1);
        dlgt.setInfluencingBounds(bounds);

        objRoot.addChild(algt);
        objRoot.addChild(dlgt);

        return objRoot;
    }
public void init() {

        AppletContext context = null;

      // If we are running as an applet we need to
      // initialize values according to the user settings in
      // the HTML file accomplished by lookForParameters().
      // Otherwise we'll just use the values used to initialize
      // the local variable declarations at the top of the block.
      //
      if (getParameter("numCards") != null) {
              context = getAppletContext();
              lookForParameters();
      }

        // Initialize the Layout Manager and create the Canvas3D
        // object.
        setLayout(new BorderLayout());
        Canvas3D c = new Canvas3D(null);
        add("Center", c);

        // Create a simple scene and attach
        // it to the virtual universe
        BranchGroup scene = createSceneGraph(c, context);
        SimpleUniverse u = new SimpleUniverse(c);

        // This will move the ViewPlatform back a bit so the
        // objects in the scene can be viewed.
        u.getViewingPlatform().setNominalViewingTransform();
```

continues

Source 7.3 *Continued*

```
            // Add the created scene graph to our universe.
         u.addBranchGraph(scene);
    }
      //
      // The following allows Shuffle to be run as an application
      // as well as an applet
      //
      public static void main(String[] args) {

        if (args.length > 0) {
            // Parse Input Arguments
            for (int i = 0; i < args.length; i++) {

                if (args[i].equals("-demo")) {
                    new MainFrame(new Shuffle(), 400, 400);
                } else {
                    System.out.println("Usage: java Shuffle -demo");
                    System.exit(0);
                }
            }
        } else {
            System.out.println("Usage: java Shuffle -demo");
            System.exit(0);
        }

    }   // END Main
} // END Class
```

Source 7.3   Complete Shuffle Applet Code (*Continued*)

Moving On

We have now completed our introduction to new types of Java 3D classes that perform action and animation. We have discussed the primary Java 3D objects designed for this purpose: behaviors and interpolators. You also have the basic idea of how to create your own custom Behavior classes in order to produce specific "triggers" from specific "conditions." Now get out there and create the next-generation 3D game! Hey, where is all of this fog coming from?

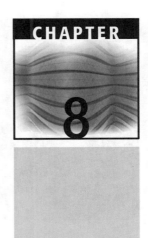

CHAPTER

8

Fog Effects

"Dense fog was blamed for a pile-up of cars on Interstate 5. Visibility was down to 15 feet."

—CNN HEADLINE NEWS

Computer-generated fog increases the realism of a scene when creating virtual weather effects or dark spooky caverns and dungeons. Fog is also used in computer graphics as a trick to increase rendering performance and scene efficiency. The further the viewer can see in a 3D scene, the more objects have to be displayed, which consumes memory and CPU cycles. Fog is used to limit the viewer's sight—whatever the viewer can't see the program doesn't have to render.

Fog Applet Description and Usage

The fog applet (Figure 8.1) is a clever illusion that keeps the viewer's attention by playing hide-and-seek with a favorite 3D object or picture. The mini-scene is created as a hazy or dark atmosphere, which simulates early morning fog or smoke. The applet controls the movement of the objects within the fog effect and the interval of revealing the object. Variations can be achieved by modifying the HTML file.

Figure 8.1   Java 3D fog.

Fog Applet Parameters Explained

When the user surfs to the Web page that contains the Fog applet, the program is invoked. One of the first things the applet program does is parse the list of attributes identified by the "param" keyword in the HTML file. Each parameter has an associated value. These values will set specific attributes in the Fog demo that will be seen at runtime.

Let's discuss how the parameter values affect the visual rendering of the demo:

FogNumSlides.   You will need to specify how many slide images you intend to flip through, then provide the appropriate parameters for each. For example, if you specify three, you will need to include FogObject1, 2, and 3; FogTexture1, 2, and 3; and FogURL1, 2, and 3. If you forget any of these supporting parameters, the program logic will fill in the gaps where it can and use default settings. These are probably *not* what you have in mind, and you will notice your oversight right away.

FogObject[n].   Used to specify the shape or object within the applet. By default, a three-dimensional cube is used. The following values can be used to change the shape:

```
value="cube"
value="rectangle"
value="sphere"
value="cylinder"
```

FogOrbitSpeed.   This parameter sets the speed at which the object "orbits" the 3D scene, around the Z-axis. The value does not change the orientation, just the speed of the object traveling along this fixed orbit. The smaller the number, the faster the orbiting speed.

```
value="15000"
```

FogSlideDelay.   This parameter will change how often the viewer sees the object in the scene—a sort of delayed effect. The value can be set from 0 to any number. Zero is off, and the object remains fixed. Time is measured in milliseconds, so 7,000 milliseconds is about 1 second.

```
value="27000"
```

FogTexture[n].   Specifies an image to lay over the provided 3D shape. This is known as texture mapping. The image or picture must be in the GIF or JPEG format. The image file value needs to use a URL reference.

FogURL[n].   Associates a URL address or local HTML file with a specific 3D object in the 3D scene. When the user clicks over the object, the browser will load the page to the specified location.

value = http://www.sun.com

Fog HTML File Explained

The HTML file for the applet is included on the book's CD. Use it to run the applet in a browser. You'll need to edit the parameter portions in the provided HTML to specify your changes. Refer to Chapter 4 for the details on interpreting the syntax of this file.

Understanding Fog Concepts

Everybody has experienced driving through fog. Your visibility is limited, and objects appear faded. Even the color of the surrounding objects is affected. If you live in the rich, fertile Central Valley of California, the fog can block the Sun's light for days, and one incredible scene is watching the fog roll into the San Francisco Bay from a high vantage point. A tall bank of white thick air crawls over the Golden Gate Bridge, engulfing it; the fog proceeds to fill the Bay until it is finally contained by the coastal mountain range surrounding the Bay's perimeter. Special weather conditions create this fog: Moist, mild air is transported over cold ground, and the air is cooled to the condensation point. The result: very dense fog.

The mystery of 3D graphics is its ability to model physical objects or phenomena, like fog, by manipulating the bits and pixels of the computer display using mathematical computation. The math has been around for some time, but until recently, the hardware didn't support 3D graphics very well, or was unable to process the amount of data within a tolerable amount of time. Remember, not too long ago, waiting 24 hours for a complex scene to render? Today's computers can render such scenes in an instant and cost under $3,000. The point is, today's graphics hardware is sufficient to simulate the real world, and computers use clever tricks to fool the eye. Take simulated fog, for example.

The human eye can see objects because light reflects off the object and back to our eyes, at close to the speed of 186,000 miles per second (Figure 8.2). When light bounces off an object, it is reflected; the effect of this reflection is variable. What does this have to do with anything? The Java 3D Fog node object attempts to represent this within a mathematical model. Reflective and attenuated light give depth and volume to objects. In computer graphics, this is called *depth-cueing*, affectionately renamed fog or smoke.

Depth-Cueing

Fog, or Depth-cueing, is a special effect used in computer graphics for added realism. It adds depth and a three-dimensional illusion to the rendering of a virtual 3D scene onto a two-dimensional hardware display (Figure 8.3). Object colors and color intensity fade to a specified value over a specified distance. An algorithm modulates the intensity of color, proportional to the distance from the viewer.

Decreasing the light intensity of distant objects in the graphic scene creates the fog "trick." As in real life, a landscape panorama will show a crisp, clear stand of trees or lake in the foreground and a dull, muted mountain range several miles away in the backdrop.

Fog effects can be added to outdoor scenes to create smoky, hazy landscapes. By changing the color, this effect can also simulate dark, deep, and

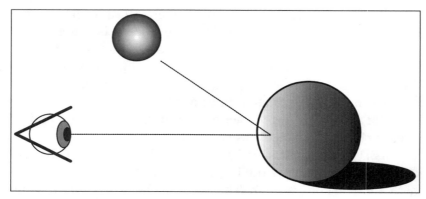

Figure 8.2 Reflected light.

Figure 8.3   Without/with fog applied.

murky ocean water. Change the color again, and it looks like smoke. Add fog to an indoor scene to create dark, creepy dungeons and labyrinths.

Java 3D Fog Node

The Fog node is grouped within the Leaf node of the Java 3D API because it has no children and is considered "atomic." The Fog node shares its place in the Scene Graph superclass, along with other friends, such as sound, lighting, and clipping, to name a few. The Scene Graph object is the common superclass, or parent, for all components under javax.media.j3d .SceneGraphObject.

The Node object class has two subclasses: Group and Leaf node objects. The Group node composes, transforms, selects, and in general, modifies its descendant nodes. The Leaf node is a collection of shape objects (Figure 8.4) and other entities, such as fog and sound. The Leaf node serves as a

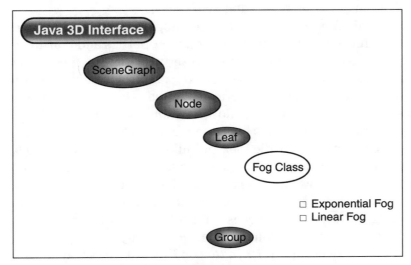

Figure 8.4   A partial class hierarchical diagram of the Leaf node.

template or framework of methods and variables for a particular kind of graphic object. "Node" is simply a term given to objects, which together form a Scene Graph.

LEAF NODE	**GROUP NODE**
Background	Billboard
Behavior	BranchGroup
Clip	Definition
Deferred Instance	Level of Detail (LoD)
Fog	Ordered Group
Instance	Coplanar
Light	Shared Group
Link	Switch
Morph	TransformGroup
Shape	
Sound	
Soundscape	
View Platform	

The Leaf node generally contains the visual, auditory, and behavioral components of the scene. The computer-generated scene really represents a hierarchy of objects, which when diagramed, looks like an upside-down tree, with branches graphed from the root. As in VRML, the Scene Graph is an ordered collection of Group nodes and Leaf nodes.

A node is any combination of information and logic that is encapsulated into an entity. The information is made up of data properties and constants used to enable/disable object features and to reserve storage elements that will be used to track the state and behaviors of the object at runtime. Sound like a Java class? It is a Java class. The term "node" has always been associated with things like org charts, control flow diagrams, and Ethernet drops on a subnetwork. But in this case, it's borrowed from VRML.

Java 3D has been provided for the task of building complex 3D scenes, which are easy to construct, and simple to manipulate the objects they contain. You can appreciate how 3D objects, their behaviors and attributes, have been organized into an object-oriented model. This beats the days when constructing 3D wireframe scenes with a list of points, when connected formed polygon shapes. You could never create complex scenes such as those seen in movies like *Terminator* or *Toy Story* this way.

Creating Fog in a Scene

Now let's get into creating some fog. Recall the basic programming template that you have seen in previous chapters. Here's the one for the fog effect, in a step-by-step procedure:

1. Create a Scene Graph.
2. Establish a Virtual Universe.
3. Establish Locale.
4. Create a new view.
5. Associate a Canvas3D object to the view.
6. Create a new BranchGroup node for the view platform.
7. Create a new BranchGroup node for the object.
8. Create a new 3D Transform object—because we want the object to move around.
9. Create a Vector object and initialize it with a value.
10. Create a new ViewPlatform object.
11. Associate the Transform object with a newly created Transform Group.
12. Attach the view to the view platform.
13. Create a 3D shape.
14. Create a Behavior object, such as rotation to spin our shape.
15. Create and schedule the Bounding volume.
16. Create a new Fog node.
17. Specify Bounds.
18. Specify scope.
19. Add the node as a child of the Root object.
20. Attach subgraphs to the Virtual Universe objects. The Scene Graph is now live.

Next, we will discuss some additional methods, constructors, and constants that provide greater functionality to set, modify, and get various Fog-related attributes and information. Source 8.1, listed at the end of this chapter, was used to generate the demonstration program. Please take the time to read through the code, as it is well documented and should help a great deal in understanding the Java 3D Fog class.

Understanding Fog Constants

The following node constants are used by the application at runtime to enable the following capabilities using the setCapability method:

```
ALLOW_INFLUENCING_BOUNDS_READ
ALLOW_INFLUENCING_BOUNDS_WRITE
```

When enabled, these flags invoke methods that read or write to the region of influence. This is an area specified to indicate in which region the Fog node is active.

```
ALLOW_COLOR_READ
ALLOW_COLOR_WRITE
```

These flags enable the application to read and write color attributes of the particular Fog node.

Fog and Related Constructors

Each of these constructors creates a new Fog node.

```
public Fog ( )
public Fog ( float r, float g, float b )
public Fog ( Color3f color )
```

The first example uses the following default values for each method parameter:

color: Black (0.0f,0.0f,0.0f), specified as a triplet of RBG values.

list of scoping nodes: Empty

influencing region: Empty

The second example constructs a Fog node with the specified fog color. The parameters represent a RED, GREEN, and a BLUE color value, each specified as a float number from 0 to 1. For example, (0 .25 0) defines a dark shade of GREEN.

The third method gets its color for the Fog node from the value at the specified x, y, and z coordinate location. There are two types of fog to select. The default is exponential, but what's the difference? Let's take a quick detour and focus on bounding volumes first, called *influencing regions*.

Influencing Region and Scope

Each Fog node needs to define just two parameters: the fog's color and the Bounds object, which defines a 3D volume or region. When an object's bounding box intersects the Fog node's region of influence, fog is applied to that object's color after lighting and texture have been applied. VRML was only capable of applying fog to a global region that engulfed all objects. By defining multiple Fog nodes, Java 3D provides greater control and detail over the scene composed of possibly numerous objects.

To manage the application of fog among several scene objects, Java 3D provides a list that can be used to identify which nodes will receive the fog effect. This is called *node scoping*. The list represents the hierarchical scope of the specific Fog node. If the list of scoping nodes is empty, fog is applied to all nodes in the scene or Virtual Universe. But, again, these objects must be within the Fog node's region of influence or selected groups of nodes, to which fog is applied (see Figure 8.5).

If the Fog node region of influence among multiple Fog nodes overlaps, the vendor implementation of the Java 3D Spec will choose a single set of fog attributes to apply to those objects that lie within the intersection. But, in general, the Fog node and its parameters closest to the object are selected.

The bounding volume specified for the Fog node can be a box, a sphere, or a *polytope* (a set of planes that define a convex, closed polygonal bounding region). A Bounds class, with a set of methods and constructors, defines the bounding region passed to the Fog methods.

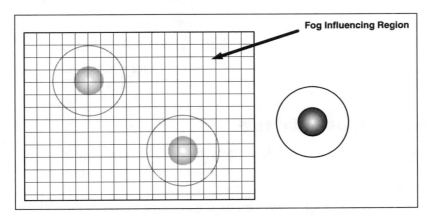

Figure 8.5 Two objects in a Fog node region, and the effect is applied.

Fog and Related Methods

To set the fog to a specified color, you use an RGB triplet or x, y, z coordinate. Get the color from a given vector.

```
setColor ( float r, float g, float b )
setColor ( Color3f, color )
getColor ( Color3f, color )
```

Next set the Fog node's influencing bounds. Get the influencing bounds information from the Fog node.

```
setInfluencingBounds ( Bounds region )
getInfluencingBounds ( )
```

Then set the Fog's influencing region to the specified bounding leaf. When set to a value other than NULL, this overrides the influencing bounds objects.

```
setInfluencingBoundingLeaf ( BoundingLeaf region )
getInfluencingBoundingLeaf ( )
```

The following method manipulates the Fog node's hierarchical scope:

`setScope( Group scope, int index )`	Specify scope at index.
`getScope( int index )`	Get scope at index location.
`addScope( Group scope)`	Append scope to node's scope list.
`insertScope( Group scope,int index )`	Insert scope at index.
`removeScope( int index )`	Remove scope at index.
`numScopes ()`	Return count of Fog's scopes.
`getAllScopes ()`	Return enumeration object of all scopes.

Linear versus Exponential Fog

The Fog node has two subnodes that apply a linear or exponential fog equation to render a varied effect. The Fog Leaf node is extended to include two additional classes (Figure 8.6). The density value is defined in the local coordinate system of the Fog node. Linear fog specifies a pair of Z-values, which direct the equation of WHEN to start the fog and WHEN to set a max-

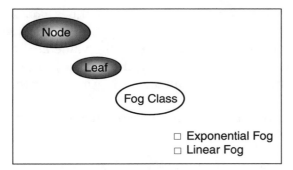

Figure 8.6   The Fog Leaf node.

imum fog density. The effect obscures the object or scene toward the back, such as the image in Figure 8.1.

Exponential Fog

The following constants are provided:

```
public static final int ALLOW_DENSITY_READ
public static final int ALLOW_DENSITY_WRITE
```

The flags are enabled by using the setCapability( ) method, after which the application can use methods to read and write the fog density values. Remember, the node has to be alive or attached to a compiled scene graph before the capability is allowed.

The following constructors are provided for exponential fog:

```
public ExponentialFog ( )
public ExponentialFog ( float r, float g, float b)
public ExponentialFog ( Color3f   color)
public ExponentialFog ( float r, float g, float b, float density)
public ExponentialFog ( Color3f  color, float  density)
```

This is how you create a new Exponential Fog node: The first constructor uses the following default value:

density: 1.0

The second method constructs a Fog node with the specified fog color. The parameters represent a RED, GREEN, and BLUE color value, each specified as a float number from 0 to 1. For example, (0 .25 0) defines a dark shade of GREEN.

The third method gets its color for the Fog node from the value at the specified x, y, z coordinate location. The fourth and fifth constructors are redundant as to how the color parameter is specified, but they add the density value as a parameter.

The Exponential Fog node provides the following methods to get or modify the density value in the Fog node:

```
public final void setDensity (float density)
public final float getDensity ( )
```

Linear Fog

As in real fog on the computer screen, from your eyes to a distance, objects are obscured and eventually hidden the farther away the objects are from you. To create this same effect graphically, a pair of distant values in the Z direction are added to the parameter list. The first Z-value represents the starting position of the fog effect in the local coordinate system of the node. The second Z-value is the position at which the scene or object will completely be obscured (see Figure 8.7).

Linear fog provides the following constants enabled with the setCapability ( ) method:

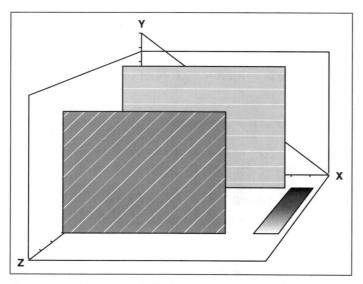

Figure 8.7 The linear gradation of fog (back to front view).

```
public static final int ALLOW_DISTANCE_READ
public static final int ALLOW_DISTANCE_WRITE
```

The values can be accessed and modified when the node is attached to a compiled scene graph and enabled.

To create linear fog, the following constructors are provided:

```
public LinearFog ( )
public LinearFog ( float r, float g, float b )
public LinearFog ( Color3f color )
public LinearFog ( float r, float g, float b, double frontDistance,
        double backDistance)
public LinearFog ( Color3f color, double frontDistance,
        double backDistance)
```

The first constructor uses the following default values. The remaining constructors use specified values for the Z distance to the front and back distance planes:

front distance: 3.5

back distance: 5.0

The second method constructs a Fog node with the specified fog color. The parameters represent a RED, GREEN, and BLUE color value, each specified as a float number from 0 to 1. For example, (0 .25 0) defines a dark shade of GREEN.

The third method gets its color for the Fog node from the value at the specified x, y, z coordinate location. The last constructors are redundant, except that a pair of Z-values are specified for the front and back distances, respectively. The fog's colors will spectrum between these two distances.

The following four methods are used to access and modify the pair of Z-values used in linear fog:

```
public final void setFrontDistance(float,  frontDistance)
public final float getFrontDistance( )
public final void setBackDistance(float, backDistance)
public final float getBackDistance( )
```

The front distance is the coordinate position at which the fog starts obscuring objects. The back distance is the position at which the fog fully obscures objects. Objects positioned closer than the front distance parameters are not affected by fog. This is also true for objects farther than the back distance value. This concludes our discussion of creating fog effect.

Summary

In summary, let's step through creating a Java 3D applet and use some of the interfaces we have discussed in this chapter. By now, you have a couple of chapters on the Java 3D API under your belt. If you are like the rest of the pack, the information is slowly soaking in. We have tried to repeat the general Java 3D API implementation framework in order for you to get a clearer and clearer understanding. Let's begin again.

We are building a Fog object. It is composed of data, as well as data and methods from other objects. We are going to access the methods of various Java 3D objects to help construct an applet. We will also add logic, so that our program can run as a standalone application. We will need to create about five logical parts of our object. The outermost part of our object is a class declaration. This will be the container that holds all of our data and methods for our Fog class.

```
public class Fog extends Applet {
```

In this instance, we are extending the Fog class as a subclass of Applet. This gives us access to all public data and methods of the Applet class! We will be reusing code from other objects. Most programmers prefer to write less code, if some is just lying around. This illustrates one of the reasons they call it object-oriented programming.

So, we have our class declaration, and we need to fill it up with stuff. Basically, we are looking at one constructor (a constructor is used to initialize the Java program), two methods, and a Main( ) method. At the top of the file are import statements that provide us access to the location of those other objects we need to build our program. These will include Java 3D objects, Java objects, and Vector Math objects. Ahhhhh math! Don't panic, because other Java objects do all of the calculations for you. Life couldn't be better.

Things kind of get stacked from the bottom up, so let's start with the Main( ) method. It's going to invoke a class that will create a window frame for us (handled by the browser, in the case of applets) and call the Fog( ) constructor all in one short order. It also passes any command-line arguments downstream, along with the 600×400 frame window size.

```
public static void main(String[] args) {
    new MainFrame(new Fog(args), 600, 400);
}
```

This is very easy to realize if the program is started as: *java Fog -demo -fast -wild.*

All of these arguments need to make it into the program, somehow. Wonder what "wild" does? Next we create the Fog( ) constructor, just above our main logic block. The constructor will create all of the core building blocks of a Java 3D program—we are talking the Universe, the Locale, and the SceneGraph—and add everything to the scene for rendering. From this constructor is called the heart and workhorse of the Java 3D program: createSceneGraph( ). This stacked on top of Main( ) and Fog( ) in our file called Fog.java.

The createSceneGraph method does a whole host of things:

- Creates the desired 3D object to be inserted in the SceneGraph.
- Creates the root of the BranchGraph.
- Creates an Appearance object, used to texture-map the object.
- Invokes the Java 3D texture loader to read in the pixel map file as the texture.
- Creates 3D geometry using the provided Java 3D utilities.
- Adds everything to the SceneGraph.
- Creates the LinearFog node. The first three parameters are color-represented as floats for the color black. The next parameter is the front plane in distance Z, which determines where the fog starts. The last parameter is the back plane in Z, and determines where the scene will be completely obscured. The front plane value must be less than the back plane value. The Linear Fog operation will graduate the color between the two planes.
- Allocates a bounding region in a spherical shape.
- Adds the Fog node to the SceneGraph.
- Returns the objRoot value, and we are done creating the SceneGraph.

Finally, we need to create a method that parses the parameters being passed from the HTML Applet interface. The lookForParameters( ) method handles all of this. Get "wild" in the HTML interface will usually set a local constant or variable that will be used somewhere later in the program logic.

Java 3D Fog Class Code

The following is the source code listing of a Fog class example. Please review the code comments for additional information and instruction.

```
// Import needed JDK classes.
import java.applet.*;
import java.awt.BorderLayout;
import java.net.MalformedURLException;
import java.net.URL;

// Import the Java 3D API.
import javax.media.j3d.*;

// Import the vector mathematics API.
import javax.vecmath.*;

// Import the needed Java 3D utility classes.
import com.sun.j3d.utils.universe.*;
import com.sun.j3d.utils.geometry.*;
import com.sun.j3d.utils.image.TextureLoader;
import com.sun.j3d.utils.applet.MainFrame;


/**-----------------------------------------------------------------
   Credits:
   Fog program by Dan Petersen and Kirk Brown
   Orbit/Rotate Behaviors provided by Dan Petersen.
   -------------------------------------------------------------*/
public class Fog extends Applet {

    // Class variables.  The default values can be overridden
    // by using the PARAMS tag when invoking the applet.
    //
    // The following is the defined HTML interface to this program:
    //
    //        <PARAM NAME="FogNumSlides" VALUE="8">
    //                Value Options: "[number of defined slides]"
    //        <PARAM NAME="FogOrbitSpeed" VALUE="2700">
    //                Value Options: "[time value in milliseconds]"
    //        smaller the number faster the orbit
    //        <PARAM NAME="FogSlideDelay" VALUE="42000">
    //                Value Options: "[time value in milliseconds]"
    //                larger the number = more delay between slides
    //        <PARAM NAME="FogObject1" VALUE="rectangle">
    //                Value Options: "[rectangle,sphere,cube,cylinder]"
    //        <PARAM NAME="FogTexture1" VALUE="tex1.jpg">
    //                Value Options: "[path to *.jpg or *.gif]"
    //        <PARAM NAME="FogURL1" VALUE="http://www.sun.com">
    //         Value Options: "[HTML page associated with slide number]"

    // Total number of slides.
    private int numSlides = 8;
```

Source 8.1 Complete Java 3D Fog Class

```
    // Orbit Speed (msecs)
    private int orbitSpeed = 10000;

    // Switch to next slide delay (msecs)
    private int delaySpeed = 90000;

    // Used to assign FogObject parameter.
    private static final int CUBE      = 1;
    private static final int RECTANGLE = 2;
    private static final int SPHERE    = 3;
    private static final int CYLINDER  = 4;

    // Array of primitives used for each "slide".
    private int[] primitive = {
            CUBE, CUBE, CUBE, CYLINDER,
            CUBE, CUBE, CUBE, SPHERE };

    // Array of texture names used by each "slide".
    private String[] texture = {
            "Tex1.jpg", "Tex2.jpg", "Tex3.jpg",
            null, "Tex4.jpg", "Tex5.jpg", null,
            "Tex7.jpg", "Tex8.jpg" };

    // Array of URLs associated with each "slide".
    private URL[] link = {
            null, null, null, null,
            null, null, null, null };

    // Applet URL image references
    URL[] imageURL = {
            null, null, null, null,
            null, null, null, null };

    // Switch group that will cycle through each Shape3D object.
    Switch slides;

    // Every object that need a Bounds will share the same bounds object.
    BoundingSphere bounds;

    Primitive[] shapes;

    boolean applet = false;

    // Examines all parameters that can be passed in to this
    // applet and updates the global state to reflect any
```

continues

Source 8.1 *Continued*

```
    // non-default settings.
    private void lookForParameters() {

        // Used to read in the parameters for the applet.
        String paramValue;

        // Running as an applet.
        boolean applet = true;

        // Find out the total number of "slides" - the number of
        // objects to switch in the scene.
        paramValue = getParameter("FogNumSlides");
        if (paramValue != null)
            numSlides = Integer.parseInt(paramValue);
        else
            numSlides = 1;

        // Allocate the needed array space.
        primitive = new int[numSlides];
        link = new URL[numSlides];
        imageURL = new URL[numSlides];
        shapes = new Primitive[numSlides];

         // Set the speed of the orbiting objects
         //
         paramValue = getParameter("FogOrbitSpeed");
         if (paramValue != null)
             orbitSpeed = Integer.parseInt(paramValue);
         else
             orbitSpeed = 2400;

        // Set the delay between slides in milliseconds
        //   7000 = 1 sec.
        //
        paramValue = getParameter("FogSlideDelay");
        if (paramValue != null)
                delaySpeed = Integer.parseInt(paramValue);
        else
                delaySpeed = 33000;

        //
        //Looks for parameter values for each slide.
        //
        for (int i = 0; i < numSlides; i++) {

            // Look for the object parameters.
            paramValue = getParameter("FogObject" + (i + 1));
```

Source 8.1   Complete Java 3D Fog Class (*Continued*)

```
            // see if this parameter was passed in.
            if (paramValue != null) {
                // Compare string
                if (paramValue.equalsIgnoreCase("rectangle") == true)
                    primitive[i] = RECTANGLE;
                else if (paramValue.equalsIgnoreCase("sphere") == true)
                    primitive[i] = SPHERE;
                else if (paramValue.equalsIgnoreCase("cylinder") == true)
                    primitive[i] = CYLINDER;
                else
                    primitive[i] = CUBE;

            }
            else
                // Default value.
                primitive[i] = CUBE;

            // Look for the texture parameters.
            paramValue = getParameter("FogTexture" + (i + 1));
            if (paramValue != null) {
                URL linkURL;
                try {
                    linkURL = new URL(paramValue);
                }
                catch (MalformedURLException e) {
                    // Bad URL.
                    linkURL = null;
                }
                imageURL[i] = linkURL;
            }
            else {
                // set it to blank
                imageURL[i] = null;
            }

            // Look for URL parameters.
            paramValue = getParameter("FogURL" + (i + 1));
            if (paramValue != null) {
                URL linkURL;
                try {
                    linkURL = new URL(paramValue);
                }
                catch (MalformedURLException e) {
                    // Bad URL.
                    linkURL = null;
```

continues

Source 8.1   *Continued*

```
                    }
                    link[i] = linkURL;
            }
            else {
                    // Default Value
                    URL weblink;
                    try {
                        weblink = new URL("http://stub");
                        link[i] = weblink;
                    }
                    catch(MalformedURLException e) {
                        System.out.println("ERROR:" + paramValue);
                    }
            }
        }

    } // END FOR loop
} // END lookForParameters

// Creates all the objects to be inserted in the scene graph.
private BranchGroup createSceneGraph(Canvas3D c,
                                    AppletContext context) {

    // Allocate the bounding sphere to be used with the all nodes.
    // The assumption is that the all nodes should be active all
    // the time.  The bounds center is set to the origin and
    // then a radius of 100 is assumed to be "sufficiently large"
    // so that all the nodes will always be within this bounds.
    //
    bounds = new BoundingSphere(new Point3d(0.0, 0.0, 0.0),100.0);

    // Create the root of the branch graph
    //
    BranchGroup objRoot = new BranchGroup();

    // This Transform Group Scales the objects so
    // they fit the scene.
    //
    TransformGroup objScale = new TransformGroup();
    Transform3D t3d = new Transform3D();
    t3d.setScale(0.2);
    objScale.setTransform(t3d);
    objRoot.addChild(objScale);

    // This will have the geometry move in a circular
    // orbit along the XZ axis.
    //
    TransformGroup orbit = new XZorbit(orbitSpeed,
```

Source 8.1 Complete Java 3D Fog Class (*Continued*)

```
        4.0f, new Point3d(0.0, 0.0, 0.0));

    // Create a wobble. yRotate will rotate all objects
    // around the Y-axis. zRotate will rotate all objects
    // around the Z-axis.
    //
    TransformGroup yRotate = new Yrotator();
    TransformGroup zRotate = new Zrotator();

    // Create the slides switch node - it will initially
    // display slide 0, the first slide.
    slides = new Switch(0);

    // Set needed capabilities:
    //   ALLOW_SWITCH_WRITE will allow the currently selected
    //   switch node child to be changed.
    //   ALLOW_CHILDREN_READ will allow the switch node to call
    //   numChildren() and getChild() methods.  Needed during
    //   picking to find the picked node and associated URL.
    //
    slides.setCapability(Switch.ALLOW_SWITCH_WRITE);
    slides.setCapability(Group.ALLOW_CHILDREN_READ);

    // Needed by the texture loader utility.
    String rgb = new String("RGB");

    for (int i = 0; i < numSlides; i++) {

        // Store URL in LocalData object and assign to this
        // primitive. Don't execute this if running -demo.
        if (applet == true) {
            LocalData ld = new LocalData(link[i]);
            shapes[i].setUserData(ld);
        }

        // Create an Appearance object.  This will be used to
        // place the texture map onto the object.
        Appearance a = new Appearance();

        // Make it a solid color surface by default.
        // Set up the coloring properties
        Color3f objColor = new Color3f(1.0f, 0.2f, 0.5f);
        ColoringAttributes ca = new ColoringAttributes();
        ca.setColor(objColor);
        a.setColoringAttributes(ca);
```

continues

Source 8.1   *Continued*

```
                   // If applet then expect URL references for the
                   // images, else we are in "-demo" mode and we'll
                   // be passing strings to the TextureLoader class.
                   // If no image is specified, then we have prepared
                   // a solid  surface (above).
                   //
                   if (applet == true) {
                      if (imageURL[i] != null) {
                         TextureLoader t =
                                    new TextureLoader(imageURL[i],
                                          new String("RGB"), this);
                          if (t != null)
                              a.setTexture(t.getTexture());
                      }
                   }
                   else if (texture[i] != null) {
                         TextureLoader t =
                                    new TextureLoader(texture[i],
                                          new String("RGB"), this);
                          if (t != null)
                              a.setTexture(t.getTexture());
                   }


              /**------------------------------------------------

                   Create the basic shape objects

              ------------------------------------------------*/

              if (primitive[i] == RECTANGLE) {
                 Primitive rect = new Box(0.25f, 0.75f, 0.75f,
                             Box.GENERATE_NORMALS |
                             Box.GENERATE_TEXTURE_COORDS,
                             a);
                 slides.addChild(rect);
              }
              else if (primitive[i] == CUBE) {
                 Primitive cube =
                          new Box(0.75f, 0.75f, 0.75f,
                             Box.GENERATE_NORMALS |
                             Box.GENERATE_TEXTURE_COORDS,
                             a);
                 slides.addChild(cube);
              }
              else if (primitive[i] == SPHERE) {
                 Sphere sphere = new Sphere(1.2f,
                        Sphere.GENERATE_NORMALS |
```

Source 8.1   Complete Java 3D Fog Class (*Continued*)

```
                    Sphere.GENERATE_TEXTURE_COORDS,
                    60, a);
            slides.addChild(sphere);
        }
        else if (primitive[i] == CYLINDER) {
            Primitive tube = new Cylinder(0.75f, 1.5f,
              Cylinder.GENERATE_NORMALS |
              Cylinder.GENERATE_TEXTURE_COORDS,
              15, 15, a);
            slides.addChild(tube);
        }
        else {
            Primitive def =
              new Cylinder(0.75f, 1.5f,
              Cylinder.GENERATE_NORMALS |
              Cylinder.GENERATE_TEXTURE_COORDS,
              15, 15, a);
            slides.addChild(def);
        }
    }
}

// This is a simple alpha object that will be used to cycle
// through each child node under the switch node.  Each child
// node is considered one "slide".
//   loopCount
//     Specifies the number of times to cycle the alpha.
//      A -1 means to cycle it infinitely.
//   mode
//     Specifies what part of the wave form (going from
//     0.0 to 1.0 or 1.0 to 0.0 or both) to use.  The
//     switchAlpha will go from 0.0 to 1.0 and then
//     restart at 0.0, so only an increasing alpha
//     value is used.  This will result in each slide
//     being displayed sequentially from 1 to the number
//     of slides and then back to slide 1.
//   triggerTime
//     Defines when (in milliseconds) to begin the
//     alpha waveform.  For the switchAlpha no delay is
//     necessary.
//   phaseDelayDuration
//     Defines a time period when the alpha value does not
//     change.  For this time alpha will be either 0.0 or 1.0
//     depending on the waveform of the alpha created.  This is
//     not used for the switchAlpha - it is set to 0.
//   increasingAlphaDuration
//     The time (in milliseconds) to vary alpha from 0.0
```

continues

Source 8.1   *Continued*

```
//      to its 1.0 value.  This value determines the frequency.
//      Set to a "reasonable" time so that each object
//      has time to be viewed.
//    increasingAlphaRampDuration
//      Used to change the rate at which alpha increases over
//      time.  For the switchAlpha object, a constant rate is
//      desired so this value is set to 0.
//    alphaAtOneDuration
//      The time (in milliseconds) to keep alpha at its 1.0
//      value. The switchAlpha object continually switches
//      between all nodes under the switch node so this value
//      is set to 0 so no delay occurs.
//    decreasingAlphaDuration
//      The time(in milliseconds) to vary alpha from 1.0 to 0.0.
//      The switchAlpha object does not use decreasing alpha so
//      this value is ignored.
//    decreasingAlphaRampDuration
//      Used to change the rate at which alpha decreases over
//      time.  The switchAlpha object does not use decreasing
//      alpha so this value is ignored.
//    alphaAtZeroDuration
//      The time (in milliseconds) to keep alpha at its 0.0
//      value. The switchAlpha object continuously switches
//      between all nodes under the switch node so this value
//      is set to 0 so no delay occurs.
Alpha switchAlpha = new Alpha(-1, Alpha.INCREASING_ENABLE,
  0, 0, delaySpeed, 0, 0, 0, 0, 0);

// This interpolator will continuously switch between all child
// nodes of the Switch group node slides.
SwitchValueInterpolator slideSwitch
    = new SwitchValueInterpolator(switchAlpha, slides);

// Assign the bounding sphere to be used with the Switch node.
slideSwitch.setSchedulingBounds(bounds);

// Add everything to the scene graph - first the orbit
// behavior, then the Yrotator, next the Zrotator and finally
// the geometry.
objScale.addChild(orbit);
objScale.addChild(slideSwitch);
orbit.addChild(yRotate);
yRotate.addChild(zRotate);
zRotate.addChild(slides);

// Create the linear fog node.  The first three components
// are the fog color - the best effect is to make this the
```

Source 8.1   Complete Java 3D Fog Class (*Continued*)

```
        // same color as the background.  The frontDistance is the
        // distance in Z that fog start while backDistance is the
        // distance in Z that everything will be completely obscured
        // by the fog. Because Z goes into the screen, the
        // frontDistance must be less than the back distance. The
        // front and backdistances were chosen to have a nice effect
        // given the viewing parameters obtained.
        //
        LinearFog lFog = new LinearFog(0.0f, 0.0f, 0.0f, 1.5, 3.0);

        // Assign the bounding sphere to be used with the fog node.
        lFog.setInfluencingBounds(bounds);

        // Add the fog to the scene graph.
        objRoot.addChild(lFog);

        // If applet setup a behavior that will determine the proper
        // URL to load when the user clicks the left mouse button
        // over a "slide".
        //
        if (applet == true) {
          PickURL pickURL = new PickURL(c, objRoot, bounds, context);
          pickURL.setSchedulingBounds(bounds);
          objRoot.addChild(pickURL);
        }

        return objRoot;
    }

public void init() {

        AppletContext context = null;

      // If we are running as an applet we need to
      // initialize values according to the user settings in
      // the HTML file accomplished by lookForParameters().
      // Otherwise we'll just use the values used to initialize
      // the local variable declarations at the top of the block.
      //
      if (getParameter("FogNumSlides") != null) {
              context = getAppletContext();
              lookForParameters();
      }
      // Create the layout manager used for this applet.
      setLayout(new BorderLayout());
```

continues

Source 8.1 *Continued*

```
            // Create the Canvas3D object used by Java 3D.
            Canvas3D c = new Canvas3D(null);
            add("Center", c);

            // Create a simple scene.
            BranchGroup scene = createSceneGraph(c, context);

            // Attach scene to virtual universe.
            SimpleUniverse u = new SimpleUniverse(c);

          // This will move the ViewPlatform back a bit so the
          // objects in the scene can be viewed.
            u.getViewingPlatform().setNominalViewingTransform();

            u.addBranchGraph(scene);
        }


    //
    // The following allows Fog to be run as an application
    // as well as an applet
    //
    public static void main(String[] args) {

        if (args.length > 0) {
            // Parse Input Arguments
            for (int i = 0; i < args.length; i++) {

                if (args[i].equals("-demo")) {
                    new MainFrame(new Fog(), 400, 400);
                } else {
                    System.out.println("Usage: java Fog -demo");
                    System.exit(0);
                }
            }
        } else {
            System.out.println("Usage: java Fog -demo");
            System.exit(0);
        }
    } // END main
} // END Class
```

Source 8.1 Complete Java 3D Fog Class (*Continued*)

Moving On

That's it for this chapter. We think this is one of the more interesting applets in the book. By using a small powerful program, the result is a new form of content for the Web. It's 3D, its curious, and it serves an interesting role as a menu.

CHAPTER
9

Texture Mapping

"Pixel, n: a mischievous, magical spirit associated with screen displays. The computer industry has frequently borrowed from mythology. Witness the 'sprites' in computer graphics, the 'daemons' in operating systems, and the 'trolls' in the marketing department."

—JEFF MEYER

Texture mapping (Figure 9.1) is the most exciting thing to happen in computer graphics within the last decade. Ten years ago, it was used in flight simulators that cost a million dollars. Five years ago it could be found on technical and scientific workstations at the cost of $30,000. Unbelievable and staggering is that today, texture mapping can be found on a $200 PC card that outperforms all the expensive versions of the past. Texture mapping is even found on Nintendo, which costs under $200 and runs on a 96 MHz chip. Texture mapping is a primary innovation that adds reality to a virtual, computer-generated picture, so in this chapter we focus on creating and implementing great texture mapping.

Sign Description and Usage

The Sign applet (see Figure 9.2) displays a simple scene consisting of a rotating billboard, which can be textured with your favorite image. The pro-

Figure 9.1   Texture mapping example.

gram backdrop can also be an image, to give the application depth and visual interest. This program is designed to animate by rotating a sign that has lighting and that demonstrates the quality of texture mapping that can be achieved with the Java 3D API.

Sign Applet Parameters Explained

The following is the defined HTML interface to this program. How to read the syntax of the provided HTML file (Sign.html) is covered in great detail in Chapter 4 so we will not repeat the discussion here and bore you to sleep.

If you have been following along, the syntax will look familiar. The first parameter sets the image for the sign. It can be in either the JPEG or GIF format.

```
<PARAM NAME="SignImage" VALUE="http://www.sun.com/Sales.jpg">
```

The second parameter is used to specify the background image or a color—you will need to choose one or the other. If you choose to use a

Figure 9.2   Sign applet.

color, the following predefined colors are available: blue, green, yellow, purple, gold, orange, black, white, medblue, and medgreen.

```
<PARAM NAME="SignBackground" VALUE="http://www.sun.com/clouds.jpg">
<PARAM NAME="SignBackground" VALUE="gold">
```

Texture Mapping Concepts

Texture mapping is a technique for attaching images called "the texture" over 3D geometric models. As mentioned, this trick was used in early flight simulators, to add realism to the training process; it has since become a core primitive in commercial computer gaming and visualization applications. Basically, a picture, or texture, is made up of pixels of various colors that form the image, which is mapped onto the 3D object made up of polygons. The excess is cut away and the seam is smoothed so it is invisible.

The mapping of the textures to a 3D shape requires special mathematical operations.

(u,v)   (T,S)   (x,y,z)   (i,j)

Basically, the color of the 3D object at each pixel is changed by its corresponding color from the texture image. The image is applied to the 3D shape by assigning texture coordinates (u,v) to the object's vertices. These *texture coordinates* map to an image index to determine each of the polygon's pixel value (Figure 9.3). As a result, the viewer sees an object that appears to be built from bricks, because of the image used to texture the 3D object. What makes it believable is the way the picture is stretched and conformed to the geometric model.

Let's use a simplified case to illustrate how texture mapping occurs. We'll map a checkerboard, bitmapped image of 8×4 pixels onto a rectangle polygon shape in 3D space, defined by four points.

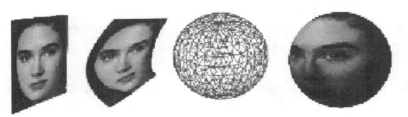

Figure 9.3 Texture mapping process.

```
       s = 0                      s = 1              u = 0  u = 1

   A  o————————————————o B        v = 0   00001111

      |0000000000000111111111111 |                  00001111

      |0000000000000111111111111 |                  11110000

      |0000000000000111111111111 |                  11110000

      |1111111111110000000000000 |         v = 1

      |1111111111110000000000000 |

      |1111111111110000000000000 |

   D  o————————————————o C

       t = 0                     t = 1
```

The upper left corner of the polygon is defined as the origin (0,0) and location (0,0) of our texture map. Moving counterclockwise, the polygon points correspond to the corners of our texture map: (0,0), (8,0), (8,4), (0,4).

Mapping occurs by specifying a transformation from the location of the texture in 2D space (s,t) to the two *surface space* vectors (u,v), which represent the axes of the 3D coordinate space of the polygonal model. The s and t coordinates are mapped to u, v coordinates. This corresponding relationship is called *texture space*. Consequently, we used (u,v) = (0,0) to map A, (u,v) = (1,0) to B, and (u,v) = (0,1) to D. This results in stretching the texture map to fill the entire polygon map.

The texture mapping process in the Java 3D API can be divided into two basic steps:

1. Take the transformed texture coordinates, plus the image, and the texture filter functions (such as blending the object color with the texture color, or modulating the object color with the texture color) and compute a texture color for each pixel in our 3D shape.

2. Apply the computed texture colors to the incoming pixel colors and, finally, render the 3D shape.

   The result will be a 3D shape wrapped with the specified texture. (The actual equation can be found in the published Java 3D API specification.)

Java 3D has two types of textures: 2D for image textures and 3D for volume textures. Both types provide a framework for managing texture data, filtering, wrapping modes, and setting a boundary color.

The Texture Object

To implement texture mapping in the Java 3D API, a Texture object is used. It is either a 2D object or a 3D texture volume, and both provide various methods for setting the object's properties and attributes. For the sake of discussion, we will limit the information to 2D texture mapping because of its common applicability to the applets used in this book. The Texture2D object is a subclass of the Texture class. It provides a method for creating a 2D texture image.

The *TextureAttributes* object is a component of the Appearance object, and its purpose is to define the texture properties when texture mapping is used. This includes various parameters and properties control values. Some of these properties are: the texture boundary (the texture can be clamped or constrained within provided coordinates, or the texture can be repeated or tiled if the provided coordinates are exceeded), magnification filters (handles mapping pixels to texel area sizes), pixel color applications, and texture quality and resolution. Consider the following code fragment:

```
Material mat  =  new Material( );
// Set  the material properties here
TextureAttributes  ta  =  new TextureAttributes( );

// Set additional texture attributes here
Appearance app  =  new Appearance( );
app.setMaterial(mat);
app.setTextureAttributes(ta);
TextureLoader tex = new TextureLoader(new String("brick.gif"),
         new String("RGB"), this);
app.setTexture(tex);

// Build a Shape with this Appearance Node containing a texture
```

The TextureAttributes Object

There are special attributes for many types of Node objects in the Java 3D API. If you remember from Chapter 3, Leaf Node objects include the actual geometry and use the attributes required to render 3D shapes. Leaf Nodes themselves do not fully describe the Shape3D object's appearance because some of that information is contained in a *NodeComponent* object (See Figure 9.4). The information may be appearance properties or floating-point and integer values. We have also discussed the Appearance object, the component object of a Shape3D node that will specify all rendering attributes for a particular shape; it is a subclass of NodeComponent. If you're confused with the reference to nodes, leafs and object groupings, you're not the

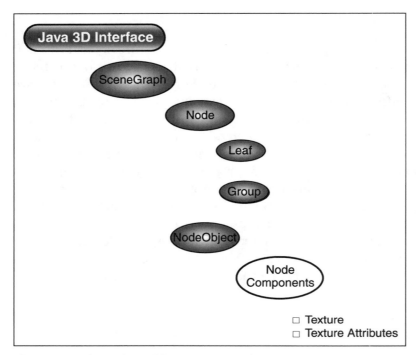

Figure 9.4 The Texture object.

only one—but we promise, it won't be on the final exam. There are diagrams and javadoc HTML links to help you find objects and to navigate the Java 3D API tree.

When implementing texture attributes and properties, these will have to be set to the Appearance object to take effect. Let's continue to clarify what we need to do to create awesome texture maps. We'll go through this step by step and inch by inch.

Step-by-Step Texture Mapping

The Java 3D API provides a convenience class called *TextureLoader* that is used to simplify the process of adding texture mapping to a 3D scene. We highly recommend using this method to simplify adding texture to the scene. Here's what you need to do:

1. Create your SceneGraph (Virtual Universe, BranchGroup, any TransformGroups needed for movement, etc.).

2. Create an Appearance object, called "ap" in our example.

   ```
   Appearance ap = new Appearance();
   ```

3. Create the texture from the provided image file with TextureLoader( ); we'll name it "tex."

```
TextureLoader tex = new TextureLoader(new String("brick.gif"),
new String("RGB"), this);
```

4. Set the texture as a component of the existing Appearance object.

```
ap.setTexture(tex.getTexture());
```

5. Create 3D shapes and specify the constructor to generate texture coordinates. The Appearance object "ap" is used in the Creation method.

```
Box shape = new Box(1.0f, 0.6f, 1.0f,
Box.GENERATE_TEXTURE_COORDS, ap);
```

6. Add the shape to the scene.

```
objRoot.addChild(shape)
```

In Chapter 4, we discussed methods for defining some geometry under the Geometry parent class. Handling texture mapping is a little different and takes a little more work. The following constructs an empty QuadArray for 24 vertices and the vertex format for coordinates. Then a method is called to initialize the object with the vertices information. Consider the following arrays of information:

```
private static final float[] boxverts = {
        // front face
         1.0f, -1.0f,  1.0f,
         1.0f,  1.0f,  1.0f,
        -1.0f,  1.0f,  1.0f,
        -1.0f, -1.0f,  1.0f,
        // back face
        -1.0f, -1.0f, -1.0f,
        -1.0f,  1.0f, -1.0f,
         1.0f,  1.0f, -1.0f,
         1.0f, -1.0f, -1.0f,
        // right face
         1.0f, -1.0f, -1.0f,
         1.0f,  1.0f, -1.0f,
         1.0f,  1.0f,  1.0f,
         1.0f, -1.0f,  1.0f,
        // left face
        -1.0f, -1.0f,  1.0f,
        -1.0f,  1.0f,  1.0f,
        -1.0f,  1.0f, -1.0f,
        -1.0f, -1.0f, -1.0f,
        // top face
         1.0f,  1.0f,  1.0f,
         1.0f,  1.0f, -1.0f,
```

```
        -1.0f,  1.0f, -1.0f,
        -1.0f,  1.0f,  1.0f,
        // bottom face
        -1.0f, -1.0f,  1.0f,
        -1.0f, -1.0f, -1.0f,
         1.0f, -1.0f, -1.0f,
         1.0f, -1.0f,  1.0f,
    };
```

To add color or texture mapping coordinates, additional arrays need to be created. Adding color information would look like:

```
private static final float[] boxcolors = {
        // front face (red)
        1.0f, 0.0f, 0.0f,
        1.0f, 0.0f, 0.0f,
        1.0f, 0.0f, 0.0f,
        1.0f, 0.0f, 0.0f,
        // back face (green)
        0.0f, 1.0f, 0.0f,
        0.0f, 1.0f, 0.0f,
        0.0f, 1.0f, 0.0f,
        0.0f, 1.0f, 0.0f,
        // right face (blue)
        0.0f, 0.0f, 1.0f,
        0.0f, 0.0f, 1.0f,
        0.0f, 0.0f, 1.0f,
        0.0f, 0.0f, 1.0f,
        // left face (yellow)
        1.0f, 1.0f, 0.0f,
        1.0f, 1.0f, 0.0f,
        1.0f, 1.0f, 0.0f,
        1.0f, 1.0f, 0.0f,
        // top face (magenta)
        1.0f, 0.0f, 1.0f,
        1.0f, 0.0f, 1.0f,
        1.0f, 0.0f, 1.0f,
        1.0f, 0.0f, 1.0f,
        // bottom face (cyan)
        0.0f, 1.0f, 1.0f,
        0.0f, 1.0f, 1.0f,
        0.0f, 1.0f, 1.0f,
        0.0f, 1.0f, 1.0f,
    };

QuadArray box = new QuadArray(24,
        QuadArray.COORDINATES|QuadArray.COLOR_3);
box.setCoordinates(0, boxverts);
box.setColor(0,boxcolors);
```

We now have our own prebuilt box shape; but it won't support texture mapping without a little more work. So let's add another array to specify the texture coordinates, then add the bit flag that declares the presence of provided texture mapping coordinates.

```
private Point2f texCoord[]= {
        new Point2f(1.0f, 0.0f), new Point2f( 1.0f, 1.0f),
        new Point2f(0.0f, 1.0f), new Point2f( 0.0f, 0.0f) };

QuadArray box = new QuadArray(24,
        QuadArray.COORDINATES |QuadArray.COLOR_3 |
        QuadArray.TEXTURE_COORDINATE_2);
```

There's not much more to it. Check out Source 9.1 for the full picture.

Related Texture Mapping Constants

The following are common constants used to specify the format of the texture being used and how it is to be saved in the texture object.

RGB.   The texture contains red, green, and blue color values. For example, the texture could be a GIF or JPEG image file.

RGBA.   The texture contains red, green, and blue color values, plus an alpha value. For example, the texture could be an RGB image file with a transparency color defined for the alpha value.

BASE_LEVEL.   This indicates that the Texture object has only one MIP map level. (See the upcoming MIP map discussion.)

The boundary mode for the s and t texture object coordinates can be set to the following:

CLAMP.   Restrains the texture coordinates within the range of $0 \ldots 1$.

WRAP.   The texture is repeated for mapping texture coordinates that fall outside the range $0 \ldots 1$.

Don't forget: When building 3D Shape objects, the following flags are used so that texture coordinates for the Shape object will be generated when the objects are created. In this case, it is assumed that a 2D texture is being used and that these flags direct the API logic to generate 2D texture coordinates for s and t.

```
GENERATE_TEXTURE_COORDS
TEXTURE_COORDINATE_2
```

The following is an example of using the flag TEXTURE_COORDINATE_2 in the creation of a 3D Shape object. In this case, we are going to provide the geometric data, color information, and texture coordinates that will be used to build a subcomponent of the 3D Shape object.

```java
public class MyTextureShape extends Object {
    private static final float[] vertices = {
    // geometry data for my 3D shape
        // front face
            1.0f, -1.0f,  1.0f,
            1.0f,  1.0f,  1.0f,
           -1.0f,  1.0f,  1.0f,
           -1.0f, -1.0f,  1.0f,
        // back face
           -1.0f, -1.0f, -1.0f,
           -1.0f,  1.0f, -1.0f,
            1.0f,  1.0f, -1.0f,
            1.0f, -1.0f, -1.0f,
        // right face
            1.0f, -1.0f, -1.0f,
            1.0f,  1.0f, -1.0f,
            1.0f,  1.0f,  1.0f,
            1.0f, -1.0f,  1.0f,
        // left face
           -1.0f, -1.0f,  1.0f,
           -1.0f,  1.0f,  1.0f,
           -1.0f,  1.0f, -1.0f,
           -1.0f, -1.0f, -1.0f,
        // top face
            1.0f,  1.0f,  1.0f,
            1.0f,  1.0f, -1.0f,
           -1.0f,  1.0f, -1.0f,
           -1.0f,  1.0f,  1.0f,
        // bottom face
           -1.0f, -1.0f,  1.0f,
           -1.0f, -1.0f, -1.0f,
            1.0f, -1.0f, -1.0f,
            1.0f, -1.0f,  1.0f, };

    private static final float[] colors = {
        // front face (red)
            1.0f, 0.0f, 0.0f,
            1.0f, 0.0f, 0.0f,
            1.0f, 0.0f, 0.0f,
            1.0f, 0.0f, 0.0f,
        // back face (green)
            0.0f, 1.0f, 0.0f,
            0.0f, 1.0f, 0.0f,
            0.0f, 1.0f, 0.0f,
```

```
        0.0f, 1.0f, 0.0f,
    // right face (blue)
        0.0f, 0.0f, 1.0f,
        0.0f, 0.0f, 1.0f,
        0.0f, 0.0f, 1.0f,
        0.0f, 0.0f, 1.0f,
    // left face (yellow)
        1.0f, 1.0f, 0.0f,
        1.0f, 1.0f, 0.0f,
        1.0f, 1.0f, 0.0f,
        1.0f, 1.0f, 0.0f,
    // top face (magenta)
        1.0f, 0.0f, 1.0f,
        1.0f, 0.0f, 1.0f,
        1.0f, 0.0f, 1.0f,
        1.0f, 0.0f, 1.0f,
    // bottom face (cyan)
        0.0f, 1.0f, 1.0f,
        0.0f, 1.0f, 1.0f,
        0.0f, 1.0f, 1.0f,
        0.0f, 1.0f, 1.0f, };

private Point2f texCoord[]= {
    new Point2f(1.0f, 0.0f), new Point2f( 1.0f, 1.0f),
    new Point2f(0.0f, 1.0f), new Point2f( 0.0f, 0.0f) };


private Shape3D shape;

public MyTextureShape( ) {
        QuadArray myshape = new QuadArray(24,
        QuadArray.COORDINATES |QuadArray.COLOR_3 |
        QuadArray.TEXTURE_COORDINATE_2);
    myshape.setCoordinates(0, vertices);
    myshape.setColors(0, colors);
    for (int i=0; i<24; i++) {
        myshape.setTextureCoordinate(i, texCoord[i%4]);
    }

    shape = new Shape3D(myshape, new Appearance());
}

public Shape3D getShape() {
    return shape;
}
}
```

A QuadArray object is created with placeholders for 24 sets of coordinates, color values, and texture coordinates. Then the object properties are initialized with the provided vertex, color, and texture coordinate data. The

QuadArray object is a component of the Shape node. Finally, it is all brought together into a 3D Shape object and returned to the method that invokes our 3D Shape constructor, MyTextureShape( ). There are several additional texture mapping flags and filters for minification, magnification, and mipmaps that are not covered here, but that are included in the Java 3D API notes.

Texture Mapping Related Constructors

The easiest way to generate a texture object is to use the convenience class provided with the set of utilities in Sun's Java 3D API.

```
public TextureLoader(String fname, String format, Component observer)
```

If that is too generic, use the Texture object constructors:

```
public Texture( )
public Texture2D(int mipmapMode, int format, int width, int height)
```

The first constructor creates a Texture object with the following default values:

boundaryModeS: WRAP

boundaryModeT: WRAP

minification filter: BASE_LEVEL_POINT

magnification filter: BASE_LEVEL_POINT

boundary color: black

texture image: null

The second constructor is an extension to the Texture object and allows the programmer to specify multiple images for each mipmap level, the data format of the textures, and dimension values.

This method constructs an empty Texture object with specified mipmap-Mode format, width, and height. Image at level 0 must be set by the application using the setImage method. If mipmapMode is set to MULTI_LEVEL_MIPMAP, images for *all* levels must be set. The parameters are:

mipmapMode. The type of mipmap for this texture, one of BASE_LEVEL or MULTI_LEVEL_MIPMAP.

format. The pixel data format of the image saved in this object. Data is read from pixels as a sequence of signed or unsigned bytes, shorts or longs, or single-precision, floating-point values, depending on type.

These values are grouped into sets of one, two, three, or four values, depending on the specified format.

LUMINANCE.   Values provided specify the brightness of color. Each element is a single luminance value. It is converted to floating-point, then assembled into an RGBA element by replicating the luminance value three times for red, green, and blue, and attaching 1.0 for alpha. Each component is then multiplied by the signed scale factor and added to the signed bias and clamped to the range [0,1].

ALPHA.   An image that contains an alpha channel causes transparent areas to be seen through the image. Often, the alpha value is used to remove the backdrop around an object within an image. Each element is a single alpha component, converted to floating-point and assembled into an RGBA element by attaching 0.0 for red, green, and blue.

LUMINANCE_ALPHA.   Each element is a luminance/alpha pair, converted to floating-point, then assembled into an RGBA element by replicating the luminance value three times for red, green, and blue. Each component is then multiplied by the signed scale factor and added to the signed bias, then clamped to the range [0,1].

RGB.   Each element is an RGB triple, converted to floating-point and assembled into an RGBA element by attaching 1.0 for alpha. Each component is then multiplied by the signed scale factor and added to the signed bias, then clamped to the range [0,1].

RGBA.   Each element is a luminance/alpha pair converted to floating-point, then assembled into an RGBA element replicating the luminance value three times for red, green, and blue. Each component is then multiplied by the signed scale factor and added to the signed bias, then clamped to the range [0,1].

Width.   The width of the image at level 0; must be power of 2.

Height.   The height of the image at level 0; must be power of 2.

Throws: IllegalArgumentException, if width or height are not power of 2, OR invalid format is specified.

Now let's take a short break to discuss the image files themselves. First, the name of the image file is passed into our program from the command-line argument or from the applet tag interface. There are a couple of things you need to know about the texture image file itself: How is it formatted? Does it have three channels for red, green and blue? Does it have an Alpha channel? The list goes on. It is also important that the image file's height and width are a power of 2, so that the image can be processed properly by the Java 3D API without generating runtime exception messages. There is also support for 3D images and textures, which are commonly used for volume rendering and visualization. The difference is that, in addition to a width and a height, they come with a depth component. But our focus in this section is on 2D images and textures.

The Graphics Interchange Format (GIF) and Joint Photographic Experts Group (JPEG) are the two most common image file formats used and recognized by the getImage( ) method. GIF images are limited to 256 colors, but support transparency. An extra channel, called Alpha, is provided to supply the transparent color value. This value is blended across the rendered image using a special mathematical computation, which produces the transparency effect. Generally, GIF files are smaller then JPEG, because of the reduced number of colors. JPEG, on the other hand, supports true color, more than 16 million colors, and grayscale images.

When loading an image, it is likely that the image source is being downloaded from a Web server. This takes time and affects our applet programs, because we need the image to be fully loaded onto the client before proceeding with the texture mapping operation. In this case, we'll rely on an AWT object called *MediaTracker*. Basically, the following is collapsed into the convenience class TextureLoader( ).

```
MediaTracker  mediatracker  =  new  MediaTracker(this);
Image bricks = getImage(getCodeBase(), "bricks.gif");
mediatracker.addImage(bricks, 0);
try
      mediatracker.waitForAll();
catch  (InterruptedException  error)
      showStatus("Problems loading the image.");
```

You can reuse the MediaTracker object for preparing multiple textures by calling multiple getImage( ) and addImage( ) methods. Note that there are issues of portability in how other platforms handle image loading. You should consider this when building cross-platform, run-anywhere applications that will require texture mapping.

Let's return to our discussion of setting up the texture mapping features in the Java 3D API.

Texture Mapping Related Methods

First we'll need to construct a class that creates a 2D array of pixels that will copy our image into the array, pixel by pixel.

```
ImageComponent2D image  =  new
      ImageComponent(ImageComponent.FORMAT_RGB, bricks);

Texture2D tex  =  new Texture2D(Texture.BASE_LEVEL,
          Texture.RGB, 64, 64);
```

To set up a texture application, you need two objects: an ImageComponent and a Texture2D object. The first object creates the array of pixels from the provided image file. Next, you set the desired image.

```
tex.setImage(0, image);
```

This method sets the specified image component to the mipmap level of 0. Level 0 is the base level. What is *MIP mapping?* You had to ask didn't you? Let's see if we can concisely define this advanced subject without causing too much confusion. MIP mapping is a technique used to provide multiple levels of texture detail by creating several resolutions of the texture (Figure 9.5). Each level is derived from the original by incrementally reducing the original to lower resolutions. The MIP map pixel corresponds to this collection, which results in a filtered value. This value is the difference between the transition from one resolution of the pixel to another, across a surface area. As textures are positioned at longer distances from the eye position, becoming very small to the viewer, only a small number of pixels will be visible. This produces odd-looking texture mapping artifacts. MIP mapping tries to eliminate these artifacts and improve the quality of the textures in the scene. For example, when a textured object is far from view, a lower resolution of texture is used on the object. This variation of texture mapping also helps to increase rendering speed. Resolution variation is defined in "levels"; the higher the mipmap level, the lower the resolution.

Next, we'll create some geometry and an Appearance object, then specify or set the texture to the Appearance class.

```
a.setTexture(tex);
tex.setEnable(true);
```

A new Shape node is instantiated by passing the Appearance Object, which also defines a texture to use. The new Shape object is added to the

Figure 9.5 MIP mapping.

SceneGraph so the viewer can see the 3D object that texture mapping applied.

One mipmap filter is *linear interpolation,* which essentially removes data information, and results in reduced texture resolution, or *Level of Detail (LoD).* Depending on the distance from the view, a mipmap level is selected to render the textured object. Again, this improves rendering performance and image quality when the textured object is very small. The Java 3D API provides a behavior class called *DistanceLOD* to do this for you. This behavior will track the ViewPlatform and compute a distance from a shape to the eye position. These distances are mapped to a Switch object that would contain various objects with varying levels of detail.

Advanced Texture Attributes

There are additional methods that allow you to manipulate the texture map even further, including texture transforms, texture modes, color blending, and perspective correction. These attributes are part of the TextureAttributes class.

```
setTextureMode( int mode)
```

The texture mode controls how the pixels of the texture image are applied to the shape color. Here are the provided constants:

BLEND.   Blends texture with material color of the shape.

DECAL.   Applies texture on top of the material.

MODULATE.   Texture pixel colors modulate the material color (for an x-raylike effect).

REPLACE.   Texture colors replace material colors.

```
setTextureBlendColor( Color4f color)
```

Textures can be blended with a given color before being applied to the shape, or set later.

```
setTextureTransform(Transform3D trans)
```

A texture transform can translate, scale, or rotate the texture coordinates (s,t,r) before the texture is applied to the shape. You use a translation to slide the image across a shape.

```
Appearance app  =  new Appearance ( );
TextureAttributes ta  =  new  TextureAttributes( );
```

```
Transform3D trans = new Transform3D( );
trans.set(new Vector3d(-1.0,0.0,0.0));
ta.setTextureTransform(trans);
app.setTextureAttributes(ta);
```

Then you reorient the texture with a rotation transform and scale the texture to repeat the image multiple times on a shape—just modify the transform that is about to perform other effects, like rotation or scaling of the texture.

```
trans.rotZ(Math.PI/2.0);      // rotate
trans.setScale(0.4);          // scale
```

To further position the texture on the 3D shape, use:

```
setCoordinate( )
setTextureCoordinates(int index, Point2f position);
```

Setting the coordinates positions the entire texture at some offset before the texture is wrapped around an object. Setting the texture's coordinates is like making a cookie cutout: When you want only a portion of the texture image to be used, you specify these coordinates, which will take the "cutout" and use it as the texture source.

Texture Mapping Code Example

To close this chapter, we provide the documented source listing (Source 9.1) for you to study. It is sometimes nice to read through code listings on paper rather than on a screen. That way you can write notes next to the code while giving your eyes a break from the bright monitor.

```
import java.applet.*;
import java.net.URL;
import java.net.MalformedURLException;
import java.awt.BorderLayout;
import java.awt.event.*;
import java.awt.Image;
import com.sun.j3d.utils.applet.MainFrame;
import com.sun.j3d.utils.universe.*;
import com.sun.j3d.utils.image.TextureLoader;
import com.sun.j3d.utils.geometry.*;
```

continues

Source 9.1 Complete Texture Mapping Code

```
import javax.media.j3d.*;
import javax.vecmath.*;

/**-----------------------------------------------------------------
   Credits:
   Sign program by Kirk Brown


   -------------------------------------------------------------*/

public class Sign extends Applet {

     // Class variables.  The default values can be overridden
     // by using the PARAMS tag when invoking the applet.
     //
     // The following is the defined HTML interface to this program:
     //
     //        <PARAM NAME="SignImage" VALUE="[URL]/Sales.jpg">
     //               Value Options: "[image file]"
     //        <PARAM NAME="SignBackground" VALUE="[URL]/clouds.jpg">
     //               Value Options: "[image file]"
     //           OR
     //               Value Options = blue,green,yellow,purple,gold,
     //                      orange,black, white,medblue,medgreen
     //

     // Pre-defined colors
     Color3f white = new Color3f(1.0f, 1.0f, 1.0f);
     Color3f black = new Color3f(0.0f, 0.0f, 0.0f);
     Color3f gray = new Color3f(0.6f, 0.6f, 0.6f);
     Color3f red   = new Color3f(1.0f, 0.0f, 0.0f);
     Color3f ambientred = new Color3f(0.4f, 0.1f, 0.0f);
     Color3f medred = new Color3f(0.80f, 0.4f, 0.3f);
     Color3f green   = new Color3f(0.0f, 0.80f, 0.2f);
     Color3f ambientgreen = new Color3f(0.0f, 0.3f, 0.1f);
     Color3f medgreen = new Color3f(0.0f, 0.5f, 0.1f);
     Color3f orange   = new Color3f(0.7f, 0.4f, 0.0f);
     Color3f ambientorange = new Color3f(0.5f, 0.02f, 0.0f);
     Color3f medorange = new Color3f(0.5f, 0.2f, 0.1f);
     Color3f blue    = new Color3f(0.1f, 0.3f, 0.9f);
     Color3f ambientblue = new Color3f(0.0f, 0.1f, 0.4f);
     Color3f medblue = new Color3f(0.0f, 0.1f, 0.4f);
     Color3f gold = new Color3f(1.0f, 0.8f, 0.0f);
     Color3f yellow = new Color3f(1.0f, 1.0f, 0.6f);
     Color3f purple = new Color3f(0.5f, 0.2f, 0.8f);
     Color3f medpurple = new Color3f(0.5f, 0.2f, 0.5f);

     // Local Variable Declarations
```

Source 9.1   Complete Texture Mapping Code (*Continued*)

```
//
String sign = new String("sign1.jpg");
String back = new String("back.gif");
Image signimg;
Image backimg;
Color3f backcolor = black;

// Need these flags because the background can be:
//      a local image source when run standalone
//      a full URL image source when run as applet
//      or just a solid color
//
boolean applet = false;
URL imageURL;
URL backURL;

// Examines all parameters that can be passed into this
// applet and updates the variable state to reflect any
// non-default settings.
//
private void lookForParameters() {

    // Running as an applet, so use full URL image names:
    //          http://www.sun.com/images/foo.gif
    //          file:///c:/images/foo.gif
    // and do something a little different when creating
    // the texture. Mainly pass an Image object versus a
    // string to TextureLoader which handles both types.
    // Default assumes standalone mode with a local image
    // source (image = true; imageURL = false;)

    // Used to read in the parameters for the applet.
    String paramValue;

    // Running as Applet, reset.
    boolean applet = true;
    sign = new String();
    back = new String();

    paramValue = getParameter("SignImage");
    if (paramValue != null) {
            URL linkURL;
            try {
                linkURL = new URL(paramValue);
            }
            catch (MalformedURLException e) {
```

continues

Source 9.1   *Continued*

```
                                     // Bad URL.
                                     linkURL = null;
                        }
                        imageURL = linkURL;
            }
            else {
                        // set it to blank
                        imageURL = null;
            }

            paramValue = getParameter("SignBackground");
            if (paramValue != null) {
               if (paramValue.equalsIgnoreCase("red") == true) {
                        backcolor = red;
               }
               else if (paramValue.equalsIgnoreCase("green") == true) {
                        backcolor = green;
               }
               else if (paramValue.equalsIgnoreCase("blue") == true) {
                        backcolor = blue;
               }
               else if (paramValue.equalsIgnoreCase("medred") == true) {
                        backcolor = medred;
               }
               else if (paramValue.equalsIgnoreCase("medgreen") == true) {
                        backcolor = medgreen;
               }
               else if (paramValue.equalsIgnoreCase("medblue") == true) {
                        backcolor = medblue;
               }
               else if (paramValue.equalsIgnoreCase("black") == true) {
                        backcolor = black;
               }
               else if (paramValue.equalsIgnoreCase("gray") == true) {
                        backcolor = gray;
               }
               else if (paramValue.equalsIgnoreCase("white") == true) {
                        backcolor = white;
               }
               else if (paramValue.equalsIgnoreCase("yellow") == true) {
                        backcolor = yellow;
               }
               else if (paramValue.equalsIgnoreCase("gold") == true) {
                        backcolor = gold;
               }
               else if (paramValue.equalsIgnoreCase("purple") == true) {
                        backcolor = purple;
```

Source 9.1   Complete Texture Mapping Code (*Continued*)

```
        }
        else if (paramValue.equalsIgnoreCase("medpurple") == true) {
              backcolor = medpurple;
        }
        else if (paramValue.equalsIgnoreCase("orange") == true) {
              backcolor = orange;
        }
        else if (paramValue.equalsIgnoreCase("medorange") == true) {
              backcolor = medorange;
        }
        else {
            // If NOT a color Must be an URL image source
            //
              URL bURL;
              try {
                   bURL = new URL(paramValue);
              }
              catch (MalformedURLException e) {
                   // Bad URL.
                   bURL = null;
              }
              backURL = bURL;
        }
     }
     else {
         // set it to blank
         backcolor = black;

     }

} // END lookForParameters

private BranchGroup createSceneGraph() {

     // Create the root of the branch graph
     //
     BranchGroup objRoot = new BranchGroup();

     // This Transform Group Scales the objects so they fit the scene
     //
     TransformGroup objScale = new TransformGroup();
     Transform3D t3d = new Transform3D();
     t3d.setScale(0.4);
     objScale.setTransform(t3d);
     objRoot.addChild(objScale);
```

continues

Source 9.1 *Continued*

```
     // Create a bounds for the background, behaviors and lights
     //
     BoundingSphere bounds =
         new BoundingSphere(new Point3d(0.0,0.0,0.0), 100.0);

   // Set up the background. Texture with an image or a solid.
   // Default is solid.
   //
   Background bg = new Background(backcolor);
   if (applet == true) {
       if (backURL != null) {
           TextureLoader bgtex = new TextureLoader(backURL,
                                    new String("RGB"),
                                    0,
                                    this);

           Background bg1 = new Background(bgtex.getImage());
           bg1.setApplicationBounds(bounds);
           objRoot.addChild(bg1);
       }
   }
   else if (back != null) {

           TextureLoader bgtex = new TextureLoader(back,
                                    new String("RGB"),
                                    0,
                                    this);

           Background bg2 = new Background(bgtex.getImage());
           bg2.setApplicationBounds(bounds);
           objRoot.addChild(bg2);

   }


   // Set up lights
   //
   Color3f lColor1 = new Color3f(0.7f, 0.7f, 0.7f);
   Vector3f lDir1  = new Vector3f(-1.0f, -1.0f, -1.0f);
   Color3f alColor = new Color3f(0.8f, 0.8f, 0.8f);

   AmbientLight aLgt = new AmbientLight(alColor);
   aLgt.setInfluencingBounds(bounds);
   objScale.addChild(aLgt);

   DirectionalLight lgt1 = new DirectionalLight(lColor1, lDir1);
   lgt1.setInfluencingBounds(bounds);
   objScale.addChild(lgt1);
```

Source 9.1   Complete Texture Mapping Code (*Continued*)

```
    // Create Appearance properties. Texture the Sign with an
    // image or else use a default.
    //
    Appearance app = new Appearance();

    // Assume a solid surface by default.
    app.setMaterial(new Material(gray, black, gray, white, 1.0f));

    if (applet == true) {
        if (imageURL != null) {
            TextureLoader tex = new TextureLoader(imageURL,
                                    new String("RGB"),
                                    0,
                                    this);
            if (tex != null)
                    app.setTexture(tex.getTexture());
        }
    }
    else if (sign != null) {
            TextureLoader tex = new TextureLoader(sign,
                                    new String("RGB"),
                                    0,
                                    this);
            if (tex != null)
                    app.setTexture(tex.getTexture());
    }

    // Create the Sign which is a rectangle
    //
    Primitive thesign =  new Box(1.0f, 0.6f, 0.1f,
                        Box.GENERATE_TEXTURE_COORDS |
                        Box.GENERATE_NORMALS, app);

    // Rotate the Sign slowly.
    TransformGroup signRot = new Rotator(new Transform3D(),
                        Rotator.SLOW);

    // Add everything to the Scene Graph
    //
    objScale.addChild(signRot);
    signRot.addChild(thesign);

    return objRoot;
}

public void init() {
```

continues

Source 9.1 *Continued*

```
          // If we are running as an applet we need to
          // initialize values according to the user settings in
          // the HTML file accomplished by lookForParameters().
          // Otherwise we'll just use the values used to initialize
          // the local variable declarations at the top of the block.
          //
          if (getParameter("SignImage") != null) {
                  lookForParameters();
          }

          setLayout(new BorderLayout());
          Canvas3D c = new Canvas3D(null);
          add("Center", c);

          // Create a simple scene and attach it to the virtual universe
          BranchGroup scene = createSceneGraph();
          SimpleUniverse u = new SimpleUniverse(c);

          // This will move the ViewPlatform back a bit so the
          // objects in the scene can be viewed.
          u.getViewingPlatform().setNominalViewingTransform();

          u.addBranchGraph(scene);
      }


      //
      // The following allows Sign to be run as an application
      // as well as an applet
      //
      public static void main(String[] args) {
          if (args.length > 0) {
              // Parse Input Arguments
              for (int i = 0; i < args.length; i++) {

                  if (args[i].equals("-demo")) {
                      new MainFrame(new Sign(), 400, 200);
                  } else {
                      System.out.println("Usage: java Sign -demo");
                      System.exit(0);
                  }
              }
          } else {
              System.out.println("Usage: java Sign -demo");
              System.exit(0);
          }
      } // END Main

}
```

Source 9.1 Complete Texture Mapping Code (*Continued*)

Moving On

Another chapter down. Only three more to go! As you can see, the Java 3D API is a very powerful and robust tool for creating wonderful 3D graphics. By now, you should be getting used to the constructs and the order of the Java 3D interface. Next we are going to liven things up and create 3D sound.

Java 3D Sound

"Am I afraid of high notes? Of course I am afraid!
What sane man is not?"

—LUCIANO PAVAROTTI

Playing music and sounds over the Web has been possible for quite some time. The audio is recorded in an audio format that is sent over the Web to an audio player on the other side of the connection. One big problem in delivering sound, however, has been bandwidth. An uncompressed audio file is huge. If, say, the file were recorded in CD quality (44.1 kHz, 16-bit stereo), it would equal 180/Kbps (kilobytes per second), or 10 megabytes per minute. To give you some frame of reference, a 28.8 modem can handle only about 200K per minute, which means the quality of the recorded audio would need to be encoded at 8 kHz/mono. It would sound like telephone-quality audio. I don't think Beethoven would have approved.

What else can be done? There have been numerous recent innovations in compression technology, which compacts the audio file, to something like a 30:1 ratio, before sending it down the wire. On the other end, the file is decompressed and played. Within a Web browser, when the user clicks on a link to an audio file, the browser requests the file from the Internet server on the other end. The request is fulfilled and sent to the browser, which then launches a helper application to play the audio. For the user, this means lots of waiting. Java has improved this process by embedding logic in the browser, which can perform the same functions as the helper applications to load and play audio segments. There are a bunch of audio formats out there on the Net, including AU (by Sun), WAV (by Microsoft and IBM), MPEG, RealAudio, ShockWave, MIDI+SBK, and others. Java 3D offers many interesting innovations to audio content that will be discussed here, including support for AIF, WAV, and AU audio formats.

Sound3D Description and Usage

The Sound3D applet (see Figure 10.1) demonstrates Java 3D sound. The program loads a specified 3D data file in the WaveFront format (*.obj) and associates a sound file, a textured image, or a URL with the 3D object. The scene can be composed of multiple objects. Users then navigate toward the objects in the scene. The closer they get, the louder the music becomes; the farther away they are from the objects, the more sound volume decreases. This applet is a lot of fun to use, and surfers will want to hang around for awhile trying out all of the sound objects.

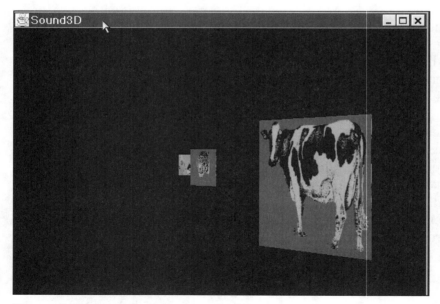

Figure 10.1   Sound3D applet.

Sound3D Applet Parameters Explained

The following is the defined HTML interface to this program. How to read the syntax of the provided HTML file (Sound3D.html) was covered in Chapter 4 in great detail, so we will not repeat the discussion here and bore you to sleep. If you have been following along, the syntax will look familiar.

NumSounds[n].   You will need to specify how many objects you plan to use in the scene.

```
value="3"
```

Poster[n].   A picture can be textured onto the 3D shape. This could be product information, people, or whatever. Remember to create the image dimensions by a power of 2 (i.e., 128×128).

```
value="http://www.sun.com/images/poster1.gif"
```

Sound[n].   The file name of the sound clip is specified and associated to a group by a numeric identification number—Sound1 goes with SoundObject1, SoundURL1, and so on.

```
value="http://www.sun.com/sounds/jazz.wav"
```

NavType.   Specify the type of navigation action of either "walk" or "examine".

```
value="walk"
```

Java 3D Sound Concepts

The Java 3D scene graph can support and contain multiple sound effects. Sound can be triggered by mouse clicks or behaviors to produce environmental sound effects and continuous sounds. In Java 3D, there are three types of sound: background, point, and cone. Java 3D also has a class to set up sound environments called *soundscapes*. The Soundscape node describes the aural area that the sound occupies. A Soundscape object has a bounding region (which can be thought of as a "room" the sound is played in). Soundscape nodes also have an *AuralAttributes NodeComponent* object. This is a class that is used to control sound properties like:

- Amplitude scale factoring to control the volume.
- Control flags to disable, repeat, or remove sound.
- Looping parameters and playback properties.

The *BackgroundSound* node defines unattenuated and nonspatialized audio that doesn't have a specific position or direction (a similar concept to ambient lighting). The next time you go shopping, listen for "happy" music playing in the background, which sounds the same no matter which aisle you travel down. The music seems to be everywhere, and the source of the music is undetectable. That's background music.

The *PointSound* node defines spatially located sound that radiates uniformly in all directions from some point in space. The listener can immediately determine the direction and distance of the sound source. This sound is like the small speaker on your laptop from which you hear crisp sound clips, dings, and ticks while using applications or playing computer games.

The *ConeSound* node defines a point sound to which the source of the audio is directed along a vector in 3D space (see Figure 10.2). The sound emits radially from a point and in a certain direction while constrained to a cone shape. This type of sound is like the police bullhorn: "You there, in the Java T-shirt! Put down that latté and behave yourself!" If you are in front of the bullhorn, you definitely hear it. But if you are 1,000 yards behind the bullhorn on an open field, you might not be able to hear what was said unless you caught an echo of the sound waves.

Sound nodes play sound data that is loaded by the *MediaContainer* class. The sound data originates from an audio file or a URL link to an audio file. Streaming audio is also supported. The MediaContainer class provides the capability to load a given sound file from local disk or a specified URL. Also,

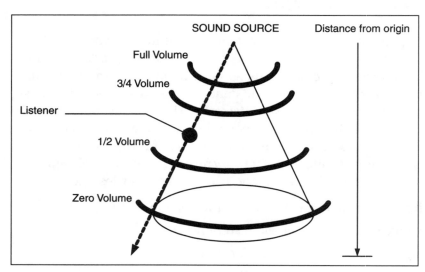

Figure 10.2   ConeSound with distance gain array.

each sound node has a scheduling bounds, a bounding volume in the shape of a sphere, box, or polytope (a volume defined by a closed intersection of half-spaces). By default, sounds do not set their scheduling bounds, and a common mistake is to forget to set them—no wonder we can't hear anything! Sounds are played when the user or object triggers the sound action by intersecting the scheduling bounds.

To add depth and realism, we can manipulate the sound environment using soundscapes and aural attributes. These classes add effects like reverberation, echoes, and Doppler effects. By using these attributes, we can create virtual music rooms. The environment can be set up as a concert hall or a small jazz club. Music played in a concert hall sounds much different from music played on a small stage in some club. Many of the top-line luxury automobiles, like the BMW 740il, have these features integrated into their stereo systems. With a push of a button, the reverb is adjusted to modify the audio signal either to absorb certain wavelengths that soften and mute the sound or to replicate the wavelength with delays to produce a bouncy, sound echo that we would expect in a large amphitheater.

The following is the class hierarchical relationship of our sound components:

```
java.lang.Object
   |
   +----javax.media.j3d.SceneGraphObject
           |
           +----javax.media.j3d.Node
                   |
                   +----javax.media.j3d.Leaf
                           |
                           +----javax.media.j3d.Sound
                           |
                           +----javax.media.j3d.BackgroundSound
                           |
                           +----javax.media.j3d.PointSound
                           |
                           +----javax.media.j3d.ConeSound
```

The following javadoc information contains some of the terms used with Sound nodes and are a useful reference with which to end our discussion on Sound object concepts.

Sound Data

Associated with each Sound node is a MediaContainer that includes audio data and information about this data. This data can be cached (buffered) or noncached (unbuffered or streaming). If an AudioDevice has been attached to the PhysicalEnvironment, the sound data is made ready to begin playing. Certain functionality cannot be applied to true streaming sound data:

- Querying the sound's duration (Sound.DURATION_UNKNOWN will be returned).
- Looping over a range of the streaming data.
- Restarting a previously played portion of the data.

Initial Gain

This gain is a scale factor that is applied to the sound data associated with this sound source to increase or decrease its overall amplitude.

Loop

Data for nonstreaming sound (such as a sound sample) can contain two loop points that mark a section of the data that is to be looped a specific number of times. Thus, sound data can be divided into three segments:

- The attack (prior to the begin loop point).
- The sustain (between the begin and end loop points).
- The release (after the end loop point).

If there are no loop begin and end points defined as part of the sound data, then the begin loop point is set at the beginning of the sound data and the end loop point at the end of the sound data. If this is the case, looping the sound means repeating the whole sound. However, these points allow a portion in the middle of the sound to be looped. A sound can be looped a specified number of times after it has been activated before it is completed.

The loop count value explicitly sets the number of times the sound is looped. Any nonnegative number is a valid value. A value of 0 denotes that the looped section is not repeated but is played only once. A value of −1 denotes that the loop is repeated indefinitely.

Changing the loop count of a sound after the sound has been started will not dynamically affect the loop count currently being used by the sound playing. The new loop count will be used the next time the sound is enabled.

Release Flag

When a sound is disabled, its playback normally stops immediately, no matter what part of the sound data was currently being played. By setting the Release Flag to True for nodes with nonstreaming sound data, the sound is allowed to play from its current position in the sound data to the end of the data (without repeats), thus playing the release portion of the sound before stopping.

Continuous Flag

For some applications, it's useful to turn a sound source off but to continue "silently" playing the sound so that when it is turned back on the sound picks up playing in the same location (over time) that it would have been if the sound had never been disabled (turned off). Setting the Continuous flag to True causes the sound renderer to keep track of where (over time) the sound would be playing even when the sound is disabled.

Enable Sound

When enabled, the sound source starts playing and thus can potentially be heard, depending on its activation state, gain control parameters, continuation state, and spatialization parameters. If the continuous state is True, even if the sound is not active, enabling the sound starts the sound silently playing, so that when the sound is activated, the sound is (potentially) heard from somewhere in the middle of the sound data. The Activation state can change from active to inactive any number of times without stopping or starting the sound. To restart a sound at the beginning of its data, you reenable the sound by calling setEnable set to True.

Setting the enable flag to True during construction will act as a request to start the sound playing as soon as it can be started. This could be close to immediately in limited cases, but several conditions, detailed in the following, must be met for a sound to be ready to be played.

Scheduling Bounds

A sound is scheduled for activation when its scheduling region intersects the ViewPlatform's activation volume. This is used when the scheduling bounding leaf is set to Null.

Scheduling Bounding Leaf

When set to a value other than Null, this scheduling bounding leaf region overrides the scheduling bounds object.

Prioritize Sound

Sound priority is used to rank concurrently playing sounds in order of importance during playback. When more sounds are started than the AudioDevice can handle, the sound node with the lowest priority ranking is deactivated (though it continues to play silently). If a sound is deactivated (because a sound with a higher priority was started), it is automatically reactivated when resources become available (e.g., when the sound with a higher priority finishes playing) or when the ordering of sound nodes is changed due to a shift in a sound node's priority.

For example, assume we have eight channels available for playing sounds. After ordering four sounds, we begin playing them in order, checking if the channels required to play a given sound are actually available before the sound is played. Furthermore, say the first sound needs three channels to play, the second sound needs four channels, the third sound needs three channels, and the fourth sound needs only one channel. The first and second sounds can be started because they require seven of the eight available channels. The third sound cannot be audibly started because it requires three channels and only one is still available. Consequently, the third sound starts playing silently. The fourth sound can and will be started since it only requires one channel. The third sound will be made audible when three channels become available (i.e., when the first or second sound finishes playing).

Sounds given the same priority are ordered randomly. If the application wants a specific ordering, it must assign unique priorities to each sound.

Methods to determine which audio output resources are required for playing a Sound node on a particular AudioDevice and to determine the currently available audio output resources are described in the AudioDevice class.

Duration

Each sound has a length of time specified in milliseconds that it can run (including the repeating loop section) if it plays to completion. If the sound media type is streaming, or if the sound is looped indefinitely, then a value of −1 (implying infinite length) is returned.

Number of Channels Used to Play Sound

When a sound is started, it might use more than one channel on the selected AudioDevice on which it is to be played. The number of Audio-Device channels currently used for a sound can be queried using getNumberOfChannelsUsed().

Preparing a Sound to Be Played

Sound data associated with a Sound node, either during construction (when the MediaContainer is passed into the constructor as a parameter) or by calling setSoundData(), can be prepared to begin playing only after the following conditions are satisfied:

1. The Sound node has nonnull sound data associated with it.

2. The Sound node is live.

3. There is an active view in the Universe.

4. There is an initialized AudioDevice associated with the PhysicalEnvironment.

Depending on the type of MediaContainer the sound data is, and on the implementation of the AudioDevice used, sound data preparation could consist of opening, attaching, loading, or copying into memory the associated sound data. The isReady() query method returns True when the sound is fully preprocessed so that it is playable (audibly if active, silently if not).

Playing Status

A sound source will not be heard unless it is both enabled/started and activated. While these conditions are meet, the sound is potentially audible, and the isPlaying() method will return a status of True. If a sound is enabled before it is activated, it begins playing silently. If a sound is enabled, then deactivated while playing, it continues playing silently. In both of these cases, isPlaying() returns False, though the isPlayingSilently() method returns True. When the sound finishes playing, its sound data (including all loops) is implicitly disabled.

Creating 3D Sound

To add 3D audio to your programs you need a couple of components. The following basic template can be used:

1. Create and initialize an instance of the JavaSoundMixer AudioDevice and attach it to the PhysicalEnvironment via SimpleUniverse.

```
public SoundDemoApplet( ) {

    // Parse commandline arguments

    // Set Layout Manager
    // Create Canvas3D object
    // Create SimpleUniverse object

    AudioDevice  adev =
            u.getViewer().createAudioDevice();

// Create SceneGraph
// Add scene BranchGraph
}
```

2. Preload the various audio sounds before they are needed using a MediaContainer class.

3. Create the bounding volume that will be used with the Bounding-Sphere class.

4. Create one or more of the Sound nodes and set class properties.

5. Set the SchedulingBounds object using the created bounding volume.

You'll find complete source code for the Sound3D applet at the end of this chapter. It illustrates how these steps fall nicely into place.

MediaContainer Object

The MediaContainer object defines all sound data: cached state flag and associated sound data. Currently, this references the media in the form of a URL path to the sound data. In future releases, this will include references to Java media sound API objects. The following is the class diagram showing the MediaContainer class relationship.

```
java.lang.Object
   |
   +----javax.media.j3d.SceneGraphObject
        |
        +----javax.media.j3d.NodeComponent
```

```
              |
              +----javax.media.j3d.MediaContainer
String path  =  getCurrentDirectory( );
MediaContainer  song  =  new MediaContainer(path + "hiddyho.wav");
song.setCacheEnable(true);
```

A full explicit path can be defined and amended to the string name of our sound file. This is passed to the media container, after which the Media-Container is instructed to cache this data so it will be ready to go.

MediaContainer Constants

There are a few constants that can be set on the MediaContainer class:

ALLOW_CACHE_READ. Specifies that this object allows the reading of its cached flag.

ALLOW_CACHE_WRITE. Specifies that this object allows the writing of its cached flag.

ALLOW_URL_READ. Specifies that this object allows the reading of its sound data.

ALLOW_URL_WRITE. Specifies that this object allows the writing of its URL path.

The following are the MediaContainer constructors:

```
MediaContainer()
MediaContainer(java.lang.String path)
MediaContainer(java.net.URL url)
```

The following are the MediaContainer methods:

getCacheEnable(). Retrieves the Cache Enable state flag.

getURL(). Retrieves a URL.

setCacheEnable(boolean flag). Sets Cache Enable state flag. Allows the writing of sound data explicitly into the MediaContainer rather than just referencing a JavaMedia container.

setURL(java.lang.String path). Sets local file.

setURL(java.net.URL url). Sets a URL.

Background Sound

The BackgroundSound node defines unattenuated and nonspatialized audio that doesn't have a specific position or direction. The audio from a background sound comes from all directions at a constant volume. Java 3D supports the implementation of multiple background sound nodes. The node sits underneath and extends the Java 3D Sound node.

```
java.lang.Object
   |
   +----javax.media.j3d.SceneGraphObject
        |
        +----javax.media.j3d.Node
             |
             +----javax.media.j3d.Leaf
                  |
                  +----javax.media.j3d.Sound
                       |
                       +----javax.media.j3d.BackgroundSound
```

The following are the provided BackgroundSound constructors:

```
BackgroundSound( )
BackgroundSound(MediaContainer  soundData,
    float  initialGain);
BackgroundSound(MediaContainer soundData,
          float  initialGain,
          int  loopcount,
          boolean  release,
          boolean  continuous,
          boolean  enable,
          Bounds  region,
          float  priority)
```

The following are the parameters:

soundData.   Sound data associated with this sound source node.

initialGain.   Amplitude scale factor applied to sound source.

loopCount.   Number of times loop is repeated.

release.   Flag denoting playing sound data to end.

continuous.   Denotes that sound plays silently when disabled.

enable.   Sound switched on/off.

region.   Activation bounds.

priority.   Playback ranking value.

Consider the following source code listing that will create the sound object:

```
MediaContainer  soundtrack  =  new
MediaContainer("i_feel_good.au");
soundtrack.setCacheEnable(true);
float volume = 20.0f;

BackgroundSound  sound  =  new
        BackgroundSound(soundtrack,volume);

sound.setCapability(PointSound.ALLOW_ENABLE_WRITE);
sound.setCapability(PointSound.ALLOW_INITIAL_GAIN_WRITE);
sound.setCapability(PointSound.ALLOW_SOUND_DATA_WRITE);
sound.setCapability(PointSound.ALLOW_SCHEDULING_BOUNDS_WRITE);
sound.setCapability(PointSound.ALLOW_CONT_PLAY_WRITE);
sound.setCapability(PointSound.ALLOW_RELEASE_WRITE);
sound.setCapability(PointSound.ALLOW_DURATION_READ);
sound.setCapability(PointSound.ALLOW_IS_PLAYING_READ);
sound.setCapability(PointSound.ALLOW_LOOP_WRITE);

sound.setSchedulingBounds(new BoundingSphere(
    new  Point3d(0.0,0.0,0.0),
    100.0);
```

Point Sound

Point sounds emit audio in all directions from a point. The sound waves are attenuated: the volume of the sound fades as the viewer moves away from the point sound position. A scene can have multiple point sounds playing, and they are useful for adding sound effects to your scene.

```
MediaContainer  laser  =  new  MediaContainer("lasergun.au");
Point2f [ ]  fader = {
    new Point2f(0.0f, 1.0f, 0.0f),  // Full volume
    new Point2f(0.0f, 1.5f, 0.0f),  // 3/4
    new Point2f(0.0f, 2.0f, 0.0f),  // 1/2
    new Point2f(0.0f, 2.5f, 0.0f),  // 1/4
};
TransformGroup tg  =  new TransformGroup( );
PointSound  zap  =  new  PointSound( );
zap.setSoundData(laser);
zap.setEnable(true);         // start playing
zap.setLoop(1);          // play twice(zero-based value)
zap.setPosition(new Point3f(0.0f,1.0f,0.0f));
zap.setDistanceGain(fader);
zap.setSchedulingBounds(bounds);
group.addChild(zap);
```

Cone Sound

A Cone sound emits audio from a point toward a direction. The shape of the sound is constrained to a cone. This is useful in simulating speakers and intercoms. ConeSound is an extension of the PointSound class.

```
MediaContainer  laser  =  new  MediaContainer("lasergun.au");
Point2f [ ]  frontgain = {
    new Point2f(0.0f, 1.0f, 0.0f),  // Full volume
    new Point2f(0.0f, 1.5f, 0.0f),  // 3/4
    new Point2f(0.0f, 2.0f, 0.0f),  // 1/2
    new Point2f(0.0f, 2.5f, 0.0f),  // 1/4
};
Point2f [ ]  backgain = {
    new Point2f(0.0f, 1.0f, 0.0f),  // Full volume
    new Point2f(0.0f, 1.5f, 0.0f),  // 3/4
    new Point2f(0.0f, 2.0f, 0.0f),  // 1/2
    new Point2f(0.0f, 2.5f, 0.0f),  // 1/4
};
Point2f [ ]  fader  =  {
    new Point2f(0.0f, 1.0f, 0.0f),  // Full volume
    new Point2f(0.0f, 1.5f, 0.0f),  // 3/4
    new Point2f(0.0f, 2.0f, 0.0f),  // 1/2
    new Point2f(0.0f, 2.5f, 0.0f),  // 1/4
};
TransformGroup tg  =  new TransformGroup( );
PointSound  zap  =  new  PointSound( );
zap.setSoundData(laser);
zap.setEnable(true);        // start playing
zap.setLoop(1);         // play twice(zero-based value)
zap.setPosition(new Point3f(0.0f,1.0f,0.0f));
zap.setDirection(new Vector3f(1.0f, 0.0f, 0.0f));
zap.setDistanceGain(frontgain, backgain);
zap.setAngularAttenuation(fader);
zap.setSchedulingBounds(bounds);
group.addChild(zap);
```

The attenuation angles are in a range from 0.0 to PI radians. This is used to set the audio's frequency as it varies when played at an angle away from the listener. A trumpet being played at 90 degrees from your ears will sound much differently from the trumpet blowing toward you head-on.

Sound3D Applet Source Code

Source 10.1 is self-documenting code that adds a few interesting objects, such as a custom behavior and several sound objects.

```
import java.applet.*;
import java.awt.*;
import java.awt.event.*;
import com.sun.j3d.utils.applet.MainFrame;
import com.sun.j3d.utils.universe.*;
import javax.media.j3d.*;
import javax.vecmath.*;
import java.io.*;
import com.sun.j3d.loaders.*;
import com.sun.j3d.utils.behaviors.mouse.*;
import com.sun.j3d.utils.geometry.*;
import com.sun.j3d.utils.image.*;
import java.net.MalformedURLException;
import java.net.URL;

/**-------------------------------------------------------------------
   Credits:
   Sound3D program by Kirk Brown

   Sound3D creates a virtual sound scape which contains spinning
   posters related to the music source emmiting from the area
   and direction of the poster. There can be several areas that
   can be specified. As the user moves their mouse closer to a sound
   source, the volume attenuates based on the distance between the
   viewer and the sound source. This way a user can "walk" up to a
   sound source for a preview and walk away to discontinue. The idea
   would be to create numerous sound posters, like the CEO discussing
   their vision, or a friendly receptionist's welcome or a virtual
   jukebox with top performers.

   The viewer uses a special behavior that allows the user to fly
   through a simple "flat" scene by transforms that only affect
   the X and Z planes. Navigation is restricted to the movement
   along the X or Z axis or "forward", "back", "left" and "right".
   This is accomplished by pressing down the left mouse button and
   dragging it around.

   -------------------------------------------------------------------*/

public class Sound3D extends Applet {

      // Class variables.  The default values can be overridden
      // by using the PARAMS tag when invoking the applet.
      //
      // The following is the defined HTML interface to this program:
```
continues

Source 10.1 Complete Sound3D Applet Code

```
    //
    //        <PARAM NAME="numSounds" VALUE="3">
    //        <PARAM NAME="Sound1" VALUE="[URL]bigBand.wav">
    //        <PARAM NAME="Sign1" VALUE="[URL]dorsey.jpg">
    //
    //        <PARAM NAME="SoundBackground"
    //               VALUE="http://www.sun.com/images/clouds.jpg">
    //                    Value Options: "[URL][image file]"
    //               <PARAM NAME="Ground" VALUE="black">
    //                    Value Options = blue,green,yellow,
    //                                        purple,gold,
    //                                        orange,black,white,
    //                                        medblue,medgreen
    //

    // Pre-defined colors
    Color3f white = new Color3f(1.0f, 1.0f, 1.0f);
    Color3f black = new Color3f(0.0f, 0.0f, 0.0f);
    Color3f gray = new Color3f(0.6f, 0.6f, 0.6f);
    Color3f red   = new Color3f(1.0f, 0.0f, 0.0f);
    Color3f ambientred = new Color3f(0.4f, 0.1f, 0.0f);
    Color3f medred = new Color3f(0.80f, 0.4f, 0.3f);
    Color3f green   = new Color3f(0.0f, 0.80f, 0.2f);
    Color3f ambientgreen = new Color3f(0.0f, 0.3f, 0.1f);
    Color3f medgreen = new Color3f(0.0f, 0.5f, 0.1f);
    Color3f orange   = new Color3f(0.7f, 0.4f, 0.0f);
    Color3f ambientorange = new Color3f(0.5f, 0.02f, 0.0f);
    Color3f medorange = new Color3f(0.5f, 0.2f, 0.1f);
    Color3f blue   = new Color3f(0.1f, 0.3f, 0.9f);
    Color3f ambientblue = new Color3f(0.0f, 0.1f, 0.4f);
    Color3f medblue = new Color3f(0.0f, 0.1f, 0.4f);
    Color3f gold = new Color3f(1.0f, 0.8f, 0.0f);
    Color3f yellow = new Color3f(1.0f, 1.0f, 0.6f);
    Color3f purple = new Color3f(0.5f, 0.2f, 0.8f);
    Color3f medpurple = new Color3f(0.5f, 0.2f, 0.5f);

    // Declare constants and variables
    private int numSounds = 4;

    private static String[] pimage =
        { "poster1.jpg", "poster2.jpg", "poster3.jpg", poster4.jpg"};
    private URL[] imageURL =
        { null, null, null, null };

    private String backimage = new String("clouds.jpg");
    private URL backURL = null;
```

Source 10.1   Complete Sound3D Applet Code (*Continued*)

```
private String[] psound =
     { "Classical.wav", "FastDance.wav",
       "SweetDreams.wav", "Rockin2.wav" };
private URL[] psoundURL =
     { null, null, null, null };
private MediaContainer[] media =
     { null, null, null, null };

private Color3f backcolor = black;
private Color3f groundcolor = gray;

private boolean applet = false;

// Array of card objects
Box[] poster = new Box[4];
TransformGroup[] posterTrans = new TransformGroup[4];

// Examines all parameters that can be passed in to this
// applet and updates the global state to reflect any
// non-default settings.
private void lookForParameters() {

    // Used to read in the pramaters for the applet.
    String paramValue;

    // Running as an applet
    applet = true;

    paramValue = getParameter("numSounds");
    if (paramValue != null) {
            numSounds = Integer.parseInt(paramValue);
            // Program designed only to support max of
            // 8 sounds.
            if (numSounds > 8)
                numSounds = 8;
    }
    else {
            numSounds = 1;
    }

    paramValue = getParameter("SoundBackground");
    if (paramValue != null) {
       backimage = new String();
       if (paramValue.equalsIgnoreCase("red") == true) {
               backcolor = red;
       }
       else if (paramValue.equalsIgnoreCase("green") == true) {
```
                                                              continues

Source 10.1 *Continued*

```
                    backcolor = green;
            }
            else if (paramValue.equalsIgnoreCase("blue") == true) {
                    backcolor = blue;
            }
            else if (paramValue.equalsIgnoreCase("medred") == true) {
                    backcolor = medred;
            }
            else if (paramValue.equalsIgnoreCase("medgreen")== true) {
                    backcolor = medgreen;
            }
            else if (paramValue.equalsIgnoreCase("medblue") == true) {
                    backcolor = medblue;
            }
            else if (paramValue.equalsIgnoreCase("black") == true) {
                    backcolor = black;;
            }
            else if (paramValue.equalsIgnoreCase("gray") == true) {
                    backcolor = gray;
            }
            else if (paramValue.equalsIgnoreCase("white") == true) {
                    backcolor = white;
            }
            else if (paramValue.equalsIgnoreCase("yellow") == true) {
                    backcolor = yellow;
            }
            else if (paramValue.equalsIgnoreCase("gold") == true) {
                    backcolor = gold;
            }
            else if (paramValue.equalsIgnoreCase("purple") == true) {
                    backcolor = purple;
            }
            else if (paramValue.equalsIgnoreCase("medpurple") == true)
{
                    backcolor = medpurple;
            }
            else if (paramValue.equalsIgnoreCase("orange") == true) {
                    backcolor = orange;
            }
            else if (paramValue.equalsIgnoreCase("medorange") == true)
{
                    backcolor = medorange;
            }
            else {
                // If NOT a color Must be a URL image source
                //
```

Source 10.1 Complete Sound3D Applet Code (*Continued*)

```
                    URL bURL;
                    try {
                                bURL = new URL(paramValue);
                    }
                    catch (MalformedURLException e) {
                        // Bad URL.
                        bURL = null;
                    }
                    backURL = bURL;
            }
        }
        else {
            // set it to blank
            backcolor = black;

        }

            paramValue = getParameter("Ground");
        if (paramValue != null) {
            if (paramValue.equalsIgnoreCase("red") == true) {
                    groundcolor = red;
            }
            else if (paramValue.equalsIgnoreCase("green") == true) {
                    groundcolor = green;
            }
            else if (paramValue.equalsIgnoreCase("blue") == true) {
                    groundcolor = blue;
            }
            else if (paramValue.equalsIgnoreCase("medred") == true) {
                    groundcolor = medred;
            }
            else if (paramValue.equalsIgnoreCase("medgreen")== true) {
                    groundcolor = medgreen;
            }
            else if (paramValue.equalsIgnoreCase("medblue") == true) {
                    groundcolor = medblue;
            }
            else if (paramValue.equalsIgnoreCase("black") == true) {
                    groundcolor = black;;
            }
            else if (paramValue.equalsIgnoreCase("gray") == true) {
                    groundcolor = gray;
            }
            else if (paramValue.equalsIgnoreCase("white") == true) {
                    groundcolor = white;
            }
```

continues

Source 10.1 *Continued*

```
        else if (paramValue.equalsIgnoreCase("yellow") == true) {
                groundcolor = yellow;
        }
        else if (paramValue.equalsIgnoreCase("gold") == true) {
                groundcolor = gold;
        }
        else if (paramValue.equalsIgnoreCase("purple") == true) {
                groundcolor = purple;
        }
        else if (paramValue.equalsIgnoreCase("medpurple") == true)
{

                groundcolor = medpurple;
        }
        else if (paramValue.equalsIgnoreCase("orange") == true) {
                groundcolor = orange;
        }
        else if (paramValue.equalsIgnoreCase("medorange") == true)
{

                groundcolor = medorange;
        } else {
                groundcolor = gray;
        }


    // Allocate the needed array space.
    psoundURL = new URL[numSounds];
    imageURL = new URL[numSlides];

    // Look for the parameter values for each slide or set defaults
    for (int i = 0; i < numSlides; i++) {

            paramValue = getParameter("Sound" + (i + 1));
        if (paramValue != null) {
            URL soundURL;
            try {
                            soundURL = new URL(paramValue);
            }
            catch (MalformedURLException e) {
                // Bad URL.
                psoundURL[i] = null;
            }
            psoundURL[i] = soundURL;
        }
        else {
                    // set it to blank
                    psoundURL[i] = null;
        }
```

Source 10.1 Complete Sound3D Applet Code (*Continued*)

```
            paramValue = getParameter("Sign" + (i + 1));
            if (paramValue != null) {
                URL signURL;
                try {
                              signURL = new URL(paramValue);
                }
                catch (MalformedURLException e) {
                    // Bad URL.
                    imageURL[i] = null;
                }
                imageURL[i] = signURL;
            }
            else {
                    // set it to blank
                    imageURL[i] = null;
            }

    } // END for loop

} // END lookForParameters

public BranchGroup createSceneGraph() {

        Vector3f lDir1  = new Vector3f(-1.0f, -0.3f, -1.0f);

    // Create predefined poster positions (max 8) in
    // a clock-like layout.
    //
    Point3f[] position = {
       new Point3f(0.0f, 0.0f, 0.0f),     // 0
       new Point3f(0.0f, 0.0f, 20.0f),    // 1
       new Point3f(20.0f, 0.0f, 0.0f),    // 2
       new Point3f(10.0f, 0.0f, -10.0f),  // 3
       new Point3f(0.0f, 0.0f, -20.0f),   // 4
       new Point3f(-10.0f, 0.0f, -10.0f), // 5
       new Point3f(-20.0f, 0.0f, 0.0f),   // 6
       new Point3f(-10.0f, 0.0f, 10.0f)   // 7
    };

    // Create a distance gain array for each point sound
    // that will be located in the middle of each poster
    // object(s). This will control the sound volume in
    // relation to the distance between the viewer and the
    // poster. If the user is less than 2.0f from the center
    // of the poster, they will hear full volume and so on
```

continues

Source 10.1   *Continued*

```
            // until at 10.5, the sound will shut off. It might be
            // possible to hear multiple sounds, some stronger and
            // some weaker since our sources may overlap just a bit
            // when more than 1 sound is specified in our 60x60x60
            // Universe.
            //
            Point2f[] distgain = {
                        new Point2f( 2.0f, 1.0f ),    // Full volume
                        new Point2f( 5.0f, 0.5f ),    // Half volume
                        new Point2f( 9.9f, 0.25f ),   // Quarter volume
                        new Point2f( 10.5f, 0.0f )    // Zero volume
                    };

        // Create the root of the branch graph
        BranchGroup objRoot = new BranchGroup();

        // Create a TransformGroup to scale all objects so they
        // appear in the scene.
        TransformGroup objScale = new TransformGroup();
        Transform3D t3d = new Transform3D();
        t3d.setScale(0.7);
        objScale.setTransform(t3d);
        objRoot.addChild(objScale);

            // Create the transform group node and initialize it to the
            // identity.  Enable the TRANSFORM_WRITE capability so that
            // our behavior code can modify it at runtime.  Add it to the
            // Scale Transform group of the subgraph.
            TransformGroup objTrans = new TransformGroup();
            objTrans.setCapability(TransformGroup.ALLOW_TRANSFORM_WRITE);
            objTrans.setCapability(TransformGroup.ALLOW_TRANSFORM_READ);
            objScale.addChild(objTrans);

    BoundingSphere bounds =
            new BoundingSphere(new Point3d(0.0,0.0,0.0), 100.0);

    // Set up the background which is a large Sphere that has a
    // texturemap or a solid inner surface. When the user looks
    // around, the scene will appear uniform.
    //
    Appearance a = new Appearance();
    Material m = new Material(backcolor,
                    black, backcolor, white, 80.0f);
    m.setLightingEnable(true);
    a.setMaterial(m);
```

Source 10.1   Complete Sound3D Applet Code (*Continued*)

```
        if (applet == true) {
    if (backURL != null) {
        TextureLoader t = new TextureLoader(backURL,
                                     rgb, this);
            if (t != null)
                    a.setTexture(t.getTexture());
    }
}
else if (backimage != null) {

    TextureLoader bgtex = new TextureLoader(backimage,
                              new String("RGB"),
                              0,
                              this);
    if (bgtex != null)
                    a.setTexture(bgtex.getTexture());
}

Sphere bubble = new Sphere(30.0f,
            Sphere.GENERATE_NORMALS |
            Sphere.GENERATE_TEXTURE_COORDS,
            60, a);

objScale.addChild(bubble);

// Create the transform group for the sound
//   objects within our scene.
TransformGroup soundgroup = new TransformGroup();
soundgroup.setCapability(TransformGroup.ALLOW_TRANSFORM_WRITE);
soundgroup.setCapability(TransformGroup.ALLOW_TRANSFORM_READ);
poster = new Box[numSounds];
objTrans = new TransformGroup[numSounds];

// Create Sound and Poster objects.
//
for (int i = 0; i < numSounds; i++) {

    Appearance app = new Appearance();

    // Prepare possible solid lit color poster
    Material mat = new Material(pcolor,
                black, pcolor, white, 80.0f);
    mat.setLightingEnable(true);
    app.setMaterial(mat);

    // If applet then expect URL references for the
```

continues

Source 10.1 *Continued*

```
            // images, else we are in "-demo" mode and we'll
            // be passing strings to the TextureLoader class.
            // If no image is specified, then we have prepared
            // a solid lit poster surface (above).
            //
            if (applet == true) {
               if (imageURL[i] != null) {
                 TextureLoader pt =
                         new TextureLoader(imageURL[i],
                                  new String("RGB"), this);
                 if (pt != null)
                       app.setTexture(pt.getTexture());
               }
            }
            else if (texture[i] != null) {
                 TextureLoader pt =
                         new TextureLoader(texture[i],
                                  new String("RGB"), this);
                 if (pt != null)
                       app.setTexture(pt.getTexture());
            }

            poster[i] = new Box(0.45f, 0.55f, 0.01f,
                         Box.GENERATE_NORMALS |
                         Box.GENERATE_TEXTURE_COORDS,
                         app);

            // Create the transforms needed to locate the poster
            // objects within our scene.
            Transform3D t = new Transform3D();
            tr.setIdentity();
            tr.setTranslation(new Vector3f(position[i]));
            posterTrans[i] = new TransformGroup(tr);

            // Rotation transform for the poster at slow speed.
            //
            posterRot[i] = new Rotator(new Transform3D(),
                                       Rotator.SLOW);

            // Add the poster object to the position transform
            posterTrans[i].addChild(poster[i]);

            // Add the position transform to the rotator.
            posterRot[i].addChild(posterTrans[i]);

            // Add the rotator to the scaled branch group transform
            objScale.addChild(posterRot[i]);
```

Source 10.1 Complete Sound3D Applet Code (*Continued*)

```
                            // Preload the sounds
                            //
                if (applet == true)
                    MediaContainer media[i]  =
                            new MediaContainer(psoundURL[i]);
                else
                    MediaContainer media[i]  =
                            new MediaContainer(psound[i]);

                media[i].setCacheEnable(true);

                PointSound sound[i] = New PointSound();
                sound[i].setSoundData(media[i]);
                sound[i].setEnable(true);
                sound[i].setLoop(Sound.INFINITE_LOOPS);
                sound[i].setPosition(position[i]);
                sound[i].setInitialGain(0.5f);
                sound[i].setDistanceGain(distgain);
                sound[i].setSchedulingBounds(bounds);
                sound[i].setCapability(Sound.ALLOW_ENABLE_WRITE);
                sound[i].setCapability(Sound.ALLOW_INITIAL_GAIN_WRITE);

                objScale.addChild(sound[i]);

            } // END for loop

            // Set up the ambient light
            AmbientLight ambientLightNode = new AmbientLight(white);
            ambientLightNode.setInfluencingBounds(bounds);
            objScale.addChild(ambientLightNode);

            // Set up the directional lights
            Vector3f light1Direction  = new Vector3f(10.0f, -10.0f, 0.0f);
            Vector3f light2Direction  = new Vector3f(10.0f, 10.0f, 0.0f);

            DirectionalLight light1 = new DirectionalLight(white,
                                                        light1Direction);
            light1.setInfluencingBounds(bounds);
            objScale.addChild(light1);

            DirectionalLight light2 = new DirectionalLight(white,
                                                      light2Direction);
            light2.setInfluencingBounds(bounds);
            objScale.addChild(light2);

            return objRoot;
```

continues

Source 10.1   *Continued*

```
    }

public void init () {

        // If we are running as an applet we need to
        // initialize values according to the user settings in
        // the HTML file accomplished by lookForParameters().
        // Otherwise we'll just use the values used to initialize
        // the local variable declarations at the top of the block.
        //
        if (getParameter("numSounds") != null) {
                lookForParameters();
        }

        setLayout(new BorderLayout());
        Canvas3D c = new Canvas3D(null);
        add("Center", c);

        // Create a simple scene and attach it
        // to the virtual universe .
        BranchGroup scene = createSceneGraph();
        SimpleUniverse u = new SimpleUniverse(c);

        // This will move the ViewPlatform back a bit so the
        // objects in the scene can be viewed.
        u.getViewingPlatform().setNominalViewingTransform();

        //
        //   Get the viewing platform created by SimpleUniverse.
        //   From that platform, get the inner-most TransformGroup
        //   in the MultiTransformGroup.  That inner-most group
        //   contains the ViewPlatform.
        //   The inner-most TransformGroup's transform will be
        //   changed by the walk behavior.
        //
                ViewingPlatform viewingPlatform =
                        universe.getViewingPlatform( );
        viewTransform =
                        viewingPlatform.getViewPlatformTransform( );

        //
        //   Create a "headlight" as a forward-facing directional light
        //   Set the light's bounds to huge.  Since we want the light
        //   on the viewer's "head", we need the light within the
        //   TransformGroup containing the ViewPlatform.  The
        //   ViewingPlatform class creates a handy hook to do this
        //   called "platform geometry". The PlatformGeometry class is
```

Source 10.1 Complete Sound3D Applet Code (*Continued*)

```
//   subclassed off of BranchGroup, and is intended to contain
//   a description of the 3D platform itself and a headlight.
//   So, to add the headlight, create a new PlatformGeometry
//   group, add the light to it, then add that platform
//   geometry to the ViewingPlatform.
//
BoundingSphere allBounds = new BoundingSphere(
                  new Point3d( 0.0, 0.0, 0.0 ), 100000.0 );

PlatformGeometry pg = new PlatformGeometry( );
headlight = new DirectionalLight( );
headlight.setColor( White );
headlight.setDirection( new Vector3f( 0.0f, 0.0f, -1.0f ) );
headlight.setInfluencingBounds( allBounds );
headlight.setCapability( Light.ALLOW_STATE_WRITE );
pg.addChild( headlight );
viewingPlatform.setPlatformGeometry( pg );

// Build the scene root
BranchGroup scene = createSceneGraph();

// Build a transform that we can modify
sceneTransform = new TransformGroup( );
sceneTransform.setCapability(
        TransformGroup.ALLOW_TRANSFORM_READ );
sceneTransform.setCapability(
        TransformGroup.ALLOW_TRANSFORM_WRITE );
sceneTransform.setCapability(
        Group.ALLOW_CHILDREN_EXTEND );

sceneTransform.addChild( scene );

scene.addChild( sceneTransform );

//
// Create a pair of behaviors to implement two navigation
// types:
//
//    - "examine":  a style where mouse drags rotate about
//      the scene's origin as if it is an object under
//      examination.  This is similar to the "Examine"
//      navigation type used by VRML browsers.
//
//    - "walk":  a style where mouse drags rotate about
//      the viewer's center as if the viewer is turning
//      about to look at a scene they are in.  This is
```

continues

Source 10.1 *Continued*

```
            //        similar to the "Walk" navigation type used by
            //        VRML browsers.
            //
            //  Aim the examine behavior at the scene's TransformGroup
            //  and add the behavior to the scene root.
            //
            //  Aim the walk behavior at the viewing platform's
            //  TransformGroup and add the behavior to the scene root.
            //
            //  Enable one (and only one!) of the two behaviors
            //  depending upon the current navigation type.
            //
            walkBehavior = new WalkViewerBehavior(
                    viewTransform,  // Transform group to modify
                    null );         // Parent frame for cusor changes
            walkBehavior.setSchedulingBounds( allBounds );
            scene.addChild( walkBehavior );
            walkBehavior.setEnable( true );


            //
            //  Compile the scene branch group and add it to the
            //  SimpleUniverse.
            //
            scene.compile( );
            u.addBranchGraph( scene );

    } // END init

    //
    // The following allows the program to be run as an application
    // as well as an applet
    //
    public static void main(String[] args) {
        if (args.length > 0) {
            // Parse Input Arguments
            for (int i = 0; i < args.length; i++) {

                if (args[i].equals("-demo")) {
                    new MainFrame(new Sound3D(), 400, 400);
                } else {
                        System.out.println("Usage: java Sound3D -demo");
                    System.exit(0);
                    }
            }
        } else {
                System.out.println("Usage: java Sound3D -demo");
                System.exit(0);
```

Source 10.1   Complete Sound3D Applet Code (*Continued*)

```
        }

    } // END Main

}  // END class
```

Source 10.1 *Continued*

Moving On

Now you are ready to add some new kinds of sounds to your Java 3D programs. We have covered many types of sound classes to choose from and some examples to get you started. We are finished with this chapter and are now ready to move onto 3D text.

CHAPTER

11

3D Text and Fonts

"P-O-T-A-T-O-E . . . Potatoe."

–DAN QUAYLE

Web sites are a common place to find nice logos designed using interesting professional fonts (see Figure 11.1). These headings, headers, and attention grabbers often simulate 3D graphics—they spin, they scroll, they animate. Some even contain textures and light sources. Anyone can throw a Web page together, but its success depends on content and delivery. They're everything. A user's first reaction to a great Web site is visual: shouts of Wow! Cool! echo over the wire. But graphics and text need to have the right balance. Too much text and the Web page becomes a stale textbook. Too many blinking and flashing components and the Web page becomes an irritating commercial. Java 3D can provide some very interesting 3D text and imagery to keep your visitors glued to your Web page.

Java 3D does support fonts! But a spell checker is NOT included! The 3D Font class uses 3D glyphs to create the 3D fonts. The 3D glyphs are constructed from Java 2D font objects, which are then extruded to create depth and the 3D shape. Java 3D uses a couple of components to accomplish this feat. The Font3D object determines the appearance of the desired text, which is used when creating Text3D Geometry objects. Text3D objects require a Font3D object, a text string, and a text position value (the point in 3D space where the text string will be placed).

Figure 11.1   3D text.

TieRack Description and Usage

This applet (see Figure 11.2) reminds us of a tie rack, hence its name. There are several text strings stacked one on top of the other. Each of the "racks" swings around in a circle, with one end fixed at the Y-axis. The applet is passed five different parameters: a text string, and the desired font, text color, text size, and a URL associated with the text string. When the user clicks on the text "rack," the browser loads the specified Web page. This is a great applet to use when creating 3D menus using the 2D Text objects.

TieRack Applet Parameters Explained

This again is our familiar applet interface, where each parameter has an associated value. The basic parameter format consists of Tie[identifier][rack id].

Figure 11.2   TieRack applet.

NumRacks. The number of text strings specified in the HTML parameter file. Each unique text string is referred to as a "rack."

TieString[n]. Specifies the text string that will be rendered.

TieColor[n]. Specifies the color of the text string.

TieFont[n]. Specifies the name of the font to be used. Java 3D supports the following: Times, Helvetica, Courier, Serif, Sans Serif

TieSize[n]. Specifies the font size.

TieURL[n]. A URL to link to the text string.

Text Concepts

The Java 3D API provides support to add text to the 3D scene in a couple of ways. There is a Text2D class, which is fairly simple and provides an easy method for labeling scene objects or when some simple text is needed. The other object is the Text3D class. It is created from the Font3D object and provides a very nice form for logos and prominent labels. One of the components of the Text3D object is the Font3D class, which contains 3D glyphs used to render the 3D text. The product of the Text3D object looks more like a 3D shape. It has depth and volume and is treated like other Geometry objects.

TieRack Source Code

Let's take a look at the Text2D object that is used in the Java 3D Source 11.1.

```
// Import needed JDK classes.
import java.applet.*;
import java.awt.*;
import java.net.MalformedURLException;
import java.net.URL;

// Java 3D classes
import javax.media.j3d.*;
import com.sun.j3d.utils.applet.MainFrame;
import javax.vecmath.*;
import com.sun.j3d.utils.universe.*;
import com.sun.j3d.utils.geometry.*;

/**-------------------------------------------------------------
```

continues

Source 11.1 Complete Java 3D TieRack Code

```
        Credits:
        TieRack program by Kirk Brown

        A group of text labels can be stacked in an animated fashion.
        The user can click on any "rack" and jump to an associated URL
        which will load in the browser. This program is a type of 3D menu
        that will animate and capture the user's attention.


-------------------------------------------------------------------*/
public class TieRack extends Applet {

    // Class variables.  The default values can be overridden
    // by using the PARAMS tag when invoking the applet.
    //
    // The following is the defined HTML interface to this program:
    //
    //   <PARAM NAME="NumRacks" VALUE=2>
    //   <PARAM NAME="TieString1" VALUE="About The Company">
    //   <PARAM NAME="TieColor1" VALUE="GREEN" or "0.0 0.1 0.0">
    //   <PARAM NAME="TieFont1" VALUE="HELVETICA">
    //   <PARAM NAME="TieSize1" VALUE="36">
    //   <PARAM NAME="TieURL1" VALUE="www.sun.com/about.html">
    //   <PARAM NAME="TieString2" VALUE="Products">
    //   <PARAM NAME="TieURL2" VALUE="www.sun.com/products.html">

    // Pre-defined colors
    Color3f white = new Color3f(1.0f, 1.0f, 1.0f);
    Color3f black = new Color3f(0.0f, 0.0f, 0.0f);
    Color3f gray = new Color3f(0.6f, 0.6f, 0.6f);
    Color3f red   = new Color3f(1.0f, 0.0f, 0.0f);
    Color3f ambientred = new Color3f(0.4f, 0.1f, 0.0f);
    Color3f medred = new Color3f(0.80f, 0.4f, 0.3f);
    Color3f green   = new Color3f(0.0f, 0.80f, 0.2f);
    Color3f ambientgreen = new Color3f(0.0f, 0.3f, 0.1f);
    Color3f medgreen = new Color3f(0.0f, 0.5f, 0.1f);
    Color3f orange   = new Color3f(0.7f, 0.4f, 0.0f);
    Color3f ambientorange = new Color3f(0.5f, 0.02f, 0.0f);
    Color3f medorange = new Color3f(0.5f, 0.2f, 0.1f);
    Color3f blue    = new Color3f(0.1f, 0.3f, 0.9f);
    Color3f ambientblue = new Color3f(0.0f, 0.1f, 0.4f);
    Color3f medblue = new Color3f(0.0f, 0.1f, 0.4f);
    Color3f gold = new Color3f(1.0f, 0.8f, 0.0f);
    Color3f yellow = new Color3f(1.0f, 1.0f, 0.6f);
    Color3f purple = new Color3f(0.5f, 0.2f, 0.8f);
    Color3f medpurple = new Color3f(0.5f, 0.2f, 0.5f);

    // Total number of racks
```

Source 11.1   Complete Java 3D TieRack Code (*Continued*)

```
    private int numRacks = 3;

    // Array of text strings for each "rack"
    private String[] textstring =
        { "LINKS", "PRODUCT INFO", "CONTACT US" };

    // Array of color values for each "rack"
    private Color3f[] textcolor =
        { red, blue, medpurple };

    // Array of Font types used by each "rack"
    private String[] textfont =
        { "Serif", "Serif", "Serif" };

    // Array of Font size used by each "rack"
    private int[] textsize = { 120, 120, 120 };

    // Array of URLs associated with each "rack"
    private URL[] textlink = { null, null, null };

    boolean applet = false;

    // Examines all parameters that can be passed in to this
    // applet and updates the global state to reflect any
    // non-default settings.
   private void lookForParameters() {

        // Used to read in the parameters for the applet.
        String paramValue;

        // Running as an applet
        applet = true;

        paramValue = getParameter("NumRacks");
        if (paramValue != null)
            numRacks = Integer.parseInt(paramValue);
        else
        // Default
        numRacks = 1;

        // Allocate the needed array space.
        textstring = new String[numRacks];
        textcolor = new Color3f[numRacks];
        textfont = new String[numRacks];
        textsize = new int[numRacks];
        textlink = new URL[numRacks];
```

continues

Source 11.1 *Continued*

```
            // Look for the parameter values for each rack
            //
            for (int i = 0; i < numRacks; i++) {

              // Looks for text string parameter values
              paramValue = getParameter("TieString" + (i + 1));
              if (paramValue != null)
                textstring[i] = paramValue;
              else
                textstring[i] = new String("HTML ERROR");

              // Look for text color parameter value
              paramValue = getParameter("TieColor" + (i + 1));
              if (paramValue != null)
                if (paramValue.equalsIgnoreCase("red") == true) {
                        textcolor[i] = red;
                }
                else if (paramValue.equalsIgnoreCase("green") == true) {
                        textcolor[i] = green;
                }
                else if (paramValue.equalsIgnoreCase("blue") == true) {
                        textcolor[i] = blue;
                }
                else if (paramValue.equalsIgnoreCase("medred") == true) {
                        textcolor[i] = medred;
                }
                else if (paramValue.equalsIgnoreCase("medgreen") == true) {
                        textcolor[i] = medgreen;
                }
                else if (paramValue.equalsIgnoreCase("medblue") == true) {
                        textcolor[i] = medblue;
                }
                else if (paramValue.equalsIgnoreCase("black") == true) {
                        textcolor[i] = black;
                }
                else if (paramValue.equalsIgnoreCase("gray") == true) {
                        textcolor[i] = gray;
                }
                else if (paramValue.equalsIgnoreCase("white") == true) {
                        textcolor[i] = white;
                }
                else if (paramValue.equalsIgnoreCase("yellow") == true) {
                        textcolor[i] = yellow;
                }
                else if (paramValue.equalsIgnoreCase("gold") == true) {
                        textcolor[i] = gold;
                }
```

Source 11.1   Complete Java 3D TieRack Code (*Continued*)

```
            else if (paramValue.equalsIgnoreCase("purple") == true) {
                textcolor[i] = purple;
            }
            else if (paramValue.equalsIgnoreCase("medpurple") == true) {
                textcolor[i] = medpurple;
            }
            else if (paramValue.equalsIgnoreCase("orange") == true) {
                textcolor[i] = orange;
            }
            else if (paramValue.equalsIgnoreCase("medorange") == true) {
                textcolor[i] = medorange;
            }
        else
            textcolor[i] = red;

        // Look for text font parameter value
        paramValue = getParameter("TieFont" + (i + 1));
        if (paramValue != null)
            textfont[i] = paramValue;
        else
            textfont[i] = new String("Times");

        // Look for text size parameter value
        paramValue = getParameter("TieSize" + (i + 1));
        if (paramValue != null)
            textsize[i] = Integer.parseInt(paramValue);
        else
            textsize[i] = 120;

        // Look for URL link parameter value
        paramValue = getParameter("TieURL" + (i + 1));
        if (paramValue != null) {
            URL linkURL;
            try {
                linkURL = new URL(paramValue);
            }
            catch (MalformedURLException e) {
                // Bad URL.
                linkURL = null;
            }
            textlink[i] = linkURL;
        }
        else {
            // Default Value
            URL weblink;
            try {
```

continues

Source 11.1   *Continued*

```
                     weblink = new URL("http://www.sun.com");
          }
          catch (MalformedURLException e) {
                     // Bad URL.
                     weblink = null;
          }
          textlink[i] = weblink;
      }

   }  // END of loop

} // END LookForParameters

// Creates all the objects to be inserted in the scene graph.
//
public BranchGroup createSceneGraph(Canvas3D c,
                                    AppletContext context) {

   // Array of text objects in the scene
   Shape3D[] textobj;

   // Array of transform groups for behaviors
   TransformGroup[] objTrans;

   // Array of text transform groups
   TransformGroup[] textransg;

   // Array of 3D matrices
   Transform3D[] textrans;

   // Array of text appearance objects
   Appearance[] textapp;

   // Array of text polygon attributes
   PolygonAttributes[] textpa;

   // Array of Alpha objects
   Alpha[] textalpha;

   // Array of Interpolator objects
   RotationInterpolator[] rotator;

   // Create the root of the branch graph
   BranchGroup objRoot = new BranchGroup();

   BoundingSphere bounds =
      new BoundingSphere(new Point3d(0.0,0.0,0.0), 100.0);
```

Source 11.1   Complete Java 3D TieRack Code (*Continued*)

```
    // Create a Transformgroup to scale all objects so they
    // appear in the scene.
    TransformGroup objScale = new TransformGroup();
    Transform3D t3d = new Transform3D();
    t3d.setScale(0.4);
    objScale.setTransform(t3d);
    objRoot.addChild(objScale);

    // Set up the background
    Color3f bgColor = new Color3f(0.0f, 0.0f, 0.0f);
    Background bg = new Background(bgColor);
    bg.setApplicationBounds(bounds);
    objScale.addChild(bg);

    // Calculate Initial Y position of first text string
    // based on the total number of strings used.
    float yPos = numRacks * 0.1f;

    // Allocate needed array space
    //
    objTrans = new TransformGroup[numRacks];
    textobj = new Text2D[numRacks];
    textapp = new Appearance[numRacks];
    textpa = new PolygonAttributes[numRacks];
    textransg = new TransformGroup[numRacks];
    textrans = new Transform3D[numRacks];
    textalpha = new Alpha[numRacks];
    rotator = new RotationInterpolator[numRacks];

    // Create a bunch of text tie racks that rotate
    //
    for (int i = 0; i < numRacks; i++) {

        // Create the transform group node and initialize it to the
        // identity.  Enable the TRANSFORM_WRITE capability so that
        // our behavior code can modify it at runtime. Add it to the
        // root of the subgraph.
        objTrans[i] = new TransformGroup();
        objTrans[i].setCapability(
                TransformGroup.ALLOW_TRANSFORM_WRITE);

        textobj[i] = new Text2D(textstring[i],
                                textcolor[i],
                                textfont[i],
                                textsize[i],
                                Font.BOLD);
```

continues

Source 11.1 *Continued*

```
         textapp[i] = textobj[i].getAppearance();

         // Turn Culling off here by setting polygon Attrs. so we
         // can see the back side of the text as it swings around.
         textpa[i] = textapp[i].getPolygonAttributes();
         if (textpa[i] == null)
            textpa[i] = new PolygonAttributes();

         textpa[i].setCullFace(PolygonAttributes.CULL_NONE);

         if (textapp[i].getPolygonAttributes() == null)
            textapp[i].setPolygonAttributes(textpa[i]);

         // Position the text
         textrans[i] = new Transform3D();
         textrans[i].setTranslation(new Vector3f(-0.5f, yPos, 0f));
         textransg[i] = new TransformGroup(textrans[i]);

         // Create the rotating Behavior of different speeds
         textalpha[i] = new Alpha(-1, Alpha.INCREASING_ENABLE,
                                  0, 0,
                                  8000+(i*200), 0, 0,
                                  0, 0, 0);

          rotator[i] = new RotationInterpolator(textalpha[i],
                          objTrans[i], textrans[i], 0.0f,
                                   (float) Math.PI*2.0f);

          rotator[i].setSchedulingBounds(bounds);

         // Add everything to the scene
         objScale.addChild(textransg[i]);
         textransg[i].addChild(objTrans[i]);
         objTrans[i].addChild(rotator[i]);
         objTrans[i].addChild(textobj[i]);

         // increment yPos for next text rack
         yPos = yPos + -.4f;

         // Store URL in LocalData object and assign to this
         // primitive. Dont execute this if running -demo.
         if (applet == true) {
                 LocalData ld = new LocalData(textlink[i]);
                 textobj[i].setUserData(ld);
         }

      } // END for loop
```

Source 11.1 Complete Java 3D TieRack Code (*Continued*)

```
        // Setup picking URLs.
        if (applet == true) {
            PickURL pickURL = new PickURL(c, objRoot, bounds,
context);
            pickURL.setSchedulingBounds(bounds);
            objRoot.addChild(pickURL);
        }

        return objRoot;

    } // END createSceneGraph

    public void init() {

        AppletContext context = null;

        // If we are running as an applet we need to
        // initialize values according to the user settings in
        // the HTML file accomplished by lookForParameters().
        // Otherwise we'll just use the values used to initialize
        // the local variable declarations at the top of the block.
        //
        if (getParameter("numRacks") != null) {
            lookForParameters();
        }

        setLayout(new BorderLayout());
        Canvas3D c = new Canvas3D(null);
        add("Center", c);

        // Create a simple scene and attach it to the virtual universe
        BranchGroup scene = createSceneGraph(c, context);
        SimpleUniverse u = new SimpleUniverse(c);

        // This will move the ViewPlatform back a bit so the
        // objects in the scene can be viewed.
        u.getViewingPlatform().setNominalViewingTransform();

        u.addBranchGraph(scene);
    }

    //
    // The following allows TieRack to be run as an application
    // as well as an applet
    //
    public static void main(String[] args) {
```

continues

Source 11.1 *Continued*

```
        if (args.length > 0) {
            // Parse Input Arguments
            for (int i = 0; i < args.length; i++) {

                if (args[i].equals("-demo")) {
                    new MainFrame(new TieRack(), 450, 200);
                } else {
                    System.out.println("Usage: java TieRack -demo");
                    System.exit(0);
                }
            }
        } else {
            System.out.println("Usage: java TieRack -demo");
            System.exit(0);
        }
    } // END Main
}
```

Source 11.1 Complete Java 3D TieRack Code (*Continued*)

TieRack Source Code Explained

Starting at the beginning, a TieRack public class is declared. Our TieRack object is created when the applet is invoked, or from main() in the standalone situation. In any case, TieRack will begin to construct itself by executing the methods, along with data contained within the same pair of curly braces.

We'll use part of the Java AWT package to create a container for our program. The first thing we need to define is a layout manager for the components we will be adding to a container. A "container" is a Java class that holds components and arranges them visually in a neat, orderly fashion. One of our components is a 3D Canvas. Our interface is very simple, but it's possible to add other GUI buttons, menus, and controls with the add() method.

Command-line arguments are passed to the method that will create the top-level SceneGraph object. A SceneGraph is made up of Java 3D objects, called nodes, that are arranged in a tree structure. Next, the program needs a Virtual Universe to attach our scene graph. Java 3D provides a nice utility to simplify this procedure.

If the hardware running our program supports graphics acceleration for OpenGL or Direct3D (lower-level graphics interfaces), then scene.compile() will invoke a different set of procedures that take advantage of the accelerated hardware. The user will notice the resulting performance.

Finally, the whole scene is moved back a bit from coordinate 0,0,0 so we can see all of the action. Otherwise, we'd have to view the program running at the very edge of our computer display. That's like watching *Titanic* in between your eyeballs. So we are going to reduce the eyestrain and headaches by positioning the scene at a comfortable viewing distance. We attach the scene and we're ready to sit back and watch the show.

During the creation of the scene graph, a bunch of 3D text objects and behaviors are constructed. Basically, we parse the HTML file or command-line arguments and construct a series of text strings that are stacked on top of one another. They swing around at different speeds that remind us of the old-fashioned tie or towel racks. Each rack can have a URL associated with it. When the user clicks on the rack, the browser loads the associated URL. It's like using a new type of 3D menu.

Java 3D has two objects that are used to create text: 2D and 3D. We like to use the Text2D object for labels and text content. The Text3D object is great for logos and primary Web headers.

The Text2D Object

The Java 3D API provides a class for creating 2D text. This class creates a texture mapped rectangle that displays the text string sent by the user, given the appearance parameters also supplied by the user. The size of the rectangle (and its texture map) is determined by the font parameters passed to the constructor. The resulting Shape3D object is a transparent (except for the text) rectangle located at (0,0,0) and extending up the positive y-axis and out the positive x-axis. The Text2D class has the following relationship:

```
java.lang.Object
     |
     +----javax.media.j3d.SceneGraphObject
             |
             +----javax.media.j3d.Node
                     |
                     +----javax.media.j3d.Leaf
                             |
                             +----javax.media.j3d.Shape3D
                                     |
                                     +----
com.sun.j3d.utils.geometry.Text2D
public Text2D(java.lang.String text,
              Color3f color,
              java.lang.String fontName,
```

```
                        int fontSize,
                        int fontStyle)
```

This constructor creates a Shape3D object, which holds a rectangle that is texture mapped with an image that has the specified text written with the specified font parameters.

Text.   The string to be written into the texture map. For example:

```
String text = new String("Hello World in 2D");
```

Color.   The color of the text string. For example:

```
Color3f green = new Color3f(0.0f, 1.0f, 0.0f);
```

FontName.   The name of the Java font to be used for the text string.

```
String fontName = new String("Serif");
```

Possible font types are: Serif, San Serif, Monospaced, Times Roman, Helvetica, Courier, Dialog, Dialog Input.

FontSize.   The size of the Java font to be used. For example:

```
int fontSize = 60;
```

FontStyle.   The style of the Java font to be used. For example: Font.BOLD, Font.ITALIC, Font.PLAIN.

Here is a sample code fragment that puts everything together.

```
Shape3D GreenTitle = new Text2D("The Java 3D API",
                        new Color3f(0.0f, 1.0f, 0.0f),
                        "Courier",
                        60,
                        Font.BOLD);

Appearance app = GreenTitle.getAppearance( );

objTrans.addChild(GreenTitle);
```

In this case, we haven't yet defined the position of the text. For that, more code would be needed; here, only the basic components have been created: a text string "The Java 3D API" in green using a 60-point Courier font in bold. That's all there is to 2D text. But what about 3D text?

The Text3D Object

A Text3D object is constructed using a Font3D object passed to the Text3D( ) constructor. The Font3D object will specify a font and FontExtru-

sion component that defines the extrusion path. The Text3D object is a subclass of the Geometry object.

```
java.lang.Object
      javax.media.j3d.SceneGraphObject
            javax.media.j3d.NodeComponent
                  javax.media.j3d.Geometry
                        javax.media.j3d.Text3D
```

The Text3D object is a text string that has been converted to 3D geometry. The Font3D object determines the appearance of the 3D font. This is
demonstrated in a code fragment from the Java 3D distribution example
Text3DLoad.java:

```
TransformGroup objTrans = new TransformGroup();
objTrans.setCapability(TransformGroup.ALLOW_TRANSFORM_WRITE);
objTrans.setCapability(TransformGroup.ALLOW_TRANSFORM_READ);
objScale.addChild(objTrans);

Font3D f3d = new Font3D(new Font(fontName, Font.PLAIN, 2),
      new FontExtrusion());
Text3D txt = new Text3D(f3d, textString,.
          new Point3f( -sl/2.0f, -1.f, -1.f));
Shape3D sh = new Shape3D();
Appearance app = new Appearance();
Material mm = new Material();
mm.setLightingEnable(true);
app.setMaterial(mm);
sh.setGeometry(txt);
sh.setAppearance(app);
objTrans.addChild(sh);
```

The Text3D object here is being created and added under a Transform-
Group so that it can be moved around the scene. When implementing
Text3D, you can use a basic template:

1. Create a TransformGroup object and set the logical bits to allow
   READ/WRITE access.

2. Create a Font3D object. In this case, it describes the desired specified
   font that was parsed from the command line. A new Font object is created as PLAIN text with the default extrusion path. The font type was
   passed to the application as:

```
java Text3DLoad -f Times "SomeTextStringHere"
  if (args.length == 0) {
  usage();
  } else {
  for (int i = 0 ; i < args.length ; i++) {
```

```
         if (args[i].startsWith("-")) {
           if (args[i].equals("-f")) {
             if (i < args.length - 1) {
               fontName = args[++i];
             } else usage();
           } else {
             System.err.println("Argument '" + args[i] + "' ignored.");
           }
         } else {
           textString = args[i];
         }
       }
     }
```

3. Next, the Font3D object, some text, and position information are used to create the Text3D object.

4. A Shape3D node is needed to contain the 3D text geometry. An Appearance object is needed to specify characteristics like the color of our text; and because the 3D text will be lit, a Material object is needed.

5. Finally, the Text3D geometry is used to initialize the Shape3D node, which is then added under the TransformGroup.

Text3D Variables

The following can be set using the setCapability( ) method. For example:

```
Text3D txt = new Text3D(f3d, textString,
            new Point3f( -sl/2.0f, -1.f, -1.f));
txt.setCapability(Text3D.ALIGN_CENTER);
```

ALIGN_CENTER.   Alignment: The center of the string is placed on the position point.

ALIGN_FIRST.   Alignment: The first character of the string is placed on the position point.

ALIGN_LAST.   Alignment: The last character of the string is placed on the position point.

ALLOW_ALIGNMENT_READ.   Specifies that this Text3D object allows reading the text alignment value.

ALLOW_ALIGNMENT_WRITE.   Specifies that this Text3D object allows writing the text alignment value.

ALLOW_FONT3D_READ.   Specifies that this Text3D object allows reading the Font3D component information.

ALLOW_FONT3D_WRITE. Specifies that this Text3D object allows writing the Font3D component information.

ALLOW_PATH_READ. Specifies that this Text3D object allows reading the text path value.

ALLOW_PATH_WRITE. Specifies that this Text3D object allows writing the text path value.

ALLOW_POSITION_READ. Specifies that this Text3D object allows reading the text position value.

ALLOW_POSITION_WRITE. Specifies that this Text3D object allows writing the text position value.

ALLOW_STRING_READ. Specifies that this Text3D object allows reading the String object.

ALLOW_STRING_WRITE. Specifies that this Text3D object allows writing the String object.

PATH_DOWN. Path: Succeeding glyphs are placed below the current glyph.

PATH_LEFT. Path: Succeeding glyphs are placed to the left of the current glyph.

PATH_RIGHT. Path: Succeeding glyphs are placed to the right of the current glyph.

PATH_UP. Path: Succeeding glyphs are placed above the current glyph.

Text3D Constructors

The following are Text3D class constructors that will be called depending on which parameters are passed (type and number).

Text3D( ). Creates an empty Text3D object.

Text3D(Font3D). Creates a Text3D object with the given Font3D object.

Text3D(Font3D, String). Creates a Text3D object, given a Font3D object and a string.

Text3D(Font3D, String, Point3f). Creates a Text3D object, given a Font3D object, a string, and a position.

Text3D(Font3D, String, Point3f, int, int). Creates a Text3D object, given a Font3D object, a string, and a position.

How to create the Font3D was shown earlier. The String is your favorite group of words, and the Point3f parameter is a point in 3D space. This position will be the starting placement against which the text will be aligned.

Text3D Methods

Once the Text3D object has been created and the appropriate variable has been set, the following methods can be used to manipulate the object. For example:

```
Text3D txt = new Text3D(f3d, textString,
          new Point3f( -sl/2.0f, -1.f, -1.f));
txt.setCapability(Text3D.ALIGN_CENTER);
if  (txt.getAlignment( ) != txt.ALIGN_CENTER)
          // re-calculate text position
```

getAlignment( ). Retrieves the text alignment policy for this Text3D NodeComponent object.

getBoundingBox(BoundingBox). Retrieves the 3D bounding box that encloses this Text3D object.

getCharacterSpacing( ). Retrieves the character spacing used to construct the Text3D string.

getFont3D( ). Returns the Font3D objects used by this Text3D NodeComponent object.

getPath( ). Retrieves the node's path field.

getPosition(Point3f). Copies the node's position field into the supplied parameter.

getString( ). Copies the character string used in the construction of the Text3D node into the supplied parameter.

setAlignment(int). Sets the text alignment policy for this Text3D NodeComponent object.

setCharacterSpacing(float). Sets the character spacing used in constructing the Text3D string.

setFont3D(Font3D). Sets the Font3D object used by this Text3D NodeComponent object.

setPath(int). Sets the node's path field.

setPosition(Point3f). Sets the node's position field to the supplied parameter.

setString(String).   Copies the character string from the Text3D node into the supplied parameter.

The Font3D Object

To create a Text3D object, you need a Font3D object, which describes the "style" of the object. The Font3D object contains a couple of necessary components to help us out. To create a Font3D object, we are going to need the Font and FontExtrusion objects described in the next sections. Let's take a break here and quickly cover these important elements.

The Font class is provided by the java.awt.Font package. This Java class is used to represent a font in a platform-independent way. The following constructor is used to create a Font object.

```
Font(String fontname, int style, int size)
```

fontname.   Helvetica, Courier, Dialog, Dialog Input, Serif, Sans Serif

style.   Bold, Italic, Plain, Bold + Italic.

size.   12, 14, 18, 36, 60, and so on

The FontExtrusion Object

The FontExtrusion object is used to describe the extrusion path for a Font3D object. The extrusion path is used in conjunction with a Font2D object. The extrusion path defines the edge contour of 3D text. This contour is perpendicular to the face of the text. The extrusion has its origin at the edge of the glyph, where 1.0 is the height of the tallest glyph. Each point in the extrusion path must ensure that the current X coordinate is greater than the previous X coordinate. The following constructor is used to create a FontExtrusion object.

```
FontExtrusion(java.awt.Shape extrusionShape)
```

extrusionShape.   The Shape object to use to generate the extrusion path.

The default shape is a straight line from 0.0 to 0.2, referred to as a *straight bevel*. This parameter is used to construct the 3D contour of a Font3D object. The extrusion path describes how the edge of a glyph varies in the Z-axis.

The Font3D object is used to store extruded 2D glyphs. These 3D glyphs can then be used to construct Text3D NodeComponent objects. Custom 3D fonts, as well as methods to store 3D fonts to disk, will be addressed in a future Java 3D release. A 3D Font consists of a Java 2D font and an extrusion path, and is a child of the Java Object class.

```
java.lang.Object
   |
   +----javax.media.j3d.Font3D
Font3D(java.awt.Font font, FontExtrusion extrudePath)
```

font.   The Java 2D font used to create the 3D font object.

extrudePath.   Describes how the edge of a font glyph varies in the Z-axis.

Here is another sample code fragment that puts everything together:

```
Font3D myfont = new Font3D(new Font("Serif", Font.BOLD+ITALIC, 24),
     new FontExtrusion());
Text3D 3dtxt = new Text3D(myfont, textString,
     new Point3f( -sl/2.0f, -1.f, -1.f));
```

Moving On

Now you know how to add fonts to your programs. You're almost done! One chapter to go, to discuss some of the tools and utilities we used to create some of the content and code for the chapter applets.

Java 3D Web Tools and Utilities

"Poof, there goes the desktop computer [referring to changes that Java will bring]."

"Java technology is sufficiently close to the state-of-art."

—BILL JOY

Several Java 3D classes, tools, and utilities have been created especially for you to use. We hope they will make adding 3D to your Web site easier. Many of the applets in this book allow for the geometry to be replaced, maybe by a cool company logo or some interesting shape that has been custom-created by these tools. In any case, our goal was to leave enough flexibility in the applet designs so that you could make your Web content unique. With the creation of some new shapes and a simple edit of the featured applet's HTML file, a new Java 3D applet is born. You can't do this with GIF animations very easily. We'll first go over all of the tools available with this book. Some are easier to use than others. Some are intended for programmers who wish to reuse certain of the unique Java 3D classes and shapes that were used within the book.

Creating New Shapes

Three utilities can be used to create some shapes:

Surfacer.   A Java 3D modeling toolkit that allows the user to create 3D shapes, which are then saved to a Java source file (*.java). These shape files can be compiled and used with the book's Java 3D applets that support the import of these types of files. The Java Development Kit (JDK) is necessary to compile the Java source files. JDK can be obtained for free from Sun Microsystems (java.sun.com/).

wrl2j3d.   This utility is really a conversion filter that takes a VRML file (1.0 or 2.0) and strips the *wrl file of all of its 3D objects and creates separate class files for each shape. This is useful when you come across that great VRML scene and want to use a shape; or when you are using a VRML modeler and you want to convert the file so it can be used within Java 3D. Surfacer is the first elementary Java 3D modeler of its type. To get commercial-quality geometry, you will have to use more sophisticated modelers and somehow manipulate the file formats into the Java 3D vector file format. This is one way to get there.

ac3d.   This is a public-domain VRML modeler. Using this toolkit will enable you to create more complex shapes to use on your Web site. You create the geometry file, save it to VRML, then use the wrl2j3d filter to prepare the geometry for Java 3D applets.

Surfacer

The toolkit was created by Matt Robinson (as a graduate student at Clemson) who, while just playing around with Java 3D to see what it could do, came up with Surfacer in a short period of time. Matt can be reached at www.cs.clemson.edu/~matt for future updates and other neat stuff.

Surfacer is a simple modeler that uses a sweep generator to construct the 3D shape. After the user provides a shape profile in two dimensions, it replicates the profile in a 360-degree "sweep" about the Y-axis to fill in the missing geometry. It's kind of like a virtual lathe. Surfacer also comes with several computer-generated 3D shapes. To use this tool, open a console window and run:

```
% java Surfacer
```

If this doesn't work, you'll need to set up a correct Java environment. There are instructions on how to do this in Appendix A.

On the left side of the toolkit are preset shapes. Clicking the left mouse button over one of the menu buttons, say, Knot, will render the 3D shape. You can move the mouse over the 3D shape in the rendering window and use the mouse to manipulate the objects. Left-mouse drag rotates the shape;

middle-mouse drag scales the shape; and right-mouse drag translates the shape.

The middle window is the sweep generator. Simply hold the left-mouse button over the coordinate axis and drag to draw a profile shape. Release the mouse button and the application will render your result. Try starting your shape in different areas of the coordinate axis, or drawing straight lines, sticks, circles, and skinny rectangles, and see what happens.

When you have finished and want to save the shape, type a name for the shape in the text field and click Save. If you give it a name like MyShape, the file MyShape.java will be generated. This file can then be compiled with javac and used within some of the book's applets.

VRML to Java3D Converter

Markus Roskothen, a 3D consultant with www.infoplasm.com, contributed the VRML to Java3D Class Converter. He can be reached at markro@ vruniverse.com).

This utility converts VRML1.0 and VRML2.0 files to Java3D Shape3D classes. It was written so that small and medium-sized VRML models could be stored as Java classes. For larger files and scenes, it is recommended that you use a VRML runtime loader. You can invoke it from the command line as follows:

```
% java VrmlToJava3D <path name | name of the VRML file without
extension *.wrl>
e.g.: java VrmlToJava3D vrmlWorld
```

Executing this will produce one or more Shape3D classes, depending on the number of IndexedFaceSets in the VRML file. They are named in the following way:

```
<name of the VRML file>Shape1.java, <...>Shape2.java, etc.
e.g. vrmlWorldShape1.java, vrmlWorldShape2.java, etc.
```

All files are stored in the directory the VRML file is in. These classes are then instantiated and transformed in a main class file, which has the same name as the VRML file (e.g., vrmlWorld.java). Copy and paste the contents of this file into your application and add the TransformGroup trans0 to your scene graph. The sample file ShowVrml.java demonstrates how to use this class in a Java 3D application. Be aware of the dimensions of your VRML object and adjust the position in the scene accordingly.

At the time of writing, the program handles the VRML Transform node, the Shape node, the Appearance node, and the IndexedFaceSet node. Check www.vruniverse.com for the latest version. Note that from VRML1.0 files, only the IndexedFaceSets with their corresponding Material nodes are extracted; no transform information is retained. Therefore, it is recommended that you convert VRML1.0 to VRML2.0 files, then to Shape3D classes.

The test VRML files were produced with 3D Studio MAX R2.0 and Cosmo Worlds 2.0. If during compilation you encounter a message that "compiler has run out of memory" you might try to compile the Shape3D classes first and then compile your application. If you still get the message, you'll have to go back and reduce the polygon count or split the model into several smaller pieces. Ideally, the IndexedFaceSets in the VRML file will all have normals. If an IndexedFaceSet does not have normals, then a color-per-vertex array will be created (only for VRML2.0 files; VRML1.0 files are out of luck!) and you will get a message for each missing normal field.

AC3D

This is the shareware version of AC3D 1.94 for Windows 95/NT. Details of how to register are at www.comp.lancs.ac.uk/computing/users/andy/ac3d/reg.html.

Files include:

ac3d.exe.   The main AC3D program.

font*.ac.   AC3D font files used in the add text function. To get 3D models from TrueType fonts, use Font3D (see the manual or the AC3D page).

lib.   Some library files that TCL/TK needs (AC3D uses TCL/TK for its user interface).

tcl.   Some more files that AC3D needs for its user interface.

*.dll.   Some dll files for TCL/TK and OpenGL.

The distribution can be downloaded from the AC3D Web page: www.comp.lancs.ac.uk/computing/users/andy/ac3d.html.

Java 3D Helper Classes

The Java 3D API provides some utilities for us that are an extension of the implementation released by Sun Microsystems. These utilities are *not* part of the core API, but provide some added value to the Sun product. Many of these classes were used in previous chapter applets. Let's take a closer look at how these useful classes work.

MouseRotate Class

MouseRotate (com.sun.j3d.utils.behaviors.mouse.MouseRotate) is a Java 3D behavior object that lets users control the rotation of an object via a mouse by dragging the left-mouse button over the Java 3D object.

```
        // Create transform group, set bits
        TransformGroup transformGroup = new TransformGroup();
   transformGroup.setCapability(TransformGroup.ALLOW_TRANSFORM_READ);
   transformGroup.setCapability(TransformGroup.ALLOW_TRANSFORM_WRITE);

        // Create scene shapes (not shown intentionally.
Check out Chapter 4)

        // Add shapes to the transform group
        transformGroup.addChild(shape);

        // Add transform group to the main BranchGroup
        objScale.addChild(transformGroup);

          // Create the drag behavior node
          MouseRotate behavior = new MouseRotate();
          behavior.setTransformGroup(transformGroup);
          transformGroup.addChild(behavior);
          behavior.setSchedulingBounds(bounds);
```

MouseTranslate Class

MouseTranslate (com.sun.j3d.utils.behaviors.mouse.MouseTranslate) is a Java 3D behavior object that lets users control the translation (X, Y) of an object via a mouse drag motion with the third mouse button (Alt-Click on a PC).

```
        // Create transform group, set bits
        TransformGroup transformGroup = new TransformGroup();
           transformGroup.setCapability(TransformGroup.ALLOW_TRANSFORM_READ);

        transformGroup.setCapability(TransformGroup.ALLOW_TRANSFORM_WRITE);

        // Create scene shapes (not showm)

        // Add shapes to the transform group
        transformGroup.addChild(shape);

        // Add transform group to the main BranchGroup
        objScale.addChild(transformGroup);
```

```
// Create the translation behavior node
   MouseTranslate behavior3 = new MouseTranslate();
   behavior3.setTransformGroup(transformGroup);
   transformGroup.addChild(behavior3);
   behavior3.setSchedulingBounds(bounds);
```

MouseZoom Class

MouseZoom (com.sun.j3d.utils.behaviors.mouse.MouseZoom) is a Java 3D behavior object that lets users control the Z-axis translation of an object via a mouse drag motion with the second mouse button.

```
// Create transform group, set bits
TransformGroup transformGroup = new TransformGroup();
transformGroup.setCapability(TransformGroup.ALLOW_TRANSFORM_READ);

transformGroup.setCapability(TransformGroup.ALLOW_TRANSFORM_WRITE);

// Create scene shapes (not shown)

// Add shapes to the transform group
transformGroup.addChild(shape);

// Add transform group to the main BranchGroup
objScale.addChild(transformGroup);

// Create the zoom behavior node
   MouseZoom behavior2 = new MouseZoom();
   behavior2.setTransformGroup(transformGroup);
   transformGroup.addChild(behavior2);
   behavior2.setSchedulingBounds(bounds);
```

ObjectFile Class

ObjectFile (com.sun.j3d.loaders.objectfile.ObjectFile) is a Java 3D object for a ViewPoint .obj file. The current implementation uses only the vertex position, facet, and group data. Normals, texture coordinates, material properties, texture mapping, smoothing, and all other .obj file features are currently ignored.

```
// Load the object
TransformGroup objTG = new TransformGroup();
Transform3D objTrans = new Transform3D();
objTG.getTransform(objTrans);
objTrans.setScale( 0.6 );
```

```
objTG.setTransform(objTrans);
sceneTG.addChild(objTG);

ObjectFile f;
try {
        f = new ObjectFile("galleon.obj", ObjectFile.RESIZE,
                    (float) (49.0 * Math.PI / 180.0));
        objTG.addChild(f);
}
catch (IOException e) {
    System.err.println(e);
    System.exit(0);
}
catch (BadFileException e) {
    System.err.println(e);
    System.exit(0);
}
```

Box Class

Box (com.sun.j3d.utils.geometry.Box) is a geometry primitive created with a given length, width, and height. It is centered at the origin. By default, it lies within the bounding box, [−1,−1,−1] and [1,1,1]. When a texture is applied to a box, it is mapped counterclockwise, as on a cylinder.

```
Box box = new Box(
     3.0f,                    // X-dimension size
     2.0f,                    // Y-dimension size
     1.0f,                    // Z-dimension size
     appearance );            // appearance
```

Cone Class

Cone (com.sun.j3d.utils.geometry.Cone) is a geometry primitive defined with a radius and a height. It is a capped cone centered at the origin, with its central axis aligned along the Y-axis. The center of the cone is defined to be the center (rather than its centroid) of its bounding box. A texture is mapped onto the cone similar to that of the cylinder.

```
Cone arrowHead = new Cone(
     arrowRadius,              // base radius
     arrowLength,              // height
     0,                        // don't generate normals
     radialDivisions,          // divisions radially
     sideDivisions,            // divisions vertically
     arrowAppearance );        // appearance
```

Cylinder Class

Cylinder (com.sun.j3d.utils.geometry.Cylinder) is a geometry primitive defined with a radius and a height. It is a capped cylinder centered at the origin, with its central axis aligned along the Y-axis.

```
Cylinder obj = (Primitive) new Cylinder(
            1.0f,                   // Radius
            2.0f,                   // Height
        Cylinder.GENERATE_TEXTURE_COORDS |
        Cylinder.GENERATE_NORMALS,
            j*8+4,                  // X-divisions
            j*8+4,                  // Y-divisions
            app);                   // appearance
```

Sphere Class

Sphere (com.sun.j3d.utils.geometry.Sphere) is a geometry primitive created with a given radius and resolution. It is centered at the origin. When a texture is applied to a Sphere, it is mapped counterclockwise from the back of the sphere.

```
Sphere  moon = new Sphere(
        2.0f,                   // Radius
        Sphere.GENERATE_TEXTURE_COORDS |
        Sphere.GENERATE_NORMALS,
        60.                     // Divisions
        app);                   // appearance
```

Conclusion

Java 3D is a very powerful toolkit for creating 3D content for the Web. We hope you have come to this same conclusion and will go beyond this book to invent some really fantastic applets. We would like to hear about and see the projects you implement in Java 3D. Contact us by email at kirk.brown @sun.com. The applets shown in this book were one- to two-day projects. With the information in this book and a few weeks, your creations could be very, very interesting. As you know, the Java 3D API was not presented in its totality in this book. Other programming reference books are available with that information. Rather, we tried to provide those classes and methods specifically useful for 3D content within a Web page.

Will Java 3D become the graphics API of choice? How will graphics evolve on the desktop? What role will Java 3D play? What will the hardware vendors do to support Java 3D in the future? Will graphics accelerators take advantage and integrate Java chips to accelerate the Java 3D implementation? How will new Java compiler technology and runtime technology help performance? It will be interesting to see what happens in the next several months to answer some of these questions.

Working with 3D graphics has never been easy, but it is getting more so. There are modelers that drag and drop shapes that can be combined to form complex objects. You don't have to be a CAD professional anymore to create geometry. Imaging software is available that can slice and dice a scanned picture into just about any special effect you can think of. And the price on such advanced imaging software has dropped to under $200. Likewise, audio studio software can create some amazing sound clips, with a whole range of extras to make creating music and sound easy for those of us who never joined band in high school. This book has tried to fill in the missing component—the logic—that glues all of these effects together. Programming is complicated. There are compilers, debuggers, and weird runtime error messages, which often never point to the real problem. And then there is the API syntax to learn. We set out to create a set of logical utilities and components that could be easily constructed, together with image and sound content, hooked up to the Web and distributed across the Internet to provide a 3D experience. The result is *Ready-to-Run,* based on Java.

APPENDIX

A

Java Programming Primer

The C Programming language is a 20-year-old technology, extended with the implementation of C++ in 1983. This is a long time in computer years for a programming language to maintain popularity. But C is a very flexible and innovative compiler technology, able to take advantage of faster CPU designs, and this keeps the language in service today. But it was because of its flexibility that C laid many common traps and pitfalls in the language itself. Some said, "C gives you just enough rope to hang yourself," meaning a careless or novice programmer could produce code that was vulnerable to virus attacks, or mistakes in the program logic that would send a space rocket in the wrong direction. Senior programmers were idolized for their tricks and programming magic. There was even an unspoken contest among engineers, a sort of skills demonstration, of who could write the most compact code by using—I should say abusing—the lexical freedom of the language. The result was unreadable and difficult-to-debug logic code.

Another common problem was poorly documented code. Programmers just didn't have the time or didn't care enough to document, knowing the source code was a form of job security. Another big problem, which was very apparent to the consumers and users of the code, was memory management. Applications would consume memory and trample themselves until the hardware would lock up. The only recovery was a hard reboot. The most noticeable errors were dangling references to NULL pointers. They would cause the application to crash unexpectedly and would sometimes result in painful and long debugging sessions, a huge waste of time and effort. Back in the '70s and early '80s, there wasn't the interest in or industry vision for an Internet browser. We were still working on upgrading the green ASCII displays to graphical user interfaces with color.

Java has changed all that. The inventor and software engineer James Gosling has not only solved these age-old problems with his Java invention, but has gone on to redefine "modern programming practice." He did this by taking the best of the best from modern programming lexicons and invented a well-behaved language that was designed to run in a computer environment composed of various networked machines running many different operating systems. Actually, this was the result of Gosling's and his team's effort. The initial goal was to build a small system environment for a low-cost, hand-held computer device.

For all developers, Java offers the important advantages of software portability and simplified program development; Java is also Internet-ready. And the runtime environments are already distributed on hundreds of thousands of computers around the world. All that is needed is the Java application itself. What is even more interesting is that the World Wide Web infrastructure is used as a delivery mechanism for software vendors. Because of the Web's capability, most software vendors can obsolete distribution on floppy diskettes and CD-ROMs.

Companies like Netscape, Microsoft, and Sun Microsystems have been distributing Web browsers that support the execution of Java applications, called applets. By embedding applets into Web pages, companies are able to offer new services through the Web to their customers, employees, and key partners. These applets may process a business form automatically or provide access to a database. And because Java is platform-independent, the same Java applet is capable of executing on all the computer platforms supported by these Web browsers.

The term "Java" is used to cover all of the bases, which sometimes can confuse the unaware user. At the core of Java's capability are two components: the development environment, called the *Java Development Toolkit* (*JDK*), and the runtime environment, called the *Java Virtual Machine* (*JVM*).

The JVM is bolted onto the proprietary vendor hardware. Its implementations are different from vendor to vendor as it has been ported from one hardware platform to the next. But the defined JVM interfaces are all identical. That's why it is possible to write a Java application with the JDK and it will run on any JVM. The Virtual Machine is the key, along with independence from the underlying operating system and system resources.

A developer writes Java source code and saves it into a file with the extention *.java; CoolApplet.java, for example. The file is compiled into bytecodes to become a *.class file. These bytecodes are logical instructions for the JVM to process during the program's execution. A special version of bytecodes, called applets, are stored on a Web server. In the HTML page, a special tag is added:

```
<applet code=CoolApplet>
      ..... additional parameters here
</applet>
```

When a user visits the Web page, the <applet> tag causes the bytecode to be zapped across the network from the Web server to the Internet browser. The bytecode is loaded into memory, and security checks are performed (we wouldn't want a virus to show up) before the bytecode is executed on the local machine running the Web browser.

Once invoked, the bytecode is interpreted or, optionally, turned into proprietary machine code for a performance boost. The added performance comes from a JIT for *just-in-time* code generation. These are system operations that have been tuned for a specific piece of hardware. The front-end Java application logic doesn't know anything about them. This puts most of the performance-tuning tasks on the hardware vendors and saves the software vendors enormous amounts of development time and costs.

Another cool thing Java avoids is memory abuse by applications, sometimes called "fat apps." Java loads only the code modules, as they are needed. Dynamic memory allocation allows Java to run in environments with small memory footprints, which is just a good efficient way of handling things. If you had a C program that allocated 15 megabytes upon initialization, and additional operations consumed even more memory, you wouldn't be able to run very many applications at the same time without notable system performance degradation or, even worse, hardware lockup. If you threw in a window system, a network connection, a 32Mb system became a great source of frustration. Until Java came along, it used to be difficult to keep robust, commercial software small.

Installing the Java Development Kit (JDK)

Sun Microsystems freely distributes the JDK, which contains everything you need to start building Java applications. JDK lets you write applets and applications that conform to the Java API. To get the JDK, from a Web browser, travel to the distribution site: java.sun.com/products/jdk/. You can download the most recent version for your specified hardware platform. To run a Java 3D program, you will need version Java 2 or later. The following are the abbreviated instructions:

1. Download the Java 2 software bundle for your system platform.

2. The Windows software bundle is self-extracting. If you download a Solaris software bundle, you can extract it with the command: % sh java2-solaris2-sparc.bin. The software bundle should be extracted into the following directory structure:

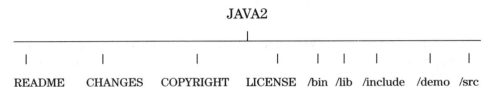

JAVA2

README   CHANGES   COPYRIGHT   LICENSE   /bin   /lib   /include   /demo   /src

The src directory shown originally appears as a src.zip file in the Solaris installation, which you must manually unzip. In Windows, the installer unzips it automatically for you.

3. Set the PATH and CLASSPATH for Windows or Solaris, as described in the section that follows.

Running Java Tools in Microsoft Windows

After installing the JDK software, you start a tool by typing its name into the DOS window with a file name as an argument. None of the Java tools are Windows programs with GUI interfaces; they are all run from the DOS command line. (For example, if you double-click on the Java Compiler javac icon, it will briefly open then immediately close a DOS window, because that is not the proper way to run it.)

You can specify the path to a tool either by typing the path in front of the tool each time or by adding the path to the startup file (autoexec.bat). For example, if the JDK is installed at C:\java2, to run the compiler on a file myfile.java, go to a DOS shell and type: **C:\java2\bin\javac myfile.java.** Or add C:\java2\bin to your path statement, then type: **javac myfile.java.**

Microsoft Windows PATH and CLASSPATH

The CLASSPATH is not required, but if it is set, it will need to be unset. You may want to update the "path" variable for convenience.

Note: For Windows NT only: If you are using Windows NT, it is preferable to make the following environment variable changes in the Control Panel: Start the Control Panel, select System, then edit the environment variables.

PATH: Add the absolute path of the java2\bin directory to your PATH statement. The PATH statement enables Windows to find the executables (javac, java, javadoc, etc.) from any current directory. To find out the current value of your PATH, at the DOS prompt type: **C:\>path**.

To change the PATH, open the AUTOEXEC.BAT file and make the change to the PATH statement. To edit the AUTOEXEC.BAT file in Windows 95:

1. Start a text editor by choosing Start, Programs, Accessories, and choosing WordPad or NotePad.

2. Choose Open from the File menu and type **c:\autoexec.bat** for the file name. This will open the file for editing.

3. Look for the PATH statement. Notice that the PATH statement is a series of directories separated by semicolons (;). Windows looks for programs in the PATH directories in order, from left to right. Look for other JDK versions in the PATH. There should only be one path to a classes.zip file. When in doubt, put the java directory at the end of the PATH statement. For example, in the following PATH statement, we have added the java directory at the end:

   ```
   PATH C:\WINDOWS;C:\WINDOWS\COMMAND;C:\;C:\DOS;C:\Java2\BIN
   ```

4. To make the path take effect, execute the following:

   ```
   C:> autoexec.bat
   ```

5. CLASSPATH Environment Variable: If you follow the default installation, you do not need to set CLASSPATH, because the tools automatically set it for you.

Refer to the README file that accompanies the JDK files for further information and installation troubleshooting.

Running Java Tools in Solaris

After installing the JDK software, you start a tool by typing its name into a shell window with a file name as an argument. You can specify the path to a tool either by typing the path in front of the tool each time or by adding the path to the startup file. For example, if the JDK is installed at /usr/local/java2, to run the compiler on a file myfile.java, go to a shell and type: **/usr/local/java2/bin/javac myfile.java.** Or add /usr/local/java2/bin to your path statement and type: **javac myfile.java.**

The PATH and CLASSPATH variables are not required, but it is helpful to know more about them. See the next section about setting these variables.

Solaris PATH and CLASSPATH

The CLASSPATH is not required, but if it is set, it will also have to be unset. You may want to update the PATH variable for convenience.

1. PATH variable: Add the absolute path of the java2/bin directory to your Unix PATH variable, as follows. The PATH variable enables Solaris to find the executables (javac, java, javadoc, etc.) from any current directory. To find out if the path is currently set for any Java tools, execute:

```
% which java
```

This will print the path to Java, if it can find it.

If you use the C shell (csh), you can set the path in your startup file (~/.cshrc) as follows, for example:

```
set path=($path /usr/local/java2/bin)
```

Then load the startup file and verify that the path is set by repeating the which command just shown:

```
% source ~/.cshrc
% which java
```

2. CLASSPATH environment variable: If you follow the default installation, you do not need to set CLASSPATH, because the shell scripts automatically set it for you.

Refer to the README file that accompanies the JDK files for further information and installation troubleshooting.

Running Applets with the AppletViewer

AppletViewer allows you to run one or more Java applets that are called by reference in a Web page (HTML file) using the APPLET tag. The AppletViewer finds the APPLET tags in the HTML file and runs the applets (in separate windows) as specified by the tags.

AppletViewer is for viewing applets; it cannot display an entire Web page that contains many HTML tags. It parses only the APPLET tag and no other HTML on the Web page. To run an applet with AppletViewer, you go to a command line for your operating system and run AppletViewer, passing in the file name or URL of the Web page as its argument.

Solaris

Here is an example of how to invoke AppletViewer on a file-based Web page in Solaris. First change to the java2 directory. Then execute:

```
bin/appletviewer demo/GraphLayout/example1.html
```

Here is an example of how to invoke AppletViewer on a URL-based Web page in Solaris. Execute:

```
bin/appletviewer http://java.sun.com/applets/NervousText/example1.html
```

Windows

Here is an example of how to invoke AppletViewer on a file-based Web page in Windows. Go to a DOS prompt, change to the java2 directory, then execute:

```
bin\appletviewer demo\GraphLayout\example1.html
```

Here is an example of how to invoke AppletViewer on a URL-based Web page in Windows. Execute:

```
bin\appletviewer http://java.sun.com/applets/NervousText/example1.html
```

Debugging Programs with the Java Debugger (JDB)

You can debug applets using the -debug option of appletviewer. When debugging applets, it's best to invoke appletviewer from the directory that contains the applet's HTML file. For example, on Solaris:

```
cd demo/TicTacToe
../../bin/appletviewer -debug example1.html
```

On the PC:

```
cd demo\TicTacToe
..\..\bin\appletviewer -debug example1.html
```

You can find documentation on the debugger and its API at java.sun .com/products/jdk/1.1/debugging/.

Compiling Java Source Code

Let's assume you have created a Java application called KillerApp.java and you're ready to compile the source into bytecode. Invoke the javac compiler by typing:

```
javac -g KillerApp.java
```

The compilation results in a new file called KillerApp.class that has been created with debugging enabled. Invoke javac -h <return> for a complete listing of options.

If you are unable to invoke javac, check your PATH setting. If you get the error that reads "Can't find classes," check the CLASSPATH setup.

Running Java Programs

Java is both a compiled and interpreted language. After the programmer creates the program file, ending in *.java, the compiler is invoked and the source code is compiled into bytecode. This is an intermediate format that is interpreted by the JVM at runtime on the client machine. The compilers must adhere to a strict Java specification that ensures portability across multiple-computer platforms. When the Java program is compiled into byte-code, a class file is generated with a *.class suffix. The runtime interpreter reads the class file and executes its instructions.

Java applets are generally small, specific programs that run within a Web browser or the developer's utility application called appletviewer. This utility is bundled with standard releases of the JDK.

Applets are constrained programs that:

- Adhere to the Java security framework.
- Relegate memory allocation and management to the JVM.

This prevents malicious hackers from playing tricks that were possible in other programming environments, such as C, C++, ActiveX, and MACRO languages. One such trick replaced keywords in your Microsoft document with something inappropriate. If the document were saved to diskette and opened by another user on a different system, the MACRO virus perpetuated itself and spread from system to system. C/C++ written programs are able to twiddle with system processes and application memory stacks to perform their unauthorized actions against a system.

Java applications are designed to run "outside" the Web browser by invocation from the command line. Unlike applets, they have a main( ) method. To run the program, the Java interpreter must be invoked:

```
% java KillerApp
```

The Java Language

Java is composed of several elements borrowed from other languages and uses a nice simple approach to object-oriented programming. Why does everything in computer science have to be so complicated? The beauty of Java is not only that it's simple, but that it's predictable. You really can't say that about C. The inventors of Java wanted to help the majority of programmers avoid their most common engineering mistakes. Because of this forethought, by default, Java increases the reliability and quality of the development effort.

What does Java do to relieve some of these programming headaches of the past? First, you don't have to deal with passing a NULL pointer, because Java doesn't have pointers. Ninety-nine percent of most system crashes probably originate in the code involving pointers or memory allocation in a program. That brings us to a second bit of good news: Java performs automatic memory allocation and reallocation, or "garbage collection," by the JVM. Java also supplies built-in error handling and security. All of this makes the job easier for programmers, allowing them to focus on solutions, rather than on mechanics.

The following subsections are not meant to be exhaustive. There are dozens of books out there on Java to choose from, and we expect you to continue your study following this introduction on the language. In case you just joined us, Java is the hottest programming language on the planet, and this chapter will point out some of its interesting features.

Comments Syntax

There are two kinds of comments to choose from. The double-slash (//) specifies that anything to the right is a comment. This can be on the same line as the source, for example:

```
y = 0; // Declare Coordinate Y
```

Comments can also be surrounded by /* */. There is also a special /** comment to identify statements intended for documentation or javadoc. The javadoc utility is run on the source code, causing HTML files to be generated by parsing documentation tags. This provides a very valuable feature of self-documenting source code. The javadoc comment starts with a /** followed by text or HTML tags until a */ is encountered. If you keep it simple, the javadoc utility will format some nice-looking HTML reference documentation. An example of adding document comments inside a *.java file would look like:

```
/**
 * The Fog leaf node defines a set of fog parameters common to
 * all types of fog.
 * It also specifies a region of influence in which this Fog node
 * is active.
 */
```

```
public abstract class Fog extends Leaf {
    /**
     * Specifies that this Fog node allows read access to its
     * influencing bounds and bounds leaf information.
     */
    public static final int
    ALLOW_INFLUENCING_BOUNDS_READ = Leaf.LAST_CAPABILITY_BIT_INDEX;

    /**
     * Constructs a Fog node with the specified fog color.
     * @param color the fog color
     * @exception CapabilityNotSetException if appropriate
capability is
     * not set and this object is part of live or compiled scene
graph
     */
    public Fog(Color3f color) {
    ....
    if(!this.capabilities.get(ALLOW_COLOR_WRITE))
                throw
                    new CapabilityNotSetException("Fog: no
capability to write color");
    }
```

Notice that the document comment has to be right above the class variable or method that is being documented. The simple method is to use comments between /** and */. There are some additional javadoc formatting tags that begin with @ and apply to the following text until another @ is encountered or the */ symbol is found marking the end of the comment.

Invoking javadoc [options] filename.java creates the HTML javadoc file.

Tokens

A small group of keywords (i.e., if, do, while, new, class) are reserved and used for selection, exceptions, decision, and control loops. Other symbols used in Java also have a special meaning. Some are listed here:

identifiers (-x1, x2, x3). Names of things that must begin with a letter, $ or "_".

literals (true, false, 25,0.113, 0xFF, "some text"). The way integers, floating points, Boolean, characters, and strings are represented in the code.

separators ([], (), {}). Used to group and separate.

operators (= + <->). Used for comparison, assignment, and mathmatical equations. Don't forget to use == for equality testing, not the equal sign (=).

Java Data Types

All variables in Java are categorized by type. There are special data types, like void and null. Void is used with methods to indicate a return value isn't expected. Null specifies the object variable isn't referencing anything. Primitive data types have a class—that is, Boolean, string, byte, integer, long. In Java, int has a 32-bit signed value; short has a 16-bit value; and byte an 8-bit value. Java provides an integral data type with a 64-bit signed value. Java also provides a single, signed 32-bit and double 64-bit floating point.

Program Structure

In Java, curly braces are used to indicate the beginning and ending of a program block:

```
void Main {
    Statements . . .
        Expressions . . .
}
```

Statements consist of expressions. Expressions are used to define data values, variables, or operations. All statements end with a semicolon (;). Multiple statements can be grouped with curly braces—{ }—to form compound statements.

A procedure is a Java method that returns the void data type. This can be easily identified when the method is declared:

```
void JavaProcedure() {
    code . . .
}
```

There are Java methods that, like C functions, return values by its declaration as a nonvoid type and by using the keyword return:

```
float BigNumberMethod(float Value) {
    code . . .
    return (Value * 0.368);
}
```

As you probably know, a Java program is constructed of different classes. Some classes are available to the entire program and others are not. A Java class not only contains data; it provides the methods that operate on the data. Another way to think of classes is as a virtual model for a real-life object. Every detail of an object is found in its class file. An object is an instance of a class.

An instructor once related this concept to the construction of a house. The architect's plans for a house are like a class. You cannot actually touch the house until it has been built. The blueprints may be the general description for several houses or instances of the plans within a large housing development. Building a home from the plans is like creating an instance of the House class. What might change from multiple instances are the variables, like paint color, carpeting, and woodwork. Though each House object was created from the same class, modifications to one object will not affect other objects of the same class; each object is separate.

Classes in Java contain methods and data. Methods simply consist of many statements and expressions to produce a desired computation. A class can have a single method and data or many methods and data. Objects are instances of a class. An object is created by instantiating, or allocating, a new record by using the new operator, which will contain the data that provides an object description.

In summary, a Java class contains methods and data variables. References to class methods and data are identified by the dot separator (.):

```
Box TheBox = new Box( );
float y;
thebox.height = 0.345;
y = thebox.WantHeight( );
```

New creates an instance of Box called TheBox, which inherits member variables and methods. To access the members of the Box class, the dot separator is used.

Java Application Life Cycle

A Java application or applet is built using a variety of objects. (Remember, an object is simply a chunk of software that describes the object.) The object has a description of its state. We can discover the object's state through its member variables. Each object is designed with a specific behavior. Object behavior is implemented through methods.

Objects are created from "blueprints," or templates, called classes. Each object will communicate with other objects by passing data and invoking member methods from one to another. The result is program computation; that is, something actually happens on the display that can be seen by the user. Once an object completes its computation, the object's resources and logic are recovered from the system memory where it was running. This is called *garbage collection*. The JVM has a process that periodically reallocates system memory used by Java objects. The garbage collector runs on a separate thread of control and passively scans the dynamic memory area looking for objects to terminate.

Before an object is collected, it has the opportunity to handle its own clean-up procedure through a finalize method. During finalization, things like opening files, socket connections, and so on can be closed and dealt with before heading for the trash heap. For example, if a class opens a file, it should also close the file when done. A well-behaved class will invoke the finalize( ) method to perform housekeeping tasks prior to termination. Let's look at the first step in creating a Java object by creating a class.

Declaring a Class in Java

Objects are created by using an instance of a class. This is done by invoking the new operator. But to do this, a class must be declared, specified, and coded. There are a whole bunch of Java core classes all ready to go, but if you want to create your own classes for your applets, what do you need to do? First, you must assemble or import Java classes that are going to be used to build this class.

```
package javax.media.j3d;
import javax.vecmath.*;
import java.util.BitSet;
import java.util.Enumeration;
```

To avoid naming conflicts and to organize a group of related objects and their interface definitions, Java defines a class library and calls it a package. All of the Java 3D classes belong to the javax.media.j3d package, because Java 3D is part of the Java Media API set. The import statement is similar to the include statement in C. The entire group of classes can be included by using the asterisk (*) wild card symbol following the class and interface names. The imported classes must have public access.

The core Java development environment provides several classes that are used in creating Java programs. Various Java APIs, such as Java 3D, also provide reusable classes in addition to the JDK. In your 3D programs, both will be used. It's a good idea to use the Java provided classes before building your own. Here is a short description of the JDK core packages, but we recommend you purchase a Java reference book for the details of each class and interface.

Java Platform 1.1.5 Core API Packages

* package java.applet   // Java applet interface

* package java.awt   // Java Abstract Window Toolkit,
                                              for GUI building

* package java.awt.datatransfer   // AWT Clipboard

* package java.awt.event   // Keyboard, mouse, window event
                                              handling

* package java.awt.image   // Image Processing

* package java.beans   // JavaBeans, for building components

* package java.io   // Input/output stream handling

* package java.lang   // Object class, class and thread
                                              support

* package java.lang.reflect   // Class member interface, the public
                                              modifier

* package java.math   // Math routines

* package java.net   // Network, sockets, URL, content,
                                              MIME

* package java.rmi   // Remote method interface to remote
                                              objects

* package java.rmi.dgc   // Extends RMI; server-side garbage
                                              collection

* package java.rmi.registry   // Database of remote objects; RMI reg-
                                              istration

* package java.rmi.server   // Remote server support; class loader

* package java.security   // Certificate, private and public keys

* package java.security.acl   // Access control list; guarded resource
                                              access

* package java.security
.interfaces   // Digital Signature Algorithm (DSA)
                                              support

* package java.sql   // SQL support

* package java.text   // Bidirectional iteration support over
                                              text

* package java.util   // Date, random, observer interface,
                                              hash, and so on

* package java.util.zip   // Open/close *.zip files and other sup-
                                              port

If you need something else, check the general list of Java APIs that specialize in areas like speech, multimedia, database, transactions, and so on. Going into each of the core Java interfaces and classes is way beyond the scope of this book. Buy a good Java resource and dive in.

Finally, we are ready to declare the class. A class consists of a *declaration* and a *body* that holds variable and method declarations. The class declaration serves three basic purposes: One, it provides a name for the class; two, it establishes access and attributes; and three, it defines its lineage to its parent. In Java, only single inheritance is supported.

The second component of a class is its body. The body contains declarations, too. Member variables and class methods are defined inside the curly braces or class body. The class state is represented by member variables. The class behavior is represented by its class methods.

The basic syntax for creating a class in Java is:

```
[modifier] class ClassName extends TypeName implements Interface {
        [variable declarations]
        [method declarations]
}
```

Class declarations sometimes involve different modifiers:

No modifier (used as default). The class can only be accessed from within the package where it is defined.

abstract. The class contains abstract methods and cannot be instantiated.

final. The class cannot have subclasses.

public. The class can be accessed outside the package where it is defined.

How to Declare Variables

When a variable is declared, it can be set to an initial value. The syntax for declaring a variable is [Data Type] [Variable Name] = [Initial Value]. A class member variable has two basic elements:

```
datatype variable_name;
```

The following demonstrates variable declaration, where each has a different meaning—in other words, watch what you are doing.

```
public class BoxClass {
        float xAxis;
```

```
        final float xOrigin=0.0;

        float ComputeBox( ) {
                float yAxis=0.25;
                        // more logic here ....
        }
    }
```

Here, other classes have access to the xAxis member variable of class BoxClass, but since the second variable declaration is within the body of the ComputeBox method, its access is local and only available within that specific method. To create a variable constant, use the final keyword that declares the variable's value cannot be changed.

How to Declare Methods

The basic method declaration has a name and a return data type:

```
returnDataType MethodName ( ) {
        // stuff here
    }
```

This is very elementary, and there are other things you can do in the method declaration, such as access modifiers and additional method attributes. Consider the following example:

```
public class Camera extends java.applet.Applet
    {
        // Member variable declaration
        float camX;
        float camY;
        float camZ;
                // Method declaration
        public boolean PositionCamera(float dx, float dy, float dz)
        {
                camX += dx;
                camY += dy;
                camZ += dz;
                return true;
        }
    }
```

The Camera class has declared three member variables: CamX, CamY, and CamZ. Since the class has been declared public, this allows other classes to access these member variables when needed. Unless a lot of thought and up-front design strategies have been applied prior to class creation, it is a good idea to declare classes and methods public initially. Then when everything is working, go back and crank down the access modifiers as needed. Making mistakes in the selection of modifiers early on will generate errors and you will waste time debugging the problems.

A single method is provided in the example Camera class that allows the application to move the virtual camera's position. Three floating point coordinates for x, y, and z are passed as parameters when the PositionCamera method is invoked.

The method is declared as public and returns a Boolean value when it successfully assigns the parameter values to the class member variables. No doubt, other class methods will be interested in this change of state or behavior of the Camera class. Let's now see how this class interface might be used by other classes.

Initialization

Most classes provide initialization routines for the object that is instantiated from itself. These methods are called *constructors*. These methods are easy to identify because constructors have the same name as the class name. Multiple class constructors will have a different number and type of arguments, even with the same name. The Java compiler keeps track of everything.

Let's continue to see how a constructor is created.

Constructors

Constructors are identified as unique from one another by the number and type of arguments they define. Look at the following constructor for the Fog Node class (Fog.class).

```
public Fog()
public Fog(float r, float g, float b)
```

Notice these multiple constructors all have the same name as their class name. The first construct initializes a new Fog object with default parameters. The second specifies the fog color of the new Fog object.

```
Fog densefog = new Fog(0.0, 0.0, 1.0);
```

The compiler knows which constructor to use when an object is created from the Fog class. In this case, the constructor was defined with the three-color parameters for red, green, and blue.

Well, with much of the background and context out of the way, we are ready to start using all of these "Lego" parts to actually do something interesting.

Using and Calling Class Variables and Methods

Basically, for using and invoking variables and methods you do two things:

1. Modify, reference, and manipulate the object's member variables.

2. Call the object's methods.

Consider the following group of examples:

1. Fog densefog = new Fog(0.0, 0.0, 1.0);

2. densefog.r = 0.25;

3. PointSound bsound1 = new PointSound( );

4. MediaContainer sample1 = new MediaContainer( );

5. sample1.setCapability(MediaContainer.ALLOW_URL_WRITE);

6. sample1.setURL("javaone_sounds/duke_C_48m.au");

7. bsound1.setSoundData(sample1);

On line 1, a new Fog object is being created, and the color is being set by a constructor from the Fog class (three RGB values). On line 2, the red value is being modified. (Note: Sometimes class interfaces are not obvious, so you need to become familiar with each of the classes you are using. A good reference book will do the trick, or keep your browser loaded with the provided javadoc HTML files.)

Lines 3 and 4 create a couple of objects that are initialized to default parameters, since parameter values are absent. Again, you have to know what this means for each class interface.

Line 5 is more interesting. The MediaContainer class contains member variables, which are constant. They are being referenced here using dot notation to set a capability in the instantiated object sample1. Remember, if the class member variable is public, other classes can use the variable. We didn't give our sample a class name, but it's implied here.

The rest of the examples show how methods that passed parameters are called. For example, a message containing a reference to an audio file is sent to the method setURL for processing; setURL could be declared within the same file or, in this case, from javax.media.j3d.MediaContainer. This method was inherited when sample1 was created with the new operator. In the *.java file, the method is declared as:

```
/**
    * Set URL
    * @param path string of URL containing non-cached sound data
```

```
    * @exception CapabilityNotSetException if appropriate capability is
    * not set and this object is part of live or compiled scene graph
    */
   public final void setURL(String path)
```

Creating Subclasses

In Java, all classes are derived from another class; the derived class is called a *subclass*. The subclass was created from the *superclass*, or parent class, as it is sometimes called. The top class on the Java pile is called the *Object class*. When referring to a class hierarchy, the Object class would be the root. A derived class is called a *leaf*. Branches of the class hierarchy are often called *nodes*. The term *ancestor* is also used to denote a superclass of its child or subclass. The terms are loosely thrown around and mixed, for historical reasons stemming from other programming languages.

A subclass will inherit the state and the behavior of its superclass in the form of variables and methods. To create a subclass is simple. Like a class, the subclass is declared but uses the extends operator.

```
class BabyBearClass  extends BearClass {
         // class body
}
```

Overriding Methods

As a Java program grows in size and complexity, its performance and efficiency keep programmers awake at night thinking how and where improvements can be made. Since Java is object-oriented, a great deal of analysis goes into code reuse. That's where overriding a method comes into play.

As discussed in the previous section, subclasses have a parent. Subclasses also inherit the member variable and methods from their parent. Occasionally, there may be a situation in which the subclass needs to replace or enhance the parent class implementation of a method, rather than replicate the effort.

To replace a method completely, you declare the method in the subclass, in exactly the same way it is declared in the parent class—use the same name, arguments, and return type. For example:

```
public class MyBox extends Box {
      void ComputeBox ( ) {
            // logic here
      }
}
```

The MyBox class member method ComputeBox overrides or replaces the method implementation of its parent Box.

A common practice for enhancing parent methods is to override constructor methods to provide additional initialization that is unique to the subclass. For example:

```
class TopClass {
      float factor = 0.25;
      public float init( ) {
            float y = 0.45;
            return y;
      }
}
class SubClass extends TopClass {
      public float init( ) {
            float y = super.factor * super.init();
            return y;
      }
}
```

The parent's constructor is declared init( ). Using *super* invokes the overriding method with additional modifications. Methods declared *static* or *final* by the parent or superclass cannot be overridden by a subclass.

Error Handling

Program errors in Java are called *exceptions*, and they are "thrown" from the logic code that detects them. When an error occurs in Java, it can be "caught" and managed by a special exception handler. Here's how you create and throw an exception:

```
public class NotSetException extends NoSuchFieldError {
    /**
     * Create the exception object with default values.
     */
     public NotSetException(){
     }

    /**
     * Create the exception object that outputs message.
     * @param str the message string to be output.
     */
     public CapabilityNotSetException(String str){
          super(str);
     }
}
public class Box {
```

```
            if (!box.y == NULL)
                throw
                new NotSetException("Box: missing value for y");
    }
```

To catch an exception, an exception handler needs to be built. It has three components: try, catch, and finally. First you declare the try block around the statements that might throw an exception:

```
try {
      // Java code
}
```

Next, link the exception handling with the try block by declaring the catch block immediately after it.

```
        try {
            // Java code that might throw an error
        } catch ( ExceptionThrowableObject variable) {
            // print something to standard out
        }

public String ColorReport() {
        StringBuffer str=new StringBuffer("Color Object:");
        Color3f color=new Color3f();
        try {
            getColor(color);
            str.append(" Get Color="+color);
        } catch (NotSetException e) {
            str.append("Caught getColor");
        }
        return new String(str);
    }
```

These two examples demonstrate the pattern to use with exceptions. The first is generic; the second implements an object, which returns a string containing the value that was attempted to be retrieved using getColor. All of this is very useful in debugging problems as well as handling them gracefully.

Finally, you add the finally block to handle dangling system resources that need to be handled, like open files or a socket connection.

```
try {
        // Java code that might throw an error
} catch ( ExceptionThrowableObject variable) {
            // print something to standard out
} finally {
        if ( condition != null) {
                // Handle the condition
```

```
        } else {
            // Condition NOT present, relax!
        }
    }
```

The Abstract Object

The tour is almost over, and like a good vacation, there hasn't been enough time to see everything. But there is one more important concept in the Java language that we need to push through before we go home. Certain classes and methods need to be protected from being subclasses or from overriding class methods. This can be achieved by specifying the class or methods using the final modifier. You probably feel better already. If you create the perfect class and are feeling pretty darn proud of yourself, declare the class as:

```
final class PerfectClassDontMessWithIt {
```

If somebody tries to subclass your beautiful creation, the Java compiler will complain. The same goes for attempts at method-overriding a final method. If a hacker tries to create an evil twin subclass of a proper superclass within your program, and the hacker swaps the bad one for the good one, look out! Extra care and thought need to be exercised regarding the design and security aspects of each class you create. It's easy to set everything to public during the initial development phase, when building everything. But don't forget to go back and implement proper access controls.

Abstract classes and methods are just the opposite. They need to be declared abstract because they are designed to be subclassed or overridden.

```
abstract class 3DObject {
```

What does it mean to be an abstract class versus, say, a public class? Classes are implemented to represent some object that we often find all around us. In this complex world, objects sometimes don't fit into a neat package of "purpose." The object has an abstract identity. It is often difficult to design a class for an object, like a "machine." Does it make sense to instantiate the object "machine?" It's too vague, too generalized.

But it does make sense to create a generic machine object that cannot be instantiated or extended, but can be subclassed. That leaves room for the derived subclasses to define additional detail to describe specialized characteristics, like gears, hydraulics, and electronics. Abstract classes can also contain abstract methods that can be shared across the superclasses' children. In the case of the machine, an abstract pivot method would come in handy.

```
abstract class Machine {
     float x, y, z;
     void pivot( float newx, float newy, float newz) {
           // some pivot code
     }
     abstract void turn();
}
class Gear extends Machine {
     void turn() {
           // implement some new behavior for turning
     }
}
```

Abstract classes and methods are great for creating object interfaces.

Creating an Interface

An interface is a bunch of abstract methods and constant values used to define basic common behavior of a superclass, which can be reused and enhanced by its children. The result is a defined relationship among the class hierarchy. To define an interface involves two components: the interface declaration and the body statements.

```
public interface AudioDevice extends Machine {
     // Constants
     public static final int HEADPHONES = 0;
     public static final int STEREO_SPEAKERS = 2;

     // Initialize the device. What exactly happens is up to
somebody else.
     public abstract boolean initialize();

     // Close the device when done and clean up.
     public abstract boolean close();
}
class Radio implements AudioDevice {
     // member variable, overridden initialize() method
}
```

The declaration contains the name of the interface and tells whether it extends other interfaces. The body contains the constant and method declarations for the interface. Note, you don't need to use the keyword *abstract* anymore when declaring an interface and its methods, because interfaces are implicitly abstract and none of the methods declared in the interface have implementations. That will be implemented by a subclass.

Creating Packages

Packages are collections of classes and interfaces. They make everything neat and tidy, in addition to preventing naming conflicts. To use the classes and interfaces defined in a package, the Java program needs to import the desired package.

You can create your own package using the package statement, which has only one component: the name of your package. By convention and to avoid name conflicts, the package name is given the inverse domain name of a company, plus an identifier. You create the package and then reference it with the import statement.

```
package com.ABC.robotics;
interface AudioDevice {
     // body
}
class Machine {
     // body
}
class Gear {
     // body
}
--------- RoboGear.java --------------------
import com.ABC.robotics.*;
import java.io.*;
public class RoboGear extends Gear {
     // body
}
```

Comparing Java Applets to Applications

We've come to the last stop on the tour! We end with a clarification of terms and an example of a Java application and a Java applet. A Java application is a standalone program that runs outside of a browser. Applets need the support environment of a Java-enabled browser in order to work. Applets use special HTML tags that reference the applet from an HTML page.

The Java application has a program structure similar to those found in C programs. The Java program is invoked by the Java interpreter at the command line:

```
% java MyJavaApp -help
```

The interpreter calls the application's main( ) method and the arguments are parsed.

```
class MyJavaApp {
    public static void main(String[] args) {
       String arg;
       int i = 0;
       while (i < args.length) {
            arg = args[i++];
            if (arg.equals("-help")) {
                 System.out.println("List of all arguments");
            }
       }
       System.out.println("End of the Tour!");
       // More methods following
       }
}
```

The main( ) method in turn will call other methods to perform some computation. The argument for main( ) is the standard one used to pass arguments to the program from the command line. Expected is an array of strings or command-line arguments, which are tested if present; then some action is taken.

Applets are a little different breed all around. Their arguments are specified within the HTML file using the <param> tag.

```
----------------- mypage.html --------------------------
<HTML>
<BODY>

<APPLET CODE="MyJavaApplet" WIDTH=200 HEIGHT=200>
<PARAM NAME=arg1 VALUE="help">
</APPLET>

</BODY>
</HTML>

--------------------- MyJavaApplet.java ----------------

class MyJavaApplet extends Applet {
     String listargs;

     public void init() {
          listargs = getParameter("arg1");
          if (listargs == null) {
               listargs = "help";
          }
     }
```

```
        System.out.println("End of the Tour!");
        // More methods following
}
```

The *.html file and the compiled file (MyJavaApplet.class) are located in the same directory. When the browser opens mypage.html, the Java applet will be run.

A whole host of issues regarding security, server-side communications, applet-to-applet communications, and the applet program structure cannot be properly addressed here. Besides, the tour has now concluded.

APPENDIX

B

What's on the CD-ROM?

The *Ready-to-Run Java 3D* CD-ROM contains many Java 3D programs and their companion HTML files that can be added to Web sites. Each Java 3D program can be run as an applet or as a standalone application. The main reason the programs were designed to run standalone was so you could quickly see what the Java 3D looked like simply by typing (for example, running as standalone):

```
% java -mx64m Planets -demo
```

The same program could be invoked within a browser by clicking on the HTML file (Planets.html) provided on the CD-ROM.

In addition to Web 3D applets, the CD-ROM provides many useful utilities, tools, and resources to help you create 3D Web content. For example, AC3D is a 3D modeling application used to create 3D shapes for export to the VRML format, which can then be imported into the Java 3D applet, javaVRML, introduced in Chapter 4. We suggest that after installing the CD-ROM, you open a browser and load the HTML page called GettingStarted.htm.

The CD-ROM is partitioned into several directories. The chapter directories contain applets. The CD is organized this way:

/programs.   These are the Java 3D Web applets. Each chapter has related applets, starting with Chapter 4; for example:

    /ch4

    /ch5

/util.   This directory contains useful tools for building 3D Web content.

/resources.   This directory contains images, textures, and links to other 3D Web resources.

/src.   This directory contains source code listings for all Java 3D programs. Each chapter has related source listings.

    /ch4

    /ch5

What Are Freeware and Shareware?

Freeware is software that is distributed by disk free of charge, over bulletin board systems and the Internet. There is no charge for using it, and it can be distributed freely as long as its use follows the license agreement included with it.

Shareware (also known as user-supported software) is a revolutionary means of distributing software established by individuals or companies too small to make inroads into the more conventional retail distribution networks. The authors of shareware retain all rights to their software, under copyright laws, while still allowing free distribution. This gives users the chance to freely obtain and try out software to see if it fits their needs. Note: Shareware should not be confused with public-domain software, even though they are often obtained from the same sources.

Hardware Requirements

As the Java 3D programs execute on a Sun one day, on Windows another day, the idea is the same: Java code executes in the same way across multiple 3D platforms. Somebody summarized this capability by changing the Java motto, "write once, run everywhere" to "write once, render everywhere."

So, besides OpenGL or Direct3D, the Java3D API requires the Java 2 environment and JVM. The four components needed to develop and run Java 3D programs are:

- Java 3D
- Java 2 or later
- OpenGL or Direct3D
- Java Plug-in

Java Development Kit, Java 2 software comes in several releases:

- Win32 for Windows 95, Windows NT 4.0 for Intel, and Windows 98. A 486/DX or faster processor and at least 32 megabytes of RAM are recommended.
- Solaris/SPARC. Only Solaris versions 2.5.1 and 2.6 are supported. At least 64 megabytes of RAM are recommended.

On all systems, you should have 65 megabytes of free disk space before attempting to install JDK software. If you also install the documentation download bundle, you need an additional 85 megabytes of free disk space. After installation, the download packages are no longer needed; and because each take up about 8 megabytes, you can reclaim an additional 15 megabytes by removing the class source code, the demos, and other options. The Win32 installer allows you to install the essential JDK software without the options. The JDK software can be obtained for free at java.sun.com/products/.

Java 3D API Implementation

This version of Java 3D for WindowsNT 4.0 and Windows95 requires the following:

- Java 2
- OpenGL 1.1 from Microsoft or a hardware accelerator that supports OpenGL 1.1. Contact your hardware vendor, or download it from www.opengl.org/.

Installing the Book's Software from the CD-ROM

To install the software on Windows, follow these simple steps:

1. Start Windows on your computer.
2. Insert the CD-ROM to your CD-ROM drive.

3. From Netscape Navigator or Internet Explorer browsers, type the following into the address text field: file://D:\index.html.

4. Follow the screen prompts to complete the installation.

To install the CD to your Solaris hard drive, complete the following steps:

1. At the command-line prompt (with the CD inserted in the drive) type: % volcheck <return>.

2. Change directories: % cd /cdrom/cdrom0.

3. Open a browser and type in the following address: file:///cdrom/cdrom0/index.html.

4. Follow the simple menu prompts to complete the installation.

Using the Software

The CD-ROM provides several Java 3D applets that will be added to existing or newly created HTML files, served from a Web server, and used by Web surfers who happen to click on the file containing the Java 3D applet. What actually happens is described in Chapters 1 and 4.

You will want to locate the Java 3D applet on a Web server and modify an existing or new Web page to include the 3D applet. Use the provided HTML files for each applet as a reference. Modify the PARAM or parameters in the HTML file to customize the applet for your Web site. You can also reference the appropriate chapters in this book that describe how to use each Java 3D applet in detail, along with their parameter attributes. You will need to create the HTML files to support a new plugin for Java. The following is an excerpt from the Java Plug-in product Web page:

On Internet Explorer. The first time a user's Web browser comes across a Web page that is enabled for the Java Plug-in product, it automatically downloads and installs the Java Plug-in software (and hence the latest implementation of the Java Runtime Environment, JRE) on the user's system. From that point forward, the browser will automatically invoke the Java Plug-in software every time it comes across Web pages that support the technology, which is completely transparent to the end user.

On Netscape Navigator. The first time a user's Web browser comes across a Web page that is enabled for the Java Plug-in product, it redirects the user to a Web page to download and install the Java Plug-in software on the user's system. From that point forward, the browser will automatically invoke the Java Plug-in software every time it comes across Web pages that support the technology, which is completely transparent to the end user.

The Java Plug-in defines a "tag" that needs to be specified in the HTML page that will host the Java 3D applet. There are instructions for Netscape-only environments or Microsoft-only environments in the Java Plug-in documentation that can be referenced from its Web site (java.sun.com/products/plugin). The following covers both environments to avoid confusion and to simplify the discussion. This information was taken directly from the setup and installation notes.

In an Internet/intranet environment, an HTML page is likely to be browsed from many different platforms, for example, Microsoft Explorer or Netscape Navigator. You should activate Java Plug-in only on the correct browser and platform combination; otherwise, you should use the browser's default JVM. (It is possible that some Web pages will contain both of old Java version applets and new Java 3D applets.) You can achieve this using the Java Plug-in tags:

<OBJECT> for Microsoft Explorer browser

<EMBED> for Netscape Navigator browser

<APPLET> for the latest Sun Microsystems HotJava browser

The original (before Java 3D was invented) Java APPLET tag looked like this:

```
<APPLET code="XYZApp.class" codebase="html/" align="baseline"
width="200" height="200">
<PARAM NAME="model" VALUE="models/HyaluronicAcid.xyz">
 </APPLET>
```

This invokes the "XYZApp" applet inside the browser window with area of 200×200 pixels and passes one parameter called "model," which points to a local file named "HyaluronicAcid.xyz".

The following is an example of an equivalent Java Plug-in tag. We'll be using a script to determine the browser environment so we can invoke the Java Plug-in correctly for multiple platforms. This example includes comments, and uses it as a template that can be cut and pasted when creating Java Plug-in Web pages. Don't be intimidated by all of these characters; their sequence and meaning can be mastered in a short period of time. Furthermore, each Java 3D applet in the book is accompanied by an HTML page that is all ready to go. Just cut and paste it into your favorite HTML page.

```
<!-- The following code is specified at the beginning of the <BODY> tag.
-->
<SCRIPT LANGUAGE="JavaScript"><!--
    var _info = navigator.userAgent; var _ns = false;
```

```
        var _ie = (_info.indexOf("MSIE") > 0 && _info.indexOf("Win") > 0
                         && _info.indexOf("Windows 3.1") < 0); //-->
</SCRIPT>
<COMMENT><SCRIPT LANGUAGE="JavaScript1.1"><!--
      var _ns = (navigator.appName.indexOf("Netscape") >= 0
            && ((_info.indexOf("Win") < 0 && _info.indexOf("Win16") < 0
            && java.lang.System.getProperty("os.version").indexOf("3.5") < 0)
            || _info.indexOf("Sun") > 0)); //-->
</SCRIPT></COMMENT>
 <!-- The following code is repeated for each APPLET tag -->
 <SCRIPT LANGUAGE="JavaScript"><!--
      if (_ie == true) document.writeln('<OBJECT
      classid="clsid:8AD9C840-044E-11D1-B3E9-00805F499D93"
      width="200" height="200" align="baseline"
 codebase="http://java.sun.com/products/plugin/1.2/jinstall-12-
win32.cab#Version=1,1,0,0">
      <NOEMBED><XMP>');
      else if (_ns == true) document.writeln('<EMBED
      type="application/x-java-applet;version=1.2" width="200"
height="200"
      align="baseline" code="XYZApp.class" codebase="html/"
      model="models/HyaluronicAcid.xyz"
      pluginspage="http://java.sun.com/products/plugin/1.2/plugin-
install.html">
      <NOEMBED><XMP>');
 //--></SCRIPT>
      <APPLET code="XYZApp.class" codebase="html/" align="baseline"
           width="200" height="200"></XMP>
      <PARAM NAME="java_code" VALUE="XYZApp.class">
      <PARAM NAME="java_codebase" VALUE="html/">
      <PARAM NAME="java_type" VALUE="application/x-java-
applet;version=1.2">
      <PARAM NAME="model" VALUE="models/HyaluronicAcid.xyz">
      No Java 2 support for this APPLET!!
 </APPLET></NOEMBED></EMBED></OBJECT>

 <!--
<APPLET code="XYZApp.class" codebase="html/" align="baseline"
         width="200" height="200">
<PARAM NAME="model" VALUE="models/HyaluronicAcid.xyz">
      No Java 2 support for this APPLET!!
</APPLET>
-->
```

Although this tag seems complicated compared to the old APPLET tag, it is not. Most of the Java Plug-in tag is the same regardless of the applet used. Thus, for the majority of cases, a webmaster can just copy and paste the Java Plug-in tag.

The first block of the script extracts the browser and platform. We recommend that you determine the browser and platform on which the applet is running. You do this by using JavaScript to extract first the browser name, then the platform, once per HTML document. The second block of the script replaces the APPLET tag. You must replace each APPLET tag with a similar block of code. The script replaces the APPLET tag with either an EMBED tag or OBJECT tag, depending on the browser. It would be nice if everybody could agree on the same tag names, but since they can't, a little more work is needed. You use the OBJECT tag for Internet Explorer (IE) and the EMBED tag for Netscape Navigator. Finally, the original APPLET tag is included as a comment at the end. It is always a good idea to keep the original APPLET tag in case you want to remove the Java Plug-in invocation when browsers eventually support Java 2 or later.

Let's review what we just said. The first JavaScript establishes the browser and the platform on which the browser is running. You must do this because, currently, Java Plug-in supports only Windows 95/98, Windows NT 4.0, and Solaris. Note that Windows NT 3.51 is the only Win32 platform that Java Plug-in does *not* support. Java Plug-in should be invoked only on the supported browser and platform. The script sets the variable _ie to True if the browser is Internet Explorer. It sets the variable _ns to True if the browser is Navigator. (Note that all variable names in the JavaScript start with an underscore, to avoid conflicting with other JavaScript variables on the same page.)

To detect the correct browser, the JavaScript evaluates three strings in the JavaScript's Navigator object: userAgent, appVersion, and appName. These strings contain information about the browser and the platform. By looking at some examples of the userAgent string, you can easily see how to evaluate userAgent and use it to determine the browser.

Remember that this block of JavaScript should be put at the top of the <BODY> of the HTML file, so that other JavaScripts can reference the variables _ie and _ns. This JavaScript is the same in all HTML files, and it is needed only once for each HTML body.

The second block of HTML tags are the corresponding OBJECT and EMBED tags that are mapped from the data in the APPLET tag. Note that JavaScript outputs the OBJECT tag when the browser is IE running on Windows 95/98 or Windows NT 4.0. If the browser is Navigator 3/4 on Windows 95/98, Windows NT 4.0, or Solaris, then JavaScript also outputs the EMBED tag, though with a slightly different syntax. (The mechanism for detecting the browser and the platform was described in the previous section.) Finally, the symbols <!-- and --> are used for comments in HTML.

Accessing JDK and Java 3D over the Web

The components required for JDK and Java 3D can be grabbed from the Web. For more instructions, you can either load index.html, provided on the book's CD-ROM, or go to java.sun.com/products and select Java 2, Java3D, and Java Plug-in to download. Follow the download and installation instructions provided on the Sun Web site for Java 2 or later, and Java 3D.

Verify that your Sun Solaris environment is ready to use the Java 3D applets by performing the following checks:

Sun Spare System with 24-Bit Frame Buffer

1. To verify, at the shell prompt type: % **/usr/openwin/demo/GL/ ogl_install_check.**

2. If successful, the following will be displayed, indicating 24 bits or greater.

```
OpenGL Library: Detail Status Report
      Number of color bits (R/G/B/A):  8/8/8/0
      Frame Buffer Depth (GL_DEPTH_BITS):  28
```

3. If the command fails to execute, install OpenGL 1.1 or later and retest.

Solaris 2.5 (Sunos 5.5) or Later

1. To verify, at the shell prompt type: % **sysdef.**

2. Upon success, the following is returned (Solaris 2.6 example):

```
      *
      * Utsname Tunables
      *
5.6 release (REL)
      steamboat node name (NODE)
SunOS system name (SYS)
      Generic version
```

Java 2 or Later (Available from java.sun.com/products/jdk)

1. To verify, at the prompt type: % **java -version.**

OpenGL 1.1 Runtime for Solaris or Later (Available from www.opengl.org)

1. To verify, at the shell prompt type: % **/usr/openwin/demo/GL/ ogl_install_check.**

User Assistance and Information

The software accompanying this book is provided as-is, without warranty or support of any kind. Should you require basic installation assistance, or if your media is defective, please call our product support number at (212) 850-6194 weekdays between 9:00 A.M. and 4:00 P.M. EST. Or we can be reached via email at wprtusw@wiley.com.

To place additional orders or to request information about other Wiley products, please call (800) 879-4539.

Index

Sun Microsystems, Inc.
Binary Code License Agreement

READ THE TERMS OF THIS AGREEMENT AND ANY PROVIDED SUPPLEMENTAL LICENSE TERMS (COLLECTIVELY "AGREEMENT") CAREFULLY BEFORE OPENING THE SOFTWARE MEDIA PACKAGE. BY OPENING THE SOFTWARE MEDIA PACKAGE, YOU AGREE TO THE TERMS OF THIS AGREEMENT. IF YOU ARE ACCESSING THE SOFTWARE ELECTRONICALLY, INDICATE YOUR ACCEPTANCE OF THESE TERMS BY SELECTING THE "ACCEPT" BUTTON AT THE END OF THIS AGREEMENT. IF YOU DO NOT AGREE TO ALL THESE TERMS, PROMPTLY RETURN THE UNUSED SOFTWARE TO YOUR PLACE OF PURCHASE FOR A REFUND OR, IF THE SOFTWARE IS ACCESSED ELECTRONICALLY, SELECT THE "DECLINE" BUTTON AT THE END OF THIS AGREEMENT.

1. **LICENSE TO USE.** Sun grants you a non-exclusive and non-transferable license for the internal use only of the accompanying software and documentation and any error corrections provided by Sun (collectively "Software"), by the number of users and the class of computer hardware for which the corresponding fee has been paid.

2. **RESTRICTIONS.** Software is confidential and copyrighted. Title to Software and all associated intellectual property rights is retained by Sun and/or its licensors. Except as specifically authorized in any Supplemental License Terms, you may not make copies of Software, other than a single copy of Software for archival purposes. Unless enforcement is prohibited by applicable law, you may not modify, decompile, reverse engineer Software. You acknowledge that Software is not designed or licensed for use in on-line control of aircraft, air traffic, aircraft navigation or aircraft communications; or in the design, construction, operation or maintenance of any nuclear facility. Sun disclaims any express or implied warranty of fitness for such uses. No right, title or interest in or to any trademark, service mark, logo or trade name of Sun or its licensors is granted under this Agreement.

3. **LIMITED WARRANTY.** Sun warrants to you that for a period of ninety (90) days from the date of purchase, as evidenced by a copy of the receipt, the media on which Software is furnished (if any) will be free of defects in materials and workmanship under normal use. Except for the foregoing, Software is provided "AS IS". Your exclusive remedy and Sun's entire liability under this limited warranty will be at Sun's option to replace Software media or refund the fee paid for Software.

4. **DISCLAIMER OF WARRANTY.** UNLESS SPECIFIED IN THIS AGREEMENT, ALL EXPRESS OR IMPLIED CONDITIONS, REPRESENTATIONS AND WARRANTIES, INCLUDING ANY IMPLIED WARRANTY OF MERCHANTABILITY, FITNESS FOR A PARTICULAR PURPOSE, OR NON-INFRINGEMENT, ARE DISCLAIMED, EXCEPT TO THE EXTENT THAT THESE DISCLAIMERS ARE HELD TO BE LEGALLY INVALID.

5. **LIMITATION OF LIABILITY.** TO THE EXTENT NOT PROHIBITED BY LAW, IN NO EVENT WILL SUN OR ITS LICENSORS BE LIABLE FOR ANY LOST REVENUE, PROFIT OR DATA, OR FOR SPECIAL, INDIRECT, CONSEQUENTIAL, INCIDENTAL OR PUNITIVE DAMAGES, HOWEVER CAUSED REGARDLESS OF THE THEORY OF LIABILITY, ARISING OUT OF OR RELATED TO THE USE OF

OR INABILITY TO USE SOFTWARE, EVEN IF SUN HAS BEEN ADVISED OF THE POSSIBILITY OF SUCH DAMAGES. In no event will Sun's liability to you, whether in contract, tort (including negligence), or otherwise, exceed the amount paid by you for Software under this Agreement. The foregoing limitations will apply even if the above stated warranty fails of its essential purpose.

6. **Termination.** This Agreement is effective until terminated. You may terminate this Agreement at any time by destroying all copies of Software. This Agreement will terminate immediately without notice from Sun if you fail to comply with any provision of this Agreement. Upon Termination, you must destroy all copies of Software.

7. **Export Regulations.** All Software and technical data delivered under this Agreement are subject to US export control laws and may be subject to export or import regulations in other countries. You agree to comply strictly with all such laws and regulations and acknowledge that you have the responsibility to obtain such licenses to export, re-export, or import as may be required after delivery to you.

8. **U.S. Government Rights.** If Software is being acquired by or on behalf of the U.S. Government or by a U.S. Government prime contractor or subcontractor (at any tier), then the Government's rights in Software will be only as set forth in this Agreement; this is in accordance with 48 CFR 227.7201 through 227.7202-4 (for Department of Defense (DOD) acquisitions) and with 48 CFR 2.101 and 12.212 (for non-DOD acquisitions).

9. **Governing Law.** Any action related to this Agreement will be governed by California law and controlling U.S. federal law. No choice of law rules of any jurisdiction will apply.

10. **Severability.** If any provision of this Agreement is held to be unenforceable, this Agreement will remain in effect with the provision omitted, unless omission would frustrate the intent of the parties, in which case this Agreement will immediately terminate.

11. **Integration.** This Agreement is the entire agreement between you and Sun relating to its subject matter. It supersedes all prior or contemporaneous oral or written communications, proposals, representations and warranties and prevails over any conflicting or additional terms of any quote, order, acknowledgment, or other communication between the parties relating to its subject matter during the term of this Agreement. No modification of this Agreement will be binding, unless in writing and signed by an authorized representative of each party.

For inquiries please contact: Sun Microsystems, Inc. 901 San Antonio Road, Palo Alto, California 94303

Java™2 Software Development Kit Version 1.2 Supplemental License Terms

These supplemental terms ("Supplement") add to the terms of the Binary Code License Agreement (collectively the "Agreement"). Capitalized terms not defined herein shall have the same meanings ascribed to them in the Agreement. The Supplement terms shall supersede any inconsistent or conflicting terms in the Agreement above, or in any license contained within the Software.

1. **Limited License Grant.** Sun grants to you a non-exclusive, non-transferable limited license to use the Software without fee for evaluation of the Software and for development of Java? applets and applications provided that you: (i) may not redistribute the Software in whole or in part, either separately or included with a product; and (ii) may not create, or authorize your licensees to create additional classes, interfaces, or subpackages that are contained in the "java" or "sun" packages or similar as specified by Sun in any class file naming convention. Refer to the Java Runtime Environment Version 1.2 binary code license (http://java.sun.com/products/jdk/1.2/jre/index.html) for the availability of runtime code which may be distributed with Java applets and applications.

2. **Java Platform Interface.** In the event that Licensee creates an additional API(s) which: (i) extends the functionality of a Java Environment; and, (ii) is exposed to third party software developers for the purpose of developing additional software which invokes such additional API, Licensee must promptly publish broadly an accurate specification for such API for free use by all developers.

3. **Trademarks and Logos.** Licensee acknowledges as between it and Sun that Sun owns the Java trademark and all Java-related trademarks, logos and icons including the Coffee Cup and Duke ("Java Marks") and agrees to comply with the Java Trademark Guidelines at http://www.sun.com/policies/trademarks.

4. **Source Code.** Software may contain source code that is provided solely for reference purposes pursuant to the terms of this Agreement.

Java™ Runtime Environment Version 1.2 and Java 3D 1.1 Reference Implementation Supplemental License Terms

These supplemental terms ("Supplement") add to the terms of the Binary Code License Agreement (collectively the "Agreement"). Capitalized terms not defined herein shall have the same meanings ascribed to them in the Agreement. The Supplement terms shall supersede any inconsistent or conflicting terms in the Agreement, either above or contained within the Software.

1. **License to Distribute.** You are granted a royalty-free right to reproduce and distribute the Software provided that you: (i)distribute the Software complete and unmodified, provided that the Software is distributed with your Java applet or application ("Program"); (ii) do not distribute additional software intended to replace any component(s) of the Software; (iii) do not remove or alter the Agreement, any proprietary legends or notices contained in the Software; (iv) only distribute the Software subject to this Agreement; (v) may not create, or authorize your licensees to create additional classes, interfaces, or subpackages that are contained in the "java" or "sun" packages or similar as specified by Sun in any class file naming convention; (vi) agree to indemnify, hold harmless, and defend Sun and its licensors from and against any claims or lawsuits, including attorneys' fees, that arise or result from the use or distribution of the Program.

2. **Trademarks and Logos.** You acknowledge as between you and Sun that Sun owns the Java trademark and all Java-related trademarks, logos and icons including the Coffee Cup and Duke ("Java Marks") and agrees to comply with the Java Trademark Guidelines at http://java.sun.com/trademarks.html.

To use this CD-ROM, your system must meet the following requirements:

Platform/Processor/Operating System. Windows 95/98, Windows NT, Solaris 2.x.

RAM. 32Mb or greater.

Hard Drive Space. 30Mb.

Peripherals. Direct 3D or OpenGL supported hardware graphics accelerator is desirable for optimal performance.